ISRAEL'S DEFENSE LINE

Her Friends and Foes
in Washington

ISRAEL'S DEFENSE LINE

Her Friends and Foes in Washington

I.L. Kenen

106369

P3 *Prometheus Books*

700 East Amherst Street
Buffalo, N.Y. 14215

Published 1981 by Prometheus Books
700 East Amherst Street, Buffalo, NY 14215

Copyright © 1981 by I. L. Kenen

Library of Congress Catalog Number: 81-81866
ISBN: 0-87975-159-2 (cloth)
ISBN: 0-87975-145-2 (paper)

Printed in the United States of America

Contents

Foreword   *vii*

Acknowledgment   *xi*

Introduction   *1*

1   Autobiography   *5*

2   American Jews Close Ranks   *7*

3   We Protect the Past   *20*

4   Stateless and Nameless   *26*

5   Truman Has Fine Eyesight   *34*

6   The Battle for the Negev   *56*

7   We Begin to Lobby   *66*

8   The Downgrading of Israel   *92*

9   Organization of the Lobby   *106*

10   The Arab Lobby   *114*

11   Arms for the Arabs—None for Israel   *122*

12   The Suez War and the Threat of Sanctions   *131*

13   The Collapse of Containment   *138*

14   Aid for Arabs Up—Aid for Israel Down   *143*

15   The Issue of Discrimination   *145*

16   The Freedom of the Seas   *148*

17   A Multitude of Promises   *154*

18 Israel's Texas Friend *173*

19 The Road to War *188*

20 We Travel a Lonely Road *194*

21 The Great Divide *203*

22 Erosion and Attrition *210*

23 The Rogers Plan *230*

24 The Violent and Violated Truce *245*

25 Sadat Trades Allies? *252*

26 We Strengthen Israel *263*

27 An End to Carrot and Stick *270*

28 Soviet Jews *279*

29 Complacency *288*

30 The Yom Kippur War *300*

31 My Final Year *316*

32 Conclusion *329*

Index *333*

Foreword

I. L. Kenen and I have been friends and colleagues for almost 40 years. We both came to New York in 1943 from Midwest cities—he from Cleveland and I from Pittsburgh. We had no knowledge then that we shared a common objective: to work with organizations bent on a saner, warless world, especially to focus on the plight of European Jewry in Nazi-occupied lands and to seek a refuge, preferably Palestine, for Jews fortunate enough to escape the ravages of Hitlerism.

I had accepted the invitation of Henry A. Atkinson, general secretary of the interfaith Church Peace Union (now CRIA: Council on Religion and International Affairs) and the World Alliance for International Friendship Through the Churches, to resign my pastorate in Pittsburgh and join his staff, devoting part of my time to the program of the newly organized Christian Council on Palestine (CCP) as its executive secretary. In 1942 I had helped establish the CCP, a sizable committee of ministers, mostly Protestant, led by ecumenical statesman Atkinson as chairman and supported by such distinguished men as theologians Reinhold Niebuhr and Paul Tillich, the *Christian Herald*'s editor, Daniel A. Poling, and *The Churchman*'s Guy Emery Shipler, Johns Hopkins archaeologist William Foxwell Albright, Methodism's Bishop Francis J. McConnell and Ralph Sockman of New York's Christ Church, the Community Church's John Haynes Holmes, and the Unitarian Pierre van Paassen, in company with hundreds of other eminent clergymen.

Our purpose was to arouse Christian concern and action in the light of Hitler's avowed intention to exterminate all Jews everywhere; and to draw attention to Palestine as the only available refuge, the area promised by the

Balfour Declaration of 1917 and sanctioned by the League of Nations in 1920.

Kenen helped us cooperate with the American Palestine Committee (APC), another non-Jewish organization, founded in 1932 and revived in 1942 under the co-chairmanship of Senators Robert F. Wagner of New York and Charles McNary of Oregon. The APC was now strengthened by hundreds of representatives and senators, university presidents, editors, governors, mayors, labor leaders (AFL's William Green and CIO's Philip Murray), the U.S. Chamber of Commerce president, Eric Johnston, Harvard's Carl J. Friedrich, former Secretary of State Sumner Welles (Maryland state chairman), and Helen Gahagan Douglas (national secretary).

We were grateful for Kenen's assistance, particularly when we merged the activities and programs of the Christian Council on Palestine and the American Palestine Committee to form the American Christian Palestine Committee of which I was co-director and later chairman of the executive council. Like his successor at the American Zionist Emergency Council, Harold Manson, Kenen helped us greatly.

As I read his absorbing account of those pre-Israel years, I recall Kenen's calm and tenacity in the face of opposition, his ability to ignore peripheral skirmishes and discern the core of the issues.

In 1951, Kenen began a new and challenging career—that of a congressionally registered lobbyist for Americans who wanted to aid Israel. He was a founder of the American Israel Public Affairs Committee (AIPAC), which sought to ensure Israel's survival, to secure aid for the fledgling nation, and to present Israel's case intelligently and factually in Washington circles, especially to Congress.

I watched Kenen in action over the years as I served churches, taught in universities, wrote books, and lectured; and each time I returned to the arena of issues affecting Israel I found him steadfastly adhering to the cause he had espoused. I was impressed by his stamina and single-mindedness as he contended against hostile forces in Washington and across the country wherever anti-Israel, pro-Arab pressure groups like the American Friends of the Middle East turned their guns on him.

It is gratifying to note that two outstanding Jewish institutions of higher learning have rewarded Kenen for his intellectual gifts, his zeal, and his loyalty. In 1976 President Alfred Gottschalk of Hebrew Union College–Jewish Institute of Religion conferred upon him the degree of Doctor of Humane Letters, *honoris causa*; and in 1977 President Avraham Harman made him an Honorary Fellow of the Hebrew University of Jerusalem.

My one regret about Kenen's work is that he did not have the kind of support from Christians, either politically or financially, which he could well have used and certainly deserved. The American Christian Palestine Committee, once so influential, slowly faded away in the late 1950s and early 1960s, ceased publication of its house organ and journal of opinion, *Land Reborn,* and terminated its activities, lacking both funds and leadership.

The tragic inadequacy of Christian support for Israel was revealed most dramatically and devastatingly by the silence of the churches, save for a few prophetic souls, at the time of the Six-Day War in early June 1967. But in that year Franklin H. Littell of Temple University organized Christians Concerned for Israel (CCI). Recently CCI has been superseded by a dynamic, swiftly growing organization, headed by Littell as chairman and with Isaac Rottenberg as executive director. This new group, the National Christian Leadership Conference for Israel (NCLCI), serves as an umbrella for all pro-Israel Christian groups in the United States. One can but hope that this new unit will finally awaken the conscience of Christian America.

Kenen's determination to create lasting bonds between America and Israel has impressed both former Secretary of State Henry A. Kissinger and Senator Daniel P. Moynihan.

Dr. Kissinger finds this book "fascinating and informative" and notes that "through the vicissitudes of Mideast diplomacy Kenen conducted himself honorably and with quiet but strong conviction."

Like Kissinger, Moynihan comments on Kenen's devotion to the cause of strengthening America's ties with Israel. He has written: "Kenen has much to teach us about the friendship of two nations he loves deeply, Israel and America. His life has been dedicated to that cause, of which his book is a fine chronicle . . . that could not have been told by anyone else."

Kenen's book has also been praised by many of those who shared his work and aspirations, among them former Senator Jacob K. Javits, Representative Jonathan B. Bingham, and Father Robert F. Drinan.

We owe Kenen a debt of gratitude for this absorbing account of what selfless and enlightened men and women in the United States were able to do to strengthen the defense line not only of Israel but of democracy itself in the entire Middle East.

CARL HERMANN VOSS

Acknowledgment

I thank many colleagues for their contributions to this book: Esther Chesney, Rita Lefkort, Leonard J. Davis, and Moshe Yuval; and for their encouragement: Dr. Carl Hermann Voss, Dr. Howard M. Sachar, David Appel, and my son, Dr. Peter B. Kenen.

I. L. KENEN

ISRAEL'S DEFENSE LINE

Her Friends and Foes
in Washington

Introduction

The Washington lobby for Israel made a decisive contribution in the struggle to establish Israel, to sustain her, and to help her achieve peace. This book tells the story of how and why our lobby came into existence, the role played by the American people and the American Jewish community in particular.

Our Jewish community faced a challenge in 1942. Numbed and helpless bystanders as Adolf Hitler waged his demoniacal war against the Jewish people, embittered by our failure to rouse the democracies to deter Hitler, to rescue and open doors to those who might be saved, American Jews assumed their responsibility during World War II. Despite the opposition of the Department of State, they made a commitment to establish an independent Jewish state where Jews could live in freedom and security.

American Jews numbered six million. Six million Jews were lost in the Holocaust. Six hundred thousand Jews were living in Palestine, and, as the war neared an end, that small remnant faced the possibility that solemn promises would be violated, and that they too would be abandoned to their foes.

During the First World War, many American Christians and Jews, as well as the United States government, had been sympathetic to the restoration of the Jewish national home in Israel. But American diplomats cooled with the rise of Arab nationalism, the discovery of oil, and the growing vulnerability of the Middle East—first to the Nazis, later to the Communists, and, in recent years, to anarchic terrorists.

In the decade preceding World War II, the British government was guilty of ignominious appeasement of the Nazis; and then of the Arabs, because they feared that Arab leaders would join the Axis. Breaching World War I

1

commitments, the British restricted Jewish escape from the Nazis at a time of dire Jewish need. The White Paper of 1939 was threatening establishment of the Jewish state by restricting immigration and the transfer of land to Jews. To our deep dismay, our own government collaborated with the British.

An aroused American Jewish community began to close ranks in 1942 to challenge U.S. policy. That was the beginning of the American Jewish struggle to save the life of the Jewish people, to assure self-determination for the Jews of Palestine, to assure self-respect for the Jews of America. Uniting forces, we waged an intensive campaign to win the support of Congress, the political parties, the media, the church, and the campus—culminating in victory at the United Nations in 1947.

We had to overcome a powerful opposition: the pervasive petro-diplomatic-military complex, an imperious conglomerate of pro-Arab diplomats, oil men, and Cold War militarists. They vainly opposed the U.N. partition resolution in 1947 and then tried to reverse it in 1948. Fortunately, Congress and the American press and people supported the nascent state of Israel, and the White House overruled the pro-Arab forces in the Departments of State and Defense.

Our pro-Arab diplomats habitually apologized to Arab leaders for their failure to block Israel's establishment, to prevent President Truman's recognition, and to restrict her territory to handkerchief dimensions. They found a scapegoat; they attributed Israel's victory to the pressures of the Zionist lobby. Regrettably, they fed the Arab illusion that Israel was a temporary apparition that would vanish when the American people freed themselves from the influence of the tiny Jewish minority. That illusion has never died.

The struggle between 1943 and 1948 to win popular support was not a lobbying effort in the strict sense of the term. The target was the United Nations, not Congress. But we did establish a lobby in 1951.

In 1950, Israel appealed for American financial assistance to help absorb the huge influx of Jewish refugees and immigrants between 1948 and 1950. Always worried about Arab reaction, our State Department was then adamantly opposed to any economic aid for Israel, which, it insisted, would deepen Arab bitterness. Accordingly, Israel's American friends concluded that they must appeal directly to Congress for enabling legislation. That was the beginning of the pro-Israel lobby, now called the American Israel Public Affairs Committee (AIPAC), which I directed from its inception in 1951 until 1975.

There are myths about our lobby. It was not organized by the Israeli government. It was formed by, and representative of, American Jews, with the support of Christian leaders. It was not required to register with the Department of Justice as an agent of a foreign principal. However, since it was active on Capitol Hill, it did register with Congress under domestic lobbying laws. Another myth pertained to the extent of its influence and its alleged invincibility. The lobby encountered many difficulties and suffered some defeats in its long struggle for constituency and support.

Our lobby was not the first American effort to advocate U.S. support for other countries. Americans sympathetic to Ireland fought for Irish home rule. American Czechs rallied to President Masaryk's call for the establishment of Czechoslovakia. For many years lobbies were stigmatized by pejoratives. But many other organizations have exercised their right to petition Congress, not only on domestic issues but on international issues as well, a trend strengthened by the growing consciousness of ethnic identity and cultural pluralism.

We reactivated the many friends who had helped win the 1947–1948 U.N. battle and expanded that constituency. We always tried to resolve the issues that divided Washington and Jerusalem, for our major objective was to strengthen bonds between the United States and Israel in the moral, economic, and strategic interests of both countries.

In addition to aid for Israel, we were concerned with aid for Soviet Jews, the Arab boycott, the blockade of the Suez Canal, the energy crisis, the secret CIA subvention to our pro-Arab opposition, the Jackson-Vanik amendment, and aid for Arab refugees.

Israel was a victim of the Cold War. The Soviets courted the Arabs with arms and aid, beginning in 1955, while our own government refused to *sell* Israel any arms until 1962 and to *grant* her any arms until 1973. Thus Israel was forced to go deeply into debt, and for two decades has had a huge per capita foreign currency debt — by far the highest in the world.

During that period, all the Great Powers, at one time or another, provided weapons to Israel's hostile neighbors. In addition to the imbalance of arms, there was an imbalance of pressures. The many Arab diplomats in Washington could swamp the small Israeli embassy staff; and the reports from American diplomats, reflecting the views of the many Arab governments to which they were assigned, far outweighed those that came from America's embassy in Tel Aviv. It was up to Congress to rectify both imbalances.

The United States had a double moral standard. Competing with Moscow for Arab favor, Washington voted for U.N. resolutions censuring Israel for her retaliation to terrorist attacks by the Arabs, who were immune from any reproach. The U.N. itself, manipulated by the expanding Soviet-Arab–Third World bloc, was cheapened and corrupted.

American taxpayers put up substantial funds to redeem the Arab refugees from the neglect of the Arab states, which were parsimonious in their philanthropy, prodigal in their arms procurement and, worst of all, supportive of Arab terrorists.

For many years U.S. aid to the Arab states exceeded U.S. aid to Israel, and U.S. tax policies enabled a huge oil cartel to invest tax-free billions in Arab economies.

Until her spectacular victory in the Six-Day War, Israel was written off as a liability to U.S. policy, while the United States sought to contain the Soviet Union by rallying and subsidizing unstable and undemocratic Arab regimes in abortive defense pacts. The United States sought to rely on strongmen like Nasser and feudal bigots like Faisal. The U.S. government thought it could buy Arab friendship, if not alliance, but learned that Arabs could not be bought but only rented.

The United States was ranged with reaction in helping to repel democratic forces that might have sought social change. In the Middle East, as elsewhere, the United States was reproached as an ally of the past, a posture exploited by radicals oriented to Moscow.

Following Israel's 1967 victory, many U.S. military and intelligence experts came to regard Israel as an asset. Even so, U.S. diplomacy resorted to the carrot and the stick to induce Israel to make territorial and political concessions to the Arab states.

The U.S. attitude worsened in 1973, when Arab mastery of pushbutton war challenged Israel's qualitative superiority. American policy was now clouded by doubts and reassessments because of expanding Arab power: oil, petrodollars, arsenals and terror—the ominous threats of the loaded purse, the sophisticated missile, and the empty U.S. gas tank.

Our country squandered arms in the scramble for oil.

* * *

In 1975, I retired as chairman of AIPAC and as editor of the *Near East Report,* which I founded in 1957. But one cannot retire from a cause in time of peril.

Like many millions around the globe, I was optimistic about the prospects of peace when Egypt's President Sadat appeared in Jerusalem on November 20, 1977. But then I became critical of President Carter's tilt toward the Arabs, the pressures for a "comprehensive" settlement, the belabored and dubious attacks on the alleged illegality of Israeli settlements, the campaign to divide the American Jewish community, the off-the-cuff improvisations, the attempt to weaken Prime Minister Begin, the effort to isolate the pro-Israel lobby, the uncritical exaltation of Sadat, the subservience to the Saudis, the counterproductive reinstatement of the Soviet partnership with its astonishing abandonment of Resolutions 242 and 338, and the obsequious courtship of the Palestine Liberation Organization, so reminiscent of British appeasement in the 1930s.

Israel's position continued to deteriorate and many feared that Israel could not possibly survive because of rising Arab expectations and power.

Aware of the urgent need to combat the spreading and well-financed Arab propaganda and to warn against the repetition of past blunders, I continued to write a weekly column for the *Near East Report,* of which I am editor emeritus. I hoped that the 1980 national election would lead to a reconsideration of policy. It may prove to have been a turning point.

Chapter 1

Autobiography

Almost all my life has been committed to the cause of Israel's restoration and survival, a fortunate coincidence between occupation and commitment. I inherited legacies from my father, a life-long Zionist, and from my mother, a pioneer trade unionist. My father was born near Kiev, my mother near Bialystok. They both came to the United States in 1891, and to Canada in 1904.

My father's life story epitomized the tragic history of his generation. He fled from Czarist pogroms; he was a prisoner of the Communists; his settlement in Palestine was barred by Anglo-Arab policy and, residing in Europe, he perished soon after Nazis conquered the Warsaw ghetto.

Born in 1905, I organized the first Young Judea Club in Toronto in 1917 under the influence of Henrietta Szold, the founder of American Hadassah. Anna Raginsky, my sister, founded the first chapter of Canadian Hadassah.

At the University of Toronto I majored in philosophy, but I was attracted to journalism and joined *The Toronto Star* in 1925. I emigrated to Cleveland the following year, in the dubious perception that "Toronto the Good" was the city of the past and that Cleveland was the city of the future. I became the City Hall reporter, political writer, and State House correspondent for *The Cleveland News*.

A year later I married a childhood sweetheart, Beatrice Bain, a fellow student at the University of Toronto. She gave me 42 blessed years and shared my devotion to Zionism. For more than a quarter of a century, she was office manager of Hadassah's national convention staffs. Our greatest blessing was our son, Peter, now an international economist at Princeton. His wife, Regina, is a professor in the social sciences at Trenton State.

Bebe died of cancer in 1969 at the age of 63. My second wife, Bernice Taube, was widely known for her humanitarian, civic, and cultural interests. We were married in 1970. She died of cancer in 1976, at the age of 62.

* * *

I was never content to be just a reporter and I championed many causes during the Depression and the decade of democratic retreat in Europe.

In 1933, I offered the motion to establish what became Local No. 1 of the American Newspaper Guild in Cleveland, in a struggle to win the five-day forty-hour week, minimum wages, and severance pay for newspapermen. Despite my newspaper's conservatism, I advocated slum clearance, old-age pensions, minimum wage laws for women, unemployment compensation, and public ownership of the Cleveland transit system; and I opposed a regressive sales tax. I was elected to the Guild's international executive board and was a co-winner of its Heywood Broun Memorial Award. I studied law at night and was admitted to the Ohio Bar, but I never practiced.

The international scene commanded my deepest concern. By the mid-1930s it was tragically evident that a paralyzed America was isolationist and that we preferred collective indecision to collective security.

I became president of the Cleveland Zionist District in 1941. In 1943, I left newspaper work to become the director of information for the American Emergency Committee for Zionist Affairs in New York. I was outraged because the West had done nothing to assist Jews to escape from the impending Holocaust, and I was embittered by the long failure of the United States to insist that the Vichy French rescind the Nazi discrimination laws after American forces liberated North Africa in 1942. As I saw it, a Jewish state was indispensable to the security and freedom of the Jewish people.

In the next seven years, I served as executive director of the American Jewish Conference, and as information director for the Jewish Agency at the U.N. and for the first Israeli U.N. delegation. In 1951, I went to Washington to spearhead the Washington lobby for Israel, which later became the American Israel Public Affairs Committee (AIPAC), and to establish the *Near East Report*. I "retired" in 1975, but I continue my work as honorary chairman of AIPAC and as editor emeritus of the *Near East Report*.

Thus, my Zionist experience, my activities as lobbyist for good causes, and my acquaintanceship in the newspaper world all equipped me for my Washington service: the struggle to close a dark chapter in Jewish history and to turn a new page illuminated by redemption and regeneration.

Chapter 2

American Jews Close Ranks

EARLY U.S. ATTITUDE

We won support in Washington because many Americans, Christians as well as Jews, had favored our cause for many decades.

President Truman stressed the extent of public support in a 1952 speech to a Jewish audience in New York. The sponsoring organization had asked me to suggest a text. "I take great pride in the fact that I was selected by destiny to be the first to recognize the new Jewish state," I wrote.

I doubt whether Truman ever saw that draft, for his speech bore no resemblance to it. On the contrary, he almost seemed to be arguing with me when he declared: "I take no special credit for recognizing the State of Israel on the day it was born. I did what the people of America wanted me to do."

Zionism was a Christian theme long before it became a Jewish political movement. The cause of Zion was cherished by early American colonists who worshiped the Bible, the law it preached, the language in which it was written, and the Holy Land whose history it told. Their scholars spoke Hebrew and even considered its adoption as the official language. The Puritans believed in the return of the scattered Jewish nation, which the prophets had predicted. Christian missionaries sought converts to hasten fulfillment of the prophecy. As early as 1818, our second President, John Adams, wrote:

"I really wish the Jews again in Judea, an independent nation, for, as I believe, the most enlightened men of it have participated in the amelioration of the philosophy of the age."

That letter was addressed to Major Mordechai Manuel Noah, a Jewish journalist, soldier, and diplomat. Seven years later, Noah proposed a

7

temporary Jewish homeland on Grand Island in the Niagara River, but no one answered Noah's messianic call. Only the Holy Land then appealed to pious Jewish sentiment.

Support for the concept of a Jewish state was countered by the rise of rationalism—the Enlightenment—which theoretically promised equality for Jews everywhere. Jews had begun to win emancipation in Western Europe and the Americas. However, disabilities were not so swiftly removed. Discrimination in Eastern Europe flared into pogroms whenever it pleased government purpose or mob passion.

In 1889, the Reverend William E. Blackstone of Oak Park, Illinois, visited Palestine and Syria and was convinced that "the land of Palestine is capable of remarkable development, both agriculturally and commercially." On March 5, 1891, he presented a petition to President Benjamin Harrison. It was signed by 413 leading Americans, a veritable "Who's Who" which included judges, governors, churchmen, congressmen, editors, and business leaders. They appealed for an international conference "to consider the Israelites' claim to Palestine as their national home, and to promote in all other just and proper ways the alleviation of their suffering condition."

The signatories included two Rockefellers, John D. and William. However, that was long before Standard Oil of California discovered an almost abandoned Saudi Arabian well, which gushed up a vast ocean of oil in 1937 and which came to be known as "Lucky Seven"—the fourth holiest place in the Arab world. It was also before the first World Zionist Congress in 1897.

Many Jews came here in flight from persecution. They were preoccupied with the struggle to learn a language and a new way of life and to earn a living. Many believed that the attainment of equality would solve all problems. Some rose swiftly in business and society and assimilated. Many were enslaved in sweatshops and turned to Socialism, not to Zionism, as their panacea. Paradoxically, most religious Jews, both in America and Palestine, spurned Zionism. Reform Judaism rejected nationalism, preaching that Jews had a universal mission. This country was to be their Zion, and Washington would be their Jerusalem. The ultra-Orthodox Jews also rejected political Zionism. While they believed in the restoration of Israel, they insisted that man must not push the hand of God. In the last century, they dominated Palestine and still exercise theological control over personal status in Israel. A tiny extremist sect in Jerusalem—the Neturei Karta—even today wages bitter war against the state which refused to wait for the Messiah.

A great number of Jews in Eastern Europe responded to the dramatic summons of Theodor Herzl, the visionary journalist who founded the modern-day Zionist movement, revolted by the infamous Dreyfus trial and the bigotry it exposed.

Many of the indifferent and hostile were jarred in the 1930s. Most German Jews had rejected Zionism, and the Munich rabbis had commanded Herzl to move his Zionist Congress to Basel. Twenty-five years later, their horrified children were to witness the beer putsch and Hitler's rise to power. The most assimilated Jewish community in Europe was the first to be attacked.

The Nazi war convinced many American Jews that Zionism was essential, not only to regain Jewish rights in Palestine, but to restore Jewish status and dignity everywhere. American Zionism had eloquent advocates: Justice Louis D. Brandeis, Justice Felix Frankfurter, philosopher Horace Kallen, Louis Lipsky, and rabbis in the Reform movement like Stephen S. Wise and Abba Hillel Silver who perceived no conflict between Zionism and Americanism. In our pluralistic country, thoughtful men could pledge allegiance to the United States and simultaneously acknowledge debt and loyalty to many cultures, peoples, and religions.

In 1917, the British, with the concurrence of President Wilson, had issued the Balfour Declaration, which promised restoration of the Jewish national homeland and which was incorporated in the League of Nations Mandate.

Congress swiftly approved the Balfour Declaration. It then unanimously voted for the Lodge-Fish resolution of 1922, in response to the appeal of a pioneering Zionist lobby, which included Louis Lipsky, Elihu Stone, Abraham Goldberg, and Dr. Herman Seidel of Baltimore. Unfortunately, Congress was soon to close the doors to immigration with cruel and invidious quota legislation, which many years later doomed Jews in Europe to Hitler's gas chambers.

The British had dishonored their trust. Jewish immigrants to Palestine in the 1920s were met with Arab terror, strike, and massacre, which the intimidated British then appeased.

The French had ousted Faisal from Syria. As a consolation, the British appointed him ruler of Iraq; his brother Abdullah became the Emir of Transjordan, the eastern area of Palestine, which Winston Churchill then severed from Palestine. Churchill's action sharply reduced the area of the future Jewish national home. The British and French arbitrarily fixed the northern frontiers between Palestine, Syria, and Lebanon.

Britain dispatched many commissions to Palestine, attempting to justify its curbs on Jewish immigration and settlement and to curry Arab favor. In 1929, Jews were massacred by rioting Arabs in Jerusalem, near the Western Wall, and in Hebron and Safed. British failure to protect these Jews provoked a storm of indignation in the press, in the pulpit, and in Congress. Senator William E. Borah (R-Idaho), Chairman of the Senate Committee on Foreign Relations, denounced British perfidy at a mass meeting in Madison Square Garden. However, the America of the twenties had become isolationist, and the Department of State failed to act.

In May 1932, shortly before Hitler came to power, congressmen established the pro-Zionist American Palestine Committee, headed by Senator William H. King (D-Utah). Vice President Charles Curtis, Senator Borah, and Senator Claude A. Swanson (D-Virginia), a ranking minority member, were honorary chairmen.

Many Jews sought refuge in Palestine, where Arabs intensified strikes and terrorism between 1937 and 1939. In 1938, an international refugee conference at Evian offered the Jews no solution; the State Department insisted that the question of Palestine was taboo and kept it off the agenda. American diplomats shared British fears that Arabs would join the Nazis if substantial numbers of Jews were permitted to enter Palestine.

The Roosevelt Administration remained scandalously silent in 1939 when the British issued the infamous White Paper, which drastically restricted Jewish land purchase and settlement in Palestine and limited Jewish immigration to 75,000 over the next five years, thereby portending doom for the Jewish state. A Capitol Hill protest was signed by 28 senators and by 15 of the 25 members of the House Committee on Foreign Affairs.

On April 30, 1941, Senator Robert F. Wagner (D-New York) revived the inactive American Palestine Committee. Senator Charles L. McNary (R-Oregon), minority leader, was co-chairman, and membership included 68 senators and more than 200 representatives. The Committee issued an eloquent declaration in 1942 to celebrate the twenty-fifth anniversary of the Balfour Declaration.

Many of Hitler's future victims might have been saved if the British had not set a terminal date on Jewish immigration into Palestine. Neutral nations might have opened their doors and provided a temporary haven if there had been assurances that Jewish refugees had a future destination and would not become permanent charges. The White Paper was a death warrant for many Jews.

AMERICAN JEWS UNITE

American Jews have a multiplicity of organizations serving diverse religious, philanthropic, cultural, and educational views and needs, but they have never created one permanent national Jewish organization to express the views of the totality. The American Jewish Conference came closest. It was conceived in 1942, and its liquidation, in 1948, came after it helped to win its major objective—the restoration of the Jewish state. It died in success—perhaps because of it.

When World War II began, the Jewish Agency for Palestine opened an office here, and American Zionists established the American Emergency Committee for Zionist Affairs. It included leaders of the Zionist Organization of America and of Hadassah, the Women's Zionist Organization. Also included were Labor Zionists, Religious Zionists, and small Zionist parties. Many other Jewish organizations were primarily concerned with domestic issues, and these bodies were generally described as "non-Zionist."

The State Department opposed this resurgence of Zionist activity; the

British went so far as to protest that an American Palestine Committee dinner might incite the Arabs and prejudice the war against the Nazis.

We Zionists agreed that our major objective was to defeat Hitler and that we must not be diverted from it, but we accepted the epigrammatic dictum of Israel's David Ben-Gurion, who had said, "We shall fight the White Paper as if there were no war and we shall fight the war as if there were no White Paper."

We appealed to our government to rescue Jews from Hitler. Manifestly, an open Palestine could provide the major avenue of escape, and Jewish organizations—both Zionist and non-Zionist—were united in demanding abrogation of the White Paper. American Jews, however, were divided on the issue of Jewish statehood. While almost all were opposed to the White Paper, some doubted that a Jewish state could ever be established, and some were strongly opposed.

Washington was not convinced that most American Jews favored a Jewish state. Accordingly, Zionists themselves had to decide whether to fight for the maximal objective or to compromise. In 1942, they convened an emergency conference in the Biltmore Hotel in New York, where Ben-Gurion successfully appealed for a clear and firm declaration, the "Biltmore Platform," which advocated establishment of a Jewish Commonwealth.

Dr. Chaim Weizmann, president of the World Zionist Organization and of the Jewish Agency for Palestine, and the scientist who had negotiated with the British for the Balfour Declaration, made the rounds of government and organization offices.

Leaders of the influential American Jewish Committee held diverse views. Some feared that establishment of the Jewish state would compromise their loyalty to the United States; some argued that the Jews could not have their own state as long as they were in the minority. Some did not want to antagonize our government, and others urged the Zionists to lower the standards of their objectives in order to preserve "Jewish unity."

Some belonged to the American Council for Judaism, a small remnant of the anti-Zionist wing of nineteenth-century Reform Judaism which was led by Lessing Rosenwald, a Philadelphia philanthropist, and by Rabbi Elmer Berger of Flint, Michigan, an inveterate foe. They strongly opposed a Jewish state because they rejected the concept of Jewish "peoplehood."

Weizmann was unable to reach an agreement with the Committee, and Jewish disunity weakened efforts to spur Washington to act.

Early in 1943, B'nai B'rith President Henry Monsky, a dynamic Omaha lawyer, convened a preparatory session in Pittsburgh of what was to become the American Jewish Conference, in the hope of establishing a consensus. He was the logical spearhead because his organization had the largest national Jewish membership and was one of the oldest.

To the New York session in 1943 came 123 delegates, representing 64 national Jewish organizations, and 379 delegates elected by 77 Jewish communities and 59 regions at local inter-organizational meetings which had convened for this purpose. The Conference agenda included three issues: the implementation of the rights of the Jewish people in Palestine, the rights and status of Jews in the post-war world, and immediate measures to rescue the Jews of Europe from Hitler. Throughout the spring of 1943 these issues were debated in national organizations and in communities.

During this campaign, I left for New York, on July 12, 1943, to become the public relations director of the American Emergency Committee for Zionist Affairs (AECZA). I witnessed the deep division in national Jewish leadership on the following evening.

At a meeting of Zionist and American Jewish Congress leaders, I was startled to hear Wise, the veteran chairman of both the Congress and AECZA, recommend postponement of the Conference because of the invasion into Europe. He also feared that the public might resent a Jewish conference on post-war planning at a time when casualty lists were mounting. The question was temporarily put aside.

In Palestine, the British were staging trials against gunrunning, and *The New York Times,* then strongly anti-Zionist, carried dispatches implying that an ulterior motive of the Jewish war effort was self-militarization in order to fight the Arabs. I drafted a long indignant statement which *The Times* featured in full. Our Committee, traditionally reticent under Wise-Goldmann leadership, was surprised by this initiative, but I was encouraged by Lipsky and Meyer Weisgal of the Jewish Agency—both veteran journalists— to take the offensive against our detractors, mobilizing a host of friends who had been silent much too long and who were eager to be activated.

Our major concern was due to the recurrent reports that Roosevelt wanted the Conference postponed, as Wise had indicated, and that the State Department had drafted a letter urging us to abstain from political action and post-war planning until after the war. Washington was alarmed that a pro-Zionist declaration would inflame the Arabs, provoke riots, and necessitate the diversion of seven divisions to protect the Jews in Palestine. Anti-Semites could then blame the Jews for prolonging the war and its casualties.

It was difficult to attack an unpublished letter, which, in fact, Roosevelt decided not to send. However, the omnipotent Drew Pearson did break the story in his column, enabling me to tell friendly editors and columnists that "we will not go underground with the hopes of the Jewish people."

In a tactical move to stave off the threatened letter, Under Secretary of State Sumner Welles, one of Zion's best friends in Washington, appealed to Wise for a postponement of the Conference. Wise urged our Committee to agree, but it was sharply divided. Wise slipped me a note requesting my opinion. "I disagree," I wrote back. "Jews will not understand. Somewhere we must stop our retreat and make a stand." Wise had another motive. He hoped for a compromise with the American Jewish Committee, whose leaders, he feared, would bolt the Conference if the maximal position prevailed. The majority of our Committee rebuffed him.

By this time, I was beginning to realize that the AECZA was not really a decision-making body but, like most umbrella committees, a loose federation of sovereign organizations, each of which could insist that debatable questions be referred to its governing bodies for ratification.

Soon after I arrived in New York, Silver, a fellow Clevelander, responded to a growing national draft that encouraged him to become the Council's chairman and to inaugurate a dynamic policy. Wise would serve as cochairman, creating a check and balance coalition. Differences erupted within hours after the American Jewish Conference opened its five-day session at the Waldorf-Astoria Hotel on Sunday, August 29.

In his keynote speech, Wise stressed the need to open the gates of Palestine to Jewish immigration, but he made no reference to a Jewish Commonwealth. Judge Joseph Proskauer, president of the American Jewish Committee, at once seized the opportunity to indicate that the Conference might emerge with a united program. The following morning, at a closed meeting of Zionist leaders, Silver furiously upbraided Wise. Wise fought back and offered his resignation, and I think Silver would have been willing to accept it, but Judge Louis E. Levinthal of Philadelphia and others defended Wise. This was the first of many climactic confrontations.

That night Silver insisted on reinstating the demand for the Jewish Commonwealth, rejecting the pressure for compromise. A magnificent orator—one of the world's greatest—he took the platform to thunder:

"If I agree with certain people, that is unity. If I ask them to agree with me, that is disunity."

The tumultuous ovation killed compromise.

The Palestine Committee of the Conference then voted for the Commonwealth resolution, 60 to 2, notwithstanding ominous reports, relayed from the White House, that Washington would not be pleased.

On Wednesday night, in a moving and dramatic celebration, the 501 Jewish leaders in the hall—there was only one absentee and that was due to a last minute Army call—voted with near unanimity for the Biltmore resolution.

There was no roll call; there was a show of hands. There were four negative votes, those of the American Jewish Committee, and 19 abstentions, announced by delegates of the Jewish Labor Committee (16) and the National Council of Jewish Women (3).

The Conference had been organized by a secretariat of representatives of major organizations, including Weisgal, Maurice Bisgyer, Jane Evans, Lillie Shultz and the Conference's administrative secretary, Jesse Calmenson. Now staff had to be recruited to implement the Conference program. A five-day conference and a set of resolutions submitted to Secretary of State Cordell Hull were not enough. An interim committee was elected and commissions were appointed. I joined the staff in December 1943, soon becoming its executive secretary.

Meanwhile, Silver had changed the AECZA's cumbersome name to the American Zionist Emergency Council. He was enlarging its staff and establishing local Zionist Councils to form a political and public relations offensive to capture the support of congressmen, clergy, editors, professors, business, and labor. In Cleveland, Silver and I had met infrequently while we were presidents of rival Zionist organizations which almost never cooperated, but I now learned that Silver, who rarely recognized peers, was most considerate and supportive of staff.

The Silver-Wise feud persisted. A champion of liberal causes for a generation, Wise had Roosevelt's friendship, but Silver feared that Roosevelt assumed that he carried the American Jewish community in his pocket, thanks to Wise's strong identification with him and with the Democratic party. Thus Silver felt compelled to tilt toward the GOP.

FRUSTRATION

Many critics have indicted my generation for its alleged apathy and inactivity to rescue Jews from the Holocaust. I offer no defense of our inability to move the Roosevelt Administration, but this criticism has been unjust.

At the preparatory session of the Conference, the agenda was broadened to include the urgent issue of rescue, but long before the Conference convened the following year there were protest demonstrations in many cities. I helped to stimulate and organize a mass meeting which brought 12,000 people to the Cleveland Public Auditorium in December 1942, under the auspices of the Jewish Community Council. We were balked by military leaders who constantly vetoed our appeals for rescue on the non-debatable grounds of military necessity, but they could not still our protests.

The Conference had three commissions to implement its resolutions on Palestine, post-war rights, and rescue. The Rescue Commission was by far the most active, for it was broadened to include the representatives of all concerned Jewish organizations. It was headed by two co-chairmen, Herman Shulman, a brilliant New York lawyer, and Rabbi Irving Miller of Long Island. I was its secretary. Our executive aide was an activist and veteran journalist, Meir Grossman, who had once been a lieutenant to Vladimir (Ze'v) Jabotinsky, the Revisionist leader, but who had organized his own State party after Jabotinsky withdrew from the World Zionist Organization. Lipsky, who admired Grossman, had put him to work at my side as director of our overseas relations.

What made our task most difficult was that the United States almost lost World War II at Pearl Harbor before it began. It was many months before the United States could have acted, even if it had sincerely wanted to, although it could have received many more Jewish refugees than it did. Its pre-war posture was indefensible.

The Conference sent delegations to Washington for sessions with John Pehle of the War Refugee Board, with State and Treasury officials, and with members of Congress. We attacked the State Department and issued a denunciation of Assistant Secretary of State Breckenridge Long's labored defense of U.S. immigration procedures—my memorandum to which Professor Benjamin Halpern, now of Brandeis University, made a major contribution. I drafted a statement for Wise for the House Foreign Affairs Committee in which we favored the opening of Palestine as the most feasible sanctuary. We also urged our own country to open its doors. The claim that we did not because we feared that this would somehow obstruct our drive for a Jewish state is an absurd and malicious canard which has been circulated by anti-Zionists, King Hussein, Arab propagandists, and the Neturei Karta. It has been belied by the resolutions and activities which we undertook in 1943, by our formal congressional testimony, and by top officials who dealt with the issue at the time: Pehle and the veteran George Warren of the State Department.

We helped to fill Madison Square Garden with mass demonstrations many times. We sponsored the tragic memorial meeting marking the first anniversary of the revolt in the Warsaw Ghetto. We appealed for food and supplies for Jews in occupied territory. We insisted that our government pressure the British to open Palestine and to clear escape routes. We urged cooperation with the underground to help in smuggling Jews across borders. We pleaded with neutral and satellite countries to provide havens. We called on the Administration for psychological warfare to encourage the Hungarians to shield Jews and to warn the Nazi war criminals that they would be punished; Washington agreed and we brought some 50,000 Jews to Madison Square Park to hear the Adminstration's warnings in an effort to save the threatened Jews of Hungary.

Our Post-War Commission was headed by the late Dr. Maurice Eisendrath, who represented the Union of American Hebrew Congregations, and by Chaim Greenberg, a Labor Zionist idealist. Dr. Alexander Kohanski was the Commission aide. The Commission advocated an international bill of rights, insisted that war criminals be punished, called for the restoration of rights and property for the Jews of Europe, and demanded reparations from the Nazis.

THE POLITICAL STRUGGLE

Silver became the first chairman of our Palestine Commission and was later succeeded by Professor Milton Handler of Columbia University. While the Zionist Council handled the day-to-day work on a massive scale, the Conference Commonwealth Resolution was all-important as a persuasive exhibit of the views of the American Jewish community. Monsky, the Conference spokesman, was invariably the lead-off witness at public hearings and demonstrations. We had our own office and staff in Washington. The demonstrated unity of the American Jewish community helped to win many non-Jews for Israel.

Monsky's co-chairmen were Wise and Rabbi Israel Goldstein. Our executive committee chairman was Lipsky, the Rochester-born Zionist, who helped to preserve the parliamentary integrity of the Conference, the dignity of its public utterances, and the diplomacy of its organizational relationships. He was a trenchant writer, a persuasive orator, and he had a commanding intellect. He helped us to produce impressive publications, which included the monthly Conference Record and "The Nazi War Against the Jews," an anthology of the Nuremberg documents.

The American Jewish Committee made good its threat to secede. This was resented by many American Jews, and some of the Committee's leaders and affiliated organizations resigned in protest. On the same Sunday afternoon that the Committee announced its secession, I released the resignation statements of influential Committee members. These included Rabbi B. L. Levinthal of Philadelphia, one of the five founders of the Committee, Judge Morris Rothenberg, and Mrs. David deSola Pool of New York. Others followed their example.

But within three years, by 1946, Committee leaders were endorsing the Jewish state and cooperating with the Jewish Agency for Palestine. In fact, the Committee was always ready to cooperate with the Conference, if not to belong to it, but this inevitably complicated organizational relations. It juxtaposed the Conference and the Committee as equals. While constituent members of the Conference, such as B'nai B'rith, the American Jewish Congress, and others, were ready to subordinate and submerge their organizational identity in the Conference, the Committee sought to equate itself with the Conference, thus retaining its own separate public relations personality and outranking Conference constituents.

In later years, the Committee helped our work, and I became a member of its executive committee in Washington.

Two other organizations hampered our efforts. The American Council for Judaism included some ninety ultra-Reform rabbis and laymen who were able to gain newspaper space because the press invariably features and exaggerates minority dissent. Even as the Conference convened, the Council issued a press release gratuitously insisting that the Conference did not speak for it, which, of course, we never presumed to do.

Although the Council insisted that Judaism was a religion only, its qualifications to offer testimony on this issue were questioned by religious authority of the major Jewish rabbinical bodies—Reform, Conservative, and Orthodox—whose presidents repeatedly condemned the Council's actions as a disservice to American Jews and to Israel.

Also disconcerting were the activities of a series of revolving committees organized in quick succession by Palestinian Jews, whose leader, Peter Bergson (Hillel Kook), represented the Irgun Z'vai Leumi, Menachem Begin's organization in Palestine. The Committee for a Jewish Army was followed by the Emergency Committee to Save the Jews of Europe, by the American League for a Free Palestine, and by the Hebrew Committee of National Liberation.

These committees had a flair for publicity. They purchased advertising space, had literary talent, held public conferences, and submitted legislation to Congress. They confused many people because they diluted and watered down programs, resorting to palatable and ambiguous euphemisms in order to win broad support. They rarely spoke of a Jewish state and they differentiated between the "Hebrews" of Palestine and the Jews of the United States, a strange distinction which few Jews could understand and which sounded very much like the separatism of the American Council for Judaism.

In May 1944, the Hebrew Committee for National Liberation opened an "embassy" in Washington, acting as "trustee" for the "Hebrew nation." We characterized the Committee as "an irresponsible adventurer" which lacked a mandate from the Jewish National Assembly in Palestine, and we charged that its bizarre ideology would fragmentize the Jewish people.

"One Jewish group hits another," was the off-hand press report.

In 1956, Bergson returned to Washington to promote Israel's cause, but the Israeli embassy disavowed this activity by Israeli citizens and congressmen swiftly withdrew sponsorship.

Our Conference Palestine resolution demonstrated the unified support of the American Jewish community and helped the American Zionist Emergency Council to win Congress early in 1944.

On January 27, Representatives James A. Wright (D-Pennsylvania) and Renulf Compton (R-Connecticut) introduced a resolution reaffirming the 1922 Lodge-Fish resolution and calling for free Jewish immigration and colonization in Palestine and its reconstitution as a free and democratic Jewish commonwealth.

Six days later, an identical resolution was sponsored by Senators Robert Wagner (D-New York) and Robert A. Taft (R-Ohio). Floor leaders of both Houses, Senators Alben W. Barkley (D-Kentucky) and Wallace H. White, Jr. (R-Maine), and Representatives John W. McCormack (D-Massachusetts) and Joseph W. Martin (R-Massachusetts), endorsed the resolutions.

There was opposition from the Council for Judaism and from spokesmen for Arab groups. An American Jewish Committee memorandum urged abrogation of the White Paper and an amendment to provide for an international trusteeship responsible to the United Nations. It asked that "final determination of this controversial question [of the Jewish Commonwealth] be deferred."

Within a few days, on February 23, General George C. Marshall, Army Chief of Staff, presented the military's objections at an executive session of the Senate Committee on Foreign Relations. The House Committee on Foreign Affairs deferred action because Secretary of War Henry Stimson had written that the War Department considered that "action at this time would be prejudicial to the successful prosecution of the war."

We then appealed to Roosevelt for a statement opposing the White Paper, which was scheduled to end Jewish immigration on March 31.

Roosevelt received Wise and Silver during the course of a conference convened in Washington by the American Palestine Committee, a Christian body, on March 9, and authorized them to issue a statement, in which for the very first time — after five years — the Administration made it clear that it had never approved the White Paper. They announced:

> The President is happy that the doors of Palestine are today open to Jewish refugees and that when future decisions are reached full justice will be done to those who seek a Jewish national home for which our government and the American people have always had the deepest sympathy, and today, more than ever, in view of the tragic plight of hundreds of thousands of homeless Jewish refugees.

That summer both national political conventions adopted their first pro-Zionist planks.

The Republican platform plank declared:

> In order to give refuge to millions of distressed Jewish men, women and children driven from their homes by tyranny, we call for the opening of Palestine to their unrestricted immigration and land ownership, so that in accordance with the full intent and purpose of the Balfour Declaration of 1917 and the resolution of a Republican Congress in 1922, Palestine may be constituted as a free and democratic commonwealth. We condemn the failure of the President to insist that the Mandatory of Palestine carry out the provision of the Balfour Declaration and of the mandate while he pretended to support them.

The Democratic plank declared:

> We favor the opening of Palestine to unrestricted Jewish immigration and colonization and such a policy as to result in the establishment there of a free and democratic Jewish commonwealth.

There was a significant difference. Both planks called for immigration and a commonwealth, but the GOP omitted the word "Jewish."

The military ban on action did not last long. Stimson wrote to Wagner and Taft on October 10, 1944, that military considerations were not as strong a factor as they had been. "In my judgment, political considerations now outweigh the military, and the issues should be determined upon the political rather than the military."

A few weeks later, Roosevelt endorsed the Democratic plank. He wrote:

Efforts will be made to find appropriate ways and means of effectuating this policy as soon as possible. I know how long and ardently the Jewish people have worked and prayed for the establishment of Palestine as a free and democratic Jewish commonwealth. I am convinced that the American people give their support to this aim. If reelected, I shall help to bring about its earliest realization.

And on his return from the Middle East, shortly before he died, Roosevelt reaffirmed his position. On March 16, 1945, he said:

"I made my position on Zionism clear in October. That position I have not changed and I shall continue to seek to bring about its earliest realization."

It remained for Harry Truman to be the first head of state to help bring the Jewish state into being and to recognize it.

Chapter 3

We Protect the Past

THE U.N. CHARTER CONFERENCE

When the United Nations met in San Francisco in 1945 to write its charter, we won our first clash with the Arabs by an overwhelming 25 to 5 vote.

Mindful of our ignominious isolationism of the 1920s when Washington refused to join the League of Nations, the State Department enlisted nongovernmental organizations to participate as consultants to the U.S. delegation at San Francisco, in the hope of rallying the American people for ratification of membership in the new world body.

Although the Jews had been the first people attacked by Hitler, and the most grievously wounded, they had not yet won statehood and status and were thus ineligible for participation in this first U.N. conference.

As the war neared an end, the American Jewish Conference applied to the State Department for the right to be present at the San Francisco meeting; the purpose of our physical presence would be to call attention to our diplomatic absence. Our demand was echoed at some eighty Jewish rallies across the United States which were sponsored jointly by the American Jewish Conference and AZEC.

We called on Francis Russell at the State Department to describe the broadly representative character of our organization, and we were selected as one of the thirty-six consultant bodies. Proskauer protested that the American Jewish Committee had earlier won a commitment from Roosevelt; other organizations similarly complained about their exclusion. The State Department then raised the number of consultant bodies to forty-two in order to make room for both majority and minority groups: Jews, lawyers, churchmen, veterans, etc. Many other disappointed organizations received invitations to serve as "advisers."

I drafted a memorandum for submission to the U.N. delegations, and Weisgal sent it to Abraham Klein, a Canadian Jewish poet, who lifted my prose into a dramatic epic.

"It is time," Klein wrote, "that the Four Freedoms should repay their debt to the Ten Commandments. . . . It is elementary justice that the voice of the most wronged of people should be heard. . . . The duty to speak for the survivors . . . is peremptory." He reminded world leaders that "an outmoded doctrine of sovereignty tolerated a member, deemed of the family of nations, to perpetrate with impunity every manner of atrocity." He recalled that a million and a half Jews had fought in the armies of the United Nations and that none had fought in the ranks of the enemy. He continued: "Every nation which had declared war against the Axis . . . will be represented. We ask that right also for the first victims of Nazi aggression."

The document was translated into Spanish, Russian, and French, and circulated to all delegations.

Our leadership included Monsky, the official consultant to the U.S. delegation, and two associate consultants, Goldstein and Lipsky. We were joined by leaders of many affiliated organizations and by international bodies: the Board of Deputies of British Jews, the World Jewish Congress, the Jewish Agency for Palestine, and the Canadian Jewish Congress.

Future Israeli diplomats were on hand: Arthur Lourie, who later became U.N. ambassador; Dr. Jacob Robinson, a brilliant international lawyer; Eliahu Epstein, later Elath, Israel's first ambassador to the United States; Reuven Shiloah, later an Israeli minister; and Gershon Agron, *Jerusalem Post* editor and later mayor of Jerusalem.

I opened a one-room office in the old Butler Building, where we were able to obtain space for our incoming colleagues because the building—a medical center—was soon to be demolished to make way for Magnin's department store. By the end of the week we needed the entire floor and a large attic civilian defense storage room for daily conferences.

On VE Day in May, while rejoicing crowds danced through the streets below, some thirty Jewish leaders solemnly prayed in that bare barn-like attic in a memorial service to the victims of the Holocaust. On that day, the press estimated six million Jews dead in Europe—and on that day, world leaders were not yet ready to consider the future of the survivors.

It was incongruous and galling to watch the sycophantic reception accorded the five participating Arab delegations, while we sat high above in the gallery of the San Francisco Opera House. The Arabs were latecomers. They had declared war against the Axis in the closing weeks of the war in 1945—Egypt on February 25, Syria on February 27, Lebanon on February 28, and Saudi Arabia on March 2—only because that was required for U.N. membership. During most of the war they had been—at best—neutral, sitting on the fence waiting to see who would win. Some had collaborated with the Nazis: Iraq, which had gone over to the Axis in 1941; Syria, which had been dominated by the Vichy French; and Egypt, whose leaders had cooperated with Nazi and Italian fascists.

Press agentry, purchased by the international oil companies, invested the gowned Arabs with glamour. California was their stage. San Francisco's smart society, urbane visiting diplomats, and sophisticated socialites obsequiously greeted them. Ben Swig's Fairmont Hotel prudently sent its dainty, chic Oriental elevator operators away on a long vacation. ("The glamour is robe deep," I bitterly reported to New York.)

We faced dangers more critical than glamour. Here were five enemies of Zion participating in discussion and debate inside committees and the Assembly.

Obviously, the U.N. charter could not itself provide for or prevent the establishment of a Jewish state, but hostile maneuver could complicate and obstruct it. We were apprehensive that the U.N. would some day replace the British Mandate with a U.N. trusteeship, and we feared that the rights our people had won under the League of Nations Mandate could be prejudiced in negative and ambiguous language composed by indifferent or antagonistic diplomats.

Accordingly, the Jewish Agency and the Conference proposed our own amendment to the charter in an attempt to safeguard the existing rights of peoples in areas which might be placed under trusteeship.

The U.S. delegation, headed by Commander Harold Stassen, accepted the principle of our proposal, but the five Arab states opposed it, and that led to a battle over a preposition and a plural. We had written about the rights of "the peoples *in* the area." The Egyptian delegation wanted to substitute "the people *of* the territory." We were fighting for *both* peoples, Jews and Arabs; they were concerned only with the Arab claim to Palestine. The press gave wide publicity to the debate over what came to be called the "Palestine clause."

At that time many San Francisco Jews were anti-Zionist, and the American Council for Judaism had attracted membership of the older settlers. Rabbi Berger, the Council's executive head, came out to hold a press conference, which he opened by ostentatiously unfurling a tiny U.S. flag. He had an audience of seven, mostly Jews, including myself.

I had invited the press to hear Monsky and Goldmann explain our proposals to more than one hundred correspondents. Either by coincidence or by design, Bergson's competitive group scheduled a press conference at the same hour. It was poorly attended.

All this rivalry—the Jews versus the Arabs and the organizational competition—mystified the press. A veteran Cleveland colleague, columnist Peter Edson, asked me for an interview, and I explained that our organization was the most representative of American Jewry. He wrote a widely syndicated article for the Newspaper Enterprise Association (NEA) which brought a rebuke from the leading local Reform rabbi, Irving F. Reichert, who was then a vice chairman of the Council. Six other San Francisco rabbis then signed a letter confirming the accuracy of Edson's article. The local Jewish community was embarrassed by this rash of publicity, and Dr. Reichert did not reply. A decade later, however, he repudiated the Council. In later years, I spoke in his Temple on several occasions, for San Francisco soon became a stronghold for Israel's cause.

The U.N. took its time and there was a long delay. Most of our Jewish leaders had little to do in San Francisco. Some had paid a courtesy call on Jan Masaryk, the Czechoslovakian diplomat, a warm friend of the Jews. They had addressed their organizations' local chapters and some had delivered sermons in synagogues. All went home, and two of us, Epstein of the Jewish Agency and I, were left alone as we waited for the Trusteeship Committee's verdict.

Early one morning, our long wait was suddenly interrupted by an urgent call from New York. *The Times* had carried a lengthy report that the Russians intended to oppose our amendment. The AZEC wanted Lipsky and Goldmann to fly back to San Francisco, and I was to arrange for the necessary airplane priorities. I was rebuffed by U.S. officials at the Fairmont because all westbound planes were jammed. The war had shifted to the Pacific. Besides, I was informed, our organization had been allowed more priorities than any other, except for the Rotary Club. I insisted that I had inherited Monsky's place as consultant to the U.S. delegation, that I was entitled to two associates, and that the officer must telephone LaGuardia airport and find two seats. He reluctantly complied but warned that these would be our last priorities.

Epstein went to see Peter Fraser of New Zealand, the chairman of the Trusteeship Committee, and I called on Benjamin Gehrig of the U.S. delegation. Both reassured us. They explained that the mails from Moscow were slow and that we had no reason to fear an adverse Soviet vote.

We gave Lipsky and Goldmann our welcome news at dinner that evening, whereupon the peripatetic Goldmann promptly asked me to arrange for a priority to enable him to fly back to New York as soon as possible. I told him that he would have to walk back and explained why. He then made me an offer:

"If you can get me the priority, your future in the Jewish state is assured"—surely an extravagant promise from one whose own future in the Jewish state was far from certain.

I protested: "Is it really fair to condition my future on my ability to get you an airplane priority? Suppose I fail. Is there not a consolation prize?" "Of course," he assured me. "If you fail, we make you at least the Consul General in Cleveland." "What is so special about being Consul General in Cleveland?" I asked. "Ah," he replied, "then Dr. Silver will have to come to you."

One day my office received a telegram from New York advising Goldmann that the AZEC had voted that he must remain in San Francisco until the last Arab had left. It was signed by Wise as the chairman of the AZEC. A few minutes later there was another telegram addressed to Goldmann: "In view of the forthcoming meeting with Truman, it is imperative that you return as quickly as possible for consultations." It, too, was signed by Wise in the name of the American Jewish Congress. Obviously Goldmann had called his secretary to solicit the second telegram, which enabled him to justify his request for a return priority. By an odd coincidence, the priority came through on the very day that the Trusteeship Committee voted to approve what became Article 80 of the U.N. charter.

The Committee had rejected the Egyptian amendment 25 to 5, as well as other amendments which would have advanced Arab claims.

As finally adopted, the Article provided that nothing in the trusteeship system "shall be construed in or of itself to alter in any manner the rights whatsoever of any states or any peoples or the terms of existing international instruments in which members of the United Nations may respectively be parties." There was a disconcerting sequel. In 1948, when the United States reversed its stand on the U.N. partition resolution and called for a U.N. trusteeship, Senator Warren Austin (R-Vermont) cited Article 80 as justification, and I concluded that we had made a disastrous blunder at San Francisco. I rationalized that our position in 1945 had been a defensive one, but now that it had become dynamic in 1948 and we were pressing for change, our 1945 formula could be used against us.

For many years I wrote off our San Francisco experience as a self-inflicted disaster. But then in 1977, thirty-two years later, much to my astonishment former Under Secretary of State Eugene V. Rostow repeatedly cited Article 80 to defend Israel's settlements in the West Bank, contending that the area was still governed by the terms of the original Mandate and that the language of Article 80 permitted both Arabs and Jews to reside in the West Bank, as was the case during the British Mandate. I frequently referred to Article 80 in 1978, when we challenged the Carter Administration's contention that Israeli settlements were illegal and an obstacle to peace.

We had other interests in San Francisco. The American Jewish Committee had joined us in our drive for Article 80 and we, in turn, joined with the Committee and many other organizations to appeal for an international bill of rights, one of the 1943 objectives of the American Jewish Conference.

In response, the proposed U.N. charter was amended to include, as a major U.N. purpose, "the promotion of universal respect for and observance of human rights and fundamental freedoms for all without distinction as to race or sex or language or religion."

We were disappointed, for we would have preferred "protection" to "promotion." What an extraordinary difference that word might have made! Centuries of Jewish persecution called for an international body which would be empowered to combat the rise of new Hitlers. We naively believed that the new world organization of democracies that had triumphed over Hitler might want to have that power. On the other hand, who could have then imagined that some day the U.N. might degenerate and welcome a Yasir Arafat to its podium, denounce Zionism as racist and become an instrument to propagate anti-Semitism rather than to castigate and curb it.

Chapter 4

Stateless and Nameless

RESTORING LIFE

In 1945, the world's cameras focused on the barbarism of Buchenwald, Bergen Belsen, Auschwitz, Dachau, and many other death factories where Hitler's gauleiters had won the war of the Holocaust. They revealed the annihilation of millions of Jews and the desolation and despair of the surviving remnant.

There were mass graves. Some were low, flat, oblong mounds, concealing piles of skeletons; some were shallow ditches, convenient backdrops for a machine gun census. The armies of liberation, slicing the barbed wires of the concentration camps, had found heaps of half-dead bodies—living skeletons. Their breath, muscles, and bones had to be revived, and they had to be taught to stand up and to come alive.

Only the strongest had lived. Some died even as liberators neared, and some perished at the hands of the liberators themselves because the Nazis were diabolical. When American troops approached, the Nazis herded 3,500 Jews into cattle cars in order to cover the retreating Nazi troops. They were bombed by American planes, and 500 lay dead and wounded in the wooded no-man's-land between German and American armies.

No-man's-land. That is where the Jews of Europe were found and tried to find themselves, and they were no land's people. They had no firm ground under their feet; they had no permanent roof over their heads; they belonged to no place. Few were willing to recognize them for what they were—Jews.

The concentration camp Jew had dreamed that he would soon walk free. In absurd fantasy, just beyond the barbed wire, was Palestine.

But now, when "liberators" came to his bunk, he was bewildered. For they asked him: "Who are you and what are you?"

"We are Jews," the skeletons answered.

"No, no," the soldiers remonstrated. "We mean, what is your nationality? Where were you born? What are you? Not your religion. Your nationality."

"We are Jews," they said, once again.

"No, no. Are you Lithuanians? Are you Poles? Are you Latvians? Where were you born? Don't you understand?"

It was the liberators who could not understand their plight, their fears, their hopes.

The inability to recognize the ethnic identity of the Jews had political implications.

Diplomats knew what was ahead. The Department of State and the British Foreign Office knew that the Jewish remnant would press to open Palestine. It would be better not to recognize them as Jews and to repatriate them to Eastern Europe.

We were in San Francisco on VE Day, but in New York, Grossman, my Conference colleague, entrained for Washington. He met Representative Emanuel Celler (D-New York) and other New York congressmen, and urged them to propose that our Conference be permitted to send special envoys to bring the greetings of American Jews to Jewish DPs and to assure them that we were deeply concerned about their future.

They cabled the request to General Eisenhower and submitted it to the United Nations Relief and Rehabilitation Agency (UNRRA) and the War and State Departments. The displaced persons were receiving relief from the Army, from UNRRA, and from the American Joint Distribution Committee, but we wanted to lift morale, rights, and dignity, and to deliver the promise of swift liberation from barbed wire enclosures.

Permission was deferred because, it was argued, Jews were a religious group and, if Jewish liaison officers were allowed to go over, there would have to be Protestants and Catholics as well.

Someone who was much more powerful helped to disclose that Jewish DPs were really Jews. Responding to appeals that Jewish DPs be allowed to go to Palestine at once, Truman sent Earl G. Harrison, dean of the University of Pennsylvania Law School and the U.S. representative on the Intergovernmental Committee on Refugees, to make a special survey in June 1945. Bisgyer and I talked with Harrison before he left, but he did not need our briefing. His shocking report was published in the fall:

"As matters now stand, we appear to be treating the Jews as the Nazis treated them except that we do not exterminate them."

Three months after VE Day, Harrison reported, guarded Jewish DPs were living behind barbed wire fences in the former Nazi camps, in total idleness and with no opportunity, except surreptitiously, to communicate with the outside world. They lacked medical supplies, and their 2,000-calorie diet included 1,250 calories of black, wet, unappetizing bread. The death rate was high. Many wore the hideous striped pajama concentration camp garb; others wore SS uniforms. There was no organized effort to reunite scattered families.

"The first and plainest need of these people is a recognition of their actual status and by this I mean their status as Jews," Harrison wrote. He stressed that most Jews wanted to leave Germany and Austria as soon as possible, and that Palestine was their first choice. For them, "it is nothing short of calamitous to contemplate that the gates of Palestine should soon be closed."

Our request embarrassed the Establishment, and it filibustered. It had been filed on May 12; the War Department withheld approval until July 28. UNRRA acted on September 21 – just eight days before the Harrison report. The State Department delayed passports for weeks. Our six Conference representatives finally reached the camps in November and December.

They met bitter reproach. Why had they taken so long? Why had they abandoned European Jewry?

Harrison's report swiftly brought reforms as the Jewish DPs were separated from ex-Nazis and ex-collaborators. At the same time their number began to rise as many streamed into the American and British zones of Germany. They had found a haven in the Soviet Union during the war and had returned to Poland, which they now found intolerable, partly because of a recrudescent anti-Semitism, and partly because the new leftist society frowned on both traditional orthodoxy and nationalism. Others came from Hungary, Czechoslovakia, and Rumania. Some were disillusioned leftists who had encountered anti-Semitism in the Soviet Union.

At first, the U.S. military were disposed to halt these new refugees, but the War Department ruled that they be allowed temporary shelter. The British disagreed. Lieutenant General Sir Frederick S. Morgan, the British chief of UNRRA in Germany, fired the first political shot in what became a year-long fusillade, on January 2, 1946. He "exposed" the Jewish exodus as a conspiracy financed by a sinister organization that provided food, clothing, and funds. We protested to Director General Herbert Lehman of UNRRA, but Morgan survived our attack. Judge Simon Rifkind, whom Truman named as the civilian adviser to the Army on Jewish affairs, derided Morgan's charges as poppycock.

Restless, venturesome DPs began to travel the underground railroad to Palestine aided by the Palestinian Jews who had served in the British Army and by emissaries of the Haganah. The British tried to head them off, detaining refugee ships in European ports and ordering the Royal Navy to intercept others in the Mediterranean.

We invited their elected spokesman, Dr. Zalman Grinberg, to address the third session of the American Jewish Conference in February 1946, in Cleveland. He was the chairman of the Central Committee of the Liberated

Jews of Europe. He had learned English by listening to the BBC. This intense, dark-eyed doctor — an envoy from purgatory — did much to reunite our Jewish communities.

"I know that you have your Zionists, anti-Zionists and your non-Zionists," he would tell American Jewish audiences. "We do not ask you to change your point of view, but we do want you to know that we think we know what is best for us. We want to go to Palestine to live with our own people in a state of our own. We do not want to live in strange lands among strange people."

I took Grinberg to Washington to meet Lehman and General John H. Hilldring, chief of the Civil Affairs Division of the War Department. He appealed for farmlands to be cultivated by the Jews in the camps. (This request had previously been turned down.) He asked for all-Jewish hospitals; Jewish DPs did not want the ministrations of German doctors because of their past "treatment" by German "scientists."

While they had no U.S. visas to offer him, reporters invariably asked Grinberg whether he and his fellow DPs would like to emigrate to the United States, and his answer shocked them.

"The Jews in Germany do not wish to go to America because they fear that what happened to them in Europe may happen to them over here." Pressed, he would explain: "We Jews were as well integrated into our communities as you are in America and you must understand our psychological reaction to strange places and strange people."

We told him that he sounded unreasonable, but he soon could point to unpleasant evidence. We went into the House gallery and, within his first twenty minutes, he heard John Rankin (D-Mississippi), a rabid anti-Semite, denounce Adolph Sabath, the beloved Jewish legislator from Illinois, some twenty times. A pale Grinberg counseled me: "Pack your bags and come with me to Palestine — now."

Rifkind resigned in May of 1946. His successor, Rabbi Philip S. Bernstein of Rochester, author of a widely read book, *What the Jews Believe,* wanted to simplify communication lines with American Jewish organizations. He designated my office as his post office, and I became convenor of a small working committee, which included representatives of the Conference, the Committee, the Congress, the JDC, and the Jewish Agency. We met regularly to consider DP problems and to receive and reply to Bernstein's letters.

The Kielce pogrom in Poland on July 4 brought a new flood of panic-stricken Jewish refugees into the American camps in Germany — as many as 3,900 in one night.

Our five organizations appealed to Washington to keep the door open. Bernstein went to Poland and reported that 100,000 Jews were on their way. He urged the Army to receive them, which it did over British protest. He invited five Jewish leaders to Frankfurt to meet with General Joseph T.

McNarney and to express thanks for the Army's cooperation. We were in Paris at this time offering our views to the Paris Peace Conference. The five were Goldmann, Wise, Jacob Blaustein of the Committee, Judge Philip Forman of the JDC, and I.

The invitation came on Monday to visit Frankfurt for a Friday lunch. When I asked our embassy in Paris for permits to enter Germany, the clerk protested that she needed six weeks to process my request. I insisted that she send a cable, and, much to her amazement, the permits came by Wednesday; we were soon on our way to Frankfurt. I had telephoned my Washington aide to expedite them, and he later revealed that he had simply gone to the War Department, posed as a representative of the State Department, and demanded immediate action on our cable. He had then personally carried the cable to the State Department, where, posing as a representative of the War Department, he again received swift attention.

En route to Frankfurt, I asked Blaustein how the Committee, which by that time had come out for partition in Palestine, could reconcile its support for a Jewish state with its past hostility.

"We were opposed to a Jewish state in an area where Jews would be in the minority," he explained. "But if there is partition and Jews become a majority in the area allotted to them, we would have no objections."

I pointed out that the Conference and the Committee were now in agreement on most questions. And I went on: "I guess all that separates you and me now is about $40 million."

Blaustein, who was the head of Amoco, modestly demurred. "Please don't exaggerate my assets," he protested. "But don't you underestimate my liabilities," I retorted. Many years later I learned that prior to our trip, while still in Washington, Blaustein had most eloquently urged our government to keep the borders open.

We visited McNarney in his huge I. G. Farben office, which, mysteriously, had never been bombed during the war, and we received the welcome assurance that the border would remain open. We toured some of the DP camps to assure inmates that liberation would come soon.

Wise and Goldmann made speeches. Goldmann said, "I see a ray of light at the end of the tunnel." Few others did. The DPs fervently sang Hatikvah. They were led by a spirited Christian woman from Norway, Mathilde Oftedal, a dedicated social worker who had come from Oslo to serve UNRRA.

A one-woman rehabilitation army, she besieged the authorities and demanded better facilities. She commandeered a whole village so that the DPs could live normally outside barracks. She transformed Lindenfels, a former mountain retreat for Nazi officers, into a children's village. There, several hundred boys and girls marched past a "reviewing stand" to salute the American visitors. They sang a sad, pathetic camp melody: "We have worked long enough for strangers. Tomorrow, we shall work for ourselves."

The number of Jewish DPs in the American zone had now risen from 45,000, when the war ended, to about 200,000.

The dread question kept arising. What would happen if the DPs could not get out of Germany? Could they live with former Nazis?

The Cold War had begun and it was already clear in 1946 that East and West were cultivating the erstwhile Nazis. In that competitive appeasement, Jews might be forced once again to take last place in the queue.

In November 1945, I had gone to London and Paris to work with the Board of Deputies of British Jews and the World Jewish Congress to draft proposals for submission to the peacemakers on rehabilitation, reparations, compensation for property, the disposition of heirless property, and human rights.

The war against the Jews of Europe was far from over. Jews were still dying in the aftermath of victory, of disease and hunger and, some of them, of sheer weariness – a spiritual death.

In London, I had read "Perish Judah" scrawled in ugly letters on fences which boarded up the rubble of the tenements in which Jews had been buried in the blitz.

Jewish children were being baptized in France by free-thinking Jews, who hoped thus to spare them from anti-Semitism in the future. Jews who emerged from the underground to reclaim their rights, their shops, and their apartments were resisted by the new "owners," who had a vested interest in anti-Semitism. I saw the freshly-chalked sign "Mort Aux Juifs" on the Great Synagogue in the Rue de la Victoire.

Most strange was diplomacy's refusal to recognize the existence of the Jewish people, as a people.

The Intergovernmental Committee on Refugees was holding its first meeting since the war, in a Paris palace. My companion was a shy and sensitive scholar, Dr. J. C. Flaiszir, an expert for the Board of Deputies, who later, renamed Jacob Talmon, became a world-renowned scholar at the Hebrew University. We submitted our memorandum, but far more eloquent was a unique exhibit in the foyer which attracted attention. It depicted Bergen Belsen. The artists were camp inmates who had drawn on their haunted memories to ask the world to remember with them. The admonition, "Don't forget Belsen," appeared in eight languages beneath a crude crayon and charcoal drawing which starkly portrayed the horrors of that infamy. There rose the gas chambers, the belching furnaces, the guards with their hounds and their whips, and the emaciated cadavers.

The tall and gaunt Sir Herbert Emerson, director of the Committee, made an hour-long report. In his lengthy discourse on the future of refugees, Emerson studiously avoided all reference to Jews. In a tour around the map, which included Germany, Austria, Hungary, Poland, the Balkans, England, South America, and Sosua, he made no reference to Palestine.

It was like Evian in 1938 and Bermuda in 1943 – arenas where, by State Department order, the subject of Palestine was taboo. The emphasis was on repatriation, not on resettlement. "Quite a large number wish to go back to Austria," Emerson said. "A few wish to go back to Germany. I hope that the number will increase. There must be certain conditions satisfied. They must have guarantees and be satisfied that these guarantees will be carried out and that on their return they will be able to live the full and free life of citizens, free from hatred and intolerance that were their constant companions for many years. Their confidence in the future has to be built up. This will be a gradual process. Our representatives can give a helping hand to those who do return."

He conceded that some refugees would want to settle elsewhere. The committee had sent a representative to South America who would help refugees to get there and would "help those governments to get the type of refugees they want."

Emerson appealed for cooperation to help reunite families. England was setting an example, offering a haven for immigrants who had relatives there and for young people. He vaguely referred to Jewish refugees. "This is to occupy the attention of the Joint Commission [the Anglo-American Committee of Inquiry]; namely, how to create conditions in Germany and Austria and other countries that will encourage the return of the refugees of their own free will."

When we returned on the second day, the Jewish art exhibit had disappeared, and I learned that the British had renamed the camp Hohne—a simple way to erase the memory of the Bergen Belsen nightmare.

My major task for the American Jewish Conference at Paris in the summer of 1946 was to serve as the executive officer of more than twenty leading Jewish organizations and to assist in the submission of appeals for the restoration of rights and property, as well as for reparations to the Jewish victims of the Nazis, in the peace treaties to be signed with the four ex-satellite countries: Hungary, Rumania, Bulgaria, and Italy.

Our discussions of the treaties were interrupted on June 29, 1946—Black Saturday—when the British arrested 2,900 Jews in Palestine, including Moshe Sharett, the political director of the Jewish Agency, and many of his colleagues, for alleged gun-running and other crimes against the Mandatory regime. I called on Ben Gurion, my neighbor at the Royal Monçeau, and he shouted: "There's a pogrom in Palestine. Go there. Go at once, help them. Do what you can." I did not need much convincing. I was soon on my way, the first of twenty-two visits to the future Jewish state.

I arrived in Palestine on July 4, Independence Day, and offered my assistance to Michael Comay, who was then running a public relations desk for the Jewish Agency at the Eden Hotel. He asked little help from me, and he sent me on a two-week tour of the country. I was appalled by the British suppression of human rights and their harsh restrictions on economic progress and development. Even then it was manifest that a Jewish state existed *de facto,* and that it would surge ahead once the British moved out.

I was fortunate to come out alive. Abba Eban and I almost met in a close encounter in eternity. On the morning of July 22, 1946, I was preparing to leave for Cairo on my return trip to Paris. With an hour to spare, I stopped at the King David Hotel to get a manicure. Since there was no manicurist, I left on the Egyptian Misr plane for Cairo. There, several hours later, on the veranda of the Shepheard Hotel, I read the glaring headlines which announced that Begin's Irgun had blown up the wing of the hotel which housed the British Mandatory offices. There were ninety-one dead.

I recently learned from Eban's autobiography that he had gone to the King David that afternoon looking for a barber. He arrived too late, for that wing had already been blown up. I was to meet him often under safer circumstances.

I had no desire to remain in Cairo, but it was a week before I could get a plane to Paris. I never knew why; either there were no accommodations, or the British, bitter over the Irgun outrage, held me back because of my role in the pro-Zionist American Jewish Conference.

Chapter 5

Truman Has Fine Eyesight

TO THE U.N.

Truman became President on April 12, 1945, and eight days later he assured Wise that he "would do everything possible" to carry out "the expressed policies of the Roosevelt Administration"—whatever those were—despite warnings by the diplomatic establishment that the United States had commitments to the Arabs.

Truman urged Prime Minister Churchill to raise the Palestine issue at the forthcoming Potsdam conference. Churchill had always called himself a Zionist. Out of office, in 1939, he had vehemently denounced the Chamberlain White Paper. In office, as prime minister throughout the war, he had maintained that policy.

Just before Potsdam, the British Labor Party, led by Clement Attlee, regained power. Like Churchill, when they were out of office they had denounced the White Paper and, in a December 1944 resolution, had even urged transfer of Arabs out of Palestine—a population exchange to make room for the Jews—and an extension of Palestine's frontiers. At Potsdam, the British warned Truman that huge forces would be needed to overcome Arab opposition. Upon his return, much to our dismay, Truman told the press that while he favored diplomatic action to establish a Jewish state, he had "no desire to send 500,000 American soldiers there to make peace in Palestine."

The British challenged Truman. If the United States wanted to criticize, it must assume responsibilities; they invited the United States to join an Anglo-American Committee of Inquiry which would consist of six Englishmen and six Americans. The British proposed to study how many DPs could be repatriated and which non-European countries would resettle the remainder, but Truman insisted that Palestine be the focus of the inquiry. The British reluctantly agreed.

Ernest Bevin, Labor's Foreign Secretary, exposed his own animus when, in announcing the forthcoming inquiry, he scoffed that "if the Jews, with all their sufferings, want to get too much at the head of the queue, you have the danger of another anti-Semitic reaction through it all." Infuriated, we recalled that Jews had been "at the head of the queue" when Hitler had picked his victims and marched them to the death chambers.

THE ANGLO-AMERICAN INQUIRY

American Zionist leadership testified before the Anglo-American Committee. Monsky led off, noting that an Elmo Roper poll in October 1945 showed that eight out of every ten American Jews favored a Jewish state; only one was opposed and only one was undecided. An UNRRA poll showed that more than 98 percent of the Jews in the camps designated Palestine as their first choice. Some fifty Jews designated crematoria as their second choice; for them it was Palestine or no place.

When the Committee reached London, Bevin promised to carry out any unanimous recommendations—a tactic designed to discourage controversial proposals.

Taking Bevin at his word, the Committee unanimously recommended that 100,000 certificates for immigration into Palestine be issued as rapidly as possible. As for the future, it suggested that Palestine should be neither Jewish nor Arab, that neither Arabs nor Jews should dominate each other, and that the ultimate government "shall . . . fully protect and preserve the interests of the three faiths, Christian, Moslem, and Jewish, in the Holy Land."

It proposed that the British continue to hold the Mandate until a U.N. trusteeship was established to promote Arab-Jewish cooperation. Our organization denounced this as "a sharp blow at the Jewish people and the Jewish national home."

If Truman assumed that Bevin would honor his promise to accept any unanimous recommendation, he was soon disillusioned.

Attlee demanded U.S. assistance in shouldering the military and financial burdens, and attached a new condition. There could be no large-scale immigration until the Haganah and other Jewish units were disarmed. On the one hand, the British did not want to send troops to defend Jewish immigrants. Now they proposed to disarm those who would and could.

Bevin taunted, "Americans wanted Jews in Palestine because they did not want too many of them in New York."

We charged that the establishment of the Committee of Inquiry had been an "idle gesture," for the British would accept only recommendations which accorded with their predetermined view.

In a new dilatory tactic, the British now refused to discuss the admission of immigrants unless all political aspects were considered; they proposed a new committee of experts. An impatient and angry Truman, who had offered U.S. assistance to transport and house the immigrants, had no alternative but to name American experts to join a new technical commission to produce still another report.

There was bitter reaction in Palestine, where three Jewish organizations were fighting the Mandatory. The Haganah was the underground force responsible to national leadership. Organized to defend Jewish settlement, it helped Jewish immigration, disrupting British communications, facilities, and installations, especially those used to obstruct immigration. There were two dissident groups: the Irgun Z'vai Leumi, the military arm of the new Zionist organization, a right-wing party; and the Stern group, a small terrorist wing split from the Irgun Z'vai Leumi. They were in a war against the British—not the Arabs.

In mid-1946, the increasingly repressive British began to detour "illegal" Jewish immigrants to Cyprus. Insisting that they would not use force to implement the Inquiry's recommendations, they did not hesitate to use force to block them. Attlee, who had been demanding that the Jews disarm, now intended to do it for them.

Late in July, the experts produced the Grady-Morrison plan which provided for two "semi-autonomous" provinces in Palestine with a strong British-dominated federal government. The tiny Jewish state would include only 1,500 square miles of Palestine's 10,000. The central government would control Jerusalem and Bethlehem, as well as the Negev, which the British wanted to retain because of military and mineral considerations. Jewish immigrants would trickle in at the rate of 1,500 a month. At that rate, it would take a decade to empty the camps.

Monsky joined Zionist leaders in Washington in an appeal to the Administration to shelve the proposal. Truman, who did not need much persuading, told the British that he could not agree.

On October 4, the Jewish Day of Atonement, Truman reaffirmed his appeal for the admission of 100,000 Jews to Palestine, and in a message to Attlee he endorsed a Jewish Agency proposal for partition, promising U.S. support. Several days later, Governor Thomas E. Dewey of New York likewise called for mass Jewish immigration into Palestine.

The British charged that Truman's statement might "well jeopardize a settlement of this difficult problem." Hinting that Truman and Dewey were motivated by domestic considerations, they blamed the collapse of their negotiations on the United States. Arab leaders echoed Bevin's protests, and Truman then wrote a firm letter to Ibn Saud, leaving no doubt that the United States favored the establishment of a Jewish national home.

Bevin's attacks on Truman reinforced U.S. diplomats who wanted Anglo-American collaboration. As a result, an angry and tormented Truman retired to the sidelines of the silent, where he remained for many months.

On February 7, 1947, the British offered a new program: to administer Palestine as a U.N. trustee pending complete independence within five years.

Ten days later, we appealed to the U.S. government to be our voice, but the Administration demurred. Secretary of State Marshall told us that a solution would be facilitated if there were a "free and full conference between the representatives of the British government and the Jewish-Arab leaders . . . in a conciliatory spirit."

The British then turned to the U.N.

The Jewish Agency was recruiting staff in New York and Washington, and Moshe Sharett (then Shertok) invited me to be its Director of Information. Monsky and Lipsky granted me a leave of absence from the Conference, where we were then busy on many fronts: to help put DPs to work; to prepare documentation for the peace conference with Germany and Austria, if there was to be one; to justify the demand for reparations; to liberalize U.S. immigration laws.

The Jewish Agency leadership, housed in an old East 66th Street brownstone, met almost daily. The major Zionist parties had their representatives: Silver, who headed the Agency's American section; Emanuel Neumann, spokesman for the Zionist Organization of America (ZOA); Rose Halprin for Hadassah; Chaim Greenberg for the Labor Zionists; Rabbis Max Kirshblum and Wolf Gold for the Religious Zionists; and Goldmann of the Agency. Lourie was the executive officer. We had three staff representatives: Dorothy Adelson; Lionel Gelber, a Canadian scholar; and Menachem Kahane, the Agency's representative at Geneva. We were joined by Eban, the Jewish Agency's information director in London, Epstein, Comay, Shiloah, Moshe Yuval, Moshe Toff—who was a most effective liaison with Latin America—and others who came from Jerusalem.

During the next forty months, I was the press spokesman for the Agency, and later for the Israeli U.N. delegation. Public opinion was overwhelmingly on our side and I was warmly welcomed in the press section. My responsibility was to be always available. In May 1948, when Israel invited me to join its U.N. delegation, Fern Marja of *The New York Post* wrote a page-length profile describing me as the "Pied Piper of Lake Success." The headline said: "As essential as an E in your typewriter."

VOICELESS AND VOTELESS

We had grave misgivings because we were voiceless and voteless, while the Arab League had five votes and could challenge the U.N.'s competence to make any inquiry. My first press statement stressed the Jewish Agency's right to participate and to be heard because of its official status under the Mandate. I also recalled that the Egyptians had never lifted a fez to help win World War II.

There was no assurance of status, and there was doubt that we would even have tickets of admission. At the last minute, we were advised that we would be seated in a section reserved for the public.

In 1945, we had gone to San Francisco to call attention to the anomaly that the first victims of the Nazis were not represented in the new international parliament. Now, in this special U.N. session on Palestine deciding the future of the Jewish people, we certainly had every right to participate. It occurred to me that we should dramatize the denial of status by failing to show up. Our absence would be significant. Silver accepted that idea, and when the U.N. session opened and cameramen were massed at the door to photograph the incoming Jewish leaders, they were bewildered by my arrival in an otherwise empty limousine. The afternoon press bannered the paradox: "Zionists Boycott the U.N."

Every such episode bolstered our appeal for status. There was my own unconventional position as the Jewish Agency's press spokesman. I gained admission by asking for press credentials as editor of our publication, *The Conference Record*. George Barnes and Matthew Gordon, the U.N. press officers, seated me in a long corridor near the press section which was reserved as headquarters for organization representatives. My "office" was called the "DPs Wailing Wall." This courtesy was justified as a service—not to us—but to the press, who wanted to know where to find us.

Our misgivings might have been much graver had we known then, as declassified documents revealed many years later, that Loy Henderson, who was then Director of Near Eastern and African Affairs, and his colleagues in the State Department were already drafting a plan for U.N. trusteeship over Palestine, and that Truman would not endorse partition pending the outcome of the U.N. inquiry. Cooperating with the British, American diplomats at first contended that our appearance was unnecessary because the special session would merely designate a committee to investigate the Palestine problem—purely a procedural matter. Eventually the United States agreed that the Assembly should instruct its Political Committee to grant the Agency a hearing, and this was approved by a large majority.

The Arab states threatened to walk out unless the Assembly reconvened immediately to elevate the Arab Higher Committee to the same plane as the Agency. The Assembly yielded.

There was another unnecessary debate. Which Jewish body should present the Jewish case?

The British wished to project a confusing image of a divided Jewish community, even though major Jewish bodies had emphasized the Agency's undeniable right to serve as spokesman. Other, minor Jewish organizations had been on hand, contributing to disarray, but not for long. Bergson's Hebrew Committee of National Liberation folded its press releases and disappeared. The brief appearance of the American Council for Judaism was paradoxical. Why should this organization bother with the U.N. when it was so busily insisting that American Jews had no place there because they were, in fact, represented by the U.S. delegation? Nor was it clear why the anti-Zionist Agudath Israel should be heard before a political body, as the British proposed, inasmuch as it disavowed all political action.

At that session Arab diplomats prejudiced their cause by overstatement and extremism. Totally uncompromising, they hinted that Jews already in Palestine should be deported, and they threatened war.

The *Nation Magazine*'s Associates, headed by Freda Kirchwey and Lillie Shultz, had circulated a document indicting the pro-Axis activities of the ex-Mufti of Jerusalem, who had joined Hitler in Berlin—coincidentally, on December 7, 1941, the "Day of Infamy"—to broadcast calls for the "final solution." Unabashed, an Arab spokesman, Emile Ghori of Lebanon, likened this notorious war criminal to Field Marshal Jan Smuts, George Washington, and other patriots. There was an audible gasp in the audience when he declared: "The Jews are questioning the record of an Arab spiritual leader. Does that properly come from the mouth of the people who crucified the founder of Christianity?"

After that polemic, the Committee defeated Arab proposals which called for immediate Palestine independence and which would have barred any visits to the DP camps.

Silver, Sharett, and Ben-Gurion summarized the Zionist case in less than eighty minutes, with a plea for Arab-Jewish cooperation.

American reluctance to support our cause had always been predicated on the nightmare that the Soviets intended to side with the Arabs, for Communists had always denounced Zionism as the tool of British imperialism. But on May 14, 1947, the USSR's Andrei Gromyko astonished the Assembly when he called for establishment of an Arab-Jewish state in Palestine, adding that, if that were impracticable, the Soviet Union would favor partition. The Soviets were not courting the Arabs or the Zionists; their purpose was to liquidate British influence in the Middle East. Shortly before he spoke, Gromyko had asked us for background material, and we sent him our "Nazi Germany's War Against the Jews," the compilation of relevant Nuremberg documents which the Conference had published early that year.

The Gromyko statement dissipated the Arab League's blackmail power, and it should have quieted U.S. fears that the Soviet Union intended to exploit the debate to buy Arab favor. I spent that afternoon pointing out to newspapermen that there was no longer reason to inhibit U.S. endorsement of Truman's 1946 pro-partition stand, and that we could now hope for a positive result if the United States and the USSR were agreed. The friendly *New York Herald Tribune* headlined our argument the next morning, but the U.S. delegation remained frigidly neutral, even though it was now clear that Bevin's plans had boomeranged.

THE UNSCOP VISIT

The 11-nation U.N. Special Committee on Palestine (UNSCOP), dispatched to make an investigation, was unique, for all the major powers were excluded. Also, unlike all preceding inquiries, this one was free from the control of the British. Now it was they who were downgraded.

I traveled with UNSCOP as a member of the Jewish Agency's liaison team, which was headed by Eban and which also included Toff and David Horowitz, later governor of the Bank of Israel. My assignment was to brief the American press, and I strengthened the Agency's relations with newspapermen.

UNSCOP found two peoples claiming the entire country but in agreement on two fundamental issues: both wanted independence and termination of the British Mandate. Thus, partition was the logical solution and I was optimistic that UNSCOP would recommend it, although most people were convinced that the British would try to block implementation of any such recommendation.

British rule had become brutal. On April 16, after the announcement of the special U.N. session, the British had executed four Jews, although their cases were under appeal. On the day of UNSCOP's arrival, British authorities sentenced three more Jews to death, ignoring an UNSCOP resolution appealing for clemency. Even as Weizmann testified before UNSCOP, the High Commissioner confirmed the death sentences.

The British had lost face in the Middle East, which portended an early end to their rule, but the Jews were still a minority and there were many areas from which Jews were barred by the 1939 White Paper. Consequently, in demanding a Jewish state without delay, the Jews implied acceptance of partition—which Weizmann explicitly advocated during his presentation.

Binationalism, an independent state consisting of both Jews and Arabs, was urged by Dr. Judah Magnes—president of the Hebrew University and a leader of the Ichud—by the Hashomer Hatzair, a left-wing Zionist party, and by the Communists. But none who offered equal partnership with the Arabs could produce articulate Arab partners. Magnes made a moving appeal for a binational state. As a Zionist, he said, he could not give up an inch of the country. He did not want to divide it but to share it with the Arabs. Chief Justice Emil Sandstrom of Sweden and Supreme Court Justice I. C. Rand of Canada asked whether any Arabs shared his view. He acknowledged that he spoke for none.

That evening I cabled New York that partition was assured—paradoxically because of UNSCOP's reaction to the testimony of partition's opponents.

The Arab Higher Committee, led by the ex-Mufti, boycotted UNSCOP because its terms of reference had ignored their demands for independence and self-determination; but Arabs did meet UNSCOP diplomats at private parties where they could present their views without challenge.

UNSCOP visited a school in Beersheba, where Arab students turned their heads away according to instructions. Left with little to do in empty classrooms, diplomats Enrique Fabregat of Uruguay and Jorge Garcia Granados of Guatemala and I played tic-tac-toe on the blackboard.

U.N. diplomats had been snubbed in Jaffa and in every Arab town. They were swiftly evicted from the Golden Spindle, an Arab textile factory in Ramleh, after I had called Ralph Bunche's attention to children who were operating the machines. Jewish newspapermen were denied admission to an Arab cigarette factory in Haifa, and Arab City Councilmen boycotted the UNSCOP City Hall visit.

UNSCOP wanted to see Palestine and its people, and they spent fifteen days on an extended 2,200-mile tour from Dan to Beersheba. On one occasion, I drew up a detailed log for the next journey, noting mileage and major spots of interest. My itinerary carried the U.N. delegates from Jerusalem down the Jaffa road to Tel Aviv, and north up the coastal plain to Haifa, then into the hills and on south to Jerusalem. Naively, I assumed that UNSCOP would travel clockwise. It did not occur to me that the British would prefer to exhibit the Arab parts of Palestine during the day and travel through Jewish areas by night. Much to my chagrin, the long motorcade rolled counterclockwise and my mimeographed guide sheets fluttered out of car windows.

Everywhere, Jews warmly welcomed UNSCOP, pressing their case with enthusiasm and pride, although skeptical of the outcome and cynical of their own intensity. They had hoped and fought and lost before, and they could not be persuaded that this inquiry would succeed after so many failures. They were not presenting a claim as much as they were exhibiting a conclusion, for there already was a Jewish state in Palestine—not a free state, not legally constituted, not internationally recognized, but already in existence. Jews who had morbidly feared that the world had forgotten them finally had won the world's attention and would hold it as long as they could. I felt that this was not a Committee of Inquiry at all—but rather a formal visit from the U.N. to a prospective member.

In the final days of their visit, UNSCOP members witnessed climactic outrage. On July 13, the British decreed martial law and imposed collective punishment in Netanya, where 6,000 British troops screened 12,000 residents, searching for two British sergeants who had been kidnapped in retaliation for the arrest of three young Jews waiting in the death chamber at Acre, a dead city with an entire population under house arrest. Once again, we saw Jews in a queue—this time with guns at their backs.

Throughout their stay, members had asked us when the Haganah would bring in its next refugee ship. On July 21, less than forty-eight hours before UNSCOP's scheduled departure, the 1,814-ton *Exodus,* once a Chesapeake Bay excursion steamer called the *President Warfield,* brought 4,500 weary refugees to shore.

I wrote bitter protests against the British as their destroyers rammed the ship and then towed it to Haifa, but Golda Meir toned them down. On that same day, at my request, Mrs. Sharett had invited visiting American newspapermen to lunch, but we had to call it off and go to Haifa, where UNSCOP leaders watched as the battered ship was towed in. The British claimed that the crew had refused to accept British control, whereas the crew insisted that the ship had been far out at sea and that the attack had been an act of piracy. To ram it on the high sea was wanton recklessness which imperiled the lives of its passengers, many of them women and children.

Once again the U.N. saw Jews form a queue as they filed down the gangplanks. Soldiers ransacked their parcels, bags, and briefcases, tossing out canned goods, cutlery, and bottles—potential weapons of war or suicide. The refugees could remain on the dock for a few minutes but were denied contact with the earth of Palestine and its people as they were hurried on their way to three waiting ferry boats.

My companion, journalist Ruth Gruber, and I could talk only to the young British lance corporal who knowingly explained that the root of the trouble was that Jews controlled Parliament in London and Congress in Washington. Those ubiquitous Jewish lobbies! Besides, he asked, wasn't it true that Wendell Willkie had been a Jew?

I counted thirty-seven stretchers. Two occupants were dead, and a third died a few hours later. Only these had been permitted to remain in Palestine.

The British continued to shock the world, for instead of transporting the refugees from Haifa to Cyprus, as in the recent past, they kept them in a French harbor, Port-de-Bouc, under a hot blazing sun for many days, trying to force them to disembark. Frustrated, the British shipped them back to Hamburg, where they were driven by club and truncheon to land on Germany's hated soil in full view of their former persecuters.

On that very day, August 31, UNSCOP published its findings. UNSCOP now asserted the right of Bevin's victims to make the pilgrimage which Bevin's battleships had intercepted. The long odyssey of the *Exodus* had compressed into some sixty days the history of 2,000 years of Jewish homelessness.

PARTITION

UNSCOP had left Palestine for Geneva to reach a decision, and our Jewish Agency staff followed them there. However, Eban, Horowitz, Toff, and I were late because the British civil servant who was UNSCOP's administrator had no room for us on the UNSCOP plane and we were detoured via Cairo.

Even so, we were fortunate to leave Palestine when we did. The silence was broken as sniping and counter-fusillade resumed, for the British had hanged the three young Jews.

On the eve of their execution, I had spent two hours with Izhak ben Zvi, the chairman of the Va'ad Le'umi (who later succeeded Weizmann as Israel's second president), and with Mrs. Meir, as she appealed to the British High Commissioner for clemency. A personal visit was barred, and curfew forbade a mass street protest. Telegrams and cables would not be delivered; there was only the telephone. I wrote an angry statement for the press and walked down the center of the deserted street to the Public Information Office in the David Building, exercising a quasi-legal right to ignore curfew.

The correspondents tossed away my last appeal to the world's conscience because they knew, as I did, that the conscience wasn't listening. They were more interested in the imminent reaction of the Jewish community than in my rhetoric.

Reaction was swift and terrible. Avenging the execution, members of Irgun hanged the two kidnapped British sergeants, trapping their bodies with explosives. We left Palestine just before that. A day or two later, we might have been detained by the British.

I traveled for six days with a seven-man UNSCOP subcommittee through the DP camps in Germany and Austria. No Jewish Agency officials accompanied the subcommittee, but Chairman John D. Hood of Australia accredited me as a newspaper correspondent.

The Committee did not go to observe the misery of the DPs but to probe their motives. Did the DPs really want to go to Palestine or were they propelled by Zionist propaganda? Given a free choice, would they prefer to remain in Europe or to emigrate to less troubled lands? The Committee interrogated a random cross-section of the DPs. Why didn't they want to go back from where they came? Why not to the United States? (As if visas were available.) If they were fleeing from anti-Semitism, were they not aware that there was anti-Semitism in Palestine? Was their decision prompted by outside influence and pressure?

Before they began, UNSCOP was briefed by Rabbi Bernstein at Munich. He conservatively estimated that some 75 percent of the DPs wanted to go to Palestine and that the remaining 25 percent would probably prefer to join relatives in the Western Hemisphere. But, he said, if the DPs were questioned, they would unanimously choose Palestine as their destination. That was exactly what happened. Only once did UNSCOP find anyone who had another choice.

One day the Committee was pleasantly surprised to learn that the man before them was planning to go, not to Palestine, but to Czechoslovakia. "Where are you from," they had asked. "I am from Palestine," he said. "Where are you going?"

"I am going to Czechoslovakia."

The Committeemen all leaned forward. At last, they had found a witness who could belie Zionist propaganda.

"And why do you want to go to Czechoslovakia?" They were pleased again when he said, "Because my business is there and I want to go there to carry on my business."

They asked, "What is your business?" And he replied, "I am an employee of the Jewish Agency. I am trying to help emigrants get to Palestine." Only then did the Committee notice the Jewish Agency pin on his lapel.

One day, near Dachau, we visited an old monastery which now housed some Jewish DP children. From here, we learned, some youngsters had gone off on a "picnic," never to return to the monastery. They were some of the 4,500 who had crammed into the *Exodus*. On the table we saw a black-framed photograph of the 16-year-old Hirsch Yakubovich, one of the three who had been killed on that ill-fated steamer.

What had impelled these youngsters to run away? Why had they left for Palestine? The Indian delegate, Sir Abdur Rahman, a Moslem, discovered that propaganda had been at work. It was obvious to him that the youth had been induced to leave because somebody had pinned a map of Palestine on the wall. I was constrained to interrupt his conversation with Yugoslavia's Dr. Jose Brilej to point out that no one from the United States, Iran, Czechoslovakia, India, or any place else had troubled to hang a map of his country on that wall to offer the promise of a happier future.

Some UNSCOP members questioned the circulation of Yiddish newspapers in the camps, and they were reminded that these were not concentration camps and that inmates should be free to read what they pleased.

In Vienna we visited the Rothschild Hospital, which was jammed with 5,000 Jewish refugees who had fled from Rumania because deteriorating economic conditions and anti-Semitic forces had incited hatred for the Jews, most of whom had been pauperized by the war and fascism. They were headed for the American zone in Germany. This hospital was equipped to house 1,000. The 5,000 were sleeping cot to cot — in tiers — in corridors, in cellars, and even in the courtyard.

"I shall never, as long as I live, forget the misery of this day," said a deeply moved Iranian diplomat, Ali Ardalan.

Only a year before, we had fought at the Paris peace conference for documentary safeguards to enable Jews to live in Rumania. Now, Rumanian Jews made up a new exodus to the DP camps.

It was not until our last day in Germany that the U.N. visitors saw Jews with happy faces.

We came to Bergen Belsen in the British zone where Nazi fiends had exterminated hundreds of thousands of Jews. We walked around the rectangular mounds, the common graves of 30,000 Jews whose bodies were buried by Allied forces after the camp had been liberated. We saw Germans burning what looked like the striped concentration camp clothing worn by murdered Jews some twenty-seven months ago. A solitary monument bore witness, "Earth forget not the blood shed on thee."

The acrid smoke of the smudge fires was still in our nostrils when we visited the Jewish DP camp, two miles from the cemetery. At the very railroad station where Hitler had deposited his intended victims, we now saw 390 Jews who were entraining for Palestine. They were the fortunate possessors of British-issued certificates entitling them to enter Palestine. A tall British brigadier was happily swinging a swagger stick and gaily describing the movement as "Operation Grand National!" We waved "shalom" to these joyful refugees—so different from the thousands who had been crammed into the caged ships at Haifa or who had huddled in bunks and closets at the Vienna hospital.

These scenes, the *Exodus* at Haifa and the exodus from Rumania, had a decisive impact. "We have come to the conclusion that Palestine must be opened to the Jews. There is no alternative," Hood told me.

UNSCOP unanimously recommended termination of the Mandate.

A majority report, approved by Canada, Czechoslovakia, Guatemala, the Netherlands, Peru, Sweden, and Uruguay proposed that Palestine be divided into a Jewish and an Arab state, joined in economic union, and that the Jerusalem area be internationalized under U.N. administration. During a one-year transition period, the White Paper restrictions on immigration and land purchases would be set aside to permit entry by 150,000 Jewish immigrants.

Three members—Yugoslavia, India, and Iran, which had substantial Moslem populations—offered a minority report, recommending a federal state with separate Jewish and Arab legislatures and common Palestine citizenship. Australia abstained.

DOUBLE TALK

I have often written about the 1947 fall session of the General Assembly, which voted for partition, but it was not until 1975 that I learned the inside story from declassified documents.

That session was a production in double talk on a double stage. Up front, we listened to formal discussion and debate. Backstage, American diplomacy was maneuvering to defeat the partition resolution—to substitute a plan for trusteeship with a tiny Vatican-like Jewish cultural and religious center.

According to custom, the Department of State declassifies and publishes diplomatic correspondence and documents after twenty-five years. The book recording the 1947–48 papers was published a year late, but the declassified documents were available in the National Archives. In the summer of 1975, I wrote a syndicated article describing what went on behind the scenes and disclosing Marshall's startling threat to vote against Truman if he recognized Israel.

Backstage—a caucus of the U.S. delegation on September 15—Marshall warned that acceptance of the UNSCOP recommendations would provoke "very violent" Arab reaction. Upstage—his public statement two days later—he informed the Assembly that the United States gave "great weight" to the recommendations but that it intended to propose changes. The United States wanted to reduce the size of the proposed Jewish state.

Truman instructed the delegation to support partition, in the belief that "it would open the way for peaceful collaboration between the Arabs and the Jews."

Our diplomats suspected that the Soviets would make a deal with the Arabs. On October 3, Iraqi diplomats Nuri-es-Said and Fadhil Jamali had told Ambassador Wadsworth that the Arabs intended to barter their six votes for the six Soviet votes. Accordingly, Americans were surprised when the Soviets approved the UNSCOP majority report.

The Arabs were intransigent. Jamal Husseini, vice president of the Arab Higher Committee and a cousin of the ex-Mufti, told the U.N. on November 24, 1947, that Arabs would resist the plan with the "last drop of their blood. . . . The partition line proposed shall be nothing but a line of fire and blood."

The British announced that they would not carry out any program that was not acceptable to both sides.

The Jewish Agency "most reluctantly" accepted the majority report. Reluctantly, for two major reasons. Many Jews were unhappy because the proposed Jewish state would occupy a small fraction of the 44,740 square miles of Palestine originally promised to the Jewish people in the 1917 Balfour Declaration. In 1922, the British had carved away some 35,000 square miles of Palestine, creating Transjordan in order to provide a throne for Emir Abdullah. Now, UNSCOP was recommending that the Jewish state comprise only 6,370 square miles—and there would be pressure for further surgery.

Modern Jerusalem, which had been built by the Jews, was to be internationalized, for under the partition plan Jerusalem would be deep inside Arab territory and surrounded by Arabs. Was it practical? The alternative to an international city would be a divided one. Could the Jewish half of Jerusalem stand alone, an enclave in an Arab state? The Jewish Agency leadership was divided; the majority wanted to spare Jerusalem bloodshed and destruction. By a close vote, they agreed to go along with the U.N. plan for an international *corpus separatum*.

There were misgivings about the proposed boundaries of the two states. Palestine was to be divided into six areas, three Jewish and three Arab with two cross-overs—like highway cloverleafs—which would facilitate access back and forth. (I always thought that Long Island's super-highway design, which U.N. delegates admired on their long daily journey to Lake Success, had inspired this odd and impractical scheme.) In the north, western Galilee would belong to the Arabs and eastern Galilee would belong to the Jews. In the center, the eastern area, the so-called Arab Triangle, would be part of the Arab state, while the narrow coastal area would belong to the Jews. In the south, the Negev would be Jewish, while the western area, including the Gaza strip, would be in the Arab state.

During the General Assembly debate, Sir Muhammed Zafrulla Khan, the Pakistani delegate, scoffed at this "checkerboard" division. In rebuttal, Guatemala's Granados held up a map of the "tapestry" that was then Pakistan and India.

Manifestly, the UNSCOP boundaries were feasible only if the parties accepted them, but they would vanish if either party resorted to war, because they were not defensible. It would then be necessary to shorten and straighten them and to eliminate pockets of hostility. Eventually, the 1948 Arab war did, in fact, dictate that outcome.

After the general debate, the Assembly referred the UNSCOP report to two subcommittees for consideration of the majority and minority recommendations. The United States constantly pressed Sharett and his colleagues to yield territory to the proposed Arab state, and the 6,370 square miles of the Israel-to-be was whittled down to 5,579.

One day, America's Ambassador Herschel Johnson emerged from the subcommittee to ask me a pertinent question. "How many dunams are there in an acre? Sometimes I hear four and sometimes I hear five." I fear my quip was imprecise: "It all depends on whether we are giving or getting."

On November 24, the ad hoc committee rejected the Arab demand for an all-Arab Palestine state by a vote of 29 to 12. There were 14 abstentions and two absentees. The committee then voted 25 to 13 for the partition plan, with 17 abstentions and two absentees. This was a majority, but short of the necessary two-thirds. During the next five days and nights both sides lobbied intensively for votes. Meanwhile, on September 30, the U.N. had voted to admit Yemen, raising the number of Arab League members to six and further underlining the inequity of Israel's non-membership. If the archaic and feudal land of Yemen was entitled to U.N. membership, who could bar a modern Jewish Palestine?

These were anxious days. The two Great Powers, the United States and the USSR, were ostensibly in agreement, and we could count on most Western nations. The United Kingdom, avowedly neutral, was overtly hostile. The Dominions were divided. Asian nations tended to favor the Arabs. The Arabs complained that Zionists were pressuring Western governments, but they, in turn, were exploiting Moslem populations in Latin America and in Asia to gain support. They threatened that the investments of some European countries and the status of their nationals in Arab countries might be endangered. Greece, which then had many Greek citizens in Egypt, was a conspicuous example. Its delegation disclosed to American diplomats that it had been promised the support of Moslem governments in any future controversy.

U.N. diplomats were diffident in their support for partition, leading other delegations to infer that they did not really care how they voted. The official documents later revealed that Henderson had predicted to Under Secretary of State Robert Lovett that partition would fail to win the required two-thirds vote, on the assumption that the United States would support partition but "without waving the flag."

However, the flag was unfurled because of the last minute intervention of strong Israel supporters: Ambassador Ben Cohen, Mrs. Eleanor Roosevelt, and Hilldring, who had served as Truman's private eye to watch the delegation.

Cohen had cabled, on the day before the vote, that partition might fail by a vote or two unless we made it clear to states like the Philippines, Liberia, Greece, Cuba, and Honduras, "which generally follow our leadership, how deeply we feel the proposed partition plan is the only alternative to choose. If we fail, the impression would grow that we only desire to appease political sentiment at home and that we do not stand wholeheartedly in back of our declared policy, thereby undermining our American position at home and abroad."

Truman then ordered the delegation to come to life.

The historic November 29 roll call showed 33 in favor, 13 against. There were 10 abstentions, and one absentee.

The Arab states walked out, threatening war, but it was an epic moment in the life of the Jewish people. On that day, too, the U.N. attained a pinnacle of achievement, meeting its first major test with a demonstration of strength. It succeeded far better than any one had hoped, but within months there was a shattering revelation of the U.N.'s weakness. It faltered far worse than we had feared.

* * *

I returned to my post with the American Jewish Conference which opened its fourth—and final—session in Chicago on the day of the U.N. vote. We knew that the U.N. victory might mean the end of our organization. The Conference had been created as a temporary body to fight for Jewish rights in Europe and Palestine; it was never intended to be a permanent organization, and it had no jurisdiction over issues on the American scene.

Yet the Conference had been an exemplary organization which had united American Jews and major Jewish bodies overseas. Many American Jews wanted it to become a permanent organization and to cope with domestic problems, uniting the work of Jewish defense organizations engaged in the endless battles against discrimination and anti-Semitism.

The Chicago session tried to devise a plan for a permanent organization with an enlarged scope of activities. Possibly the defense organizations could be induced to accept the Conference as an overall coordinator. For the next two months of December and January, we struggled for acceptance of a permanent Conference. Lipsky was in the vanguard, assisted by Dr. Eisendrath, the leader of the Union of American Hebrew Congregations, but the fight was futile. From the outset, we were handicapped by the non-participation of the American Jewish Committee. A second blow was the untimely death of Monsky, who died of a heart attack at an interim committee meeting of the Conference in May 1947, during a debate on the issue of future organization. As long as Monsky lived, he had sustained B'nai B'rith's interest in the Conference.

A special B'nai B'rith commission wrote *finis* to the Conference on January 31, 1948, when it voted 60 to 2 against B'nai B'rith membership. Our two Conference friends were Philip M. Klutznick, who later became the B'nai B'rith president, U.S. Ambassador to the U.N. and Secretary of Commerce; and Abram Sachar, the veteran president of Brandeis University.

On the following day, I returned to the Jewish Agency. For weeks, I had been under pressure to resume my duties, for it was evident that the U.N. would not implement partition and that we faced a life and death battle— in Palestine itself and at the U.N.

ISRAEL UNDER SIEGE

Within hours after the November 29 roll call, Arabs ambushed and killed seven Israelis on the Tel Aviv-Jerusalem road, and within the first week 105 Jews had died.

Simultaneously, pro-Arab forces mounted a propaganda offensive to reverse the partition resolution. Their coalition included Arabists and Anglophiles, oil lobbyists, missionaries, and diplomats. Secretary of Defense James Forrestal urged a bipartisan agreement to remove the Palestine issue from domestic politics. Apparently believing that Israel's supporters were motivated entirely by politics, he had no conception of the extent and depth of the American people's commitment to Israel's rebirth. Pro-Arab forces succeeded in blocking implementation of the U.N. resolution but failed to prevent Israel's establishment.

The State Department swiftly imposed a drastic embargo to prevent the flow of arms for the defense of the embryonic Jewish state. The Arabs, however, could acquire weapons from the British. The main Arab fighting force, the Arab Legion, was British-trained, equipped and commanded, and Egyptians had captured arms that had been abandoned by the British and the Axis in the North African desert.

From the beginning, it had been clear that the Security Council could not implement partition, for General Assembly resolutions are recommendations and not decisions. However, the partition resolution had provided that any attempt to resist the recommendation by resorting to force should be treated as a threat to peace, subject to Security Council action. Thus, top U.S. legal experts believed that the Council could act, but Dean Rusk had overruled them and the Council refused to shoulder any responsibility.

A five-member commission, known as the Palestine Partition Commission (PPC), representing Bolivia, Czechoslovakia, Denmark, Panama, and the Philippines—and dubbed the five lonely pilgrims—had been established to implement partition, but Bevin had told Marshall on November 28, the day before the U.N. partition vote, that the commission would not be allowed to enter Palestine until May, a mere fifteen days before the scheduled British departure.

Arabs infiltrated from bordering countries to incite rebellion and sabotage, while many Arabs began to leave Palestine as early as December, confident that they could return after an easy victory. The British withdrew their forces in stages and turned over administration of the abandoned areas to indigenous residents.

Britain's Sir Alexander Cadogan complained to the U.N. on January 21, 1948:

> The Jewish story that the Arabs are the attackers and the Jews are attacked is not tenable. The Arabs are determined to show that they will not submit *tamely* [our italics] to the United Nations' plan of partition; while the Jews are trying to consolidate the advantages gained at the General Assembly by a succession of drastic operations designed to intimidate and cure the Arabs of any desire for further conflict. . . .

Cadogan's failure to distinguish between aggressor and defender in 1948 became the chronic U.N. perception for thirty years. Arab attacks were always condoned, while Israel's retaliations were always censured.

The Jewish Agency warned the U.N. on January 15 that an international police force would be needed to implement partition, and U.N. Secretary General Trygve Lie began futile negotiations to establish one.

Arab military forces had already begun to invade Palestine and, on February 6, 1948, the Arab Higher Committee cabled that the Arabs of Palestine would "never submit or yield to any power going to Palestine to enforce partition."

On February 2, the Jewish Agency submitted a memorandum detailing the extent of Arab aggression. This was not just a civil war, but aggression by Arab governments in violation of their U.N. obligations. In a supplementary memorandum, the Agency protested that the British were arming the Arabs and disarming the Jews.

There were many outrages. On February 22, Arabs blew up an apartment house in Ben Yehudah Street in Jerusalem, killing more than 50 persons. *The Jerusalem Post* was bombed. A bomb was smuggled into Jewish Agency headquarters and 13 died; 35 young university students were slaughtered as they marched in a futile effort to rescue the Etzion area villages south of Jerusalem. In May, soon after Israel was established, I heard Mrs. Meir tell a national Jewish audience in Chicago that these unarmed youths had died with nothing but stones in their hands. It was an electrifying appeal and American Jewish support soared.

Jerusalem was surrounded, isolated, and besieged, its supply of food and water cut off, its people threatened with thirst and hunger.

On February 16, the PPC reported: "Powerful Arab interests both inside and outside Palestine are defying the resolution of the General Assembly and are engaged in a deliberate effort to alter by force the settlement envisaged therein."

The President approved a State Department proposal to convene the Security Council, but he did not fully realize its implications.

Many months before, in 1947, even as UNSCOP was preparing to leave for Palestine, Austin had recommended a U.N. trusteeship which would lead to an independent Palestine state, neither Jewish nor Arab, with limited Jewish immigration.

Later, Austin, Rusk, who was head of the Office of U.N. Affairs, and Henderson had filed a similar trusteeship plan, which proposed that the Jewish "national home" be a religious and cultural center, to be supported by world Jewry and confined to a tiny coastal strip along the Mediterranean Sea between Haifa and Jaffa.

In November and December, James Terry Duce, the top ARAMCO lobbyist, had toured the area and reported back that Azzam Pasha, the Secretary General of the Arab League, had conceded that the Jews might have such a Vatican-type state.

The shattering blow fell on March 19, when the U.S. delegation proposed that another Assembly session discuss the Palestine problem anew and, in the meantime, establish a temporary trusteeship pending a final decision. Silver denounced it as "a shocking reversal . . . which will bring confusion, is likely to lead to increased violence in Palestine, and will incalculably hurt the prestige and authority of the United Nations." Overwhelmed by public protest, an embarrassed Truman insisted that this was not a reversal. The United States, he claimed, still favored partition, but since it was blocked by conflict he had agreed that a temporary trusteeship could be established. It was not intended to drop partition but merely to defer it. Moreover, Truman was mortified because he had just given his word to Weizmann that the United States would not abandon partition.

There was a hurricane of protest, and we compiled and circulated a press book of angry cartoons. "Statehood deferred is statehood denied," we told the press. We were aided by Clark M. Eichelberger and Carl Hermann Voss.

Several thousands of years after the Jewish people had bequeathed to mankind a legacy of law and morals—a code engraved in the U.N. charter itself—that people was being proffered, not independence but guardianship, not statehood but tutelage. Now, in the 20th century of an era in which Jews had given many nations statesmen, lawmakers, and teachers, they were receiving the privilege of training themselves for the distant day when they would pass probationary tests and be deemed eligible for the right to govern themselves and to determine their own future.

By this time, many Arabs had fled from Jaffa, Haifa, Tiberias, and Safed. Arab propaganda redundantly broadcasts the fiction that the exodus was precipitated by a panic resulting from the Irgun attack on Deir Yassin, one of the two villages from which Arab soldiers and mercenaries had been fighting to blockade Jerusalem. That attack, which cost the lives of many Arab civilians, did not occur until April 9, long after the Arabs had begun to leave the country with the encouragement and example of their leaders.

Arab histories never refer to such Arab atrocities as the ambush and massacre of 77 Jewish doctors, nurses, and scientists—many of whom were burned to death—in buses on the road to the Hadassah Hospital on Mt. Scopus a few days later.

In February 1962, I broadcast an interview with Salim Joubran, an Arab citizen of Israel, who told me how the Haganah and the Histradrut had appealed with broadcasts and leaflets to Haifa's more than 50,000 Arabs to remain and live at peace with the Jews as they had for many years. U.S. diplomats confirmed this.

The General Assembly reconvened in April for an unrealistic debate on the U.S. trusteeship proposal. The doubts and delusions which immobilized the world's statesmen in New York trailed far behind the rush of events in Palestine itself. While attachés and counselors mulled over bland phrases and pacifying formulas, leaders in Israel were confronted with a grim life-or-death decision.

The United States had wished to believe that the Jews secretly wanted trusteeship as an escape from a terrible dilemma. Doubtless some American Jews may have so advised the State Department. It was imperative that the Jewish Agency expose that illusion.

The Jewish Agency and the Va'ad Le'umi announced their opposition to any proposal designed to prevent or postpone establishment of the Jewish state. They would categorically reject any trusteeship regime, no matter how brief. A provisional Jewish government would begin to function in Palestine on May 16.

On April 1, Sharett told the Security Council:

"Trusteeship means denial or at least postponement of independence. We believe that we are ripe for independence. So are the Arabs. We challenge anyone to prove that we are not. We have passed the threshold of statehood. We refuse to be thrown back."

For many months, Eban had been the silent draftsman of the Agency's delegation. Late in 1947, I had arranged for a "Town Meeting of the Air" debate, in which Sharett was to participate along with Senator Warren G. Magnuson (D-Washington), Representative Lawrence Smith (R-Wisconsin), and an Arab spokesman. The afternoon before, Sharett told me that he must withdraw because of exhaustion. He nominated Eban as his substitute. "But that young man can't open his mouth," I protested. Reluctantly, Sharett agreed to remain in the symposium.

It took me several months to discover how wrong I was. On May 1, 1948, Eban delivered a speech which utterly demolished the U.S. trusteeship plan. Sharett, who was to have delivered it, insisted that Eban must finally speak for himself. It was, Eban later wrote, the turning point of his life. It was also the disastrous turning point for Washington's ill-advised campaign for trusteeship.

In a devastating indictment, Eban wrote that the trustee would be "called upon to swim against every current of political sentiment in the country." He would be "faced with a process of virtual partition which has gathered such momentum in recent weeks that not even considerable armed force could now arrest it."

(For many years I have amused audiences by confessing my absurd misconception of Eban's forensic prowess. But after Eban came to address two Washington dinners in my honor, in 1972 and 1975, I changed the story to bewilder my listeners. I blandly took credit for his mastery of the English language by explaining that a sensitive Eban had applied himself and studied hard after he had heard of my refusal to let him go on the air. And some really believed me.)

For five weeks, the General Assembly debated vague plans to arrest the inevitable.

In New York, diplomats sought to reverse the U.N. partition decision with words; inside Palestine, Jewish soldiers were enforcing the decision with their lives. As the British withdrew, abandoning forts and public institutions, Jews and Arabs would take control in the areas assigned to them in the partition plan. Thus, the plan was being implemented despite Arab resistance and British hostility.

On April 16, 1948, Jamal Husseini told the Council that the Arabs "did not deny" that they had "begun the fighting. . . . We told the whole world that we were going to fight."

As May 14 approached, American diplomats made last-minute appeals to the Jews to desist. They proposed truces and stand-still agreements, with interim plans for a measure of Jewish immigration from the DP camps. Rusk suggested that Truman's plane, "The Sacred Cow," fly Arab and Jewish leaders to a neutral spot for a last-minute compromise, but Sharett rejected it. Sharett, who was soon to become Israel's foreign minister, went to see Marshall in Washington on May 8. The American diplomat told him that if the Jews were determined to proceed they would have to rely on their own resources. Lourie, Yuval and I met Sharett at La Guardia, where he told us that Marshall had reminded him of the defeat of Chiang Kai-shek.

We saw it all so differently. We believed that Arabs were the aggressors and that Jews were fighting to exist, but diplomatic documents reveal that Rusk was convinced that Jews were the aggressors and that the Security Council would have to decide whether the Jewish armed attack on Arab communities was legitimate or a threat to international peace. In a message to Under Secretary of State Robert Lovett, Rusk charged that the Jews would use every means to obscure the fact that it was their own armed aggression against the Arabs inside Palestine which was the cause of the Arab attack.

Rusk believed that Abdullah would cut across Palestine from Transjordan to the sea at Jaffa, would give Ibn Saud a port at Aqaba, and would make territorial concessions to the Syrians in the north, leaving the Jews the coastal strip. Fortunately, that was not the prevailing opinion at the White House.

Israel proclaimed her independence on May 14, 1948. But nothing exists if no one sees or knows it, the philosophers have written. I spent most of that day urging U.N. correspondents to write the name Israel—rather than Palestine—into their dispatches.

At 6:11 P.M. four bells heralded a news bulletin from Washington:

"The White House today announced *de facto* recognition of the provisional government of Israel."

At that moment, I was in the INS bureau. I tore the yellow bulletin from correspondent Pete Huss' hands, raced down the steps, burst into the General Assembly hall, and ran down the aisle to read the astonishing news to leaders of the Jewish Agency—Silver, Halprin, Eban, and Lourie—who were in a reserved section. They burst into a jubilant cheer, interrupting the delegate of Iraq, who was then unrealistically arguing that, inasmuch as the British Mandate over Palestine had ended at 6:00 P.M., the country had reverted to the Arabs. Arab delegates angrily demanded an explanation from disconcerted U.S. delegates.

Weizmann had written a letter in which he had appealed for Truman's recognition, and I convened a press conference to dictate the text.

In fact, as we learned years later in 1975, Clark Clifford, Truman's counsel, had recommended on May 12 that the President announce immediately that he intended to recognize Israel as soon as she came into existence and that he urge other U.N. members to do likewise, and quickly, before the Soviet Union did. Both Marshall and Lovett had objected. Marshall warned Truman that he would vote against him in the 1948 election if he did. Lovett feared that we were buying a pig in a poke but thought better of it the following day. In his autobiography, Truman wrote that the "unexpected" recognition should not have surprised U.S. diplomats if they had "faithfully supported" his policies. Truman also wrote that many career officials believe that they make policy and run the government and that they regard elected officials as temporary occupants. This struggle between the President, speaking for the American people, and career officials, executing policies to suit diplomatic convenience, did not end that evening.

In the pandemonium over Truman's action, little notice was paid to Guatemala's delegate, Jorges Garcia Granados, who went to the podium to announce that his country was recognizing Israel *de jure*. Granados had been Israel's strongest advocate in UNSCOP. It was not until thirty years later that I learned that Granados's sympathy had been enlisted by a Washington physician, Dr. Harvey Ammerman, who was then serving some embassies and who briefed him thoroughly and introduced him to Sharett. By a rare coincidence, Ammerman recently became my own doctor.

Chapter 6

The Battle for the Negev

ISRAEL UNDER PRESSURE

Truman's swift *de facto* recognition of Israel's provisional government and the Soviet Union's *de jure* recognition, which followed two days later, had an impact on the Security Council. On May 15, when Israel's delegation accused the Arab states of aggression, the U.S. delegation called Israel by her right name and condemned her attackers. Austin told the Council that the Arab armies had marched "to blot out an existing independent government," a matter of "international concern and a violation of the charter."

The Arabs and their British patrons portrayed Palestine as a land plunged into civil war because of the Zionist attempt to seize control after the British withdrawal. The British delegation insisted on referring to "the Jewish Authorities of Tel Aviv" for some eight months, and once, when Eban met Cadogan emerging from a shipboard chapel, he tartly asked whether Cadogan had been praying to the "God of Abraham, Isaac and the Jewish authorities."

The United States and the Soviet Union were united in their assessment, but they could muster only five of the seven votes required for effective action because other delegations had not yet recognized Israel.

Meanwhile, imaginative Arab communiqués had trumpeted triumphant reports that Arabs had cut Israel in two, reached the Mediterranean, and all but decimated the Israelis. A cable from Israel on the fourth day disclosed that the Israeli army—not the Arab invaders—was winning battles and gaining territory, enabling us to announce the reassuring news at a hastily called U.N. press conference.

Azzam Pasha of the Arab League had told the press in Cairo on May 15: "This will be a war of extermination and a momentous massacre, which will be spoken of like the Mongolian massacres and the Crusades."

Later, U.N. Secretary General Trygve Lie wrote in his book *In the Cause of Peace:* "From the first week of December 1947, disorder in Palestine had begun to mount. The Arabs repeatedly had asserted that they would resist partition by force. They seemed to be determined to drive that point home by assaults upon the Jewish community in Palestine."

Yet, blocking any attempt to brand the Arabs as aggressors, the British imposed the immoral truce resolution of May 29, which equated attacker and defender, directing them to freeze their positions of siege and defense. We denounced the Council's breach of duty—a non-intervention posture reminiscent of the League of Nations' abysmal failure to take collective action to halt Hitler and Mussolini in the 1930s.

The real purpose of the "truce" was to reopen the territorial question. UNSCOP had recommended that the Negev, Palestine's southern desert area, be part of the Jewish state. The British and pro-Arab Americans wanted the Negev for the Arabs in order to maintain a base there if the British were forced out of Egypt, to establish a land bridge between Jordan and Egypt, and to explore for minerals and oil.

"There ought to be a broad Arab highway to allow uninterrupted traffic within the Arab world," an American diplomat once told me. But an Israeli diplomat scoffed. Once a month, or perhaps less frequently, he said, a camel train, which was probably carrying hashish, crossed the Negev from Egypt to Jordan.

The future of the Negev had been temporarily settled late in 1947 at the White House, where, in an historic meeting, Weizmann had pointed out to Truman that the Negev was strategically important, not only to Israel but to the Free World. It would provide a land bridge from the Gulf of Aqaba to the Mediterranean which could serve as an alternative to the Suez Canal if the Canal were ever closed.

Truman had agreed. Minutes before a crucial committee vote, he had telephoned New York to instruct the U.S. delegation to resist any proposals to detach the Negev from Israel; but the fight was far from over. Israel now faced new Anglo-American pressure to cede the Negev to the Arabs. The first truce lasted four weeks. When it ended, the Arabs resumed the war. The Council then threatened sanctions in a resolution which halted the fighting.

By this time, the Israelis had won decisive victories. They had opened a new road to Jerusalem, lifting the siege of its 100,000 Jewish inhabitants, and they controlled most of the territory allotted to them under the partition plan. In addition, they had swept the Arab armies out of the Galilee and taken the northwestern area of Palestine, part of which had been assigned to the Arab state.

The Arab states had hoped to seize and divide all of Palestine for themselves. They captured parts of it and, as a result, the separate Arab state envisaged in the partition plan never came into existence. Jordan captured approximately 2,000 square miles of biblical Samaria and Judea west of the Jordan River, which then came to be called the "West Bank," and the Old City in Jerusalem, whose 1,300 Jewish inhabitants were expelled or taken as prisoners to Jordan.

The Egyptians had seized the Gaza Strip, within 40 miles of Tel Aviv, and were deployed across the Negev. Theoretically, the U.N. truce permitted Israelis to cross the Egyptian line to supply Israel's twenty-five Negev settlements, but the Egyptians were in a position to bar Israel's access.

Meanwhile, Count Folke Bernadotte of Sweden had been appointed as a U.N. mediator to supervise the truce and to promote a settlement. After a summer spent in interviewing the parties, including British and American diplomats, Bernadotte redrew the map. Israel would retain the 462 square miles of western Galilee which she had occupied in the fighting, but in an incredible nine-for-one territorial exchange Israel was to give up 3,800 square miles of the southern Negev and some 150 square miles of southern Judea. Jerusalem was to be made international. The Bernadotte proposals were premised on alleged "realism." The new boundaries would enhance compactness and defensibility, it was argued, for the old partition boundaries had proved unworkable.

For Israel, the truce had been an ugly synonym for siege—a costly burden. Forced to maintain some 15 percent of her population in the army, Israel diverted workmen and farmers from their tools and tractors and stationed them along the frontier. Using taxation and internal loans to maintain the army, Israel had to pay hard currency for weapons, food, and supplies. She had to build roads, waterlines, and telephone lines to beleaguered Jerusalem. And all this at a time when the country was inundated by refugees, who for the first time in two thousand years were freely crossing frontiers and pouring into Israel—because Israel could now issue visas. Israel had won the war but was unable to end it; the Security Council arbitrarily commanded that Arab invaders not be driven off.

When Israel protested Arab truce violations, the Council did nothing except to warn Israel to do nothing. The Council piously ruled that a truce violation by one party could not excuse retaliation by the other. This ruling was a foretaste of future inequity which was to last for many years.

As the diplomatic battle opened in Paris, Bernadotte and an aide were assassinated by terrorists in Jerusalem. This tragic outrage against a personal symbol of U.N. authority was exploited by Israel's foes. The people of Israel were collectively indicted as terrorists who were contemptuous of international law and authority, and who therefore owed reparation.

At an unforgettable Security Council session, the Syrian delegate reminded us that the "Prince of Peace" had been crucified close to the very spot where Bernadotte had been murdered. He stated that the least that Israelis could do was to accept the recommendation of their victim. Arab guilt in the death of four other U.N. officials, including the U.S. consul in Jerusalem, was never mentioned.

Within twenty-four hours after publication, the Bernadotte plan was endorsed by both Bevin and Marshall, who called it a "fair and sound proposal." That was ominous, for any plan supported by both the United States and the United Kingdom was sure to win a two-thirds vote.

An effort was made to fit the mediator's proposals into the mosaic of Western policy and strategy, as well as the map. Cold War propagandists sought to smear the nascent state of Israel, not as the legitimate offspring of the U.N., but as a bastard adopted by the Soviets.

Arab spokesmen charged that Israeli immigrants were not survivors of Nazi persecution seeking refuge, but Soviet agents and troops. Headlines reported that two crowded refugee ships, the *Pan York* and the *Pan Crescent,* had brought thousands of Russian agents from Constanza, very few of whom, oddly, could speak a word of Russian.

Israel's military successes were denounced as abominable massacres, and were portrayed in atrocity pictures. Feudal and reactionary Arab leaders were painted as ideological allies of the West and defenders of democracy, who must not be compelled to deal with Israel.

There were many anti-Israel propaganda themes: the plight of 600,000 Arab refugees; the alleged desecration of Jerusalem by infidels; the need to internationalize Haifa, so that Arab oil could flow through the pipelines to stimulate European recovery; and the need to safeguard the fabulous wealth of the Negev—the phosphate, the oil, and the uranium—from the Israelis. We were constantly on the defensive.

We tried to ignore the abuse. We attacked the inequity and immorality of the plan, and warned against extortion and blackmail.

I circulated a memorandum showing that the Bernadotte plan would cut Israel to less than one-twentieth of the size of Palestine, in what would be the fourth partition. The U.N. partition resolution had reduced the size of the Jewish state to 5,579 square miles, and the Bernadotte plan proposed to reduce Israel to only 2,124 square miles, as compared with the original 44,740. Abdullah was already affluent in deserts and his acquisition of the Negev might condemn it to perpetual aridity.

There were already twenty-five Jewish agricultural settlements in the Negev; its soil was arable, and many new Jewish immigrants could be established there. We hoped that oil or other mineral resources might be found and utilized to stabilize Israel's economy. With new rail and highway communication across the Negev and the expansion of commerce and industry, the Gulf of Aqaba could become Israel's outlet to Africa and to the Indian Ocean—the window looking to the Orient.

Furthermore, we questioned the U.N. General Assembly's competence in projecting a new plan which amputated territory of a sovereign state without its consent. Some Western statesmen agreed, but John Foster Dulles, a senior member of the U.S. delegation and later Secretary of State, believed that the boundaries had to be fixed by negotiation between the parties, and that the U.N. could not arbitrarily impose them.

The embarrassed Arab governments had not yet revealed to their own people the extent of Israel's victory and their own military defeat and political impotence; such revelations could spell disaster for them. The Arabs attacked the U.N. truce as the reason for their inability to accomplish Israel's destruction.

Much of the Arab mythology was swept away by General William Riley, head of the U.N. Truce Supervisory Organization, who came to Paris late in the session and exposed the extent of the Arab defeat.

Before the debate, there were curious maneuvers over procedure. The United Kingdom and the United States favored immediate action, but we contended that it would be impossible to give objective consideration to the report so soon after Bernadotte's violent death.

The Arab delegations opposed the Bernadotte plan, despite its advantages, because the plan implied recognition of Israel's existence.

This unprecedented combination of Arab and pro-Israel delegations defeated the British demand for early debate, and the question took its normal place on the agenda. However, the parties then reversed their positions. The U.S. and U.K. delegations now favored postponement of discussion until after the 1948 presidential election. Counting on Truman's defeat, they figured that a lame duck president would hesitate to challenge or curb them.

We were told to be realistic and consistent. If Israel claimed western Galilee by right of acquisition and the necessities of defense, then Israel must concede the Negev to the Arabs. It was argued that Israel had lost control of the Negev to the Egyptian armies. We countered that Egypt was holding the Negev in violation of a U.N. resolution and in defiance of the Security Council.

Argument was fruitless; Israel took dramatic action by sending a supply convoy on October 14 to the Israeli settlements south of the Egyptian forces. The Egyptians tried to block it, but their armies were fragmented and surrounded. (One of the larger fragments, at Faluja, included a young Egyptian officer named Gamal Abdel Nasser.)

Israel now controlled most of the areas originally allotted to her in the partition plan, and the facts on the ground were consistent with Israel's claim. The Negev clash was a crushing blow for the Bernadotte plan, for the disposition of the military forces no longer squared with its territorial recommendations.

The British would not yield so easily. They and the Chinese delegation co-sponsored a resolution threatening sanctions against Israel if she failed to withdraw to previous positions.

The Security Council faced a demand that it impose sanctions against the youngest and smallest of states—a state which had been summoned into existence by the U.N. itself. It was the Egyptian army that had invaded Palestine and it was the Israeli army that was defending itself and ejecting an invader. For sixteen weeks the Egyptians had violated the truce, and Israeli action had been taken in retaliation against a wrong and in affirmation of a right. Grotesquely, Israel was ordered to withdraw her army inside her own territory or suffer sanctions.

Back home, Truman had been disturbed about Marshall's endorsement of the Bernadotte proposal. In Philadelphia that summer, the Democratic party had spelled out a platform plank on Israel, which included the following paragraph:

"We approve the claims of the State of Israel to the boundaries set forth in the United Nations resolution of November 29 and consider that modifications thereof should be made only if fully acceptable to the State of Israel."

Truman proposed to issue a statement reaffirming that plank, but Marshall explained that the Bernadotte plan had been intended primarily to encourage Arab-Israel negotiations, and that he wanted Israelis and Arabs to consider the situation to be a flexible one. Truman withheld comment until he heard that the U.S. delegation had announced its intention to support the British-Chinese resolution threatening sanctions. He reacted on October 17, during the Security Council debate, with a sharp cable to Paris:

"I request that no statement be made or no action be taken on the subject of Palestine by any member of our delegation in Paris without specific authority from me in clearing the text of any statement."

Truman's stunning reversal of the delegation was unpublished, but I received a cable from friends in New York confirming it and we wanted the press to break the story. When the Security Council resumed debate in the Palais de Chaillot, I went up on the platform and passed a note to Gordon, the U.N. press officer. "Truman has reversed the U.S. delegation," I wrote. Gordon passed the note to Barnes, his chief, who was also sitting at the table. Barnes passed it to Bunche, the acting mediator who had succeeded Bernadotte, and Bunche passed it on to Cadogan.

I then descended from the stage and told correspondents who met me in the aisle that Truman had reversed the delegation. "How do you know?" I was asked. "Bunche has just passed a note to Cadogan," I replied. "Have you seen it?" "I certainly have," I assured them, whereupon the press broke the story—its authorship undisclosed.

Truman's intervention blocked the threat of sanctions. Dewey, his rival for the presidency, accused him of failure to stand by the Democratic platform, which impelled the President to deliver a strong speech in New York on October 28:

"The subject of Israel must not be resolved as a matter of politics in a political campaign. I have refused consistently to play politics with that question. I refused, first, because it is my responsibility to see that our policy in Israel fits in with our foreign policy throughout the world. Second, it is my desire to help build in Palestine a strong, prosperous, free and independent democratic state. It must be large enough, free enough, and strong enough to make its people self-supporting and secure."

An amended British resolution was finally adopted, but it was swiftly superseded by a new resolution which called upon both sides to negotiate an armistice.

In the Assembly debate, the Bernadotte proposals were defeated by the alliance of pro-Arab and pro-Israel delegations. All references to the mediator's proposals were stricken from the resolution which the Assembly adopted. So too, in an effort to win Arab votes, were all references to the partition resolution and to the state of Israel. What finally emerged was a vague resolution establishing the Palestine Conciliation Commission and calling upon the parties to negotiate with each other or through the Commission. The resolution also included the highly controversial Article 11 which dealt with Arab refugees.

Israel celebrated the anniversary of the partition resolution by applying for membership to the U.N. on November 29, 1948. While we had no assurance of winning, I argued that this was an appropriate time to try, because everyone expected it on the anniversary date. Israel's application was championed by the United States, the Soviet Union, and by three other delegations, but it lacked the necessary majority.

On that same day, in a long letter to Weizmann, Truman reaffirmed his opposition to any territorial changes which were unacceptable to Israel. The President also disclosed that the United States intended to make a loan to Israel through the Export-Import Bank. He promised to transform *de facto* recognition into *de jure* recognition after Israel's elections, which were scheduled for January 25, and he called for direct Arab-Israel negotiations.

Once the Paris ordeal ended, many nations were ready to extend diplomatic recognition. When the U.N. session began, only fifteen nations had done so, and there were only two recognitions in the next three months. Then Canada broke the ice, and within two months twenty-six more nations had recognized Israel. Most of these were in the Western Hemisphere and in Europe.

Diplomacy so often trails the facts, for protocol often dims perception, especially when the facts are revolutionary.

THE BATTLE IS RENEWED

Fighting flared anew late in 1948. On December 21, six days after the Assembly left Paris, the Israelis told the U.N. that the Egyptians were again blocking the roads to the Negev settlements. Israel considered herself free to act in defense of her territory and charged that Egypt was refusing to accept the Council's November 16 resolution which had called for armistice agreements. Israeli forces knifed through the Negev and into Sinai. They might have reached the Suez Canal, but that was not their objective. Instead, they wheeled westward to cut off Egyptian retreat, to pocket Egyptian forces, and to expel them from Palestine.

London and Washington moved to halt the Israeli advance. The British threatened to come to Egypt's defense under the Anglo-Egyptian treaty of 1936, which permitted British forces to be stationed in the Suez Canal zone. Truman sternly called on Israel to withdraw from Egypt without delay. By January 2, Israel had withdrawn her forces, but the crisis was not over. On the same day, Egyptian planes dropped bombs on Jerusalem for the first time in the city's history. A few days later, the British sent squadrons of Spitfires into the Negev, and five were shot down by Israeli pilots. One of the pilots we later learned was Ezer Weizman. The British demanded compensation and threatened further military action. They landed troops in the Jordanian port of Aqaba to confront Israeli troops at Eilat.

Sir Terence Shone of the British delegation delivered a note of protest to Lourie, who authorized me to inform the press that he had rejected it because it was addressed to the "Jewish Authorities of Tel Aviv."

Cooler heads prevailed in London. The U.S. government and the British public were critical of the Bevin government, which survived a "no confidence" motion by a slim margin.

The crisis and its alarms had a positive result. On January 7, 1949, Egypt agreed to negotiate an armistice agreement under Bunche's auspices. That night Lourie and I were on television to hail a major turning point; we now expected peace.

Threatened with invasion, the Egyptians apparently preferred to come to terms with Israel rather than to accept Bevin's proffered assistance. British influence and policy had collapsed, climaxed by the misadventure of the reconnaissance flights, and paralleled by Israel's steady diplomatic advance.

Israel held her first election on January 25, and the United States now extended *de jure* recognition and a $100 million Export-Import Bank loan, raising the status of the U.S. mission in Israel to an embassy. Four days later, the British granted her *de facto* recognition.

At Rhodes, Bunche, tireless member of the U.N. Secretariat, brought Israel and her Arab adversaries to the armistice table to negotiate agreements, one by one. Wisely, Bunche insisted that the Arabs come one state at a time instead of *en bloc*. Moreover, he once told me, he warned the parties that the sessions would continue until they were successfully concluded, and that any party which walked out of the negotiation would have to bear responsibility. Agreements were signed with Egypt on February 24, with Lebanon on March 23, with Jordan on April 3, and with Syria, the most difficult state, on July 20. Bunche won the Nobel Peace Prize.

On March 4, 1949, the Security Council voted nine to one to recommend Israel's admission into the U.N.; Egypt voted no. The British abstained, expressing doubts about Israel's adherence to U.N. resolutions.

If London had loyally accepted the U.N. partition resolution, there would have been no war and no problems of boundaries, refugees, or Jerusalem. This protestation of concern for U.N. resolutions ill became those who had led the attack upon them.

On May 11, the General Assembly ratified Israel's admission, by a vote of 37 to 12, after a long ordeal of attack and interrogation by the Arab states and their friends on the three major issues: boundaries, refugees, and Jerusalem. Thus, the ordinary tests for admission to the U.N. were not enough. In future years, the U.N. was so eager to include everyone, under the principle of universality, that it seated new states within hours of birth. In the case of Israel, adversaries sought to extort concessions as a price.

Eban responded to the barrage and Israel's enemies gained little comfort. On May 11, I was privileged to accompany Sharett, Eban, Lourie, and others, as a member of Israel's first U.N. delegation, amid a tumultuous reception by a host of friends, who, disregarding protocol, turned the austere Assembly into joyous pandemonium.

As Bunche shaped the armistice agreements at Rhodes, the new Palestine Conciliation Commission (PCC) opened negotiations at Lausanne to transform the armistice agreements into permanent peace treaties, but the Commission blundered into stalemate. It failed because it did not emulate Bunche's successful tactic and because it represented great power interests. Also, parallel with the negotiations at Lausanne, the United States was pressuring Israel to make sweeping concessions to the Arab states.

Bunche was responsible to the U.N. In contrast, the PCC included delegates of three countries—Turkey, France, and the United States—who were responsible to their own governments. Each country had a special interest. Turkey was a Moslem country on the shores of the Mediterranean. France sought to regain the influence it had lost in 1945 and faced critical problems in North Africa. The United States was suffering from a guilt complex because the Arabs accused it of being Israel's chief patron.

From the outset, U.S. representatives urged Israel to accept the return of a substantial number of Arab refugees prior to a peace settlement and to offer territorial concessions in line with the Bernadotte plan.

Now, with the United States as their protagonist, the Arabs had no incentive to negotiate.

At Rhodes, Bunche had insisted on direct talks between Israel and her adversaries, one by one. At Lausanne, Jews and Arabs did not meet; each side met with the PCC separately. The inevitable result was the reuniting of the Arab League coalition and the stiffening of Arab opposition to any kind of settlement. No Arab country could move to end hostilities, for the Arab line was fixed by the most extreme; to recede from it was to betray the united Arab front and to invite obloquy.

The Arabs insisted that Israel make sweeping concessions before they would meet with her. Thus, they were offering a novel concept—the doctrine of a non-liability war, under which an aggressor could always afford to go to war in the comfortable knowledge that defeat would cost nothing. If his war failed, he could return to claim the rights offered in the original settlement that he had rejected.

I have often contrasted Bunche's success with the PCC's failure. In 1977, I was especially critical of the Carter Administration's insistence on a comprehensive settlement involving the Palestinians, rather than on bilateral talks between Israel and Egypt. On October 3, 1977, testifying before the Senate Committee on Foreign Relations—before Sadat visited Jerusalem—I argued that the demand for a comprehensive settlement of the Palestine question as a condition of an Israeli-Egyptian peace would veto the achievement of the major goal—the peace which both Egypt and Israel needed and so earnestly desired.

Chapter 7

We Begin to Lobby

ON CAPITOL HILL

The lobby for Israel, known as the American Israel Public Affairs Committee (AIPAC) since 1959, came into existence in 1951. It was established at that time because Israel needed American economic assistance to enable her to absorb the huge influx of refugees who poured into the country soon after statehood.

Unfortunately, the Department of State was then opposed to any U.S. grant to Israel because it feared the resentment of the Arabs, who were not requesting U.S. aid. American policy was inhibited by the fear that the Arabs would align with Moscow in the Cold War. The negative attitude of the State Department forced us to appeal to Congress, even as we had done in the struggle for statehood between 1943 and 1948.

In her first three years, Israel's 650,000 Jews absorbed 600,000 Jewish immigrants. Many had rotted in displaced persons camps in Germany, Austria, and Italy since the war's end in 1945. Many had emerged from squalid Middle Eastern ghettos like those in Yemen and Iraq, and many had come from other lands. The people of Israel could not pay the huge absorption cost; Jews everywhere had to share that responsibility.

Several thousand American Jewish leaders met in Washington late in 1950 to devise a four-point program to finance refugee resettlement and to stimulate Israel's economic development. They agreed to increase donations to the United Jewish Appeal, to encourage private investment, to launch Israel bonds to develop the country's economic infrastructure, and to request the United States to include Israel in its vast overseas aid program.

The multi-billion-dollar Marshall Plan had revived a war-stricken Europe, but only a minuscule amount had been allotted to the Middle East.

Truman was sympathetic to Israel's needs, but he could not overcome the State Department's opposition. The United States had already reflected his sympathy with a $135 million Export-Import Bank loan, repayable—and long since repaid—in dollars. In addition, the United States had provided Israel with such surplus commodities as potatoes and butter. These were loans and sales, however, and not grants.

There was no alternative but to appeal for congressional legislation. Truman thought that special legislation could be avoided because the foreign aid law permitted him to transfer 10 percent of aid appropriations from one area, such as Europe, to another, such as the Middle East. But Secretary of State Dean Acheson was then adamantly opposed to that solution.

Israel needed to make a crucial policy decision. Although her pro-Western orientation was never questioned, she had always avoided formal identification with either of the Cold War powers. Now Israel turned to the West.

Israel's case was compelling. Population had doubled in three years and was expected to triple in six. Citizens had made tremendous sacrifices. They had suffered heavy casualties to win independence, had paid high taxes, and had to accept austerity, wage and price controls, and strict rationing. Despite rising agricultural and industrial production, the country was buffeted by violent inflationary pressures. Her 1951 landscape was scarred with *maabarot*—ugly clusters of shacks, tin huts, and tents—which provided crude shelters for bitterly disillusioned immigrants. American Jews had made unprecedented contributions, but these were far from adequate and the new country verged on bankruptcy.

Israel's cause was reinforced by both moral and strategic considerations. The oil-endowed Middle East was vulnerable to attack from without and subversion from within. The area was underdeveloped and its people were underprivileged. Israel was the one country in the region whose government and people supported free institutions. A pilot plant, she would stimulate other peoples to emulate her and to labor for development, higher standards, and democracy's freedoms.

We believed that some Arab leaders might be encouraged to make peace with Israel if America tangibly supported Israel's progress and welfare, and we were convinced that the Arabs would make peace if Israel remained strong.

Israelis began looking for a lobbyist to promote the necessary legislation. Lipsky called their attention to my qualifications, for I knew many community leaders, newspapermen, and congressmen, and was familiar with Arab-Israel issues.

On Saturday, December 9, Eban asked me to draft a speech for a U.N. diplomat who, we had been told, would advocate our cause in the debate over Jerusalem. Rita Grossman, my assistant, and I worked with Eban in his apartment until 3:30 A.M. I dictated, Rita typed, and Eban rewrote. As we were finishing, Eban told me that he had heard my name in a new context. Would I leave the Israeli delegation for six months to lobby for aid on Capitol Hill?

My first reaction: "Do I go back to an American salary?" In earlier posts, I had been paid $10,000 to $12,000 a year. But, as a "diplomat" employed by Israel, I had been reduced to a munificent $7,800, with which I had been content because there was a fringe benefit—a cherished cause.

There were other questions. Should I continue my registration as an agent of the Israel government? Was it appropriate for an embassy to lobby? Embassies talked to the State Department, and American voters talked to their congressmen. An American lobbyist should work for an American organization, and, in fact, that was Lipsky's idea. He wanted me to return to the American Zionist Council as its executive director, and he believed that the Council should direct the congressional battle for aid. Lipsky decried the impropriety of lobbying by an agent of a foreign government, who would be handicapped because a foreign agent must report all expenditures, label all documents, and refrain from criticism of the United States. He contended that the American Jewish community, which had waged a magnificent campaign for the U.N. partition resolution, should be re-enlisted. The Council had already started an educational campaign for aid to Israel, but no legislation had been projected.

At first, Eban did not agree with Lipsky. He preferred that I act for an *ad hoc* committee of American Jewish organizations and that I take a leave of absence from the Israeli government for six months or a year, and then return to the next U.N. Assembly. Eban was preparing to direct both the embassy in Washington and the U.N. delegation in New York.

Later that same Sunday, I saw Lipsky, who was disappointed because I did not want to become the AZC director. At midnight, I met Sharett and Teddy Kollek at Penn Station, from where they were Washington-bound. Kollek, I learned, had nominated me for the post. On the following Tuesday, Lipsky, Goldmann, and I discussed the names of many distinguished Americans who might lead the proposed *ad hoc* committee. Our first choice was Rifkind, but he had been unable to accept such a time-consuming enterprise. There were suggestions that Judge Samuel Rosenman, Roosevelt's former legal counsel, serve as chairman, and that Murray Gurfein, another future jurist, act as vice chairman. Imaginations soared as we debated many other improbabilities: Albert Lasker, George Backer, Marshall Field, Paul Porter, Mark Ethridge, Milton Eisenhower, Clark Clifford, John W. Davis, Donald Nelson, Telford Taylor, and Jonathan Daniels. Most of them would have been astonished if they had known they were under consideration for a lobbying assignment for Israel.

Finally, the persistent Lipsky prevailed, and on January 31, 1951 it was decided that I should leave the Israeli government and spearhead the lobbying campaign for the Zionist Council.

On February 13, I notified the Department of Justice that I was withdrawing as an agent of a foreign principal, and I then filed with the Clerk of the House and the Secretary of the Senate in conformity with domestic lobbying law.

There were the inevitable personnel and organizational clashes.

In New York, Rabbi Jerome Unger knew that Lipsky expected me to succeed him as the AZC executive director, and, since he did not wish to be succeeded, he did not want me to operate in New York. In Washington, the AZC's special counsel was a veteran Bostonian Zionist, Elihu Stone, who was on excellent terms with Moshe Keren, Israel's minister at the Embassy. Stone did not relish a rival in Washington. To please Stone, Keren proposed to chair and coordinate a three-man committee comprised of Stone, Keren and myself, but Lipsky rejected the proposal. Under no circumstances would the AZC serve as an agent of the Israeli government.

AIPAC owes a debt to Lipsky. He was then in his seventy-fifth year—gruff, acerbic, and abrasive. A brilliant journalist and parliamentarian, he was one of this century's top Zionist leaders, whose epigrammatic pen and decisive gavel quickly crystallized policy and terminated debate. He had testified before Congress way back in 1922 to win endorsement of the Balfour Declaration; he was no novice on the Hill.

We enlisted the cooperation of all major Jewish organizations, both "Zionist" and "non-Zionist," such as the defense organizations. They were unwilling to lobby, but they agreed to find prominent constituents to open congressional doors for us. We decided to promote a separate bill authorizing a $100 million grant for Israel as a magnet to attract support. We would canvass Congress for sponsors and introduce the bill by March 1. Later, our bill would be offered in the form of an amendment to the Administration's overall foreign aid bill.

I met leaders of the Israel Industrial Institute in New York, including Rosenman; merchant Fred Lazarus, Jr., of Columbus, Ohio; Barney Balaban, the Paramount Pictures magnate; and the Committee's staff director, Dr. Josef Cohn, an aide to Weizmann. Lazarus sent a letter to Ohio Republican congressmen whom both of us knew: Clarence J. Brown, Sr., Mrs. Frances P. Bolton, and John M. Vorys. Balaban offered the assistance of a highly experienced volunteer, Louis Novins, his aide, who had once served the Anti-Defamation League (ADL) and who had been executive vice-chairman of the Freedom Train.

In Washington, I enlisted organization representatives: Herman Edelsberg of B'nai B'rith; David Brody of the ADL; Joseph Barr and Warren Adler of the Jewish War Veterans; Marcus Cohen of the American Jewish Committee; Olya Margolin of the National Council of Jewish Women; and Denise Tourover of Hadassah.

We had a small but gifted staff. Rita Grossman was my executive assistant from May 14, 1947, when she joined the Jewish Agency delegation at the U.N., until 1965. Ruth Ludwin, who later married Actor Lou Jacobi, was my New York secretary. Marian Perlov was the lone executive in the Washington office when I took over. Fred Gronich, a former army officer who had succeeded Mickey Marcus as Ben-Gurion's civilian adviser on military affairs, toured southern states looking for cooperative local leaders. The five of us alerted constituents to send letters and telegrams.

My task was complicated by organizational competition. ADL executives recruited by Novins wanted to assume responsibility for finding community leaders, but veteran Zionists were naturally unwilling to withdraw from the role which they had performed so effectively in the pre-state period. A host of friends rapidly expanded, duplicating efforts to win support.

Zionist leaders complained that we were not publicizing or taking credit for our work. Lipsky admonished them: "We stand squarely behind legislation — never in front of it." I observed that precept, and for a decade my name never appeared in the press. In those days "lobbying" was a pejorative, but there are many peoples' lobbies today, and I like to think that we helped to popularize the people's right to petition their government, both on domestic and international affairs.

Lipsky left AIPAC a significant legacy. He inscribed on its letterhead: "The Committee conducts public action with a view to maintaining and improving friendship and good will between the United States and Israel." That objective has always guided AIPAC.

As a result of Novins's long-distance telephone calls, February 8 was a very busy day. Wayne Morse of Oregon, then a Republican, was one of the first senators I saw. He was eager to sponsor our bill, but his face fell when I asked him to be a co-sponsor. I explained that we were asking Ohio's Robert Taft (Mr. Republican) to be the GOP lead-off man. Morse was a notorious loner and therefore not likely to recruit a following, although he was always one of the first to help us. Coincidentally, I ran into Taft that same day and he readily agreed to take second place to a Democrat. I also called Alabama's Democratic Senator John Sparkman, whom I had known at the U.N. in 1949 and who was reintroduced to me by William Bloom, a Tuscaloosa merchant who had helped him in his campaign.

Karl Baehr, an executive of the American Christian Palestine Committee (ACPC), Novins and I called on Senator Paul H. Douglas (D-Illinois). In the meantime, Silver met Taft, his fellow Ohioan. I followed up with a detailed memorandum, and now we had our two top sponsors — Douglas and Taft. Although he was a consistent budget-cutter, Taft urged me to raise our request from $100 million to $150 million, for, he explained, the amount would be slashed by Congress. (I had met Taft twenty years earlier, in 1931, when I had covered his drive to modernize Ohio's tax laws in the State Senate.)

I visited many old friends on the Hill and in New York, including John Oakes of *The New York Times,* and Harry Baehr of the *The New York Herald Tribune,* and both publications carried excellent editorials. I wrote to Stassen, recalling his help at the San Francisco U.N. conference; he promised support.

We consulted the two Jewish congressmen on the House Foreign Affairs Committee, Representatives Jacob K. Javits (R-New York), and Abraham A. Ribicoff (D-Connecticut), and their reactions frequently differed. Javits favored the bill which authorized aid to Israel; Ribicoff preferred a regional approach.

Oveta Culp Hobby, who had led the American WACs and was a Houston publisher, came to Washington to host a dinner party for Eban and the Texas Democratic senators, Tom Connally, chairman of the Senate Committee on Foreign Relations, and his youthful colleague, Lyndon B. Johnson. Connally was grumpy and antagonistic, but he promised that Israel's cause would be heard.

Democratic leader Wiley Moore of Atlanta arrived with his friend Abe Goldstein to dine with Eban and Georgia's two Democratic senators, Walter F. George, who later succeeded Connally, and Richard B. Russell, then chairman of the Armed Services Committee.

One widely respected congressman, Brooks Hays (D-Arkansas), told me that he had been in doubt about the legislation but favored it because a Little Rock rabbi, Ira Sanders, was sympathetic to Israel.

Abraham J. Feinberg of New York, who had helped to start Truman's 1948 campaign train, telephoned many senators and their aides. He kept cautioning me to preserve bipartisan sponsorship to reflect the friendship of both parties.

Stone successfully urged the two Massachusetts Floor Leaders, McCormack and Martin, to co-sponsor the bill in the House.

We had crises. The virulent Senator Joseph McCarthy (R-Wisconsin) was then in his prime, and one of my colleagues urged Eban to invite him to be a co-sponsor. I was furious when I heard about it and I went to Douglas to urge him to veto the suggestion. Douglas emphatically agreed and warned that he would withdraw his name if McCarthy's name were added.

There was some delay because Taft insisted that the bill affirm the need to contribute to U.S. security, but Silver feared that Israel would thus become gratuitously embroiled in the Cold War. Eban and I persuaded Silver to yield, and Taft prevailed. On the following day, March 2, we began circulating the bill to enlist co-sponsors.

We had unexpected help from a former antagonist, Rose Keane, who had worked with Bergson during our differences in the 1940s. She helped us to enlist two Democratic senators: Magnuson and Guy M. Gillette of Iowa. The greatest help came from Douglas's competent and dedicated legislative aide, Frank McCulloch, who always received me warmly and counseled me wisely throughout Douglas's Senate career.

By March 29, we had won 36 senators to serve as co-sponsors—19 Democrats and 17 Republicans—representing twenty-five states.

It was different in the House, where rules did not then permit multiple co-sponsorship. There, with the cooperation of Javits and Celler, and their aides, Roy Millenson and Bess Dick (who helped us for many years), we urged congressmen to sign a joint endorsement sponsored by thirteen leading representatives—seven Democrats and six Republicans.

On May 15, Israel's anniversary, Ben-Gurion came to address the National Press Club. He had breakfast with Douglas, McCormack, Eban, and myself, and the conversation reflected a paradox. McCormack, an Irish Catholic, was contending that the basic evil in America was economic. Ben-Gurion, Labor Socialist, insisted that it was spiritual.

By that time the Administration had taken note of the congressional demonstration and had recognized Israel's proven need. In its $8.5 billion Mutual Security Program, it earmarked $125 million in economic aid for the Middle East, recommending $24 million for Iran, $23.5 million for Israel, a similar sum for all the Arab states—an equation which the Arabs resented—and about $3.95 million for Libya, Ethiopia, and Liberia. In addition, there was a separate allocation of $50 million for the Arab refugees.

The Administration justified the proposed $23.5 million for Israel by estimating that Israel's balance of payments deficit would not exceed that amount. We believed that the figure was much too low, but our request for $150 million for aid to Israel was vigorously opposed by spokesmen for the Administration, both on the Hill and in communications from the field.

American diplomats, especially those stationed in the oil countries, flooded Congress with protests. Dorothy Thompson, once an ardent pro-Zionist who had switched to the Arab side, wrote an inflammatory syndicated newspaper column warning that war would explode in ninety days if the money for Israel were appropriated. Assistant Secretary of State George McGhee told Senator William Benton (D-Connecticut), one of our thirty-six sponsors, that the Administration was unqualifiedly opposed to our bill, believing that it would make the Arabs "furious." He offered similar views to the House committee.

With the help of the gifted Shulamith Nardi, who later became the official interpreter for Israel's presidents, I wrote a memorandum which explained why Israel needed American aid. I stressed Israel's critical financial position, and I reminded Congress that most Jewish refugees had once been wards of the American government in displaced persons camps in Germany, Austria, and Italy, and that Israel had assumed the cost of their care since 1948.

Congress was then considering the Administration's request for $50 million for the Palestine Arab refugees, whose numbers had soared because every Arab who claimed to be impoverished by the war could now qualify as a "refugee," even though he had never left the country and had continued to reside in the West Bank and Gaza. The U.N. freely acknowledged that ration lists were padded. Many were born but none ever died; deaths were not reported. Ration cards had become currency, freely bought and sold.

Ignoring these flagrant abuses, our critics complained that the United States was spending only $300 a year for each Arab refugee while we were asking an average of $2,000 for each Jewish refugee. We were always confronted with spurious per capita calculations and we stressed the salient difference. The Arab states were resisting resettlement and the United Nations Relief and Works Agency (UNRWA) was using its funds merely to keep people alive. In contrast, much more money was urgently needed in Israel for resettlement, housing, education and rehabilitation.

Large Jewish families had poured in from Arab ghettos and were crammed into tiny makeshift shelters. Israel's major social problem for many years to come was that many prolific families remained in the same congested quarters and bitterly resented the larger modern accommodations which were made available for later immigrants.

Israel, we contended, should not be punished because of the enmity or the inertia of her adversaries, and aid should be allocated on the basis of need and on the ability of aid recipients to make the best possible use of it.

Despite a hostile barrage, most of the press seemed favorable, and many editorials were reprinted and circulated on the Hill. Javits asked me for a document outlining Israel's attitude on boundaries, refugees, and Jerusalem — the three controversial issues. This was the forerunner of many editions of *Myths and Facts,* a widely circulated special issue of the *Near East Report.*

As we prepared to release the names of the 164 House sponsors, I noticed that a prominent Boston Democrat, Representative John F. Kennedy, was not listed. I telephoned to suggest that he might have overlooked it and that he might be interested. His answer surprised me. He said he was opposed to economic aid to the Middle East; he believed in military aid. (That was early Kennedy.)

During Ben-Gurion's visit, the United States aimed another blow at Israel. It joined with France, the United Kingdom, and Turkey in a demand at the U.N. that Israel suspend the project to drain the Huleh marshes because of Syrian objections. The action was unjustified; Israel's right was later upheld.

Several months later, Israel won U.S. support for a major decision against Egypt. At the Security Council, Israel had protested that Egypt's blockade of Israeli shipping in the Suez Canal contravened the 1949 U.N. armistice agreement, which was intended to end the state of belligerency. Bunche had ruled that the armistice agreements "provide for a definitive end to the fighting in Palestine . . . what amounts to a non-aggression pact." I went to see Magnuson, an authority on commerce, and Maine's Owen Brewster to urge them to appeal to McGhee for U.S. support on the Canal issue. Israel won that landmark decision on September 1, a major

Eban diplomatic victory, which Egypt defiantly ignored and which the United States never really tried to enforce.

Three articulate witnesses appeared for us before the House Foreign Affairs Committee: Lipsky, Dr. Joseph Schwartz, the former head of the American Jewish Joint Distribution Committee, who was best informed on the plight of the Jews of Europe and the Middle East, and economist Robert R. Nathan, who generously interrupted a Minnesota lakes vacation in response to our request. All three were impressive. They were brief, precise, and informative. No one could match Nathan's priceless testimony, and I offered him a $500 honorarium which he rejected, offering to settle if I would buy a $2.00 ticket for an American Veterans Committee raffle.

Neither Douglas nor Taft, our top Senate sponsors, were members of the Senate Committee and Eban and I called on both to urge them to testify. When I offered to prepare a draft for Taft, he assured me that no one ever wrote his speeches. Douglas was uncomfortable because he believed that the $8.5 billion aid bill was excessive. However, contending that the bill was too generous to Europe and too parsimonious for the Middle East, Douglas proposed to add another $125 million for the Middle East. One did not erect steel walls to defend Europe and mere parapets of sand to protect the Middle East. Later, Nathan and I called on Douglas, who, unlike Taft, asked me for a draft.

Opposition forces encouraged by the State Department testified before the House Committee on July 26. Three churchmen—Clarence Pickett of the American Friends Service Committee of Philadelphia, Dr. Walter Van Kirk of the National Council of the Churches of Christ in the United States, and Monsignor Thomas J. McMahon of the Catholic Near East Welfare Association—contended that the State Department's request for $23.5 million for Israel and an equal amount for all the Arab states was unbalanced. Although both Arabs and Israelis needed to absorb and resettle vast numbers of refugees, they believed that the responsibility of the Arabs was much larger and that more money should be allocated to them.

Pickett argued that the request for $150 million for Israel was apparently based on the estimate of a large refugee influx. He did not like to see millions of people "uprooted," and—with a dash of casuistry—he feared that the appropriation would stimulate the uprooting of people from all over the world.

Javits reminded Pickett that the forecasts were based on the need to provide sanctuary for Jews from unbearable persecution in countries like Iraq and Yemen. Pickett conceded that this had been so when he visited Iraq two years before, but he insisted that things had changed. He said—with a dash of humanity—that the United States should "catch those things" before the situation became severe enough to force the Jews to leave. In fact, Iraq's attitude toward Jews became increasingly brutal in later years.

By this time, a majority of both the House and Senate Committees had publicly endorsed our bill, but they might vote differently in closed session when they came to mark up the legislation. I feared that one of our most ardent supporters might offer an amendment to provide $150 million for Israel and that it might lose.

That happened. James G. Fulton (R-Pennsylvania) moved to raise the total amount for Israel by $126.5 million, but he won only four votes. When Javits recommended an additional $100 million for Israel and $50 million more for the Arabs, he had only eight votes. Mrs. Bolton's proposal to add $100 million for the Arab refugees was also rejected.

In anticipation of such setbacks, and of the parliamentary danger that amendments to amendments might table the entire initiative, I had suggested a compromise procedure at dinner with Javits two days before the vote. Inasmuch as the bill included a separate item of $50 million for the Arab refugees, I proposed the insertion of a separate new paragraph which would earmark $50 million for the Jewish refugees. This sum would be in addition to the $23.5 million in economic assistance which the Administration had recommended and would bring the total for Israel to $73.5 million.

Javits agreed, and he passed my suggestion to Representative Walter H. Judd (R-Minnesota), one of the Committee's most influential members, who offered the compromise. It was welcomed as equitable and was approved 16 to 5.

Truman's attitude was, to say the least, bewildering. On the eve of the Committee vote, Eddie Jacobson of Kansas, Truman's one-time haberdashery partner, came to Washington and informed us that he would see the President the following day. Truman then promised Jacobson that he would call Representative Franklin D. Roosevelt, Jr. (D-New York), a Committee freshman, to his office on Thursday. That would have been too late; the Committee vote was scheduled for Wednesday. That morning, I went to the Hill and called Roosevelt out of the Committee to suggest that he call the White House to find out if Truman had anything to tell him. Roosevelt telephoned, but Truman informed him that he wasn't looking for him. Roosevelt later told me that Truman was disappointed with the Committee vote. Truman still hoped that the amount for Israel could be increased on the Floor, but he warned that his personal view was not to be disclosed.

There was harsh opposition on the House Floor. The day before, Representative H. D. Cooley (D-North Carolina), chairman of the House Agriculture Committee, and several southern colleagues had met privately with seven State and Agriculture officials who had fed them anti-Israel arguments. Thus briefed, Cooley insisted that the $50 million grant for the Jewish refugees was extravagant. He disclosed the State Department's negative attitude.

The opposition congressmen had recently attended an interparliamentary conference at Istanbul and had then gone on to Jericho, Gaza, and Jerusalem to inspect Arab refugee camps. They charged that Israel had expelled Arab refugees and had denied their repatriation, that Israel was luring

Jewish refugees with political propaganda, and that the United States had no obligation to finance this migration. Israel was not viable and could not be made self-sufficient, they predicted. Israel was aggressive and arming to seize more territory, and there was really no guarantee that Israel would be pro-West in the event of conflict.

Cooley commended Israelis for their "magnificent achievements." "Some of the best friends I have in this world are Jews," he assured Congress. Nevertheless, he could not condone Israel's "acts of terror and aggression." He had seen 60,000 Arabs in a "concentration camp" on the hills of Jericho, "the most awful sight my eyes have ever seen," as well as 200,000 in Gaza "suffering from every disease known to the human race." There were 875,000 refugees "forced to live like rats and wild animals." He belabored the invidious per capita comparison. Not all of Israel's immigrants were refugees, he insisted. They were able to board planes in Iraq. Israel did not have enough room, and Israelis were building high class apartments that would do credit to U.S. cities. The Jews were moving too fast. Blood would flow within ninety days, he warned.

Cooley was joined by Representatives William R. Poage (D-Texas), Clifford R. Hope (R-Kansas), and Henry O. Talle (R-Iowa).

One of Cooley's colleagues, H. C. Bonner (D-North Carolina), described Israel as a barren and desolate country, and he predicted a terrible explosion.

In reply, McCormack described Israel as the one nation we could rely on, while Fulton warned it would be most difficult to defend Europe unless the Free World could hold the lower flank of the Middle East. Representative Donald O'Toole (D-New York) said that Christianity owed a debt to Jerusalem. (Many distinguished Christians — Henry A. Atkinson, Daniel Poling, Reinhold Niebuhr, James Farley, Harold Stassen, and Carl Voss — had endorsed aid to Israel.)

Vorys contended that Judaism was a religion, that Jews were not a nation, and that Jewish separatism was the root cause of persecution, but Representative Charles L. Kersten (R-Wisconsin) called the Jewish people a strong bulwark against atheistic communism. A future Secretary of State, Representative Christian A. Herter (R-Massachusetts), said that the pressures on Israel were tremendous, and the conservative Judd, knowledgeable and never isolationist, pointed out that Arabs were using oil as a weapon against the West, had closed the Suez Canal, and were fixing deadlines, thereby forcing Jews to leave Yemen and Iraq. Roosevelt estimated that 700,000 Jewish refugees had entered Israel in four years.

Although supported by conservative southern Democrats and midwestern Republicans, Cooley was defeated 146 to 65.

There was another jolt. While insisting that he was not opposed to aid for Israel, Kennedy felt that too much economic aid was reserved for the Middle East, and that the United States could not afford to raise the standard of living of all peoples in the world who might be susceptible to the lure of communism. He offered an amendment to cut the $175 million total for the Middle East to $140 million.

Javits and Ribicoff attacked Kennedy's amendment, but it almost carried. The vote was close—75 to 85. A subsequent teller vote was 101 to 141.

(When Kennedy became a candidate for the Senate that fall, his office asked us to draft a speech for him endorsing economic aid.)

In the final House vote the authorization for Europe was slashed by a full $1 billion, but the amount for the Middle East was raised by $50 million because of the additional grant for Israel.

There was a setback in the Senate. As in the House, a majority of the Senate Committee on Foreign Relations had endorsed the $150 million bill for Israel, but many members were absent, and the combined Senate Foreign Relations and Armed Services Committees slashed the entire aid bill 30 percent across the board by a vote of 13 to 12. When I called Senator Henry C. Lodge, Jr. (R-Massachusetts) to protest, he explained that no one had referred to the sums earmarked for refugees because that item had not appeared in the version of the bill then pending before the Senate Committee. However, when the Committees later took up the House bill, they persisted in the 30 percent cut, thus earmarking only $35 million for each refugee allocation.

I sent a telegram urging the senators to exempt the Middle East from the overall cut, arguing that one could not apply the same percentage cuts to refugees in tents and to industry operating at 100 percent capacity.

Senator Leverett Saltonstall (R-Massachusetts) moved to increase the two refugee allocations to $45 million but was rebuffed, and the Committee compromised at $40 million. It was my first defeat.

I told Lipsky I planned to appeal to Douglas and Taft to try to persuade the Senate to raise the $40 million to $50 million on the Senate Floor. Some of my non-Zionist colleagues were protesting that I was pushing too hard, for they feared that a resentful Senate might change the grant to a loan. I insisted that we must always put up a fight. When Eban and Lipsky came to dinner at my New York apartment Saturday night, both agreed with me.

I spent all that weekend drafting a memorandum explaining why the amount should be raised and a series of individualized letters to Senate members, including isolationists and critics. A thousand special delivery letters went out to community leaders to unleash a flood of telegrams. However, our first and major task was to win the concurrence of Douglas and Taft.

On Monday morning, I was warmly received by McCulloch, who took my letter and brief into Douglas's office for what seemed to be the longest ten-minute span of my life. Douglas invited me in to give me a positive answer, and he observed, as he often told me, that Jews had helped him all his life. It took four tense days to get Taft's answer, for he was preoccupied with tax legislation.

Meanwhile, the Senate Committee released the printed transcript of the hearings on the aid bill, including the Taft and Douglas testimony. Taft,

who had insisted on writing his own statement, astonished us by his commendation of Israel's gallant army and its future role. He went so far as to
portray the Israeli army as a potential defender of the Middle East and Africa,
and even of the uranium mines in the Belgian Congo.

Israelis were stunned when they read dispatches that their forces might
some day be rushed off to Africa, yet there was an inkling of truth in that
revelation. When the Congo became independent in 1960, it received on
that day an international delegation which included Israeli doctors and
nurses on a World Health Organization mission.

We learned that Christian ministers, including Van Kirk and others in
the missionary wing, were criticizing congressmen for supporting Israel. On
the eve of the Senate vote, the American Christian Palestine Committee
reacted with an eloquent and succinct telegram reminding senators that "our
way of life has not yet won its spurs in this area except in Israel. Unresolved
problems such as those of the Jewish and Arab refugees may yet overwhelm
incipient democratic development unless we, the representatives of the
Western way of life, step in with the help necessary to bring order and a
measure of prosperity to these oppressed peoples."

The published testimony revealed McGhee's contention that the Administration did not believe that Israel's needs exceeded the $23.5 million which
the Administration had recommended.

Douglas proposed to add $60 million for economic aid for the Middle
East, but Taft would not go that high. At the same time, Douglas wanted to
reduce the appropriation for Europe, which complicated our appeal, for
many Atlantic seaboard friends supported aid to both Europe and Israel.
Thus, Saltonstall was apprehensive that a boost for Israel might be resented
by Europe's friends. He was pleased to learn, however, that Taft had agreed
to support us.

When the Senate debated the foreign aid bill, Chairman Connally effectively crushed all attempts to restore authorizations which had been deleted
in committee.

Republican conservatives tried to slash an additional $500 million from
economic aid to Europe but they lost, as did Administration supporters
who tried to boost appropriations. Senator Herbert H. Lehman (D-New York)
spoke in vain for $600 million for the St. Lawrence Seaway. Two Florida
senators sought to restore Latin American Point Four appropriations for $6
million, with invidious references to the favored position of the Near East.
Lehman wanted money restored for the International Refugee Organization. Senator Everett Dirksen (R-Illinois) proposed to slash an additional
$250 million from economic aid to Europe, and that carried.

The Douglas-Taft amendment reached the Floor late in the day. Douglas argued that Israel's unprecedented rate of immigration justified the $10
million increase. Brewster, Morse, and Taft joined the debate, and Senator
Irving M. Ives (R-New York) asked Taft whether or not he agreed that Israel

was the most important country in the world to the United States. Taft, forever precise, thought that this was an exaggeration and could not concur.

Connally, whose duty it was to manage the bill, abandoned the Floor and left an unpleasant chore to Russell, who argued that the amendment had not been requested by the Administration. He did, however, have kind words for the Jewish people, as did the octogenarian Senator Kenneth McKellar (D-Tennessee), who was wheeled into the chamber to explain that he wanted to vote for the amendment to help the Jews because they had suffered so much from Arab attacks.

Russell referred to the misery and poverty of the Arab world, but Brewster contrasted Arab poverty with enormous Arab oil wealth. Morse pointed to area tension. Within weeks, the premier in Iran, Jordan's King Abdullah, and a Lebanese ex-premier had all been assassinated.

Douglas had intended to ask for a roll call, but I discouraged him because the Senate's attitude had been so negative on previous items, and he changed his mind. Watching from the gallery, I was at first mystified by the comings and goings of Gillette, who, I came to realize, was escorting our friends in from the cloak room for the impending vote, even as he was courteously ushering opponents out of the chamber.

It was difficult to count the standing vote, but we estimated that it was 15 to 10 and that the yeas included Douglas, Taft, McKellar, Humphrey, Brewster, Ives, Bridges, Moody, Hendrickson, Lehman, Morse, Gillette, and Benton; the nay votes, it seemed to me, included Russell, Connally, Smathers, Holland, Long, and McFarland. McFarland's vote showed that the Administration had done nothing to win the Democratic Floor Leader.

There were congratulatory cables from my former Israeli colleagues, including a message from Sharett on September 10, 1951: "I hasten to send you my affectionate greetings on the remarkable achievement of which you may justly feel proud."

The fight was not ended. We had won a breakthrough in the authorization bill, but we still had to win favorable action on the appropriation. All such recommended authorizations must be reexamined by appropriations committees, which ask whether the budget can afford them.

On September 27, while canvassing the House Appropriations Committee, I was alarmed by the influential Representative Albert Gore (D-Tennessee), one of our co-sponsors. He had glowingly introduced Ben-Gurion to Tennessee audiences in April, but he had since visited the Arab refugee camps with Cooley, Poage, Senators William Smith (D-North Carolina) and Homer Ferguson (R-Michigan). For more than an hour, Gore taxed me with Arab arguments. I promised him the answers within twenty-four hours.

I telephoned Rita Grossman and asked her to come to Washington. We worked all that night preparing a 10,000-word brief in reply to Gore's attacks. We also appealed to constituents of Cooley, Bonner, and other southern congressmen to head off another Floor struggle.

Later, Gore assured me that he would not oppose the appropriation. Cooley did renew the attack in the general debate, and was answered by Judd and Herter, but he offered no amendment and the bill went through easily.

On the next day, I delivered letters to the Senate Appropriations Committee, and over the weekend I obtained assurances from 12 of the 21 members that they would vote favorably. However, the Senate Committee voted 10 to 9 for a flat five percent cut across the board. We telegraphed 65 key constituents throughout the country, urging the full appropriation, and we were confident that the House would restore the Senate's cut.

On the eve of the Senate vote, I delivered an indexed memorandum, giving the answers to all controversial issues, to Max Kampelman, who was an aide to a youthful Minnesota Senator, Hubert H. Humphrey. I asked that the Senator stand guard for us on the Senate Floor, and that he did for the next quarter of a century, until his death.

While both $50 million refugee appropriations were retained without reduction, there was a percentage cut in the Administration's economic aid request. Accordingly, the $23.5 million in economic aid originally programmed for Israel was cut to $15 million, and the Arab states suffered a similar reduction.

Thus, Israel received $65 million instead of $73.5 million. Even so, that was a decisive victory, for we had been able to increase aid for Israel over the open opposition of the Department of State.

THE SECOND ROUND

There was a revolutionary change in U.S. policy in 1952, when Washington, now aware of Israel's needs, recommended a larger authorization.

In November 1951, Israel applied for $126 million. I cautioned Israel's leaders that this would be regarded as excessive, for American aid could not continue indefinitely. Israel must retrench and adopt a selective immigration policy. She had to emphasize resettlement rather than relief, stimulate productivity, and live frugally.

Israel was then facing a crisis both in economics and morale. Early in 1951, Israel had been inundated by 120,000 Jews from Iraq. An extreme drought, followed by unprecedented floods, had forced large-scale commodity purchases. Tightly rationed Israelis were barely subsisting. As a result, Israel was the first country to receive any of the 1951 aid funds. Because Israel was on the brink of default, the Department of State had released $25 million by an exchange of letters before final congressional action.

In the meantime, I had resigned from the AZC late in October 1951. I had gone to Israel for a nine-week visit to learn more about the country's future as well as to decide about my own. The question I had to resolve was whether I should rejoin the Israeli diplomatic service or resume the work that I had done in Washington. I attended an Ulpan, an intensive Israeli language program, to brush up on Hebrew, which I had studied in my youth.

Congressmen began to visit Israel after the 1951 session, and I cautioned Israelis to give them a warm welcome. Ben-Gurion had been reluctant to receive them and to be photographed with them. However, he did recognize the status of two Republican leaders: Martin, who had sponsored the aid bill, and Leonard Hall, the next GOP national chairman. He invited them to lunch along with Ambassador Monnett B. Davis. Ben-Gurion bewildered us when he predicted that Eisenhower would be nominated by both the Republican and Democratic conventions.

Sharett was mystified when I proposed that Israel establish forty-eight seacoast settlements, naming them after the forty-eight states—a public relations tactic. In 1949, I had persuaded a reluctant Tel Aviv City Council to name a street for New York's liberal Mayor Fiorello LaGuardia. Now, in 1951, I proposed that Safed name a street after Ida Littman Javits, mother of the congressman. That was not so difficult because Safed was her birthplace, but it was complicated because there was no budget for street signs. I offered to pay for them.

Washington was then planning a Middle East defense command, and Javits proposed to deliver a radio speech urging Israelis to participate. I drafted notes for him, but when he attempted to clear them with Ambassador Davis, he was surprised to learn that Washington intended no such invitation to Israel lest it alienate the Arabs.

Before I left, I visited Ben-Gurion to voice my fear that the huge immigration could impoverish both economy and culture, as well as disturb stability. There was already a gap between Sephardim and Ashkenazim. Would there also be a gap between parents and children because shacks and slums provided no room for both generations? I recalled that American Jewish urban society had suffered social casualties in the early 1900s because children had taken to the streets, had resisted parental authority, and had become outcasts. Brushing my fears aside, Ben-Gurion insisted that the army would instill democratic discipline. To a limited extent, that was sound. But the cultural gap, which alarmed me in 1951, continues to be Israel's dominant domestic problem. Quality and equality are still urgent goals.

I came to realize that my future would be limited if I opted for a diplomatic career. Many of Israel's foreign service staff were young, ambitious, and, unlike myself, multilingual and equipped to represent Israel in many lands. There was little likelihood that I would ever be assigned to countries of my origin and residence, such as Canada and the United States. Moreover, I had spent twenty-three days escorting congressional visitors—Ribicoff, Celler, Javits, Fugate, Keating, O'Toole, Barrett, and Fein—and it became evident that my future lay in Washington. I became convinced that I could be more useful in Washington than at the U.N. or in Israel.

In January, I flew home and told Lipsky that I would resume work for the AZC. I notified the Department of Justice of my activities in Israel, for which I had drawn no salary, and I was assured that there was no need to register for that period. I registered anew with Congress as a domestic lobbyist for the promotion of friendly relations between Israel and the United States and economic aid to the area.

Since the Administration was now preparing to advocate aid for Israel, our task differed from 1951, when we had fought to increase aid. Now our task would be to ward off cuts.

I met Arthur Z. Gardiner, the economic operations adviser in the State Department's Office of Near Eastern Affairs, and was surprised by his positive response. He had a high regard for the officials he had met in Israel the previous fall, and the Israeli program was moving very quickly.

"Israel needs aid," he told me. "Its trade deficit is $297 million." Regardless of the complaint that aid to Israel alienated the Arabs, Gardiner said that it would be "villainous" to reduce aid to Israel after she had been encouraged to take all her immigrants. He later testified with skill and eloquence.

Meanwhile, the Administration told Congress that Israel faced "serious difficulties" because of efforts to establish a modern state while integrating large numbers of immigrants from diverse cultural backgrounds. Heavy development expenditures had contributed to inflation, and foreign exchange reserves had been depleted to import half the country's food and nearly all its capital goods requirements.

Technical cooperation would spur development and productivity. The United States promised experts in agriculture, transportation, health, industry, and public administration to develop projects expanding power, irrigation, transportation, and industrial facilities, and to furnish housing, seed, tools, equipment, livestock, and other items for productive employment.

The Administration and the U.N. then hoped that Arab refugees could be resettled in Arab lands, and the U.N. had voted to set aside $200 million for their "reintegration" in the next three years, along with $50 million for relief. Of this total, it was expected that the United States would allocate $150 million.

Accordingly, the Administration's 1952 economic assistance program for the Middle East was $196 million. Of this, $76 million was to be used for the relief and resettlement of Jewish refugees in Israel, and $65 million for the Palestinian Arabs—the first installment of the three-year U.N. program. In addition, Israel was to receive $3 million for technical assistance.

Anticipating criticism of the appropriations for the Arab refugees, Secretary of State Dean Acheson emphasized the need for resettlement rather than repatriation. It was a major tragedy that the Arab states rejected this call for resettlement and insisted that the refugees be held in camps waiting for the day of their return and Israel's disappearance. In a moving statement, Acheson told the House Committee that we must "heal the most terrible sore . . . in that area—the pressure of the 850,000 Arab refugees. . . . They do not see how to build a future. This group of people represents a terrible danger to the Middle East." He called on Arab countries to settle them: "*You think people are liabilities. People are assets.* People are the greatest assets there are, but people have to be put on some piece of land. They cannot live like birds in the air. . . . This country of yours is now in a condition where it cannot receive people on the ground because it needs irrigation. A large part of it is desert and waste, but cooperate with us and you can have water development, which will make this land capable of sustaining people. You can remove these thousands of refugees from their tents and their misery, where they constitute a threat to all of us. Put them on this land which is developed. Put some of your own people on the land which is developing too. And then you will have a strong economic life, which can support whatever military effort you can make. This is forward-looking. This is hopeful. And that is what we are trying to do."

But nobody seemed to be listening.

From the beginning, we have favored economic aid to raise living standards for both Israel and the Arab states. We lobbied for the allocations for both the Arab and Jewish refugees. I stressed these themes in an address before the National Conference on International Economics and Social Development in Washington on April 3, 1952, and I warned against dangers that would surely grow if we neglected human needs.

Nine new states had won sovereignty in the Middle East since World War I. However, sovereignty did not mean food or medicine for the hungry and the sick. Economic progress should not be permitted to lag behind political advance. Emblems of nationalism were becoming symbols of frustration. Class cleavage was wide and stark. Like the landscape, there were oases of wealth and wastelands of poverty. In this fertile field, the fascist demagogue, seeking to maintain vested privilege, and the communist agitator, bent upon subversion, could sow together to reap a harvest of hatred. There was the threat that legitimate nationalism would be perverted into hostility for the West, the major constructive force in the region.

The United States was being denounced as the heir of nineteenth-century imperialism. This was a propaganda assault our country had to disperse, not by words but by bringing to the people themselves the techniques of training, public health service, and the constructive utilization of resource. America wanted nothing more than to help free people stand on their own feet. The Western world had poured $2 billion into the region to extract its oil. It would cost far less to help the Middle East make the most of its precious but wasted water—to irrigate its parched soil, to develop power, to arrest erosion, and to conquer the desert.

Nothing has changed much since 1952, except that the gap between the oil sheiks and the lowly fellahin has widened, and substance is squandered on weapons. How different it might all have been if Acheson's view had prevailed!

No one of consequence came before the congressional committees to attack aid for Israel, but congressmen were well briefed by opposition lobbyists and we were appalled by their hostility, as revealed in the transcript of the hearings.

The indictments against Israel were diverse and perverse: Israel had "expelled" the Arab refugees and therefore should be charged with the responsibility of the Arab appropriation as well as her own. Israel had taken abandoned Arab property and had paid no compensation. Israel was receiving a disproportionate share of aid on a *per capita* basis, in contrast to that given to the Arabs and in relation to her importance to the United States.

There were many harsh complaints and critics. Senator Alexander Smith (R-New Jersey) stated: "You are going to give the Jews a higher standard of living than the Arabs that are kicked out." Representative Omar Burleson (D-Texas) maintained: "850,000 people have been spilled out into the desert because we supported a political proposition which put them there."

To his credit, Gardiner replied effectively. He contended that the Israeli government ran its import system efficiently and ably. People lived close to the subsistence level, with hardly enough food to go around. Gardiner said that "under the rations . . . last autumn, factory workers could not carry out a full eight-hour day's work. In that economy, there were very few nylons, there were practically no automobiles, there was very little luxury." On alleged expulsion: "Why all these people left is in dispute. They were not all expelled. Some fled because there were massacres perpetrated by terrorist groups, which the Jewish authorities admit occurred, and which they disavow. Others left because people do leave when there are contending armies crossing their farms and fields."

He added that Israel had welcomed back many Arab refugees and that Arabs enjoy civil rights in Israel, including the franchise and membership in Parliament. Gardiner spoke of the great hope for Israel, whose population he described as "intelligent, determined, and well-read." He warned that there might be another explosion if Israel were abandoned. He described Israel's armed forces as "exceedingly effective." Israel could produce as many as 200,000 soldiers at short notice—many of whom were thoroughly trained during the last war. Many had marched with General Montgomery.

Representative Edna Kelly (D-New York) responded to a charge that Israel had not unfrozen blocked Arab bank accounts by pointing out that 120,000 Jews had lost their property when forced to leave Iraq in 1951. (I had called Eban's attention to this criticism, and he notified the State Department on May 15 that Israel was prepared to discuss release of the Arab funds.)

By September 1951, Gardiner estimated, Israel had a shortage of at least 157,000 dwelling rooms, and that more than 100,000 immigrants were in tents, crude huts, barracks, and tin shanties. The "permanent" housing for refugees consisted of an expandable one-room unit of reinforced concrete or concrete blocks, costing about $2,100 a unit. These, Gardiner said, were being built at a rate of about 40,000 units a year.

I circulated a 16-page memorandum in response to this new hostile barrage, in which I wrote: "Israel is a growing country seeking to resettle large numbers of newcomers, to create an industrial society, and to build an effective defense force. In contrast, the Arab economies, largely rural, are without plans for large-scale development and the technical ability to carry them out." I pointed out that most Arab governments had adequate dollar reserves—income from oil, cotton, and tourism. The American taxpayer had no reason to lengthen the motorized caravans of rich Arab rulers.

American support of Israel should not alienate the Arab world. The map of Moslem discontent reached from Pakistan to Casablanca, with little evidence that Israel's establishment caused the tensions which convulsed this vast expanse. Every conflict which separated the Arabs from the West had preceded the advent of Israel; none would be resolved if Israel were to disappear. "The facts reject the thesis that aid to Israel is a basic cause of Arab hostility. Arab animus is directed chiefly against England—the country which refused to implement the U.N. partition decision and which later even declined to vote for Israel's admission to the United Nations. We do not promote normal economic and political relations in the area if we join one party in a blockade of the other. On the contrary, we promote the peace of the region if we break blockades and if we summon all the parties to partnership in joint programs for the common development of the entire region."

I also stressed America's national interest as I noted the pertinent comment of the National Security Council on September 13, 1951:

"The United States has security interests in the Near East of which Israel is an integral part. It is in the interest of the United States that Israel remain free and independent, as well as friendly to the United States. Since its establishment as a state on May 14, 1948, Israel has developed an increasingly pro-Western foreign policy. Existing strains and tensions in the economy of Israel are already severe, and curtailment of U.S. technical and economic assistance under these circumstances would adversely affect U.S. security interests."

The House Foreign Affairs Committee slashed 20 percent from military assistance to Europe and 10 percent from defense support to Europe, but the two refugee allocations were untouched.

The Senate Foreign Relations Committee warned that aid to Israel was an emergency measure to be terminated as soon as practicable, and it recommended a change in emphasis from relief to development. The Committee estimated that of the 669,000 immigrants who had entered Israel since 1948 approximately 272,000 had been assimilated with respect to employment and housing, while about 396,000 were in various degrees of assimilation. The current decline in immigration promised progress. Foreign exchange reserves were exhausted, and Israel lived from day to day on receipts and short-term borrowings. Prices were soaring, and industry was crippled by the lack of foreign currency for raw materials.

The Senate Committee voted a 12.6 percent across-the-board cut, slashing the program for the Palestine refugees from $65 million to $56.772, and cutting the amount for refugees in Israel from $76 million to $66.38 million; Israel's technical assistance program was cut from $3 million to $2.62 million. The Committee endorsed the U.N. objective to shift rapidly from relief to resettlement of Arab refugees, as did other congressional committees in later years.

We defeated hostile initiatives in the House.

Representative Thurmond Chatham (D-North Carolina), an unceasing critic, proposed to reduce the refugee allocations for both Israel and the Arab refugees to $50 million each, which was the 1951 figure. Many participated in the debate, including Kennedy, who had caused us difficulty in 1951, and who was now a candidate for the Senate to unseat Lodge. Kennedy made a strong pro-Israel speech. He recalled a meeting late in 1951 during which Ben-Gurion had been asked whether the Arab states might fear aggression from Israel. Ben-Gurion had replied: "How could a country like Egypt, with a population of 20 million, fear invasion by a small nation of less than two million?" Besides, he had said, "We were once in Egypt and have no desire to return."

Before the Chatham $50 million–$50 million amendment came up, Judd, the author of that same proposal in 1951, now offered an amendment to reduce the amount for Israel to the $65 million requested for the Arab refugees. His amendment was defeated by a combination of Israeli supporters and friends of Chatham—a *viva voce* vote—and that assured defeat for the Chatham amendment by a teller vote of 103 to 66. At first, I thought that Judd's move was an unfriendly act, but I was wrong. Later, Judd wrote an explanation: "If my amendment to establish equality at $65 million was rejected, then almost certainly the Chatham amendment to establish equality at $50 million would also be rejected, and the figure would remain at $76 million. Javits and I had agreed on the same strategy in the Committee previously and it had worked. We hoped it would also work in the House, and I was happy that it did."

In the final figures, after conference committee compromises, Israel was allocated $70.228 million earmarked for relief and resettlement of refugees and $2.772 million for technical assistance—a total of $73 million. The Administration's original request had totaled $79 million. Its total Mutual Security request had been pared from $7.9 billion to slightly more than $6 billion. Thus, the result for Israel was much better than I had feared. Yet I wrote to our constituency that many congressmen, like our own Jewish leaders, had begun to doubt Israel's economic viability. There had to be progress in Israel, and fortunately there was; but we were headed for a rude setback in Washington in 1953.

THE CONVENTIONS AND THE CANDIDATES

As the Truman Administration neared an end, we aimed to ensure continuation of bipartisan support for Israel by testifying before both national conventions at Chicago, and later by urging presidential and congressional candidates to endorse their party platforms.

I drafted a Middle East plank requesting continued aid for Israel and showed it to Javits and candidate Taft, who approved it. We sent copies to Ives, Javits' New York colleague; to Herter, who was Eisenhower's representative on the Republican platform committee; to Dulles, who was to be Eisenhower's Secretary of State; and to Martin.

Conventions invariably pose two major problems. First, State Department officials urge the committees to be "evenhanded" and noncomittal; second, only a few congressmen are present. Most local politicians who win election as delegates are mainly interested in domestic rather than foreign policy issues. (Naturally, we could win stronger planks from the out-of-office party, which is less susceptible to State Department counsel.)

Javits submitted our plank to the 15-man subcommittee and was challenged by Philip Toomin of the anti-Zionist American Council for Judaism (ACJ), who put up a straw man and knocked him down. He argued that there was no Jewish vote, that our officials had been misled by pressure groups to favor Israel, and that American prestige had deteriorated. Private philanthropy should be continued, he conceded, but should not be confused with aid or with U.S. political relations.

I had not intended to testify, but I now asked for the floor to stress that we never claimed to speak on behalf of any Jewish vote; we were urging economic support for both Arab states and Israel, and for the resettlement of both Arab and Jewish refugees—all in the national interest of the United States.

Opposition forces hoped that Republicans would accept and exploit their contention that Truman's pro-Israel policy had alienated the Arab world, and they planted an alarming rumor and a press report to the effect that the platform would echo this partisan condemnation.

Merwin K. Hart, a notorious anti-Semite, accused our government of stirring up civil war in Palestine, forcing out 700,000 Arabs who had been our friends, and then lending Israel $100 million.

Dorothy Thompson and her newly established American Friends of the Middle East (AFME) urged Republican leadership to shun pro-Israel statements and to oppose declarations favoring any Middle East country. Fearing that the Committee might concur and offer platitudes rather than pledges, we telephoned friends in the home towns of subcommittee members, asking them to stimulate telephone calls and telegrams appealing for acceptance of our plank.

We met Senator Richard Nixon, a member of the Committee, who was soon to be nominated for the vice presidency, and he promised to help, warning, however, that the Committee members were inexperienced and that we should concentrate on the candidates. He said that Dulles would doubtless have the final word.

I visited Taft headquarters to argue with his partner, attorney John B. Hollister of Cincinnati, who questioned aid to Israel, even though his own candidate had championed it so strongly.

We alerted Ives and Brewster upon their arrival in Chicago. Brewster was indignant when he heard that the platform might attack Truman's aid to Israel. "This is the most foolish thing I ever heard of," he said.

Ives checked and criticized generalities in the subcommittee's draft. When he read it to me over the telephone, I complained about the lack of any reference to *support* for Israel. Ives renewed his effort for an explicit commitment, but the opposition warned that if the United States financed Israel's resettlement program, it would have to feed every starving Arab in the Middle East, and surely that flouted the party's stand for economy and against "give away" programs.

The few congressmen on the Committee supported Ives, but local bankers and businessmen were thinking of taxpayer reaction—including their own. And why should a Republican convention virtually endorse Truman's policy?

The Committee did strengthen the plank. It affirmed friendly interest for Israel, but there was no pledge of support. On the other hand, General Douglas MacArthur's grim, isolationist, and self-exalting keynote speech had included a charge that the Administration had lost friendship in the Middle East, and the platform did go out of its way to note that the Middle East and much of Africa seethed with anti-American sentiment.

Text of the 1952 Republican Plank

The Republican Party has consistently advocated a national home for the Jewish people since a Republican Congress declared its support of that objective 30 years ago. In providing a sanctuary for Jewish people rendered homeless by persecution, the State of Israel appeals to our deepest humanitarian instincts. We shall continue our friendly interest in this constructive and inspiring undertaking.

We shall put our influence at the service of peace between Israel and the Arab states, and we shall cooperate to bring economic and social stability to that area.

In August, candidate Nixon visited an Israel Bonds exhibit while in New York. After completing his tour of Israel's products, he dictated an enthusiastic statement about Israel into a tape recorder. Inexplicably, the tape was blank and his words were lost to posterity—a bizarre rehearsal for the future.

On July 28, Nixon wrote to Lipsky: "I was delighted that I had the opportunity to participate in the drafting of this platform. I am proud that our country has been an effective champion, as you so ably expressed it, in the settlement of Jewish refugees in Israel and the development of that country."

THE DEMOCRATIC CONVENTION

Long before the Democratic convention, I drafted a Middle East plank for Abraham Feinberg. He turned it over to Charles S. Murphy of the White House staff, who relayed it to the platform committee. Naturally, I did not submit this text when I addressed the committee, but spoke in general terms.

Once again, I was caught in the crossfire of personality and organizational clashes. Chicago Jewish leaders wanted to know why they should not testify as they had in 1944. Celler was irate because I refused to give him the exact language of our plank for his own presentation, and Lipsky, my 72-year-old chairman, had to fly to Chicago to placate him. I simply could not explain that all such formality was superfluous and that it would be most absurd and embarrassing for Celler to submit the same text which the committee already had received from the White House.

I also had difficulty with Paul Ginsberg of Atlanta, the head of the Jewish War Veterans (JWV), who wanted me to endorse Russell's presidential candidacy. I explained that we never endorsed candidates. Moreover, I reminded him that Russell had opposed the Douglas-Taft amendment on the Senate floor in 1951.

My statement to the platform committee was attacked by Herbert T. Schaffner of the American Council for Judaism, who, like Toomin at the GOP convention, denied that I was speaking for him and that there was a Jewish vote. Schaffner's gratuitous slur provoked a caustic reaction from Lehman, who admonished him that aid to Israel was recognized in Congress as helpful to the United States and that there had never been any effort to appease, placate, appeal to, or secure the support of the "Jewish vote."

Chairman McCormack interrupted Schaffner to remark: "We are all one people, not a race." While he was an Irish American, it was his being an American that was most important to him. He asked Schaffner whether he wanted to pursue his statement, and Schaffner reluctantly withdrew.

Sparkman complimented me on our statement. And Brooks Hays, one of my most cherished friends, was pleased that the Zionist Council supported a regional program including aid for the Arabs. He rejoiced that anti-Arab emotionalism was no longer evident, but he was puzzled by the

ACJ, for he had admired Julius Rosenwald and knew Lessing Rosenwald as the son of the great philanthropist. I explained that other members of the same family, William Rosenwald and Mrs. Adele Levy, were generous contributors to the UJA.

The platform committee accepted our proposal without change. We then urged the candidates to endorse their party's plank.

Eisenhower's attitude was unclear; he had avoided references to Israel in the past. We called this to the attention of many of his friends—Max Rabb, Lodge's campaign chief; Rabbi Judah Nadich, Eisenhower's first adviser on Jewish affairs; Javits; and many others. At the same time we recalled his dramatic role in the liberation of the survivors of the Holocaust, an experience which had profoundly moved him and had impressed Ben-Gurion.

I strongly believed that any Eisenhower statement should be offered in the context of a general foreign policy speech to a national audience, affirming that aid to Israel was an integral part of our foreign policy and was not dictated by domestic politics. We always tried to counter the Arab smear that Israel was a New York ballot box creation.

Senator Arthur Vandenberg (R-Michigan) promised an Israeli correspondent that Eisenhower would strengthen existing policy, and we received similar assurances from Lodge and others. Nevertheless, we had ample reason to be concerned. In February 1947, Eisenhower had been the honored guest at the opening of the UJA campaign in Washington. He had stressed the need for volunteer action to alleviate the hardship and suffering of victims of persecution in Europe, but he had avoided any reference to Palestine, which was then on the U.N. agenda.

The Intermountain News of Denver reported that Eisenhower spoke of the need to win Arab friendship, without mentioning Israel, at a press conference in Denver on June 24, 1952. He urged a NATO type of unification in the Middle East and in the Far East. In the Middle East, he said, "you have a problem of just cold hatred to us and there we have got to win friends before we even talk with them."

The Saturday Evening Post of April 19, 1952, quoted Eisenhower to the effect that "we must support the legitimate aspirations of the Moslem world or else I don't see how we can hold true to our doctrine that we do not want to dominate anyone." In contrast, Governor Adlai E. Stevenson, the Democratic nominee, had made an eloquent pro-Israel statement when he introduced Eban at the Chicago stadium on April 30, 1952.

Finally, on September 17, the Jewish New Year, there was a message from Eisenhower: "Here in America we have watched the establishment and development of the modern state of Israel. This, too, is part of the miraculous history of the Jewish people. I look forward confidently to the progress of democracy in Israel, to the stabilization of her economy and her growing contribution to the Free World."

On October 14, Eisenhower sent a message to a dinner honoring Ives, in which he commended Ives' "magnificent efforts on behalf of the valiant state of Israel. . . . The state of Israel is democracy's outpost in the Middle East and every American who loves liberty must join the effort to make secure forever the future of this newest member in the family of nations. We pray that a strong Israel and her Arab neighbors will join in the creation of a just and lasting peace which will bring to all an era of prosperity and enlightenment."

The long-awaited Eisenhower statement was finally released on October 19, after Silver visited him at Columbia University. It resembled his greeting to Ives. However, the media featured an attack by Silver on Truman and all but ignored the Eisenhower pro-Israel pronouncement.

Lipsky then notified both campaign headquarters that the AZC was nonpartisan and could not circulate the statement of one candidate without the statement of the other—and we did send out both.

Two months before the elections, Lipsky urged our constituents to request pro-Israel statements from local candidates. In addition, my colleagues and I visited many communities, especially those represented by congressmen on the Foreign Affairs and Appropriations Committees, and in central states which were unenthusiastic about foreign aid—Iowa, Indiana, Illinois, and Ohio.

However much we tried, it was not always easy to avoid partisan involvement. I was rebuked by Humphrey that year because a Minneapolis Jewish leader had sent out a fund-raising letter in which he quoted a letter from me in praise of Judd. I explained to Humphrey that my letter, written in 1951, had dealt with Judd's 1951 initiative on the first grant for Israel and was certainly not a political endorsement.

Text of the 1952 Democratic Plank

We seek to enlist the people of the Middle East to work with us and with each other in the development of the region, the lifting of health and living standards, and the attainment of peace. We favor the development of integrated security arrangements for the Middle East and other assistance to help safeguard the independence of the countries in the area.

We pledge continued assistance to Israel so that she may fulfill her humanitarian mission of providing shelter and sanctuary for her homeless Jewish refugees while strengthening her economic development.

We will continue to support the tripartite declaration of May 1959, to encourage Israel and the Arab states to settle their differences by direct negotiations, to maintain and protect the sanctity of the Holy Places and to permit free access to them.

We pledge aid to the Arab states to enable them to develop their economic resources and raise the living standards of their people. We support measures for the relief and reintegration of the Palestine refugees, and we pledge continued assistance to the reintegration program voted by the General Assembly of the United Nations in January, 1952.

All this activity reflected our fear that no matter who was elected President we were headed for hard times in Washington. We soon had confirmation of our deepest apprehensions.

Chapter 8

The Downgrading of Israel

THE ARMS CONFLICT

During the first year of a new presidential term, the petro-diplomatic complex invariably pressures the incoming administration to downgrade Israel and to court Arab friendship. That has been true in every first year except 1965, when Lyndon Johnson was beyond Arab reach.

After the election, dust settles on the platforms and Israel's foes use inoffensive euphemisms to urge Washington to be "more impartial, more evenhanded." I always believed that we had been less than impartial and evenhanded in the past and more prone to be "neutral" between aggressor and victim.

In 1953, we feared that Eisenhower and Dulles would be receptive to pro-Arab counsel and would pressure Israel to make concessions to Arab demands, and they did. Disagreements surfaced as U.S.-Israel relations plummeted to a new low. We had battles over economic and military aid, water, territory, terrorism, Jerusalem, refugees, and sanctions. The Soviet Union ruptured relations with Israel, reverting to its classic anti-Zionism and anti-Semitism, and Washington armed the Arab states and denied arms to Israel.

Much earlier, the Truman Administration had proposed a Middle East Defense Command—a tenuous extension of NATO. It intended to join Turkey, France, Great Britain, and three Commonwealth countries to promote cooperation and to defend the region from external aggression. Washington wanted Egypt to be the center and Israel was to be excluded.

In 1952, the United States formally agreed to sell arms to both Israel and

Egypt. Some U.S. arms were then sold to Egypt, but Israel's application gathered dust.

The United States coaxed the Arabs to join. "In the Middle East we are at a stage really preceding the North Atlantic Treaty in Europe," Acheson said in 1952. "We must, first of all, get these people to work together . . . to see a picture of what the defense of the Middle East would look like if worked out by the proper military authorities, and then get them working in an atmosphere of trust."

Secretary of State John Foster Dulles was determined to proceed. In 1953, he requested $100 million for military assistance in the Middle East, exclusive of Greece, Turkey, and Iran. Since the previous Administration had tended to split aid funds on a fifty-fifty basis, I naively assumed that $50 million would go to Israel and an equal sum to the Arab states.

The House Foreign Affairs Committee struck the entire $100 million from the bill after it had elicited testimony that all $100 million was intended for the Arabs. It declared that plans for the Middle East Defense Organization "had not yet reached a degree of maturity that warranted the authorization." The Senate Foreign Relations Committee retained the $100 million arms authorization, but urged the Executive Branch to make "every effort to bring about a termination of recrimination and economic aggression." According to custom, the conference committee split the difference and recommended $50 million.

I then lobbied for a further reduction, arguing that food was more important than arms in the Middle East and that economic stability was the first line of defense. I appealed to leading members of the two Appropriations Committees to cut another $20 million from the military aid program and to earmark it for economic aid. The Committees agreed, and later Assistant Secretary of State Henry Byroade reproached Lipsky, complaining that we Zionists had deprived him of $70 million in arms funds. The proposed $100 million had shrunk to $30 million.

Unrealistically, the Administration had failed to take into account which peoples in the area were prepared to join the Free World and to contribute to its defense. To deny arms to those willing to bear them until some artificial Middle East command was conjured into existence would be like refusing arms to volunteers until all the draft dodgers had been rounded up and conscripted for duty.

In July 1952, General Mohammed Naguib gained power in Egypt in revolt against King Farouk, and U.S. diplomacy calculated that the new military dictatorship could be won for a pro-Western defense arrangement. Assured of U.S. backing, Naguib would reach an accord with the British on the Sudan, and they would negotiate British withdrawal from the Suez Canal area. Egypt would then assume responsibility for defense of that waterway with U.S. arms.

We warned that it was folly to arm the Arab states unless they ended their Suez blockade and war against Israel. Naguib had no political party and no mass following, and without American economic aid and arms he must surely fail. He did, and in April 1954 he was replaced by Nasser and placed in protective custody.

If the United States wanted an effective Middle East defense, it would need more than the Arab states because Israel was the only land link between Africa, Asia, and Europe. Israel had excellent airports and seaports, loyal people, and an orientation to the Free World.

The entire Middle East landscape was then aflame with many conflicts: the Anglo-Iranian over oil; the Anglo-Egyptian over Suez and Sudan; the French-Algerian over North Africa; the Arab-Israeli war; and the never-ending Arab-Arab wars.

Democratic cloakrooms at the Capitol were rife with gossip that Republicans intended to reverse U.S. allegiances around the globe and that Dulles would favor Germany over France, Pakistan over India, Japan over China, and the Arab League over Israel.

THE BREAK WITH THE SOVIETS

Aiming to block the Middle East defense organization, the Soviets now openly turned against Israel, bidding for Arab favor. In 1947 and 1948, they had supported the Israelis at the U.N. — ignoring Arab resentment and hoping to undermine British power in the Middle East.

Communists had never made headway in Jewish Palestine — neither before nor after Israel's establishment — not only because of the ideological incompatibility between communism and Zionism but also because the tiny Communist party inside Palestine had branded Jewish nationalism as imperialist. Free to enter Israel's national elections, the party never polled more than four percent of the vote.

In 1951, the Soviets had joined the United States and Israel at the U.N. to order Egypt to keep the Suez Canal open to all shipping, as a matter of self-interest. They did not begin to veto pro-Israel resolutions until 1954.

In the early 1950s, there was a recrudescence of Soviet anti-Semitism as the Soviets determined to liquidate Jewish culture, institutions, and communal life. There were show trials in Communist Czechoslovakia — anti-Zionist, anti-Israel, and anti-Semitic. Rudolph Slansky, Secretary General of the Czechoslovakian Communist party, was prosecuted for conspiracy. Eleven of the fourteen accused party leaders were Jews. Eight were executed, and three were imprisoned for life.

The Prague trials had nothing to do with Judaism, but the prosecution emphasized the Jewish origin of the defendants, seeking to link them with a pro-Western, pro-Zionist conspiracy directed against world communism — Stalin's version of Hitler's Big Lie.

The accused were enemies of Israel. Slansky told a friend, "When I have to deal with matters affecting the state of Israel, I have to conceal my own hatred."

The Soviets were barring Jews from important offices and delegations. A Jewish DP told me his story in 1946. A member of the Young Communist League in Rumania during the war, he had survived and had gone to Russia to enroll in its diplomatic school. He had heard anti-Semitic smears in the streets and trolley-cars. He had been told that Jews had evaded front-line duty during the war. Finally, he had been instructed to change his name if he planned a diplomatic career. He fled from Russia to the DP camps and then went on to Israel—where, incidentally, he did change his name, as did most Israelis, to enter public life.

The Communist radio charged Jewish doctors with conspiracy against Soviet leaders, linking them with American imperialists—specifically the Joint Distribution Committee (JDC).

Eban appealed to the Free World to rally to Israel's support. There was no echo from the State Department.

Several days later, twenty-three senators offered a resolution denouncing Soviet anti-Semitism, but without reference to the Soviet break with Israel. We urged the sponsors to offer a substitute resolution. The senators explained that their resolution preceded the Soviet break, and they agreed that silence about Israel would be misconstrued. They strengthened the condemnation of Soviet anti-Semitism, and they added two additional paragraphs— one reaffirmed American sympathy for Israel in view of the Soviet break; the other reaffirmed American friendship for both the Arab states and Israel and called for peace to promote regional defense and development.

While we were trying to strengthen the resolution, there was a counter effort to weaken it. The State Department was complaining to the senators that their original resolution would be exploited by Communist propaganda to prove that America was anti-Arab and that it should be broadened to refer to all types of Communist discrimination and oppression. We advised our Senate friends to let the issue drop, for we saw no point in a debate over a fleeting and ineffective resolution.

Soon thereafter, State Department officials insisted that my fears had been groundless and that the Department was primarily concerned with the reaction of Eastern Europe. They thought that if our government aligned itself with Zionism or Israel at this stage it would lend credence to Soviet propaganda that Zionism was a servant of the West. Accordingly, the new administration had remained silent following the Soviet break with Israel, not because of Arab reaction but because of public opinion in the satellites.

DULLES REVERSES U.S. POLICY

An AZC committee called on Eisenhower in March 1953. We urged him to defer sending arms to Egypt or to any other Arab state as long as they maintained their blockade, boycott, and state of war against Israel. We appealed for financial assistance to Israel on a level commensurate with the program of the last two years.

In 1951 and 1952, aid for Israel had been earmarked in the congressional legislation. Now we were concerned by the Administration's decision to ask for a lump sum for the Middle East; we feared a drastic reduction in the amount for Israel.

Lehman and Javits went to see Byroade on April 29 to urge the Administration to disclose the Israeli allocation to the House Foreign Affairs Committee. More important, they also asked for a commitment that the Administration would not use the foreign aid program as a weapon to force Israel to cut or suspend immigration, to surrender territory, or to admit Arab refugees. Nor would it alter the military balance between Israel and the Arab states. Byroade said that he anticipated no difficulty and promised to consult Dulles, but their apprehensions were soon to be confirmed.

Most frightening was the speech which Dulles delivered on June 1, 1953, after his return from a trip to the Middle East, where he had handed Naguib a pearl-handled revolver as a symbolic first installment of U.S. aid. Everywhere, he said, he was tongue-lashed with anti-Zionist imprecations, which he had himself gratuitously provoked when he declared: "We must do what we can to allay the resentment of the Arabs caused by the creation of the state of Israel." That ill-considered statement, it seemed to me, would surely encourage the Arabs to resent all the more in order to extort U.S. concessions.

Dulles also disseminated Arab propaganda claims. He said: "Today the Arab peoples are afraid that the United States will back the new state of Israel in aggressive expansionism. They are more fearful of Zionism than they are of communism, and they fear the United States lest we become the backer of expansionist Zionism."

I was astonished to hear Dulles talk of Zionist "expansionism," for he was well aware that Israel had accepted the U.N. recommendations in 1947 and had been attacked by the Arabs. He had supported us at the U.N. session in Paris in 1948, and, in his autobiography, he took credit for helping to block the Bernadotte plan. He had written: "Strong nations which want peace cannot buy it by throwing bits of weaker nations into the jaws of ambitious despots. That only makes them more rapacious."

Nor was it helpful for Dulles to talk about the repatriation of Arab refugees — so unlike Acheson in 1952 — because this emphasis would impede acceptance of resettlement, which was the only sensible and equitable solution in view of the mass exodus of 700,000 Jews from Arab countries.

Israel soon became an unmentionable. When AID Administrator Stassen addressed a UJA dinner in Washington, he refrained from any reference to Israel, the UJA, or the Jewish people. One of America's leading Jewish philanthropists told me several days later in New York that he had been frightened by Stassen's speech. And Eisenhower himself neglected to mention Israel or Zionism in a message to the ZOA convention in August.

There was a calculated snub when the AZC was dropped from the list of non-governmental organizations that were regularly invited by the State Department for briefings on foreign policy issues. The new list was top-heavy with business organizations. I protested against our exclusion, recalling our role at the U.N. charter conference and our visit with the President, and we were reinstated.

The Administration's bias was vividly exposed when the House Foreign Affairs Committee took up the foreign aid bill and Javits put two hard questions to Gardiner, our erstwhile State Department friend, who now tilted toward the Arabs. "What do we expect from the Arabs? What do we represent to them that we want them to do?" Javits asked.

Gardiner replied: "We would like to see the Arab states develop their economies. We would like to see them better off materially. We would like to see them grow more food. We would like to see them continue to develop their mineral resources, and particularly their oil, in an orderly, effective way. We still place high value on the importance of that resource to the Free World in general.

"We would like to see them develop more stable governments. We would like to have them develop the police, the gendarmerie and the military forces which would increase their resistance to subversion. We would like, in due course — and it will take many years — to develop genuine defensive strength in that region so that it does not remain a power vacuum."

Gardiner did not think it necessary to ask the Arabs to change their anti-Israel policy, or to help settle displaced Palestinians, in contrast with the reply he gave when Javits asked, "What have we represented to Israel that we want of her?"

"We would like Israel to develop and maintain the resources of its country. We would like to see Israel take steps to compensate the Arab refugees. We would like Israel to unfreeze still further the frozen bank accounts of the Arabs. We would like to see Israel reach terms with the United Nations regarding the division of the waters of the Jordan River so that it will be possible to erect in the Jordan Valley structures for a dependable supply of water which will increase the agricultural potential of the Jordan Valley.

"We would like to see Israel consider still further possibilities of repatriation of the Arab refugees, realizing full well that repatriation can only be a partial solution of the Arab refugee problem.

"We would like to see Israel adopt a more conciliatory attitude toward the Arabs and to be ready to suggest measures of conciliation, bearing in mind the fact that Israel has been the victor in the struggle between the Jews and the Arabs.

"We would like to see Israel take steps to reassure the Arabs that it has no further intentions to expand the state of Israel."

The Administration had abandoned any pretense of impartiality and had ceased to call for an Arab-Israel peace—a policy which emboldened Arab militants to obstruct her development and to press their war for Israel's destruction.

THE CLASH OVER JERUSALEM

When Israel was established, she wanted to locate the capital in Jerusalem, where the last Jewish Commonwealth had been ruled some twenty centuries before, but the United States refused to recognize Jerusalem as the capital. Instead, it opened its embassy in Tel Aviv, encouraging other countries to follow suit.

This complicated diplomatic life for Israel. Some government offices were in Jerusalem, while the Foreign Ministry remained in Tel Aviv. Finally, soon after Dulles's visit in 1953, Israel moved her capital to Jerusalem. In the ensuing uproar of protest, Congresswoman Frances Bolton of Ohio vehemently denounced Israel's "greatest blunder" and told me that the United States would "never, never, never" recognize Jerusalem as Israel's capital. Yet a sovereign nation may decide where to locate its capital, and Israel's decision was one for her—and not for the United States—to make. "Would Americans politely acquiesce if other countries boycotted Washington and opened their embassies in Philadelphia or Boston?" some asked.

There is a legend that Israel acted at that particular moment because of a misunderstanding. When Dulles was in Israel he was informed of Israel's intention. He replied: "Don't do it while I'm around." According to this version, the Israeli who heard Dulles's colloquial reply took him literally to mean that Israel would be free to act once he had left the area.

Israelis protested that, in addition to their own boycott, the United States lobbied with other countries to dissuade them from establishing their embassies in Jerusalem.

THE STRUGGLE OVER AID

Meanwhile, we worried about the amount of aid to be budgeted for Israel. Shortly after Congress adjourned, the Administration proposed to reduce Israel's share in the 1953-1954 grant aid appropriation to about $55 million. Stassen had told the Congress that he thought Israel should receive closer to $70 million, the previous year's figure.

The Administration was then diverting additional funds to Iran, reducing the amount available to Israel and the Arab states to about $100 million.

We protested to Senators Homer Ferguson (R-Michigan), Gillette, and Humphrey and urged Representatives Robert B. Chiperfield (R-Illinois) and Javits to help replenish the fund. In mid-September, I called on Gardiner to complain, but now we faced a counter-complaint. Gardiner charged that Israel was diverting Jordan River waters to build a canal for irrigation and to create water power. The Arabs were complaining to the U.N., and Gardiner warned that Israel stood to lose more in aid because of this action than because of the transfer of funds to Iran.

On September 25, Dulles told the Israelis that they must stop the project, and aid to Israel was suspended. We could not make an effective public protest because the United States and Israel had agreed to keep the suspension of aid secret. However, on October 14, *The New York Times* broke a story from Tel Aviv hinting that aid was being withheld.

We went public the next day. I circulated a background memorandum cataloguing U.S.-Israeli differences on all fronts: arms to the Arab states; diversion of aid from Israel to Iran; the boycott of Jerusalem; U.S. pressure on the water canal; and the overall deterioration of the Administration's attitude toward Israel.

THE CONFLICT OVER WATER

We must recall the historical background of the canal controversy, for nothing is more vital to Israel than water.

When Britain and France assumed the Mandates for Palestine and Syria, they drew the boundary line east of the upper Jordan River and Lake Kinneret in order to deny Syria any riparian rights, and thus guarantee that Palestine could always control its own water supply. David Lloyd George, former Prime Minister, had warned that the British would not otherwise accept the Mandate. He had written: "The waters of Palestine are essential to its existence. On the other hand, these same waters are of no use to anyone holding Syria."

President Wilson had gone much further. He proposed that the northern boundary include the Jordan River valley and the western and southern slopes of Mount Hermon. This would have meant that the waters of the Litani River would have flowed south into Israel and would have been available to irrigate the Negev and Sinai deserts. Wilson asked Secretary of State Robert Lansing to submit this view to the British and the French. Unfortunately, the Department of State did not agree.

In the 1940s the Zionists had proposed a Tennessee Valley Authority-type plan for the Jordan Valley. The author was an eminent American soil conservationist, the late Dr. Walter C. Lowdermilk. The purpose of this plan was to generate power and to pump water to irrigate the dry southern area of the country. I released details of this project on behalf of the American Jewish Conference at the request of one of its authors, Dr. Neumann, in 1944.

Mindful of the British-French agreement, draftsmen of the 1947 partition plan carefully fixed the Israel-Syria boundary to follow the old international frontier, but during the 1948 war the Syrians had rapidly reached the edge of Lake Kinneret; the narrow intervening strip was defenseless. They seized about two square miles of territory on the banks of the lake and the river.

For their part, Israelis had occupied a number of Lebanese villages. During the armistice negotiations between Lebanon and Israel, Bunche asked Israel to withdraw to the old frontier. Israel was agreeable, providing the Syrians would likewise withdraw their military forces from the water's edge to the old frontier. Bunche insisted that the parties should negotiate one agreement at a time.

Accordingly, the Lebanon-Israel armistice agreement was speedily consummated as Israel abandoned the occupied villages. However, the Syrians were not as obliging. They refused to withdraw their troops from the water's edge, in order to claim riparian rights and obstruct Israeli development. After protracted negotiations, the Syrians finally agreed to evacuate their troops, but only on condition that a substantial area be demilitarized. Subsequently, the Syrians never lost an opportunity to challenge Israel's sovereignty over the demilitarized area and the lake.

Could Israel undertake development projects in demiltarized zones? "Yes," Bunche wrote to the Israelis on June 29, 1949. "In respect to the question of economic development, I may also assure both parties that the U.N. will also ensure that the demilitarized zone will not be a vacuum or wasteland."

If the Israelis had suspected how the Syrians intended to harass and impede their projects, they would never have agreed to the establishment of demilitarized zones. They had naively expected that the armistice agreements would swiftly lead to peace agreements and had never dreamed that demilitarized zones would always be sources of conflict.

Gunfire from Syrian slopes and the Golan Heights had aimed to prevent Israel from draining the Huleh Lake peat marshes in 1951. Syrians then argued that elimination of the Huleh Lake would tip the military balance against them. Fortunately, the U.N. ruled in Israel's favor.

General Riley, the U.N. Chief of Staff in Jerusalem, wrote to the Security Council on May 2, 1951: "I feel that the U.N. should never impede progressive work. I have never found fault with the Huleh concession. I never will. It is not a matter which affects Syria or the U.N."

Despite these early rulings, Dulles took another tack in 1953. In that year, Israelis began to build a waterfall canal alongside the Jordan River near the B'not Yakov bridge in northern Galilee. By accelerating the flow of the water downward from 40 feet above sea level to 600 feet below sea level, they intended to generate hydroelectric power which would drive the waters west and south to irrigate Israel's central plain and parched Negev. The

Syrians then threatened war. The U.N. Chief of Staff in Jerusalem, Vagn Bennike, differed from Bunche by insisting that the Israelis halt construction until they had reached an agreement with the Syrians. To his discredit, Dulles backed him by withholding economic aid from Israel.

Meanwhile, TVA, at the request of UNRWA, had completed a development plan to satisfy the water needs of all the countries concerned. This was not revealed to the Israelis until October 19. It was then charged that the Israelis were proceeding with their own water plan in defiance of the U.N. The Israelis retorted that they had never seen the plan until it was published.

Later, a committee of prominent American engineers who served as Israel's consultants found no conflict between the Israeli plan and the U.N. proposal. Nevertheless, Israel was the target of inspired press attack.

Israel was willing to suspend her project until she reached agreement with the U.N.'s Bennike, but Israel could not accept the Bennike-Dulles demand that she reach agreement with the Syrians, who would never concur in any such project. Recalling that her position had been upheld in the 1951 Huleh decision, Israel denied that she was diverting water in defiance of the U.N.

On October 22, I circulated a report emphasizing that the project was inside Israeli territory and would not affect Syrian landowners, that Syria's protest was without foundation, and that Bennike had no authority to permit Syria to veto Israel's economic development.

The United States had never taken similar punitive action, such as withholding aid, against the Arab states, despite their refusal to make peace and despite Egypt's defiance of the 1951 Security Council order to open the Suez Canal. Yet during this crisis between the United States and Israel, the United States was preparing to increase economic aid, and even to make military aid available, to Egypt.

The controversy over water rose to a bitter and hysterical climax because of a tragic coincidence—the attack by Israeli border settlers on the Jordanian village of Kibya to avenge the murder of Israeli civilians.

Shortly after midnight on October 13, Susan Kanias, thirty-two, lay asleep with her six children on the floor of her cottage at Moshav Yahud, a mile from the Jordanian border. Her mother occupied the only bed in the room, which was dimly lit by a kerosene lamp. Kanias was away from home because he worked weekdays in the Negev, returning home for the Sabbath. At Susan Kanias's side were two children, Benjamin, eighteen months, and Shoshana, four.

A Mills bomb was lobbed into the middle of the room. The mother and children close to her bore the full impact. The children died instantly. Mrs. Kanias lingered on for some hours in the hospital. Her eldest son, Ashe, was injured in the ear by a bomb fragment.

All work was halted for the funeral of Susan Kanias and her children. Angry Israeli villagers raided Kibya. Arabs charged that they had suffered 66 fatalities. As usual, the murder of the Israelis was virtually ignored by a world which descended with one-sided fury upon the Israelis. By this time terrorism against Israelis was taken for granted by a permissive society. The vital statistics bear repetition.

Since the United States, Britain, and France had "guaranteed" Arab-Israel borders in 1950, Israel had suffered these casualties at Jordan's hands: 421 men, women and children killed and wounded; 130 cases of sabotage; 866 armed attacks, and 3,263 robberies.

In 1952, Arab violations of the armistice agreements had resulted in 135 Israeli casualties, including 60 killed. In addition, there were 3,742 illegal border crossings. Between January and June of 1953, there were 93 Israeli casualties, including 26 killed. Passenger vehicles had been attacked, and houses had been blown up.

The gravity of the situation may be assessed by the decisions of the Israel-Jordan Mixed Armistice Commission. In a 12-month period, up to June of 1953, the MAC ruled against Jordan in 159 cases, and against Israel in 25.

Both Senator Styles Bridges (R-New Hampshire), chairman of the Senate Appropriations Commitee, and Senator Ferguson, chairman of the Republican Policy Committee, intervened with the State Department at our request, but to no avail.

The Department turned congressional friends against Israel by exploiting the Kibya incident and her alleged defiance of the U.N. Bridges was told that the whole matter was within the jurisdiction of the U.N., and that therefore he must not intervene. Ferguson was told that aid had been withheld because of an alleged violation of a 1949 agreement.

Javits and Ives decided to lead a group of American Jewish leaders to call on Dulles to protest. I drew up a list at Javits's request. It included William Rosenwald, who was bewildered by my call. "Why do you want me?" he asked. "Because I want Mr. Dulles to know that Lessing Rosenwald is not the only philanthropist who bears the honored Rosenwald name." There were also Rosenwalds who strongly supported Israel. He agreed to come.

The group included Ives and Javits — who were accompanied by Bernard Katzen; Maxwell Abell, President of the United Synagogue of America; Matthew Brown of Boston, a leading member of the American Jewish Committee and later a judge; Mrs. Rose Halprin of Hadassah; Klutznick of B'nai B'rith; Lipsky; Rosenwald; and Bernard H. Trager, chairman of the National Community Relations Advisory Council. The meeting on October 26 lasted more than an hour.

After Ives and Javits voiced concern about U.S.-Israel tensions, Dulles offered a 15-minute reply. He had been raised with a deeply religious background and had been nurtured and influenced by the Old Testament, the basis of Judeo-Christian civilization. As Secretary of State, Dulles represented the interests of all Americans, but saw no inconsistency between such a position and that of regarding the descendants of the prophets in a favorable light. He had gone to the Middle East in May searching for peace and had discovered that the existing hatreds and tensions now made that impossible. He conceded that Egypt hated the British more than it hated the Israelis, and that Lebanon and Syria hated the French more than they hated the Israelis. The United States would have no influence if Arabs continued to believe that we were wholly pro-Israel.

Dulles had been about to announce an allocation to Israel and to other countries, when, on September 21, Bennike had ordered suspension of the canal project. On September 25, he had met with Eban, reinforcing Bennike's request. He resented Eban's reply. Instead of suspending work on the canal, Israel started three eight-hour shifts.

Dulles had told Eban that the Department could not allocate aid to Israel while the issue was pending at the U.N. He emphasized that no aid grants were being made to any Arab states.

If Israel suspended the water project, the United States would immediately allocate economic aid to Israel. The United States had to support the U.N. and to dispel the Arab notion that the United States backed Israel, right or wrong. The United States urgently wanted peace in the Middle East because of the tremendous military importance of its oil. NATO and SAC could not function without it. The U.S. action served the interests of both the United States and Israel.

Javits reminded Dulles that Egypt had defied the Security Council for several years, yet economic sanctions had been applied only to Israel.

Mrs. Halprin recalled that Article 8 of the Israel-Jordan armistice agreement provided for Israel's access to Mount Scopus, the site of the Hadassah Hospital.

Brown argued that the State Department's action was contrary to common law jurisprudence.

Abell recalled continuing Arab violations, such as the refusal to permit Jews to enter Arab countries and the pressures on airlines not to land in Israel.

Rosenwald emphasized that compliance with Bennike's request was impossible, since no Arab state was willing to negotiate with Israel.

Lipsky declared that the State Department was in an impossible dilemma. If it pursued its present course, it would be compelled to become more and more unfriendly to Israel, and in the end would still not win Arab friendship.

(Rabbi Silver also visited Dulles during this controversy.)

A deeply disturbed Dulles contended that he was misrepresented and misunderstood. He had been instrumental in the decision that led to the establishment of the state of Israel, but he had received only criticism in return. The Jewish people had not appreciated what he had done for them in this regard and had continued to criticize him over the years. It seemed to him that all we wanted was the policy of the preceding Administration, which had brought no peace but only trouble.

Eban had no alternative but to agree that Israel would temporarily suspend work on the building of the canal, pending further inquiry and decision by the U.N. The United States then lifted the ban on aid.

In the meantime, the Israelis agreed to consider an overall project under the auspices of Ambassador Eric Johnston which would allocate the waters to Israel, Jordan, and Syria according to an agreed formula that would satisfy the water needs of all.

No formal political agreement on the division of water was ever reached, yet the plan Johnston proposed actually went into effect. Johnston spent two years shuttling back and forth between Israel and the Arab states, meeting engineers, technicians, and political leaders. He proposed a unified plan which would conserve the waters of the Jordan valley basin—both the Jordan and the Yarmuk Rivers—during the rainy season, and which would release them for irrigation and power during the summer.

The Arabs were offered all the water they needed, about 60 percent of the combined Jordan and Yarmuk flow. Small allocations were to irrigate about 30,000 acres in Syria and about 8,700 acres in Lebanon in the north. Jordan was to get the major portion, enough to irrigate some 120,000 acres in the Jordan valley. The Yarmuk waters were to be diverted away from Israel into irrigation canals down the Jordan valley for the purpose of settling Jordanian farmers, including Arab refugees. In this area, Jordan could grow three harvests a year and reach world markets before anyone else.

Israel, it was estimated, would get enough water to irrigate about 100,000 acres—some in the Jordan valley and the remainder in the Negev.

The technicians representing the countries involved speedily reached agreement. There was no real obstacle. The Arabs had first call on the water; they took their allocations before the water reached Israel. However, since the scheme involved cooperation with Israel, Arab political leaders vetoed it in Cairo in the autumn of 1955, a fortnight after Nasser had reached his arms deal with the Soviet Union.

Despite the absence of a formal agreement between the parties, Jordan and Israel proceeded with their own water development plans separately, but consistent with Johnston's blueprint. Israel's project was finally completed in the early 1960s, with a green light from President Kennedy.

Meanwhile, the B'not Yakov bridge plan had to be abandoned. Soviet opposition at the U.N. blocked its approval. Its great value had been the man-made waterfall which would have created hydroelectric power, sharply reducing the cost of the diversion. Now the Israelis had to pump the water directly from the Kinneret itself to a higher level—a far more costly project. Besides, lake waters were more saline than the fresh river water in the north.

Ironically, as it turned out, the original plan had been impractical because the natural reservoir which Israel had intended to use to store the waters in the Upper Galilee turned out to be porous and therefore unusable.

Because of my interest in the water development, which went back to 1943, and my friendship with his aide, George Barnes, who had helped us at the U.N., I kept in close touch with Johnston during this period and arranged dinner parties for the leaders of our Committee at which he reported the progress of his work. At the very outset, I appealed to him to make the best possible use of the waters of the Litani River by allowing them to flow southward to irrigate the arid Sinai, a project which would have facilitated the resettlement of many thousands of people. That was not to be. The Litani was diverted westward, and wastefully, to the Mediterranean Sea.

Despite the aid controversy, Israel did not fare as badly as we had feared. Aid was cut to $54 million, of which $52.5 million was a grant and $1.5 million was technical assistance. In 1952 aid had been $73 million.

It was a stormy year and, as a result of the sharp conflict between the State Department and the Jewish community, we concluded that we must create a new organization to carry on our lobbying activity. That was early in 1954.

Chapter 9

Organization of the Lobby

THE BIRTH OF AIPAC

Our acrimonious clashes with the Eisenhower-Dulles regime over arms and water led to rumors that the American Zionist Council (AZC) faced investigation. The rumors were ill-founded but they were persistent and could not be ignored. We reorganized and established a lobbying committee — the forerunner of the American Israel Public Affairs Committee (AIPAC).

Between 1951 and 1953, I had been the Washington representative of the AZC, a tax-exempt organization. A government agency had ruled that only an insubstantial portion of AZC funds had been used for lobbying. Now, however, we heard that the State Department was busily comparing my critical 1953 memoranda with those circulated by the Israeli embassy.

"Shouldn't Kenen register as an agent of a foreign government?" a desk officer indignantly demanded of an Israeli journalist, Eliahu Salpeter of *Haaretz,* who then called me to sound the alarm. Then, late in December 1953, a Republican member of our Executive Committee, who worked in Washington, told our Committee that I might be a target.

There was no basis for the contention that we were merely parroting Israel's views. I had differences with the Israeli government, and I had not hesitated to voice them. We had a major disagreement on arms.

Some Israeli diplomats, notably Shiloah, maintained that, since the Administration planned to arm Iraq, we should immediately campaign for arms for Israel. I disagreed, arguing that we should oppose arms to every country in the area as long as possible, at least until the United States began the threatened shipments to Egypt and Iraq. My Washington colleagues concurred. So did Sharett, who overruled Shiloah. (I took a similar position in the controversy over the F-15s to Saudi Arabia in 1978.)

Nevertheless, because of the possibility that we might be subject to attack, we organized a new and separate lobbying committee in 1954, independent of AZC control and financing and thus impervious to challenge. It was named the American Zionist Committee for Public Affairs (AZCPA). There was no change in leadership or membership, but we stopped receiving tax-exempt funds from the AZC. Instead, we solicited contributions which would not be deductible from income tax.

Naively, I did not think that it would be very difficult to raise a $50,000 budget to finance our office and small staff. I became the least known and most unpopular fund-raiser in the United States. Many could not understand why the Israeli government could not subsidize this modest undertaking; they did not realize that foreign agents were limited in expression and activity. Moreover, since the budget was so tiny, prospective donors slashed their contributions proportionately—to minute sums. We were always in the red, and I often had to wait a long time for my modest $13,000-a-year salary. I frequently had to lend money to the Committee, and I had to dispense with a capable assistant. The budgetary deficit was not lifted until the Six-Day War.

Not a single contribution came during the first week, and I had to telephone a good friend—Dewey Stone, a Massachusetts philanthropist and one of Israel's pioneer supporters—for an advance of $500. After a year of frustration, and now in his 78th year, Lipsky resigned because leaders of our constituent organizations ignored his appeal for funds.

Lipsky suggested that I offer the chairmanship to another Rochesterian, Rabbi Bernstein, my 1946-1947 co-worker. Bernstein consulted a close friend, Under Secretary of State Robert Murphy, who encouraged him to accept the assignment. To my regret, Bernstein imposed a condition—he would not become involved in fund-raising. I had the highest regard for Bernstein's leadership and wisdom and the respect which he commanded in government and in the American Jewish community, and so I accepted the fund-raising responsibility.

Meanwhile, I decided to move our base and my home to Washington. My decision to establish an office in Washington preceded the threats of an investigation. The retaliation at Kibya portended a long battle. Until that time I had been commuting to the capital every week. We bought a home in Hollin Hills, Virginia, a new contemporary development, where we spent many years recarving the landscape. The house was exhibited in the National Gallery of Art in 1957 after it was selected by the American Institute of Architects as one of the ten buildings in America's future.

Gardening became my one diversion. The house was on a high hill which sloped in two directions, where the Hollin Hills landscape architect had recommended terraces to grow vegetables. I ignored his advice until I read that Byroade had claimed in a speech to the American Council for Judaism that the Jews would need the return of Arabs in order to learn how to rebuild their ancient terraces. My next-door neighbor, James Boughton, happened to be Byroade's public affairs officer, and we were partners in the ownership of a power mower. I knocked on his door and told him to tell Henry that we did not need Arabs to teach us how to rebuild terraces. I now began to saw, sink, and link old railroad ties. And four months later, after exhausting labor and help from sturdy neighbors, I gouged out seven descending terraces, which were exhibited to visiting congressmen, journalists, and diplomats for seventeen years as the "ideological terraces" of Hollin Hills.

Our lobby has always shunned partisan activity and appealed for both Republican and Democratic support. Unlike many other lobbies, we made no endorsements or campaign contributions, although we were entirely free to do so. We sought to unite Americans in support of Israel and to bring America and Israel closer together, never permitting Israel to become a partisan issue dividing the parties, if we could prevent it.

THE NEAR EAST REPORT

We took another major step in 1957. I had addressed the Jewish community in Utica to stimulate their Welfare Fund campaign, and I was surprised by a $700 honorarium. I returned it, but they insisted that I had rendered a service to their campaign and was entitled to compensation. Our accountant agreed, and that suggested a new initiative: Why not create a new and separate instrument—the *Near East Report*—a newsletter to be published independently of our lobbying committee, which would render a service to the public at large? Allen Lesser, an experienced journalist on our staff, was enthusiastic, and available.

I invested $1,000 of my own funds to finance the four-page publication, and we sold subscriptions to individuals and organizations. I insisted on editing the *Report* free from outside supervision. The newsletter—its policies and problems—was never discussed at AZCPA sessions, except for my occasional appeal for subscriptions from members of the Committee's constituent bodies. Simultaneously, I resigned from AZCPA's payroll for five years, relying on the newsletter for my income. The *Report* rapidly gained circulation because it had credibility. AZCPA paid for subscriptions for congressmen, and major organizations subscribed for their leaders. B'nai B'rith made the *Near East Report* available to students at Hillel Houses and on college campuses, which were flooded with pro-Arab propaganda. The *Near East Report* began as a biweekly; but in October 1970 we turned it into a weekly, for events were necessitating the rapid circulation of news and comment.

Much earlier, in 1964, we had begun publishing special surveys on diverse topics, such as the Middle East arms race, U.S. aid and commitments in the area, Iran, Arab refugees, candidates' statements, convention platforms, and the Arab boycott. That led to *Myths and Facts,* which has now gone through six editions. More than 750,000 copies have helped enormously to clarify the record.

In 1973, as I approached retirement, we formed a new organization called Near East Research, Inc., which purchased my interest in the *Near East Report* for the $1,000 which I had invested. I made no personal profit on this venture, although by this time circulation exceeded 30,000 and the publication had increased in value.

We came under investigation in 1962. Senator J. W. Fulbright (D-Arkansas) could not reconcile himself to our Committee's role and believed that we should register as a foreign agent. In that year, Fulbright had conducted an inquiry into the activities of foreign agents, focusing on the sugar lobby; but actually, as the sugar lobbyists assured me, he was aiming at our Committee and the *Near East Report.* Fulbright was not in a position to call me as a witness under the Senate resolution but he interrogated registered foreign agents. From the spokesmen of the Jewish Agency and Committee inquiry, he elicited the information that the AZC had used funds provided by the Jewish Agency to purchase quantities of the *Near East Report* for libraries, academicians, and other interested parties. Under these circumstances, Fulbright felt that the *Near East Report* should have been registered. We challenged that contention.

The fact was that we had ceased to receive these orders from the AZC two years earlier; the situation had become academic. Moreover, our counsel, Maurice Boukstein, pointed out that there was no reason why we could not sell *Near East Report* subscriptions directly to a foreign government or principal. Many newspapers sell subscriptions and advertising to foreign governments and receive revenues from them.

Still dissatisfied, Fulbright insisted that the FBI visit me and inquire into our means of support. I spent forty-five pleasant minutes with three FBI representatives in my office early in 1963. I pointed out that the *Near East Report* was not dependent for its existence on money that came from the Jewish Agency or Israel, that this had been a small fraction of our income, that we had managed without it between 1960 and 1963, and that we had long since discontinued any sales to the American Zionist Council, which might have been financed by subsidies from abroad. The Israeli government had limited its purchases of the *Near East Report* to about thirty subscriptions.

The FBI agents were very polite, and as they departed I offered to send them subscriptions to the *Near East Report* with our compliments. In a letter which I wrote to Fulbright's Committee at that time, I stressed that we were not agents of a foreign government; we were agents of our conscience.

Over the years, there were a number of occasions when I disagreed with Israel's policies, as this book reveals, although I generally refrained from public criticism. Nevertheless, I did communicate my views to Israelis, sometimes in their press, when I thought they were misjudging American opinion and exaggerating the influence that AIPAC had in its relations with members of Congress.

OUR WORK EXPANDS

In 1959, we had made another decision in order to enlarge constituency and support. By that time, many of our contributors were active community leaders—self-styled "non-Zionists"—and they could not understand why they should be unrecognized partners in a Zionist committee. They urged us to change the name of our Committee, substituting "Israel" for "Zionist."

I recommended to our Executive Committee that we change our name to the American Israel Public Affairs Committee (AIPAC), that we establish a National Council comprising national and local leaders of both Zionist and non-Zionist organizations, and that we enlarge our Executive Committee to include the presidents of major organizations.

While my recommendations were accepted, some Zionist leaders protested that we were surrendering control of our organization to non-Zionists. To our regret, the Zionist Organization of America (ZOA) then decided that it could no longer actively participate in AIPAC. It resumed its participation some years later.

Since our constituent organizations were always trying to expand their own membership, they were reluctant to approve my proposal that AIPAC become a membership organization. Thus, the concept of "membership" in AIPAC was not accepted for a decade—until I decided to inscribe the word "member" in our fundraising literature—without formal approval and with reluctant acquiescence by our leadership.

As for the ZOA, I always believed that the organization had blundered in 1948. It could have enlisted a host of members if it had then called itself "The American Friends of Israel." I urged Daniel Frisch, its president, to take that step in 1948 in order to breach an artificial wall between Zionists and the self-styled non-Zionists. I never accepted Ben-Gurion's view that one could not be a Zionist unless he emigrated to Israel. As I saw it, anyone who favored and helped to restore the Jewish state was, in fact, a Zionist. Churchill, for example, had told the Washington press on June 28, 1954, that he called himself a Zionist. For many of the years during which I worked in Washington, much of our support came from the so-called non-Zionists.

The press releases of some Jewish organizations stressed that they were "non-Zionist" bodies. I asked them why they thought it so necessary to make that distinction, since we were all identified with the same cause, and they agreed to desist.

Most of our affiliated organizations warmly cooperated. Over the years, I was privileged to deliver a major address to plenary audiences at eighteen national Hadassah conventions, as well as to many regional conferences. I was similarly welcomed by the Labor Zionist Alliance, the Pioneer Women, and the Mizrachi Women. I spoke often for UJA and for Israel Bonds, and I addressed the Young Leadership of UJA at seven successive annual retreats.

In due course, the presidents of most major national Jewish organizations accepted membership, in a personal capacity, on our governing body, the Executive Committee. Our National Council included local community leaders who could raise funds for AIPAC or who were on friendly terms with their congressmen.

(Why do we call AIPAC the American Israel Public Affairs Committee? Back in 1949 Israel announced that the name Israel was both noun and adjective. I circulated that announcement from our U.N. information office, but no one—except myself—ever paid any attention to it.)

Coincidentally, as our Committee was separating from the AZC, the Conference of Presidents of Major American Jewish Organizations came into existence. It was convened by Goldmann, after he had visited Washington during our 1953 conflict with Dulles and had been told by Byroade that he had received representatives of Jewish organizations five times in five days during one week. Goldmann urged that a new overall committee assume the responsibility.

I had reservations about the Presidents Conference because I thought that it was undemocratic as well as impractical to restrict its membership to organization heads. Because I was not a chairman or a president, I could not participate fully, although I attended meetings and was sometimes invited to make reports on the Washington scene. Moreover, AIPAC occasionally arranged for the Conference's Washington meetings and helped to prepare its policy statements. Some organizations, however, objected to my presence because I was a registered lobbyist.

The Conference was not effective in its early days because it could not move on any issue unless it had a consensus. In later years, particularly after the Six-Day War, it did become more assertive and vigorous, and AIPAC worked closely with it. From 1968 on, we were permitted to inform congressional committees and national convention platform committees that the Presidents Conference had endorsed, in principle, the views that we were submitting.

PERSONNEL

Bernstein was chairman of AIPAC for thirteen years, resigning in 1968 to be succeeded by Irving Kane of Cleveland, who had headed the Council of Jewish Federations and Welfare Funds as well as the National Jewish Community Relations Advisory Council. Highly regarded by the non-Zionists throughout the country, Kane was always an active Zionist, serving as treasurer of the Cleveland Zionist District when I was its chairman in the 1940s. He greatly expanded AIPAC's budget, enlisting substantial segments of the American Jewish community in its support, and I am deeply in his debt, for I had never arranged for a pension and he insisted on a plan for deferred compensation.

Kane retired as chairman early in 1974, and I then asked the Committee to elect me as chairman for the last twenty-two months of my service before my retirement at 70. I then became eligible for membership in the Presidents Conference.

When I retired as chairman of AIPAC, Leo Dunn, who had assumed leadership in New England, became chairman of our Executive Committee, and Edward Sanders, a lawyer and community leader in Los Angeles, became president. However, Sanders was offered the opportunity to join the Carter campaign and, since that was inconsistent with AIPAC's non-partisan posture, he resigned and was succeeded by Lawrence Weinberg, who had been an AIPAC leader in Los Angeles and who has wisely directed AIPAC at a very critical time in U.S.-Israel relations.

Thanks to the surge in contributions on the eve of the Six-Day War, we were able to meet expanding needs and to add staff, but because of our straitened pecuniary circumstances we could not afford large salaries. That resulted in the employment of a number of competent and dedicated young people. They included Ken Wollack, who had worked in the McGovern campaign and who is known for thoroughgoing research and inquiry on the Hill to inform his lobbying efforts; Aaron Rosenbaum, son of a distinguished Detroit rabbi, a veritable encyclopedia who served our reference room and made brilliant speeches all over the country; and Leonard Davis, a graduate of Yeshiva University, swift and energetic in his search for facts.

In addition, there were veterans. Ruth Hershman, who had been with me in the American Jewish Conference in the 1940s came to work for AIPAC in 1951 as our New York representative, which she remained for many years before her retirement. Two indispensable right hands were Rita Grossman Lefkort, who worked with me from 1948 until 1965; and Esther Chesney, who began as my secretary in 1956, assuming a multitude of duties and responsibilities, and who continues to be my most effective ally and critic to this day.

The *Near East Report* was ably staffed from the beginning by perceptive and gifted writers, including Charles Fenyvesi, who contributed to many publications and who is now with *The Washington Post*; Tina Silber, who left to join Senator Jackson's staff; Susan Levine Dworkin, who wrote many special surveys; and Wolf Blitzer, who succeeded me as editor and as

Washington correspondent for the *Jewish Chronicle* (London) and *The Jerusalem Post*.

We considered several capable people to serve as my AIPAC successor. The most outstanding was Morris Amitay, who was then a legislative aide to Ribicoff. He had been a tower of strength on the Hill, beginning in 1970 and continuing until I stepped down, as one of a group of legislative aides who helped our cause. He was excellently equipped because he was a lawyer and had served in the U.S. foreign service.

Amitay was succeeded in 1980 by Thomas A. Dine, former legislative aide to Senators Church and Muskie and one of the small group who had been helpful on the Hill. In the same year, Moshe Decter, an experienced journalist, and a pioneer in the struggle for Soviet Jewry, became the editor of the *Near East Report,* succeeding Alan M. Tigay, who resigned to become executive editor of *Hadassah Magazine.*

Chapter 10

The Arab Lobby

AN ASSIST FROM THE CENTRAL INTELLIGENCE AGENCY

The AIPAC lobby never had the Hill to itself. There has always been a pro-Arab lobby in the United States, but it has undergone revolutionary metamorphoses over the years in its composition, motivation, and financing. In fact, the Arab lobby has been financed in large part, first, by U.S. taxpayers and, more recently, by consumers.

At the outset, the Arab states had little need for their own instrument because they were championed by the American petro-diplomatic complex— the conglomerate of oilmen, diplomats, missionaries, and CIA agents. They were an impressive galaxy: James Forrestal, the Secretary of Defense; Harold B. Minor, chief of the Office of Near Eastern Affairs in 1946 and 1947 and subsequently an employee of ARAMCO; William A. Eddy, the U.S. minister to Saudi Arabia between 1944 and 1946; Wallace Murray, chief of the Office of Near Eastern Affairs for many years; Rusk; Byroade; Henderson; and many, many more.

Despite Israel's establishment, some never gave up. Debate on television offered a typical example. Parker Hart, former Assistant Secretary of State and former president of the Middle East Institute, complained to his audience: "The Zionists were always pressing and pushing me. The Arabs never did." He demonstrated by pressing back his left shoulder. A few days later, when the same television station asked me for an answer to Hart, I replied: "That's very simple. The Arabs never needed to press or push Mr. Hart."

Encouraged by American diplomats, pro-Arab Americans organized the Committee for Justice and Peace in the Holy Land to spur the 1948 campaign

114

to rescind the partition resolution, warning of a resurgence of anti-Semitism if Jews insisted on implementation. Claiming credit for the reversal, they then disbanded.

When I began to lobby in 1951, King Ibn Saud called on U.S. diplomats to finance a pro-Arab organization to counter ours. That appeal resulted in a secret CIA subvention via a paper conduit, the "Dearborn Foundation" in Chicago, in order to establish and fund the American Friends of the Middle East (AFME), whose chairman, columnist Dorothy Thompson, advertised the event on June 27, 1951. She had once eloquently championed Zionism; in 1944, I heard her tell 20,000 people in Madison Square Garden: "The opponents of Zionism are hypocrites." Unaccountably, she changed. Moreover, without disclosing that she led AFME, she syndicated her column in which she charged that the media were anti-Arab. And, despite its tax-exempt status, AFME lobbied against economic and military aid to Israel.

The CIA subvention was a secret until 1961, when Bushrod Howard, a former attorney for the oil companies, told me about it. The CIA was then sacrosanct, and I hesitated to expose the subsidy. However, in 1962, the *Jordan Times* headlined a press conference given by an AFME official, Elmo Hutchinson, a virulent foe of Israel who was formerly with the U.N. Truce Supervisory Organization. He damned Israel as "fascist, intolerant, defiant, aggressive, expansionist," and insisted that she could not possibly survive.

The *Near East Report* questioned the propriety of this diatribe. Both Robert Strong at the State Department and Myer Feldman at the White House were incredulous when I protested that Hutchinson's salary was financed by U.S. taxpayers. Feldman subsequently confirmed the allegation, but insisted that the subsidy had ended. In actuality, it was reduced, but not ended until 1967.

In 1963, the CIA had ceased to be an unmentionable. In their book *The Invisible Government,* Washington correspondents David Wise and Thomas B. Ross had disclosed how the CIA had masterminded the overthrow of Premier Mohammed Mossadegh in Iran in 1953. I then felt free to break the AFME story.

In the meantime, in June 1963, Howard submitted off-the-record testimony to the Senate Committee on Foreign Relations and the House Committee on Foreign Affairs.

One could rationalize the project — within limits. The CIA might have established AFME student counseling offices in Arab capitals as covers for intelligence operations. However, in Washington, AFME was using CIA funds to wage a propaganda offensive against Israel, and we were resentful. While we were struggling to raise a modest $50,000 to $100,000 a year to finance our lobby, U.S. subsidies to AFME reached a peak of $400,000 a year.

I published an exposé in *Myths and Facts,* a special edition of the *Near East Report,* entitled "Arab Propaganda, Line and Apparatus," in 1964. *The Nation,* and subsequently *Ramparts,* picked it up, and it finally made headlines during the congressional inquiry into CIA operations in 1967, when the subvention ended.

On March 31, 1967, Assistant Secretary of State Dixon Donnelly wrote to Rabbi Bernstein: "The President has just directed that no federal agency shall provide any covert financial assistance, direct or indirect, to American private voluntary organizations and that any such support that has been provided shall be terminated as quickly as possible."

Pro-Arab forces in this country were embarrassed by Nasser's arms deal with the Soviets in 1955, and by his nationalization of the Suez Canal. One victim was the executive officer of AFME, Reverend Garland Evans Hopkins, who sought to justify Nasser's action and was ousted. He then established a lobbying committee, the Citizens Committee on American Policy in the Near East (CITCOM), to compete with us. He was unable to raise non-tax-exempt funds to finance his work and he committed suicide.

Another loner was a ubiquitous and resourceful Arab propagandist, Dr. Mohammed Mehdi, who had resigned as director of the Arab Information Center in San Francisco to organize his own Action Committee on American-Arab Relations. An extremist, he did not attract a large following. Mehdi sought to justify Robert Kennedy's murder by Sirhan Sirhan on the ground that Kennedy had endorsed Phantom jets for Israel.

THE ARAB STUDENTS

A major AFME achievement was to spawn and activate the Organization of Arab Students on college campuses.

Many Arab students identified themselves with the extreme left as they joined in the fight against the Vietnam war. Many were in revolt against their own conservative governments. They won some support from American students in the anti-war coalition. These students rewrote history for campus publications. They appeared before church groups and they made some inroads among radical and disinterested Jewish students. They courted blacks who were allied with liberation movements, exploiting their economic deprivation. The responsible leadership of the black community resented the crude anti-Semitism of this propaganda thrust.

More recently, many black students have been preoccupied with campus issues, such as the Bakke case, the admission and advancement of black students and faculty, as well as apartheid in South Africa.

As the radical tide receded and most college students resumed their traditional apolitical postures, Arab students were isolated, except for a hard core of avowedly Marxist extremists, and their influence declined. Their cause was reinvigorated by the rise of the PLO's Yasir Arafat after the 1973 Yom Kippur War.

We were apprehensive about a vast influx of Arab students and scholars, but the record shows that few came to study the liberal arts at Ivy League schools, and that most foreign students went to engineering and medical schools—not to influence others but to train themselves for future vocations. According to the Institute of International Education, the total number of students who came here in the 1976-1977 academic year from Southwest Asia was 38,490, of whom 23,310 came from Iran. The number from Saudi Arabia, with a much smaller population, was 4,592. There were only 2,140 from Israel. Most of those who came from the Middle East were not from the Arab states, but from Iran.

At one time there were reports that the Arab states planned large gifts for Middle East studies. Their enthusiasm waned when they were given to understand that they would not be permitted to control faculty appointments or student admissions. (But large Arab gifts are still available as this is written, and in some universities the Jewish Studies program may be downgraded in the pursuit of benefactors from Riyadh.)

Israeli students did not have the time or the money to become involved in controversy with subsidized Arab students. Usually much older, they were interested in their education and rejected debates as meaningless and degrading, since Arabs were challenging their right to survive as a people. American Jewish students, for the most part, did not have the background or inclination to enter into forensic contests, but they became increasingly conscious of their own identification with the cause of Israel.

THE PRO-ARAB BLOC

I declined to debate with Arab diplomats because they would not sit with Israelis. I saw no reason why American Jews should sit with those who regarded the Israelis as a non-people. I often clashed with American spokesmen for the Arab cause at the Middle East Institute, at the Junior American Assembly at Arden House, at the American Enterprise Institute, at the Center for Strategic Studies, on college campuses, and before congressional committees. These included leading supporters of the Arabs, such as Christopher Mayhew; Elmer Berger; John S. Badeau, who had been our ambassador to Cairo; David G. Nes, who was the U.S. chargé d'affaires in Cairo when Nasser precipitated the Six-Day War; Professors Alan R. Taylor and Harry Howard of American University; and John Ruedy and Michael Hudson of Georgetown University.

Arab Americans were not as concerned about the fate of their motherlands as were the Jews about Israel. Arab emigrés were inclined toward integration and assimilation and were unlikely to maintain ties with the countries whence they came. Moreover, divisions and rivalries paralleled those of the Arab states. There was a wide diversity of religious belief, cultural and economic interest, and allegiance. In the pre-state struggle, some Lebanese

Christians cooperated with the American Zionist Emergency Council. The two religious minorities were drawn to each other.

When UNSCOP took secret testimony in August 1947, the Maronite Archbishop of Beirut, Ignatius Moubarak, told them: "Major reasons of a social, humanitarian and religious nature require the creation of two homelands for minorities—a Christian home in the Lebanon, as there has always been, and a Jewish home in Palestine. . . . Lebanon demands freedom for the Jews in Palestine, as it desires its own freedom and independence."

This alliance was to be reinstated in the 1970s when Lebanese Christians were embattled with the Syrians and the PLO and were aided by the Israelis, who opened up a "Good Fence" on their northern border.

After the Six-Day War, pro-Arab organizations proliferated. Most active were the National Association of Arab Americans (NAAA) and the Detroit-based Association of Arab American University Graduates (AAUG).

NAAA was founded early in 1972, and supported the PLO, but some of its original leaders withdrew, outraged by the genocidal war in Lebanon. It had a succession of presidents, including Professor Hisham Sharabi of Georgetown University, a Palestinian-born emigré who strongly champions the PLO. Its Director of Public Affairs was John P. Richardson, until recently associated with American Near East Refugee Aid, Inc. (ANERA), where he worked under John H. Davis, who had been Commissioner General of the U.N. Relief and Works Agency (UNRWA) and who had always insisted that the Palestinian Arab refugees had a right to repatriation. For many years, Davis repeatedly questioned Israel's right to exist. Soon after the Yom Kippur War, ANERA received a $2 million gift from the Gulf Oil Company.

Other former NAAA presidents were Richard Shadyac, Peter S. Tanous, and Joseph Baroody, who turned over the chairmanship to Sharabi. Sharabi holds the chair of Arab Studies at Georgetown University, which was financed by a $750,000 grant from Libya's Muammar Qaddafi. Subsequently, he obtained a $50,000 grant from Iraq and clashed with President Timothy Healy, denouncing him as a "Jesuit Zionist" when Healy insisted on returning the Iraqi gift. David J. Sadd is NAAA's executive director.

Over the years, six Arab Americans had been elected to the House, and one of them, James Abourezk, to the Senate. At the suggestion of Jewish friends in South Dakota, I went to see Abourezk in 1972, when he was hoping to advance to the Senate. I tried to formulate a pro-Israel statement for him and, while we failed to reach agreement, I nevertheless wrote to constituents that I thought he was sympathetic. This was a mistake. After he visited Lebanon, he became an outspoken advocate of the PLO.

Our country, Abourezk told the Washington Press Club, had alienated the Arabs, who had turned to the Soviet Union as a result of U.S. arms aid to Israel. That absurdity was swiftly challenged by a journalist in the audience. Along with Senator James A. McClure (R-Idaho), Abourezk later testified against the $2.2 billion authorization recommended by the Administration in 1973 to finance the massive airlift to Israel.

In March 1974, we reproduced an excerpt of a South Dakota TV broadcast to the effect that Abourezk had received $49,000 for thirteen speeches in 1973, including one unprecedented $10,000 honorarium. Congress later voted a drastic ceiling on honoraria.

In 1974, I informed Abourezk's contributors that I had wrongly advised them in 1972—an action which he publicly decried but which I thought was due them. He was not a candidate for reelection in 1978, but continued to serve the Arab cause, and in 1979 he was retained by Iran.

In recent years, the Arab lobby has made gains on four major fronts: in the media, at the U.N., on college campuses, and on Capitol Hill.

While most Americans deplore violence, hijacking, and terrorism, the PLO smashed its way into the headlines and on to the TV tubes, riveting the eyes and resounding in the ears of a host of Americans. The PLO may not have won sympathy and friendship, but it has been able to capture and neutralize vast audiences.

Charging that the media and banks are controlled by Jews, pro-Arabs invariably denounce the alleged failure to accord them fair treatment. At the 1975 NAAA convention I heard the audience berate four media representatives for alleged pro-Israel bias. They were reassured with statistical evidence to the contrary. Many editors are now constrained to print an equal number of letters from each side. While newspapers may receive many more pro-Israel letters than those emanating from Arab sympathizers, the reader is given the false impression that the country is equally divided. The effect is to discourage Israel's friends from writing.

I have urged audiences to write letters to the media even though they may not be printed. Too many fail to recognize that the media do keep score. They count letters from opposing factions, while maintaining parity in their columns and programs. The disappearance of many newspapers has been a setback. Many cities now have but one publisher, which makes it difficult to voice dissent.

The United Nations—the stalwart friend of 1947 to 1948—has become a disaster area. African and Asian countries have identified with the expanding bloc of Arab states, twenty-two at the last count; and Israel is isolated—an abandoned pariah—as the world's most powerful propaganda agency circulates a stream of virulent propaganda around the globe.

OIL MONEY LUBRICATES

The major revolutionary change came with the vast infusion of oil money and the activation of skilled and knowledgeable agents. They included experts in public relations and ex-diplomats and ex-legislators well-schooled in the ways of Capitol Hill, the Department of State, the Treasury, the White House, and the executive offices of our government.

The rapid growth of Arab oil power and our country's failure to reduce our dependency on the Arab oil producers aroused nightmarish fears and alarm among many who predicted that the Arabs would take over the media, the campus, our financial institutions, and our defense industries. Israel and her American Jewish friends, they feared, would become the scapegoats in a convulsion of anti-Semitism. Many of us were skeptical. Despite the long lines of deprived and impatient motorists, we insisted that few Americans would blame Jews, that many more would blame the Arabs for the embargo, the oil companies for maldistribution, and our own government for the failure to anticipate and defuse the crisis.

There were other dire forebodings—that Arab students and scholars would invade our universities, thereby controlling Arab-endowed study centers and indoctrinating future scholars, diplomats, and congressmen.

With the five-fold increase in the price of oil, the oil-rich Arab states found a simpler way to buy American allegiance: to hire American experts to pressure the U.S. government and American corporations to build their economies and toughen their defenses on the scene. This could be done at the expense of Americans. The American taxpayer had financed the first pro-Arab lobby in the 1950s. Now the American consumer, who was paying an exorbitant price for oil, would provide the petro-dollars to finance the employment of American agents to capture American opinion and power and, once and for all, to undermine and vanquish the pro-Israel lobby.

Arab states have come to realize that they can most efficiently promote their cause by hiring agents who know how to open the right doors in Washington, and they have the funds, which have been provided by the American consumer, to pay the huge cost.

The Department of Justice list included Frederick Dutton, who once served the Kennedy Administration as its congressional liaison and who received $425,100 from Saudi Arabia between April 4, 1975 and June 29, 1978.

Fulbright, another former Hill luminary, served as an agent of the Saudis for $50,000 a year and of the United Arab Emirates for $25,000 a year.

That 1978 list included the names of many more handsomely paid foreign agents who know their way around the Hill and the White House, and it disclosed the report of the PLO office, revealing a $44,360 six-month budget.

In addition to the influence which these experienced professionals may bring to bear on Congress and the Administration, there is a widespread pro-Arab lobby in the communities, mobilizing hundreds of thousands of Americans who are employed by corporations which have contracts in the Arab states.

There is a fundamental difference between the two lobbies. Could Israel have retained foreign agents to win her application for aid in 1951? By no means. She had to direct her appeal to American citizens across the country to win the interest and support of their congressmen in a clash with an unsympathetic, if not hostile, establishment. In contrast, the Arabs began their battle on the Hill with the sympathy and support of the Administration. They needed articulate Hill alumni who could open doors with the Administration's blessing. Unlike them, AIPAC had to begin with the grass roots, and it continues to rely on them.

Chapter 11

Arms for the Arabs — None for Israel

THE DUBIOUS COMMITMENT

Disregarding our widely supported protests and deep forebodings, the Eisenhower Administration began to arm Iraq in April 1954 in the ill-advised stratagem to contain the Soviet Union. Yet Washington still refused arms for Israel.

One of Eisenhower's 1952 supporters was sarcastic. "Iraq is to be armed by our government not, to be sure, with sufficient military equipment to be a threat to Israel but with just enough military equipment to resist possible Soviet aggression," Rabbi Silver told a ZOA convention on June 24, 1954.

We warned that arms for any Arab state would mean arms for all Arab states, fueling an uncontrollable intra-Arab arms race, and that the arms for Baghdad, the capital of Iraq, would eventually fall into Soviet hands, a prediction unhappily fulfilled in the 1958 Kassem revolt. This was the first major issue to confront our newly established lobbying committee.

In 1949, after Bunche had negotiated the armistice agreements, the British and French resumed selling arms to the Arab states, and the United States proposed to equip Egypt. I spent a week in Washington in January 1950 to voice concern to friends on Capitol Hill.

On May 25, 1950 — in an effort to reassure Israel — Britain, France, and the United States issued the Tripartite Declaration, which expressed opposition to an arms race. They recognized that the Arab states and Israel needed "to maintain a certain level of armed forces for . . . internal security and . . . legitimate self-defense and to . . . play their part in the defense of the area as a whole."

All the states had given assurances that they did "not intend to undertake any act of aggression against any other state."

The three governments declared "their unalterable opposition" to the use or threat of force in the area and promised immediate action in and outside the U.N. if any of the states were "preparing to violate frontiers or armistice lines."

Our government invariably cited this declaration to justify its refusal to provide Israel with arms or a security guarantee. However, Dulles's own testimony made a mockery of it in 1956, and, in 1967, after the Six-Day War, the Department of State conceded that it was an empty and unenforceable commitment since it was devoid of the reciprocal obligations of a treaty.

In 1952, the United States agreed to sell arms to both Israel, on February 27, and to Egypt, on December 10, but Israel's subsequent request was ignored. Our diplomats had set their hearts on arming Egypt—which they preferred over Iraq as the keystone of the proposed anti-Communist wall in the Middle East—because Britain's departure from the Suez Canal Zone could not long be delayed. Moreover, despite the 1949 armistice agreement, and the 1951 Security Council decision ordering Egypt to keep the Canal open, the Arab states insisted that they were still at war with Israel.

The U.N. was similarly inert, when, on March 17, 1954, eleven Jews were ambushed and murdered as their bus drove through the Scorpion Pass in the Negev. It was widely suspected that the infiltrators came from Jordan, because tracks led from the Jordanian frontier, but Hutchinson, the U.N. observer who chaired the Mixed Armistice Commission and who was soon to become AFME's mouthpiece, refused to assess blame.

THE ARMS IMBALANCE

Our new Committee's first statement, issued on March 30, dealt with the arms deal. We described Iraq as the "most belligerent member" of the Arab League, emphasizing that it had refused to sign an armistice agreement with Israel. We recalled that Fadhil al-Jamali, Iraq's Prime Minister, had told his Parliament on January 16: "Whoever called for peace with Israel would be guilty of high treason and should be hanged." On February 18, he had asserted: "The destruction of Israel will be achieved only by strengthening the Arab states." No angel of peace, Nasser himself had declared in May 1954: "Israel is an artificial state which must disappear."

More than forty senators and representatives met with Under Secretary of State Walter Bedell Smith and Byroade on March 3, warning that "the guns we give to the Arabs may be used not to advance the security of the area but to promote attack on our own essential interests." They stressed the Arabs' real needs: more bread, better utilization of land and water resources, and more orderly administration.

Many organizations joined us in challenging the Administration's decision, including the American Christian Palestine Committee and the American Association for the United Nations. There was a letter from a great number of American leaders who were distinguished in education, religion, labor, and government.

Lipsky and I clashed with Byroade, who had twice addressed chapters of the American Council for Judaism. While he conceded that Arab fears of Jewish immigration into Israel were unrealistic and "illogical," he felt that Israel must calm Arab fears with assurances, such as the admission of an unspecified number of Arabs into Israel.

Byroade continued: "When we ask the Arab states to accept the existence of the state of Israel . . . they should have the right to know . . . the magnitude of this new state. They look upon it as expansionist Zionism, which . . . will ultimately commit aggression to expand to suit its future needs."

On the eve of the 1954 national elections, our Committee circulated a questionnaire to all nominees for Congress. We did not intend to make endorsements; our purpose was to rally bipartisan support. Marshaling the arguments, we warned that a premature supply of arms to the Arab states, without conditions, would delay peace, stimulate Arab hostility, and obstruct the organization of an effective regional defense system.

We invited candidates to endorse the following statement:

I am opposed to the grant of arms to any of the Arab states unless they:
1) declare their readiness to join in the defense of the Free World against Communist aggression;
2) agree to negotiate a peace settlement with the state of Israel; and
3) in advance of any such negotiations, abandon their direct and indirect boycott and blockade of Israel, and, in the case of Egypt, the restrictions on the free movement of shipping to and from Israel through the Suez Canal.
I believe that the Administration should make a new and vigorous effort to bring the Arab states and Israel to the peace table for direct negotiations.

There was an impressive response, as 258 nominees representing 39 states endorsed the statement; 92 candidates issued their own statements or otherwise expressed reservations on the current arms policy (among them, Gerald Ford). Of these 350, 30 were candidates for the Senate and 188 were elected to the 84th Congress.

Opposition organizations published advertisements rebuking our action as an "intrusion" into U.S. foreign policy, for the Executive Branch was then widely regarded as immune from congressional challenge on foreign policy.

We quoted editorials from twenty-four leading newspapers, some of which referred to the blood-chilling pledge of Saudi Arabia's new ruler, King Saud, that the Arab nations would sacrifice "10 million of their 50 million people, if necessary, to wipe out their neighbor Israel."

The presidents of sixteen major American Jewish organizations—Zionist, non-Zionist, Conservative, Orthodox and Reform—came to Washington on October 25, 1954, to protest, and there were many large public meetings across the country.

The arming of Iraq was counterproductive. It angered Nasser and he turned to the Soviets. Nasser had wanted U.S. arms but he would not comply with the Mutual Security Act's requirement that an American military mission must accompany all such gifts. In May 1956, a special Middle East Study Mission of the House Foreign Affairs Committee, headed by Representative Clement Zablocki (D-Wisconsin), submitted a detailed report on the protracted U.S.-Egyptian negotiations, refuting Egypt's charge that U.S. conditions had impinged on Egypt's sovereignty.

Dulles shed further light on the collapse of the negotiations with Egypt before a Senate Committee in February 1956. He had first heard that Nasser might be thinking of getting arms from Czechoslovakia in June 1955, but Egypt had suspended the deal and had opened negotiations with the United States, which was then willing to sell arms to Egypt. "We gave them prices and they found that they could get arms from the Soviet bloc more cheaply on the basis of a barter of cotton, the principal export commodity. . . . Because of our big cotton exports and the likelihood of our selling competitively, they prefer to use their cotton on a barter arrangement such as this," Dulles said.

Another preposterous myth was that Nasser dealt with the Kremlin because the United States had refused to help him build the Aswan Dam. The fact is that the United States offered Egypt aid to build the Aswan Dam *after* Nasser had begun to receive arms from the Russians. Washington had then hoped to induce Nasser to discontinue or at least to reduce his purchases from the Soviet Union. The United States had proposed to grant Egypt $56 million, while the British were to put up $14 million, and the World Bank was to lend $200 million. Nasser persisted, however, in a strident propaganda war against the West in the Arab states and Africa. Preaching "positive neutralism," Nasser sought to counter the Baghdad Pact with an anti-Western alliance including Syria, Saudia Arabia, and Yemen. He also recognized Communist China. The powerful Cairo Radio incited revolt against the French in North Africa and against the British in Cyprus and Jordan.

Disillusioned, Dulles withdrew the U.S. offer and, in 1956, an enraged Nasser nationalized the Suez Canal.

Despite the failure of our arms negotiations, we tried to propitiate Nasser with economic assistance: $40 million in fiscal 1955, and $30 million in fiscal 1956.

Sensitive to criticism of the deal with Iraq, Dulles had announced on August 26, 1955, that the United States would offer security guarantees to Israel and to the Arab states if they could agree on boundaries. This seemingly attractive proposal was undermined by a built-in veto, for the guarantees could never go into effect because the Arabs would not agree on boundaries. We countered with a suggestion that the United States guarantee existing armistice lines, but Dulles refused.

The flow of arms from both East and West grew more alarming every day. Egypt won superiority over Israel in the air and would soon have it on land. England agreed to send Egypt Valentine tanks, Bren carriers, and armored cars.

For many years, Britain had subsidized Jordan's economy with $20 million a year. The British now pressured the Jordanians to join the Baghdad Pact. Egyptian agents and Communist Party agitators exploited this British blunder by inciting anti-Western riots in Amman, financed, allegedly, by Saudi oil money. The death toll rose to 56. The Englishman Glubb Pasha, who had served Jordan's Arab Legion for a lifetime, was given his walking papers.

We were then calling for arms for Israel and for security guarantees with states which wanted them. I went to Israel shortly after Nasser's deal with the Soviets and was startled by the widespread fear that war was inevitable. Sharett flew to a Geneva summit conference, and there he dramatically pleaded with the Western powers for arms. By a coincidence, I was then bound for the United States, and I met Sharett at the Athens airport on his way back to Israel. He bitterly described his frustration; he could get neither arms nor guarantees.

Meanwhile, Dulles had buoyantly spoken of collective security in an address to the U.N. on June 24, 1955. The United States, which had sought safety in 1914 and 1939 in isolation and neutrality, had come to learn that security rested on collective action. The United States was now treaty-bound with forty-four countries. "We are proud to have these multiple ties of trust and confidence. These systems conform with the Charter of the U.N.," Dulles asserted. (Many were asking why Israel could not become the forty-fifth.)

Congress was alarmed by the Administration's pro-Arab posture. Democratic and Republican congressmen signed petitions urging that Israel be allowed to purchase $50 million in defensive arms, that the Administration oppose any attempts to force Israel to surrender vital territory, and that our government speed negotiations and security guarantees.

Some 50 Republican House members, led by Hugh Scott, Albert P. Morano, James C. Fulton, Kenneth B. Keating and Edward Radwan, joined in a letter to the Secretary of State. A similar statement was signed by 101 Democrats. That totaled 151, more than one-third of the House, and included 13 members of the House Committee on Foreign Affairs. That was Scott's first major initiative, and for many years he led many battles for Israel.

SECRET DEAL WITH THE SAUDIS

Iraq was not our only Arab customer. Suddenly, there came the astonishing discovery that the United States had been selling planes to Saudi Arabia since 1952. That was revealed after eighteen Walker bulldog tanks bound for Saudi Arabia were accidentally detected on a Brooklyn pier on February 17, 1956.

The Senate Foreign Relations Committee convened on February 24 to demand an explanation from Dulles. A brilliant lawyer, he had many answers. Senators were incredulous.

Dulles was confident that Communist policies had failed. He conceded that Soviet shipments were upsetting the balance and endangering Israel, but he was still opposed to selling Israel jet planes and entering into a mutual security pact with her.

In his State of the Union message, Eisenhower had said that in the face of Communist power we must maintain an effective system of collective security . . . of warning measures and military agreements. Why, Dulles was asked, had there been such a long delay in meeting Israel's needs?

To a question from Smith, Dulles replied: "The preservation of the state of Israel is what I regard as one of the essential goals of U.S. foreign policy. It is not our only goal. And we have to combine the search for that result with the achievement of other results which are also important."

To a question from Humphrey, Dulles replied: "If I were in their position, I would be pressing for just what they have, for no country likes to be dependent on the resources and decisions of another country, and they prefer to have their capacity in their own hands."

Dulles told Sparkman that Israel's fears were unfounded. "But I admit that if I were in their position, sitting where they are, I would probably entertain much the same fears."

He explained why he opposed Israel's request. Due to her smaller size and population, Israel could not win an arms race against the Arabs who had access to Soviet bloc stocks. He pointed out that Israel had a population of about 1.7 million, as compared with approximately 32 million Arabs.

This was a new and weird doctrine. Did we hesitate to send arms to Taiwan because the population of Formosa was only 8.5 million as compared with the 580 million on the mainland? Did we deny aid to England because its people were vastly outnumbered? And how could 160 million Americans preserve a balance with the 700 million subjects of Moscow and Peking?

The Israelis had been greatly outnumbered in 1948, when they had lost 6,000 of their 650,000 people, but survival does not depend solely on numbers and space. More decisive factors are spirit, skill, and motivation.

Later the State Department reinterpreted the Dulles sophistry. Still refusing arms for Israel, it argued that the Israelis—though outgunned and outnumbered—could rely on their "qualitative superiority"—a reassurance until push buttons in the Yom Kippur War made it obsolete.

Dulles assured the senators that tanks landed at Dhahran could not cross an impassable desert to reach Israel. Nor could they be rolled against the British in the Buraimi oasis dispute. Morse pointed out that they could be shipped toward Israel by water. Dulles conceded this, but argued that the Saudis were not permitted to transfer them; he was certain that they would honor this obligation.

The exuberant Humphrey then asked what purpose they really served: "Do they just need tanks to make them feel good?"

Dulles explained that they were for training for internal security because there had been large-scale riots and disturbances and 6,000 Americans lived in the area. He then disclosed that we had been sending planes and other equipment to Saudi Arabia for more than five years. At first he mentioned "cargo" planes, but he later revised his testimony to refer to "a limited number of military aircraft of the propeller type."

This led to criticism that the agreement for the U.S. airbase at Dhahran permitted Saudi Arabia to exclude any "objectionable" individuals. The United States was required to submit a detailed list of the names and identities of personnel and employees. Dulles blundered when he went on to explain why American Jews could not be assigned to an American base. There was an audible audience gasp when he said that Saudi Arabia practices "very rigorously certain religious doctrines, and they have felt for a long time—it goes back centuries—a very particular animosity toward the Jews because they credited the assassination of Mohammed to a Jew." Dulles later revised his testimony to read: "a very particular animosity towards the Jews since the time of Mohammed." While the Secretary personally disapproved such practices, we had to recognize that Saudi Arabia was an "ally."

"We perforce accommodate ourselves to certain practices they have which we do not like; they perhaps accommodate themselves to certain of our idiosyncrasies which they do not like, but on the whole they have a pretty arbitrary rule, largely dictated by the strict tenets of the Moslem faith."

If we declined to provide the weapons the Saudis needed, we might have to give up the base (which, in fact, we did long ago).

This historic colloquy precipitated a controversy which engaged Congress for many years—the refusal of Saudi Arabia and other Arab countries to admit Jews. It led to congressional action denying aid to countries which discriminated on the ground of race or religion. Both political parties wrote anti-discrimination planks into their 1956 political platforms a few months later.

Asked how the United States could send arms to Iraq and still deny them to Israel, Dulles pointed out that Iraq was not contiguous to Israel. However, recognizing his palpable inconsistency, he acknowledged that "we were prepared to modify the policy in the case of Egypt under very special circumstances where we felt that otherwise they would get arms from the Soviet Union, where, in fact our proposal fell through."

He had no dearth of explanations. "We are holding up arms for Israel because we do not believe that the shipment would be conducive to the only worthwhile solution—a permanent peace between Israel and the Arab states."

That was still another novel doctrine. We would win peace if Israel, which wants peace, were made relatively weaker, and if the Arab states, which want war, were allowed to become stronger. This paradoxical rationalization was often advanced by U.S. diplomats who believed that Arabs might make peace with Israel if only they could lead from strength.

Morse pointed out that the Arabs could ship tanks toward Israel by water. Dulles conceded this, but contended that Saudi Arabia was not permitted to transfer them. Dulles was convinced that the Saudis would honor their obligations to us, even though, at that time, it was widely believed that Saudi money had financed anti-Western demonstrations in Jordan, only a few weeks before, when the British pressured Jordan to join the Baghdad Pact.

Confidence in Nasser's peaceful intentions? Just a month before, on January 16, Nasser had broadcast: "From the Atlantic to the Persian Gulf there is but one Arab nation, which no one will succeed in dividing again. After World War II, part of the Arab heart was snatched from the Arab body. Today, Arabs from the Atlantic to the Persian Gulf will cooperate in restoring that part."

Some weeks later, on March 13, 1956, columnist Walter Lippmann wrote in *The New York Herald Tribune:* "The question is whether or not the Arab rulers and politicians, their officers and intellectuals, will settle for anything short of the expulsion of France from North Africa, Britain from the eastern Mediterranean and the Persian Gulf, the extinction of Israel as an independent state, and the reduction of the United States to the position of a hired servant of the Saudi Arabian oil kingdom."

If Israel is to have no arms, upon whom should she rely? Dulles was asked. His answer was, "The United Nations," for after all, he declared, "Israel is a creature of the United Nations," hardly a felicitous expression in light of the U.N.'s subsequent hostility toward her.

It was pointed out that the Soviet veto could block effective action to assist Israel in a crisis, to which Dulles replied that action could be taken in the General Assembly if the Security Council were paralyzed by a veto. But, as far back as 1956, the Assembly had grown to 76, and the Soviet-Arab-Afro-Asian bloc already had a blocking third.

Could Israel rely on the 1950 Tripartite Declaration? Dulles now minimized it. This was merely a declaration by the three great powers. It was not a treaty, and Congress had never approved or reinforced it.

Dulles's explanation that the tanks were for internal security elicited Morse's charge that the Administration was playing into the hands of Soviet propaganda by extending U.S. military support to help suppress human rights and freedom in a totalitarian regime. Dulles was confident that this was not true in Saudi Arabia, insisting that past demonstrations had been of alien inspiration.

Our military deals in the feudal Middle East were symptomatic of a corrosive sickness in our foreign policy: the wishful illusion that we could strengthen democratic forces by arming the palace guard; that we could win the friendship of impoverished peoples by arming their wealthy masters; that we could hire mercenaries to defend freedom—a paradoxical dilemma which persists in today's convulsive confrontations. Bitterly, we recalled how the democracies had rejected collective security in the 1930s, preferring a collective suicide pact, which led inexorably to a collective death certificate for a myriad of Jews.

It is ironic commentary on the Dulles refusal to permit U.S. arms to go to Israel that the United States was then encouraging our allies—England, France, and Canada—to sell Israel the arms she so urgently needed.

Returning from a NATO conference early in May 1956, Dulles declared: "[It] was recognized at Paris that wide discrepancies in armed strengths would be likely to create tensions." That month, Israel received twenty-four jet fighters from France, while Canada prepared to sell her F-86 planes later in the year.

We carried our campaign to the national political conventions. In our testimony we asked for "arms to Israel as well as security treaties to guarantee the existing U.N. armistice lines against aggression and counter the Communist weapons poised on Israel's frontiers."

The Republican plank ignored arms for Israel, but the party was determined to prove that it was Israel's friend. Friendship for Israel was affirmed no less than three times. The GOP plank declared: "We regard the preservation of Israel as an important tenet of American foreign policy. We are determined that the integrity of an independent Jewish state shall be maintained. We shall support the independence of Israel against aggression. The best hope for peace lies in the United Nations. . . ."

There was less rhetoric and more substance in the Democratic plank: "The Democratic party will act to redress the dangerous imbalance of arms in the area, created by the shipment of Communist arms to Egypt, by selling or supplying defensive weapons to Israel, and will take such steps, including security guarantees, as may be required to deter aggression and war in the area."

War was not deterred. It was but three months away.

Chapter 12

The Suez War and the Threat of Sanctions

NASSER NATIONALIZES THE CANAL

The Suez War was inevitable. Israel swiftly won it late in 1956. In a monumental blunder, the United States joined the Soviet Union in 1957 in pressuring Israel to withdraw from the territory she had occupied, without requiring Egypt to make peace. Our government threatened sanctions against Israel if she did not yield.

"You may choke with rage but you will never succeed in ordering us around," Nasser had cried when he nationalized the Suez Canal.

The United States, England, and France failed to combat Nasser's action. Although united in objective, they could not agree on method, while the Soviets increased their political and military support of the Egyptian dictator.

All through early 1956, Arab terrorists based in the Gaza strip, Syria, and Jordan infiltrated Israel's frontier settlements, killing farmers, fishermen, and soldiers. On March 4, Syrians murdered four Israeli policemen in a patrol boat on the Sea of Galilee. On March 9, an Israeli villager was killed by a Jordanian infiltrator. On April 4, Egyptians killed four Israeli soldiers on the Gaza border. Israel struck back the following day at Gaza, and Egyptians counted 63 casualties. Terrorists penetrated within five miles of Tel Aviv on April 11; 14 Israelis died that week and four more were killed in an ambush near the armistice line with Jordan on April 23.

Nasser then had few American sympathizers because of the raids, his nationalization of the Canal, and the Soviet arms deal. Some compared his coup to Hitler's seizure of the Rhineland and feared an imminent attack on Israel.

131

Israel's reaction was inevitable; she struck on October 29.

Instead of blaming Egypt for the war, the Administration joined the Soviets in competition for Arab favor—an unprincipled exercise in appeasement. We were dismayed by our government's stand. We joined the Conference of Presidents of Major American Jewish Organizations in appeals to the Administration to work for a negotiated settlement and guarantees for agreed boundaries.

We had strong public support. Typical of many anti-Nasser editorials was a lengthy indictment in *The New York Times* on November 1, which declared that "it would be ridiculous to permit Colonel Nasser to pose before the U.N. or the world as the innocent victim of aggression or to hold a protecting hand over him. On the contrary, insofar as there is any one man guilty of aggression, it is the Egyptian President. . . ." And it also catalogued Nasser's crimes against the peace.

Lippmann wrote: "To ignore the Egyptian raids, to treat Israel as the aggressor and Egypt as the innocent victim . . . was a grave mistake in policy, indefensible in principle and, in fact, entirely unrealistic and impracticable."

The Security Council met on October 30. The United States and the Soviet Union offered resolutions calling for a cease-fire and withdrawals as the Soviet Union accused Israel of aggression.

The British and French, who had entered the conflict in collusion with Israel, vetoed both. Instead, they called upon Egypt and Israel to cease fire and to withdraw ten miles from the Suez Canal in order that they might occupy the area. They reinforced this call by bombarding Egyptian installations. On November 5, they landed and stationed their forces along one-fifth of the Canal.

Foreign Minister Lester Pearson of Canada suggested the establishment of a U.N. Emergency Force (UNEF) to enforce the cease-fire and withdrawal, but the Soviet Union, opposing the establishment of UNEF, proposed instead that the United States and the Soviet Union join forces to terminate the "aggression" against Egypt. Eisenhower rejected this proposal, but the Soviet Union now threatened its own military intervention.

On November 5, Premier Nikolai Bulganin warned Britain, France, and Israel that it might use rockets, which had a range of 700 miles—with British bases only 450 to 500 miles away: "We are fully determined to crush the aggressors and restore peace in the Middle East through the use of force. We hope at this critical moment, you will display due prudence and draw the corresponding conclusions from this." Five days later, the Russians warned that they would permit volunteers to go to Egypt.

The British and French accepted the U.N. cease-fire. An angry Ben-Gurion retorted that Israel would not permit the stationing of U.N. troops on her territory, protested that Egypt had violated the armistice agreement, and insisted that Israel would not withdraw without a real peace.

On the following day, threatened by the Soviet Union and under persistent U.S. pressure, Ben-Gurion reluctantly agreed that Israel would withdraw as soon as UNEF was established.

Coincidentally, on the day before Bulganin's threat to use rockets, the Soviet Union crushed the revolt in Hungary. The world failed to respond to Premier Imre Nagy's urgent appeal for help; the world was preoccupied with pressures against Israel.

The British and French completed their withdrawal on December 22. The Israelis promised to leave Sinai by January 22, but they intended to remain in Gaza in order to guard against border raids from that area and in Sharm el-Sheikh in order to prevent Egypt from renewing the blockade in the Gulf of Aqaba.

Egypt had assumed control over two islands in the Strait of Tiran — Tiran and Sanafir — back in 1950 with the concurrence of Saudi Arabia, which claimed title. On January 28, 1950, Cairo had assured the United States that passage through the narrow straits of the Gulf would be free and open. On July 1, 1951, in violation of that pledge, Egyptian patrols barred a British vessel, and Egypt began to block Israeli shipping through the Gulf as well as through the Suez Canal.

The Israelis resolved in 1956 to terminate that illegitimate action, once and for all.

In the U.N. debate, Israel kept demanding guarantees before withdrawal, but U.S. Ambassador Lodge insisted that progress toward a final settlement had to be deferred until after Israel had withdrawn.

The conflict approached a crisis on January 23, when Israel told Secretary General Dag Hammarskjold that she would not withdraw from Gaza and Sharm el-Sheikh unless her rights were protected. Israel proposed to provide civil and social services in Gaza, and ultimately to conduct a plebiscite to determine the strip's political future. In effect, this meant an Israeli trusteeship without a U.N. force.

Israel would remain at Sharm el-Sheikh until the four bordering countries — Israel, Egypt, Saudi Arabia, and Jordan — signed a treaty to safeguard freedom of navigation. In the alternative, a U.N. force could be stationed there pending a final settlement, or Israel would be satisfied with guarantees by the great maritime powers. In addition, Israel wanted Egypt to comply with the Security Council's 1951 order to permit Israeli shipping to transit the Canal.

DEBATE OVER SANCTIONS

Israel's stand precipitated the threat of sanctions. On January 24, the Afro-Asians threatened introduction of a resolution calling on all members to withhold economic, financial, and military assistance from Israel.

On February 5, the press asked Dulles about sanctions against Israel, and he replied that the United States would not take unilateral action against her. If the U.N. called for such action, "we would of course have to give them every serious consideration." He assumed that Israel's democratic institutions would compel her to show a decent respect for the verdict of the General Assembly.

Asked about Egypt and the Suez Canal blockade, Dulles said: "I would think that Egypt could also be expected to accept the verdict of the General Assembly." Dulles recalled the failure to enforce the Security Council's 1951 decision. "But I think that there is a greater recognition now of the necessity for a general compliance with the armistice."

Meanwhile, there were long and feverish negotiations between the Israelis and Dulles, and the Secretary of State tried to divide American Jews, most of whom were strongly backing the Israelis. He invited a group of major Jewish philanthropists, including leading non-Zionists, to use their influence to persuade Israel to accept the U.S. position, but they held fast and refused to qualify their support.

Dulles's equivocal comment on sanctions led to uproar on Capitol Hill. William F. Knowland (R-California), the GOP Senate leader, who was then a member of the U.S. delegation to the U.N., had been embittered by the U.N.'s failure to act against the Soviet occupation of Hungary, while it deplored Israel's move against Egypt. He read Dulles's statement as it came over the Senate cloakroom ticker and immediately protested: "To punish Israel while sidestepping the larger aggression of the Soviet Union would be most immoral and in good conscience unsupportable."

Next day, Eisenhower supported Dulles: "I personally believe that Israel has what our declaration calls a decent respect for the opinion of mankind, and I believe that she will withdraw her forces, and I would not want to speculate on the future. We are committed to the support of the U.N." Knowland would not be silenced: "I said yesterday that such sanctions would be immoral and unsupportable. What I said yesterday I repeat today. I stand on it." He repeated his statement the next day, and his views were echoed all over Capitol Hill and in the press.

Three days after Knowland spoke out, Ives and Javits announced their protest. On the following day, they were joined by Senators Sparkman and Wiley, leaders of the Senate Committee on Foreign Relations. On the next day, Representative Scott issued a statement on behalf of forty-two Republicans. Democratic representatives, led by Emanuel Celler, also issued a statement.

We wanted Lyndon Johnson, the Democratic leader, to join Knowland. Nathaniel Goodrich, who was then the American Jewish Committee's Washington representative, and I went to see George Reedy, Johnson's press aide. Reedy promised to reach Johnson as soon as possible. That Friday afternoon, my assistant and I telephoned Texas Jewish leaders to urge telegrams to Johnson.

Four days later, Reedy handed me a copy of a forceful letter which Johnson had sent to Dulles on February 11. On the Senate floor, Johnson expressed hope that the deadlock would "not revive the talk about sanctions or other methods of coercion." He called on Dulles to instruct the U.S. delegation to oppose any proposal for sanctions "with all its skill."

Johnson supported Israel's request for U.N. guarantees that the attacks would not recur once she had withdrawn her troops, and, like Knowland, he contrasted the U.N.'s gentle attitude toward the Soviet Union with its menacing threat against Israel.

Other senators joined their party leaders, including Bridges, Chairman of the GOP Policy Committee, and Saltonstall, Chairman of the Republican Conference. Both Knowland and Humphrey threatened to withdraw from the U.N. delegation. Kennedy had also sent a protest on February 11.

Johnson and members of the Democratic Policy Committee breakfasted with the President on February 19, and urged him to resist any proposal to punish Israel for her rejection of unconditional withdrawal; the U.N. could not apply one rule for the strong and another for the weak. They declared that "the merits, the justice and the morality in this situation are clear against economic sanctions." Lodge told them that the U.N. would vote sanctions unless the United States vetoed. However, he said that the United States intended to abstain.

Denying him support, the senators suggested to the President that he carry his case to the public.

Eisenhower did not refer to sanctions in his television address the following evening, but he did call for pressure to force Israel's withdrawal. At the same time he warned Egypt:

"We should not assume that if Israel withdraws, Egypt will prevent Israeli shipping from using the Suez Canal or the Gulf of Aqaba. If unhappily Egypt does hereafter violate the armistice agreement or other international obligations, then this should be dealt with firmly by the society of nations."

As for criticism of the U.N.'s double standard, Eisenhower declared that Israel's default could not be ignored because the U.N. had been unable to condemn the Soviet Union's suppression of Hungary.

"It would indeed be a sad day if the United States ever felt that it had to subject Israel to the same type of moral pressure that was being applied to the Soviet Union," he said.

Two days later, 20,000 people poured into Madison Square Garden in a demonstration of protest. We had asked Senator Douglas and Bishop James Pike to speak. Pike, who was a strong supporter of Israel's cause, and who later met his death in the Judean desert, sarcastically pointed to "a strange incongruity. Since the Russians are atheists, we are applying moral sanctions to them, but since the Israelis are imbued with a religious faith and a sense of moral value, we are open for the idea of economic sanctions for them."

While public opinion, as voiced by U.S. congressmen, was strongly opposed to sanctions against Israel, it is depressing to record that the press, which had so sharply denounced Nasser and supported Israel when the war began, now shifted and began to exert pressure on Israel to withdraw and to rely on the U.S. commitment.

Thus, *The New York Times,* on February 22, called on Israel to "put itself on the side of the angels and set itself aright with both the U.N. and the great body of world opinion."

Similarly, *The Washington Post* observed that Israel's misgivings were understandable because of past "indifference" and "pussyfooting," but that in the light of the "solemn pledge" of the United States "Israel cannot expect more, and if she cannot rely on the good faith of the United States, then she has no outside reliance of any kind."

The remarkable change in the attitude of the media reflects the ability of spokesmen for the White House and for the State Department to sway media representatives, especially those with short memories. We witnessed this phenomenon many times in our conflicts with the Administration over the years.

Under continuing pressure to withdraw, Israel finally gave her reluctant consent. She had little choice. There could be no conditions on withdrawal. However, she could state, as Mrs. Meir did, that she was withdrawing on the basis of "assumptions" that the Suez Canal would be open and that UNEF would assume control of the Gaza strip, would vigilantly protect the Gaza-Israel frontier, and would oversee the Strait of Tiran at Sharm el-Sheikh in order to ensure freedom of navigation through the Gulf of Aqaba. It was the adroit French who invented the euphemism "assumptions." Eban used to refer to them as the "immaculate assumptions." For the most part, they might have been described more precisely as "vanishing assumptions."

Contrary to Israel's expectations, UNEF did not take command in Gaza, for Nasser's forces quickly returned to resume administration and control. However, UNEF forces did guard the Gaza frontier in the attempt to curb terrorist action, which began to decline in that area. Establishment of the PLO in 1964 signaled its resumption. Nasser reinstated his blockade of Israeli shipping through the Canal in two years, in 1959, when the United States and the U.N. folded their impotent hands.

The major gain was in the Strait of Tiran, which remained open for a decade until Nasser ousted UNEF forces, precipitating the Six-Day War in 1967.

The indefatigable Johnson had never ceased pressure on the Administration. Almost daily, he would speak on the issue, either on the Senate Floor or in the country. His staff would call our office almost every day to find out whether Israel and the Administration had reached agreement. LBJ had a weapon. Until U.S.-Israeli agreement was reached, Johnson insisted on barring Senate action on the so-called Eisenhower Doctrine, which the Administration had proposed as a panacea for Middle East tensions – the request for standby authority to employ U.S. forces as he deemed necessary, in order to protect any Middle Eastern nation requesting aid against overt armed aggression from any nation controlled by international communism. He blocked passage until he was assured that Israel and the United States had agreed. Senate action came finally on March 5, after Ben-Gurion gave the order for Israel's withdrawal.

When LBJ became President years later, he faced a similar Soviet threat in the Middle East.

Chapter 13

The Collapse of Containment

THE BAGHDAD PACT MINUS BAGHDAD

The calm which followed the Suez War was evanescent and the ever turbulent Middle East exploded in 1958. Emulating Egypt's pro-Soviet and anti-American policy, Syria accused the United States and Israel of plotting against her, and on February 1, 1958, Syria and Egypt formed the United Arab Republic (UAR).

The union facilitated a three-way deal. Egypt traded cotton for wheat from Syria, which bartered cotton for Soviet weapons. Cairo Radio praised the people of Syria "who stood firm" in the face of "evil American colonialism." Saudi Arabia, whom the United States regarded as our ally, hailed the new federation.

Lebanon was threatened by civil war. Charles Malik, her foreign minister, took the U.N. floor in an unprecedented denunciation of Nasser's intrigue in the Christian-Moslem country.

Israel now faced danger on three fronts.

On July 14, 1958, the pro-Western government of Iraq was ousted in a military coup, and the Baghdad Pact to contain the Soviet Union lost its Arab linchpin. Both Lebanon and Jordan, as well as Israel, were imperiled. President Camille Chamoun appealed to the United States to fulfill its commitment to protect Lebanon under the Eisenhower Doctrine. The Administration swiftly dispatched U.S. Marines, averting the outbreak of conflict and strengthening confidence in the United States.

In the meantime, the Administration had begun a new courtship of the Arab states.

THE EISENHOWER DOCTRINE

The Eisenhower Doctrine, announced on January 5, 1957, offered $120 million in economic and military assistance to all states which subscribed to it, along with an Administration promise to help counter a Soviet threat.

The Doctrine declared that the United States was prepared to assist any nation in the Middle East dedicated to its national independence and development of its economy. It authorized the Executive to undertake programs of military assistance and cooperation, including the use of U.S. armed forces, to protect the territorial integrity and political independence of nations which requested such aid against overt armed aggression from any nation controlled by international communism.

With some misgivings, AIPAC endorsed the proposal, believing that democracy would gain in the area if the United States became its avowed defender, although Rabbi Bernstein's testimony contended that subversion was a far graver threat to these countries than aggression and that we should give priority to economic and social needs.

In fact, only one Middle East country was threatened with "overt armed aggression" from any nation "controlled by international communism." That was Israel. Egypt and Syria were receiving weapons from the Soviet Union; Israel was the only country which received none of our government's $120 million largesse.

Representative James Richards (D-South Carolina), chairman of the House Foreign Affairs Committee, allocated $118.7 million to nine countries during a 30,000-mile journey to sell the Doctrine: $67.7 million in economic aid — $52.7 million in grants, $15 million in loans — and $50 million in military aid, most of it in gifts.

Recipients of military and economic aid included Lebanon, Turkey, Iran, Pakistan, Iraq, Ethiopia, Afghanistan, and Tunisia. There was non-military aid to Libya, then ruled by King Idris.

In addition, the Administration provided Jordan with $10 million outside the Eisenhower Doctrine. There was a special $25.3 million program for Saudi Arabia, negotiated before Richards' mission.

Israel's aid program, now reduced to $25 million in loans and grants, remained unchanged in 1957, although her economic problems had become critical because of an influx of Jewish refugees from Egypt following the Sinai War and from Hungary and other countries behind the Iron Curtain. Israel needed housing for them, but that was not the type of project that would reinforce the Eisenhower Doctrine; Richards reported that Israel understood that. Nevertheless, one of the first items allocated to Arab countries was for low-cost housing and slum clearance.

The Administration had been deeply concerned about Jordan. The British had prematurely pressed Hussein to join the Baghdad Pact, and Nasser's friends in Jordan staged riotous demonstrations. "Courageous partisans,"

Pravda hailed them. Two pro-Western governments succumbed in quick succession. Hazza el-Majali, an outgoing Jordanian prime minister, charged that the rioters were Communists bribed by Saudi Arabia. Cairo demanded that Jordan spurn the annual British subsidy. Hussein had to promise to keep out of the Baghdad Pact, and Britain's Sir John Bagot (Glubb Pasha), who had built the Arab Legion and had served the Hashemite dynasty for a generation, was summarily expelled.

Jordan was promised $35 million from Saudi Arabia, Syria, and Egypt to replace the British subsidy, but both Syria and Egypt defaulted. Saudi Arabia, with U.S. aid, put up $14 million. Iraq was not interested.

While receiving arms from the Soviet Union, Syria wanted arms from the United States as well, expecting the two major powers to compete in order to "protect" her neutralism. Syria now constituted a threat to Jordan. Washington rushed Globemasters and Flying Box Cars, jeeps, guns, and ammunition to save Hussein and initiated a military aid program—a $10 million grant to enable him to purchase the weapons previously supplied by the United Kingdom. U.S. aid to Jordan totaled $30 million in a two-month period.

Israel looked the other way, as she often did when the United States helped her Arab neighbors, and ignored Jordanian rhetoric, such as that of General Hafiz Majali, Jordan's Chief of Staff, who insisted that there were no strings attached to U.S. aid and that "as soon as it becomes possible for our armed forces to prepare themselves, Jaffa and Haifa will be in our pocket. . . . There is no place in our homeland for Jews or world Zionists."

Israel's one gain in 1957 was UNEF's presence at the Gulf of Aqaba, enabling her to use the port of Eilat, but Jordan's Foreign Minister Samir el-Rifai proclaimed, on September 10, that "the Gulf of Aqaba is 100 percent Arab, and we do not recognize any right to it by any other quarter. We emphatically reject the view advocating freedom of shipping. We do not see any reason for the continued presence of UNEF."

It was a bad time for the United States, reaching an unhappy climax when the Russian Sputnik flashed across space in October of 1957. A delirious Cairo Radio boasted that the Arab crescent and the Red Moon were cousins and taunted the United States: "The enemy of mankind, freedom and peace—where is your Sixth Fleet?"

ISRAEL UNDER ATTACK

Pro-Arab propaganda was on the rise. Senator Ralph Flanders (R-Vermont) made a series of brief speeches in July and August of 1958 attacking U.S. policy. He blamed Israel for Middle East tensions, held Zionists responsible for Arab assassinations of Arab leaders, and urged a reduction in aid for Israel. He challenged the United Jewish Appeal.

I asked Johnson and Knowland to issue a joint statement repudiating the attacks, but they persuaded me that I was exaggerating Flanders' impact, and that if the two Floor Leaders joined in rebuttal it would put Flanders on page one. However, as the Flanders speeches grew more vitriolic, Javits decided to speak out. He asked me to prepare a point-by-point reply and to rally some of his colleagues to join him in a colloquy with Flanders on the Senate Floor.

Accordingly, when Flanders rose to begin his fifth speech, he was startled by a chorus of dissent from Senators Humphrey, Wiley, Douglas, Symington, Clark, Neuberger (D-Oregon), Proxmire (D-Wisconsin), and Saltonstall.

Humphrey had agreed to make a speech defending the UJA, but only on condition that I write it. I told him that he was the one senator who did not need any help from me; he was an expert on the subject. But he insisted. That day, as always, Humphrey spoke brilliantly. As he concluded, he added insult to injury by asking leave to introduce additional "notes" he had prepared for the occasion—my draft. On the following day, I met Humphrey in the Senate subway and told him that the Congressional Record showed why he would some day be President of the United States, and why I would probably remain a ghost writer.

The negative attitude of American diplomats was painfully evident. The Reverend Karl Baehr, Executive Director of the American Christian Palestine Committee, protested to the new Secretary of State, Christian A. Herter, against statements made by Ambassador Sheldon Mills in Amman. Mills had told American visitors that he had sympathized with the Jews during the Hitler era but that the Jews had committed an equally grave crime against the Arabs by driving them from their homes. If Faisal had remained alive, Zionists would not have been able to colonize Palestine. Further immigration into Israel would precipitate an explosion. A Middle East map in his office blanked out Israel.

On December 11, 1957, Edward M. J. Kretzmann, public affairs adviser in the Bureau of Near Eastern Affairs, addressed the Institute of World Affairs in California, referring to an "aggressively national Jewish state whose establishment was achieved at the expense of dispossessing close to a million Arabs."

Fulbright's Foreign Relations Committee held public hearings on Middle East policy, and the prospective witnesses, including myself, had been listed. We were speedily scratched, however. Instead, the Committee heard former Ambassador Minor, who complained that the public celebration of Israel's tenth anniversary did not reflect "impartiality." Americans had to face, "boldly and realistically, the fact that the Arabs regard the collection of private tax-free funds for Israel as an American subsidy." (Ironically, AFME, of which Minor was president, was then receiving the secret CIA subsidy.)

In 1959, Fulbright fought the confirmation of Ogden Reid, *New York Herald Tribune* publisher, as U.S. ambassador to Israel, because he regarded

Reid as a political appointee. I urged members of the Senate Foreign Relations Committee to support Reid's confirmation. Sparkman and Morse quickly agreed. Humphrey was not so easily persuaded, but finally said that he would go along. Kennedy was opposed. In the end, Reid was confirmed.

In 1958, Israel celebrated her tenth birthday. The two Floor Leaders, Knowland and Johnson, once again joined forces, this time to offer a resolution in the Senate commemorating Israel's anniversary. There was a gala celebration in New York, where Justice Felix Frankfurter and historian Henry Steele Commager delivered significant addresses. Frankfurter read excerpts from Mark Twain's *Innocents Abroad* describing the primitive and barren Palestine which confronted travelers to the Holy Land less than a century ago. Commager drew a distinction between nationalism that was "malignant" and nationalism that was "benign." The nationalism of Israel was humanistic, civilized, and devoted to peace. The nationalism of her neighbors took the form of "chauvinism, militarism, and territorial and cultural imperialism."

Chapter 14

Aid for Arabs Up—
Aid for Israel Down

COURTSHIP OF EGYPT

The United States renewed its courtship of Egypt in 1958. The aging Senator Theodore F. Green (D-Rhode Island), who had become chairman of the Senate Committee on Foreign Relations in 1957, insisted that Nasser could still be won for the West and urged denial of Israel's appeals for arms and security guarantees.

Fulbright told the Senate that the past equivocal attitude toward Egypt had been the source of much of America's Middle East troubles, but he said: "We seem to have matured somewhat in our understanding of the strong drives of Arab nationalism."

Pro-Arab organizations were active. Dr. Edward L. R. Elson, President Eisenhower's pastor and former AFME chairman, declared that it was important to keep Arabs and Israelis apart, to allow them to cool off.

Our government now began a substantial aid program for Nasser: $48 million in agricultural commodities under the PL480 program; $10 million in economic and technical assistance; and a $5 million Export-Import Bank loan for a fertilizer plant. On July 29, just three days after a violent Nasser speech, the UAR purchased $57.7 million in U.S. wheat and flour for Egyptian pounds. Aid to Egypt rose in 1959.

In addition, Egypt wanted $290 million to deepen and widen the Canal to permit transit by large tankers, which had been forced to transport their oil around the South African cape. However, Dulles insisted on freezing Nasser's dollar balances in the United States until Egypt settled with the Suez Canal stockholders whose property Nasser had nationalized.

In contrast, U.S. aid to Israel was declining as it switched from grant to loans and from the grant of surplus foods to commodity credits. By 1958 grant aid to Israel was down to $7.5 million, and in March 1959 we were dismayed to learn that even this relatively small sum was to be eliminated.

I met with members of the House Committee on Foreign Affairs to argue that it was wrong to phase out the grant aid program to Israel at a time when she was absorbing refugees from Hungary and Rumania and when her foreign currency debt was rising. The Administration contended that it was necessary to cut the budget and to include aid for new countries, whose needs, they suggested, probably exceeded those of Israel.

Six members of the House Foreign Affairs Committee sent reassuring replies to my memorandum. Humphrey publicly urged the Administration to reconsider.

Fulton, one of Israel's strongest friends, went to see Under Secretary of State C. Douglas Dillon, who suggested that if the House Committee wished aid to Israel restored it should recommend it in its report. The Administration, he said, would certainly be guided by the recommendation and it would not be necessary to amend the legislation.

Dillon reiterated this view to the Committee, which made the recommendation in its report. He expressed the same opinion when questioned by Morse in the Senate Committee and emphasized that the Administration would make every effort to remedy the psychological and political feeling that there had been some diminution of interest in Israel. The money was restored.

Chapter 15

The Issue of Discrimination

During the 1956 Senate hearings, attention had been focused on Saudi Arabia's refusal to permit American Jewish soldiers to be stationed at the Dhahran base, and there were demands on Capitol Hill to terminate the agreement which had been consummated during the Truman Administration in 1952.

Resolutions introduced in the House by Representatives Sidney Yates (D-Illinois) and Henry Reuss (D-Wisconsin) protested our government's submission to discrimination. Former Air Force Secretary Thomas E. Finletter testified that the Saudi airfield was not vital to American interests.

In the Senate, Lehman offered a resolution which declared that distinctions against U.S. citizens were incompatible with the relations that should exist between friendly nations and that every reasonable effort should be made to maintain that principle. It was adopted unanimously.

Despite this resolution and the platform declarations adopted by both parties at their national conventions, the Dhahran base agreement was renewed in 1957. On April 23, the press asked Dulles whether any effort had been made to persuade King Saud to reconsider. Dulles explained that he did not find the King's attitude "very receptive, largely perhaps because . . . he had not been given non-discriminatory treatment himself in the city of New York."

King Saud had made a state visit to the United States early in 1957, as our government sought unsuccessfully to persuade him to embrace the Eisenhower Doctrine. Eisenhower had welcomed him personally at the airport, but New York did not roll out the red carpet.

On July 8, 1959, Senator Morse offered an amendment to the Mutual Security Act to deny aid to countries which discriminate against Americans on the ground of race or religion. Liberals like Douglas, Humphrey and Javits supported Morse, but Fulbright and John Sherman Cooper (R-Kentucky) were opposed. Cooper said that this was "an unhappy situation in which we have to balance the security of our country against practices which we do not like." Kennedy offered an amendment to permit the President discretion, and Morse reluctantly accepted it.

Fulbright contended that the bill was not the proper vehicle to reform the world's moral problems. He foresaw complications, for, he told the Senate, Iceland did not admit Negroes, Norway did not admit Jesuits, and India had its "concept of untouchability." Norway abandoned its restriction in 1956.

Despite reservations, Fulbright was willing to accept the amendment and take it to conference with the House; but a suspicious Morse, knowing that Fulbright would quickly abandon the amendment in conference if he could, insisted on a roll call vote to put the Senate formally on record. To Morse's dismay, he was defeated 47 to 43.

Often a loner, Morse had not given us advance notice of his proposal and there had been no opportunity to campaign for it. It was now agreed to renew the fight when the foreign aid appropriations came up for a vote. Javits and 21 other senators joined Morse as co-sponsors, and I wrote to some 4,200 members of our Committee to rally support.

Meanwhile, there had been a favorable court ruling in New York. The Arabian American Oil Company (ARAMCO) required prospective employees to fill out applications for Saudi Arabian visas, which ask for the candidate's religion. The New York State Commission Against Discrimination had ruled in favor of ARAMCO's claim for a bona fide occupational qualification. The American Jewish Congress appealed for a court review, and the New York State Supreme Court overruled the Commission. It brushed aside the argument of the State Department, which had protested that U.S. policy in the Middle East might be jeopardized if ARAMCO were not exempted from the state's laws against discriminatory employment.

The New York court said: "If the enforcement of the public policy of New York State would embarrass the State Department in the Near East, then it should be said that the honor of American citizenship – if it remains for New York State to uphold it – will survive ARAMCO's fall from Arab grace."

Saudi Arabia, ARAMCO had disclosed, objected to the employment of Jews not only in Saudi Arabia but anywhere in the company's operations, including the United States.

Morse and Javits carried their proposals to the Senate Appropriations Committee. Morse asked me to prepare a complete statement of the history and background of the American struggle against discrimination, at home and abroad. He submitted the statement to the Committee and it was read into the Senate record. The Committee approved the amendment and it was accepted by the Senate without debate. It declared that attempts to create distinctions because of race or religion among American citizens in the granting of personal or commercial access are repugnant, and that in all negotiations arising as a result of appropriations under this act, "these principles shall be applied as the President may determine."

The amendment led to a showdown over "The Freedom of the Seas."

Chapter 16

The Freedom of the Seas

REVOLT ON THE HILL

Determined to strangle Israeli shipping, Nasser began to block ships carrying cargoes to Israel early in 1959. The United States withheld action. It regarded this issue as Hammarskjold's responsibility.

Meanwhile, Nasser negotiated an agreement with the World Bank for a $56 million loan to widen and deepen the Suez Canal. At the same time, he agreed to pay $81 million to compensate Suez Canal stockholders for nationalization. There were widespread protests from labor, Congress, and the press—challenging a World Bank loan as long as Egypt closed the Canal.

Hammarskjold won a concession. The UAR would not interfere with shipping provided cargoes were shipped f.o.b. from Israel and c.i.f. to Israel in non-Israeli ships; that is, the cargoes would be the property of the sender en route to Israel and of the buyer as soon as the cargoes left Israel. But Egypt broke its promise, confident that the loan would be approved.

Thirteen members of the House Banking and Currency Committee urged Eugene Black, president of the World Bank, to withhold the loan. On December 21, the day that it was to be approved, I telephoned many members of Congress, who were then home for the holidays. Within a few hours, 67 congressmen from 17 states had signed a joint telegram to Black and Dillon, urging deferment of the loan, but to no avail.

Two days later, Nasser celebrated the third anniversary of the Suez Canal victory at Port Said and declared: "We will reiterate here again that we will never let Israeli ships pass through the Canal."

148

As 1960 began, I wrote to our constituency, appealing for renewed support for AIPAC. I pointed out there were ominous signs of reversion in U.S. policy to the 1953-1955 appeasement period. I set forth an agenda for 1960: to make certain that the grant aid program to Israel continues; that Israel's requests for aid are not tested by Arab criteria; that her security needs are met; that her water program goes forward unimpeded by Arab threat; that Arab propaganda is answered; that the Arab boycott is challenged; and that the Suez Canal is opened. "We will ask the political conventions for positive platform declarations guiding the presidential and congressional candidates in a reaffirmation of American friendship for Israel."

I went up to the Hill early in January and found many angry congressmen. Some suggested that I draft legislation to oppose loans and grants to aggressors. I drew up a statement for inclusion in the preamble of the foreign aid bill—a declaration of policy barring aid to countries which boycott countries which also are recipients of U.S. aid.

The amendment read:

It is the sense of the Congress that inasmuch as—

(1) the United States favors freedom of navigation in international waterways and economic cooperation between nations; and

(2) the purposes of this Act are negated and the peace of the world is endangered when nations which receive assistance under this Act wage economic warfare against other nations assisted under this Act, including such procedures as boycotts, blockades, and the restriction of the use of international waterways;

(3) assistance under this Act and the Agricultural Trade Development and Assistance Act of 1954, as amended, shall be administered to give effect to these principles, and, in all negotiations between the United States and any foreign state arising as a result of funds appropriated under this Act or arising under the Agricultural Trade Development and Assistance Act of 1954, as amended, these principles shall be applied, as the President may determine, and he shall report on measures taken by the Administration to insure their application.

I consulted Morse, Javits, and Humphrey, who were sympathetic but suggested that I begin on the House side, where foreign aid authorizations originate. Besides, it might be difficult to win the Senate Committee on Foreign Relations because of Chairman Fulbright's inevitable opposition.

I took the amendment to House Committee members Leonard Farbstein (D-New York), Wayne Hays (D-Ohio), James Roosevelt (D-California), and Barrett O'Hara (D-Illinois). They also approved. The Hays-Farbstein amendment was accepted by the House Committee, 19 to 13, on the first day that the Committee began to mark up the 1961 Mutual Security authorization.

The Commitee report declared that the United States had been ineffective in urging "removal of the restrictions on the free movement of commerce through the Canal." The Committee recommended continued aid for Israel, for "against great odds Israel has continued to be a bulwark of stability in an otherwise disturbed area."

On April 7, 1959, a Greek ship, the *Astypalea,* had been forced by Egypt to yield up her cargo. The *Inge Toft,* a Danish freighter, which was held up in Port Said for eight and a half months, had surrendered her cargo on February 4, 1959.

My Israeli friends were worried about a confrontation with the Administration on this issue, but I felt that we should not discourage congressmen from expressing resentment of Nasser's aggressive policies. Moreover, we emphasized that the amendment was a statement of policy and not a categorical ban on assistance, for the President was given discretion.

The amendment was approved in the House on April 21, without debate, but Fulbright ignored it in the Senate Committee. He had reported out the foreign aid bill before the House vote.

As a result, we had to win concurrence on the Senate Floor by offering the House language as an amendment. I took counsel with Sparkman, a ranking member of the Senate Committee, who urged me to draft an amendment similar to, but not identical with, the House version. I disagreed. That would have permitted Fulbright to accept it without debate and to take it to a Senate-House conference committee, where he doubtless would have succeeded in killing it. It was clear that we would lose in conference, but an amendment identical with the one approved by the House would be inviolate.

I was in Omaha that weekend to address a Hadassah regional conference. On my return flight, I met Morse, who told me: "You must not weaken on this issue; you must call the roll. Insist on it. You must offer the amendment in exactly the same language and you must mobilize support. Be sure to round up enough co-sponsors for the amendment to give your proposal the weight it needs."

On Monday I invited eight legislative aides to lunch. They included McCulloch, Douglas's legislative assistant, and Steve May, adviser to Senator Keating. We decided to ask two leading senators to sponsor the amendment and to enlist as many co-sponsors as possible.

We all agreed on Douglas as our lead sponsor. My second choice, on the Republican side, was Cooper of Kentucky, who had always impressed me because of his judicial background. I asked Lee White, his legislative aide, if Cooper would co-sponsor, and I asked for an early answer. Javits would have been the Republican co-sponsor, but he was then in Europe for a NATO parliamentary conference. Meanwhile, May was urging me to enlist Keating as the lead-off Republican.

White's preliminary answer was that Cooper probably would co-sponsor, but a short time later he reported that Cooper had changed his mind. He would not co-sponsor, but he would support us on the Floor. We put Keating's name on the amendment.

We called our leading constituents and national Jewish organizations to appeal for co-sponsors. By Thursday, when the bill came up for debate, we had 30 co-sponsors, including John Kennedy, as well as Mike Mansfield (D-Montana) and Thomas Kuchel (R-California), the Democratic and Republican whips. Differing with Fulbright, nine members of the Senate Foreign Relations Committee—a majority—were among them.

We now sought the crucial support of LBJ, who had opposed sanctions against Israel two years earlier. We appealed to Reedy, his aide, and to Dallas friends.

The debate was swift. Fulbright registered his opposition. Douglas replied. He had once told me that he and Fulbright disagreed on such issues as civil rights, regulation of utilities, and U.S. policy toward Israel. We were trailing as the roll call began, but when Johnson voted with us, other Democrats followed his lead, some of them revising their earlier vote. We won.

Fulbright charged that the amendment would accomplish nothing "beyond the appeasement of certain uninformed minority groups in the United States," and was obviously designed for local political advantage in this country. "What it will accomplish is to annoy the Arabs and fortify them in their conviction that in any issue arising from the Arab-Israel controversy, the United States, because of domestic political pressures, will be on the side of the Israelis."

Fulbright was supported by Senators George D. Aiken (R-Vermont), Bourke B. Hickenlooper (R-Iowa), Francis Case (R-South Dakota), Cooper, and Dirksen, the Administration's leader. Cooper's opposition surprised us; we thought he had promised to vote with us. "When some sponsors talked to me about this amendment, I indicated my sympathy with its objectives," he told the Senate. "But on reflection and study, I am convinced that the amendment can have no effect toward opening the Suez Canal and I shall vote against it," he said.

Douglas, Keating, and Ernest Gruening (D-Alaska) argued that the Arab boycott and blockade had been intensified and that the United States must strengthen its policy.

Douglas detailed the increasing U.S. assistance to the UAR. Special Assistance money would be used to expand Cairo's airport and its propaganda facilities. American assistance to the UAR would exceed $100 million in 1960, not including the World Bank loan.

Off the Senate Floor, I encountered Senator Frank Lausche (D-Ohio), whom I had known when he was Cleveland's mayor. Impugning the loyalty and integrity of the amendment's supporters, he angrily declared that "somebody ought to stand up for the United States." Later, he made a similar statement on the Floor, and his colleagues, like myself, were offended.

Dirksen, speaking for the Administration, said that the proposed amendment would demonstrate favoritism and would render difficult our efforts to bring about a relaxation of tensions. It would be an effort to tie strings to our economic aid and threaten its use "as an instrument of political coercion."

On the day before the vote, Eisenhower told the press that he did not know what the United States could do to force the UAR to respect Israeli shipping rights in the Suez Canal "unless you want to resort to force . . . and I'm certain that we are not trying to settle international problems with force. We have done everything we could to make it clear that we stand by our commitments and we think that other nations should do the same, particularly when it comes to the free use of the Suez Canal."

We won by a substantial majority—45 to 25. Eventually, the total recorded in the affirmative reached 62.

Douglas offered the routine measure to reconsider, and then Johnson moved to table the Douglas motion, thus to block reconsideration and end the debate. Fulbright and his supporters tried to induce Johnson to withhold his motion to table and to permit reopening of the debate on Monday. The Arkansas senator accused the Senate of "irresponsible action."

Johnson said that Fulbright's procedure was a reflection on the Senate. He did not believe that "a single senator is going to be misled or change his convictions as a result of what is happening. . . . I see no reason for attempting to get a pressure operation going." He demanded a roll call; the motion to table was approved 40 to 29, with 31 not voting.

On the next day, Fulbright offered new amendments. He could not change the language of the freedom-of-the-seas statement already adopted, but he proposed to add a new section to the effect that the President should not regard the statement as applicable when two or more nations receiving assistance were engaged in actions detrimental to U.N. efforts to maintain peace and stability and when U.S. action would constitute partiality.

Fulbright offered a second amendment related to Arab refugees. He proposed to incorporate the language of paragraph 11 of U.N. Resolution 194 (adopted in 1948) that "refugees wishing to return to their homes and live at peace with their neighbors should be permitted to do so at the earliest practical date . . . ."

In a "Face the Nation" program, Fulbright had previously linked free passage through the Suez Canal with the problem of the Arab refugees, in an attempt to justify the blockade. He argued that the Arabs regarded Israeli cargoes as their property because the Israelis had deprived them of their land and their property.

McCulloch and I drafted a telegram for Douglas and Keating charging that Fulbright's amendment would nullify the Senate action. We deplored the attempt to impugn the motives of the majority of Congress and warned that Fulbright's amendment would be a damaging retreat and would serve as a green light to the UAR to persist in its blockade of the Canal.

Fulbright produced a letter from Acting Secretary Douglas Dillon declaring that while the purpose of the Douglas-Keating amendment "is fully consistent with the long-standing objectives of the U.S. government," its inclusion would be "counterproductive" and would have harmful repercussions on U.S. interests in the Middle East.

Concerned about the refugee problem, I sent a lengthy night-letter urging senators to oppose Fulbright's proposal. In summary, I pointed out: "It emphasizes repatriation without mentioning resettlement, which is the only logical solution for the vast majority of the refugees. It fails to call upon the Arabs to negotiate a peace settlement, the major part of the 1948 resolution from which the Fulbright amendment was extracted. It encourages extremist Arab propaganda demands as it fortifies Arab resistance to resettlement. It exposes Israel to pressures that she commit suicide by admitting a potential fifth column. It is inconsistent with authoritative reports on this issue, including the Hammarskjold study, the Taft 1953 report, the Humphrey 1957 report, the Smith-Prouty 1954 report, the Carnegie Endowment report, and many other findings. It is a disservice to Arab refugees, to Israel, and to the best interests of the United States."

The Israeli embassy was uneasy about the entire clash, and one envoy went so far as to suggest that we permit Fulbright's first amendment to pass if he would drop the second. I disagreed.

Home from his NATO conference, Javits took the Floor in forceful opposition to Fulbright's amendments, pointing out that the issue was not partiality or impartiality. The question was the honoring of international commitments.

Dealing with the second Fulbright amendment, Morse read my lengthy memorandum on the refugee problem on the Senate Floor.

Keating passionately warned that a Senate reversal would encourage Nasser and his "fellow highwaymen" to continue their "high-handed" tactics. Replying to Fulbright's smears of minority groups, pressure groups and lobbies, Keating exclaimed: "I freely admit to being a lobbyist for this amendment. Far from fearing the effects of such lobbying, I fear the effects if our nation is ever deprived of those who will lobby for what they believe is morally and legally right."

Reflecting his growing impatience with Fulbright's tactics, LBJ offered a motion to table the Fulbright amendment—an unprecedented action by a Floor Leader directed against a committee chairman. His motion carried 45 to 39, with 16 absent or not voting.

Fulbright never asked for a debate or a vote on his refugee amendment.

So we won a splendid paper victory. Despite the action taken by Congress, aid to Egypt continued. So did the blockade of the Suez Canal and so did the U.S. courtship of Egypt's Nasser. Nevertheless, this clash marked the beginning of a more articulate role for Congress in the conduct of U.S. foreign policy in the Middle East.

Chapter 17

A Multitude of Promises

Because of our many setbacks during the Eisenhower-Dulles Administration and our fear that the courtship of Nasser would endanger Israel's existence, our Committee held an all-day meeting to formulate a statement of policy which would crystallize our views and emphasize the need for a more dynamic policy by our government. We also decided to convene a national policy conference on March 26–27, 1960, in Washington. Since then, a national conference has been held every year to draw up a platform and to bring community leaders to the Capitol to visit with their congressmen and to meet officials of the Department of State.

At that first policy conference, we drew up a 1,500-word statement on American policy in which we urged:

1) Continued U.S. economic assistance to Israel and the Arab peoples to raise living standards; 2) adherence to the U.S. policy to preserve the independence and integrity of the nations of the Middle East; 3) efforts to halt Soviet arms shipments to the Middle East and to prevent an arms imbalance in that region; 4) no compromise with boycott, blockade and other warlike acts; 5) resettlement of the Arab refugees in Arab countries with compensation from Israel for their abandoned property; 6) a U.S. initiative to promote direct negotiations between Israel and the Arab states.

I testified at the Republican and Democratic national conventions, offering the planks in our policy statement. The final Republican platform was reserved; our proposals challenged their record. The Democrats enthusiastically endorsed them.

154

On my way home, Colonel Jacob Arvey, the Illinois Democratic national committeeman, invited me to a meeting with Nominee Kennedy in Feinberg's suite at the Pierre Hotel in New York on August 5 and asked me to draft our questions. Kennedy came with Myer Feldman, his administrative assistant, who later became his counsel and adviser on Jewish affairs, to meet with thirteen national leaders.

Paradoxically, questions on domestic issues were assigned to a leading Zionist, Dewey Stone of Boston. My questions about Arab-Israel conflicts were offered by Klutznick, then president of B'nai B'rith and later Kennedy's ambassador to the U.N. Economic and Social Council.

Kennedy's replies were guarded. He would try for a negotiated Arab-Israel settlement, but he would first sound out the parties. He did not know how Nasser could be persuaded to come to the peace table, but he did not intend to force Israel to accept an unsatisfactory peace.

It was necessary to maintain Israel's strength and a commitment to intervene if Israel were attacked. If the Soviet Union rejected disarmament, Israel would get the arms she needed. I asked whether the United States would provide the arms directly; Kennedy was not ready to say. However, he became the first president to do so.

He said it was absurd to ask Israel to repatriate all the refugees, but that Israel should absorb some in a peace settlement. The majority could be resettled in underpopulated Arab countries like Iraq. He agreed that a new effort was needed to open the Suez Canal. Asked for comment on Fulbright's opposition, Kennedy said, "He is a rational man but he went overboard on this issue."

On domestic issues, he denied that his father, Ambassador Joseph Kennedy, had ever been anti-Semitic. None of Kennedy's children had ever been guilty of that, and, he said, apples do not fall far from the tree. He had opposed his father's isolationism, but his father's diary repudiated any indication of sympathy with Berlin.

Kennedy's record showed that, with the exception of his opposition to economic aid for Israel and the Arab states in 1951, he had taken a pro-Israel position. He had questioned the 1954 arms shipments to Iraq and had favored U.S. aid to Israel when the Soviets armed Nasser. On February 11, 1957, the very same day that Johnson protested against the Dulles threat of sanctions against Israel, Kennedy wrote a similar letter, urging that Israel be given guarantees if she withdrew her forces and that her right to act in her own defense under Article 51 of the U.N. Charter should be recognized. This was prophetic, for Israel did invoke Article 51 in the 1967 war.

But Kennedy was not a special pleader for Israel. He also recognized the right of the Arabs to be neutral, and he believed that the United States must come to terms with Arab nationalism.

In a moving speech on Israel's tenth birthday, in 1958, before B'nai Zion, Kennedy rejected the Arab propaganda myth which holds that "without Israel there would somehow be a natural harmony throughout the Middle East and the Arab world. . . . Quite apart from the values and hopes which the state of Israel enshrines—and the past injury which it redeems—it twists reality to suggest that it is the democratic tendency of Israel which has injected discord and dissension into the Near East. Even by the coldest calculations, the removal of Israel would not alter the basic crisis in the area."

During our New York interchange, Kennedy accepted an invitation to speak at the forthcoming ZOA convention. I pointed out that U.S. policy in the Middle East was the concern of all Americans and that this speech should be delivered over national television, but I was overruled.

Many in Kennedy's audience were older than he, but he rapidly bridged the generation gap as he recalled that Herzl was only 37 when he proclaimed the "inevitability" of Israel's "triumphant reality." He said, "The Jewish people, ever since David slew Goliath, have never considered youth as a barrier to leadership."

Candidate Nixon was not present at the ZOA convention, but he sent a message reassuring Israel of his support. Unwittingly he stumbled, for he proposed to refer the issue to the U.N. and to Ambassador Lodge, unmindful of the U.N.'s anti-Israel stand in 1956 and Lodge's demands for Israel's forthwith and unconditional withdrawal. Nixon himself had made a speech in Hershey, Pennsylvania, in November 1956, praising the Administration's Suez policy as proof of U.S. willingness to stand with an African country against America's allies—England, France, and Israel—a demonstration which had won the gratitude of the "neutralist" Afro-Asian world.

Most welcome was Kennedy's promise to call a peace conference: "I propose that all the authority of the White House be used to call in a conference the leaders of Israel and the Arab states to consider privately their common problem, assuring that we support in full their aspirations for peace, unity, independence and a better life, and that we are prepared to back up this moral commitment with economic and technical assistance."

Kennedy promised friendship, economic aid, and guarantees against aggression: "The United States meant what it said in the Tripartite Declaration of 1950." He lashed out at Eisenhower's "empty and negative rhetoric," at "the series of incredible blunders which led to the Suez crisis," and at the "repudiated Eisenhower Doctrine."

Kennedy considered appointing Fulbright as his Secretary of State. Civil rights organizations opposed Fulbright because he opposed school desegregation. How could Fulbright be effective with African leaders, they asked.

We offered no protest when Kennedy chose Rusk, his brother Robert's choice. We regarded Rusk's appointment as ominous, for he had fought Israel's establishment at the U.N. in 1948. But Israel's Ambassador Avraham Harman urged me to forget the past, and never once during Rusk's eight years as Secretary did we attack him as the author of our reverses.

The Department of State sought to dampen Kennedy's ardor. They drafted position papers which reviewed all previous initiatives: the armistice agreements in 1949 (which had succeeded because Bunche had insisted that the Arabs and Israelis speak directly to each other); the PCC's vain effort in 1949–1950 to transform the armistice agreements into peace treaties (which had failed because the PCC had yielded to the Arab refusal to meet with the Israelis); the Clapp mission of 1949 to determine whether economic development might help resettle the refugees; the Tripartite Declaration of 1950; the renewed effort of the PCC in the same year; the UNRWA effort to promote a works program in 1952–1953; the arms to Iraq to cement the Baghdad Pact in 1954; the Eric Johnston water project in 1953–1955; the Dulles proposal for security guarantees with its built-in veto; and the ill-fated gesture to assist in the construction of the Aswan Dam.

All these projects having failed, the Department came to believe that time—and therapy rather than surgery—would eventually knit severed and wounded tissues. As for future options:

The Arab boycott? To exaggerate its impact would encourage Arabs to redouble their efforts. They rationalized that some Israelis welcomed the boycott, for it stimulated them to leapfrog hostile Arab frontiers.

Arms for Israel? They reiterated the pretense that "the United States had never been an arms supplier to the region," even though we had armed Saudi Arabia, Jordan, and Iraq and had offered arms to Egypt. Anyway, they argued, Israel could get supplies from the French.

A treaty to guarantee against aggression? The U.N. was on the scene with UNTSO, with the MACs, with UNEF—all "trip wires" against aggression. In the current climate, the United States was encouraging neutralism and was opposed to new pacts and alliances. Moreover, it might provoke the Russians into signing a similar treaty with Egypt.

Pressure on Nasser? To single him out would drive him closer to the Russians at a time when they were criticizing his hostile treatment of Egyptian Communists.

FREEDOM OF THE SEAS

To avoid another Floor fight on the freedom-of-the-seas amendment, I negotiated with the State Department for the inclusion of an acceptable policy statement in the forthcoming foreign aid bill. The Department agreed to include this statement:

"The Congress declares that it is the policy of the United States to support the principles of increased economic cooperation and trade among nations, freedom of navigation in international waterways, and recognition of the right of all private persons to travel and to pursue their lawful activities without discrimination as to race or religion."

Even this mild version irked Fulbright, and he complained to the State

Department's witness, Assistant Secretary Phillips Talbot, who hastened to explain that the paragraph had emanated from the White House. The State Department, he said, would not object to its deletion.

Fulbright insisted on adding a paragraph that the United States must not take sides in any controversy between countries having friendly relations with the United States. Later, in the House-Senate conference committee, Fulbright's declaration of "neutrality" was thrown out, and Congress included its own addendum:

"In the administration of all parts of this Act, these principles shall be supported in such a way in our relations with countries friendly to the United States which are in controversy with each other as to promote an adjudication of the issues involved by international law procedures available to the parties."

Sargent Shriver, Kennedy's brother-in-law, sturdily held his ground when he testified as director of the Peace Corps to the effect that he would not send the Peace Corps into any country which barred Jews. Fulbright was provoked, but Shriver was not intimidated. He was acting in conformity with the laws of Congress, he said. There would not be any religious or racial tests for Peace Corps volunteers, nor agreements with any countries which set up unsatisfactory standards.

DIRECT TALKS AND BRAZZAVILLE

We were dismayed by the Administration's opposition to our major proposal: the call for direct negotiations.

Recalling Kennedy's pledge, I urged the House Committee on Foreign Affairs to include a call for direct talks in its report on the foreign aid bill, and the Committee readily agreed. I was alarmed when I learned that State Department officials had objected.

Worse was yet to come. Seeking to combat anti-Israel resolutions, 16 nations joined at the U.N. to co-sponsor the "Brazzaville" resolution, which urged the parties to negotiate a peace settlement. The co-sponsors were: Central African Republic, Chile, Congo (Brazzaville), Costa Rica, El Salvador, Gabon, Guatemala, Haiti, Ivory Coast, Liberia, Madagascar, Netherlands, Niger, Sierra Leone, Upper Volta, and Uruguay. Mrs. Meir appealed to Rusk for U.S. support, but the U.S. delegation insisted that the resolution had no meaning and voted against it.

America's negative stand was censured on the Hill and in the press. Both *The New York Post* and *The New York Herald Tribune* charged that the United States had missed an opportunity to let the Arabs know that the international community disagreed with them.

The resolution won 34 supporters from Africa, Europe, the British Commonwealth, and the Western Hemisphere. Only two Western Hemisphere nations voted no: the United States and Cuba. There were 44 nays and 20 abstentions.

Ambassador Francis T. P. Plimpton explained that the United States was opposed to anything that might divert attention from the forthcoming Joseph E. Johnson initiative for repatriation of Arab refugees, which it regarded as simple, direct, and constructive.

Arab diplomats had accused the sponsors of selling out to Israel, to which Arsene Assouan Usher of the Ivory Coast retorted: "Saudi Arabia may be used to buying Negroes [a reference to the old slave traffic], but it can never buy us."

THE BOYCOTT ISSUE

The State Department was also reluctant to move against the Arab boycott. Early in 1961, the state legislatures of New York and California memorialized Washington to act. Brooks Hays wrote that the government disapproved the boycott, but minimized it. Only 25 U.S. ships had been blacklisted, and this because they carried "materials or instruments of war."

The State Department equated measures taken by Israel with those taken by Egypt. It pointed out that restrictive clauses in ship charters negotiated by the UAR included a prohibition against sailing in Israeli waters prior to discharge. Similarly, it continued, the Israeli government had included a clause in its Title 1, Public Law 480 cargo charter contracts forbidding transporting vessels from sailing in Arab waters or from calling at Arab ports prior to discharge. But the resemblance between these two restrictions was superficial. Israel did not want ships bringing her foods to sail in Arab waters where they would be confiscated, but she did not blacklist Arab ships as such. Thus, Israel's safeguard was a defensive measure, while the Arab prohibition was aggressive.

Surprised by indignant reaction to his letter, Hays wrote a much stronger statement, promising every effort "to facilitate progress toward resolution of the boycott problem and to eliminate discrimination in the use of international waterways."

Subsequently, the Department mustered up some spunk when Cairo threatened that Helen Hayes could not appear in Thornton Wilder's "The Skin of Our Teeth" in Cairo if she persisted in a Tel Aviv performance. The State Department rejected the ultimatum. Miss Hayes played in Israel and then in Beirut, skipping Cairo.

THE JOHNSON INITIATIVE

The conventional propaganda myth of the time was a strategem based on wishful thinking. The problem of the Arab refugees could be solved if only Israel conceded their right to repatriation, in which event most of them would opt for compensation and resettlement elsewhere. That was the premise of Kennedy's peace initiative—the Johnson plan to permit the Palestinian refugees freedom of choice. They could opt for return to Israel, for resettlement in another Arab country, or for emigration abroad.

The proposal had been advocated in a staff study in the Senate Foreign Relations Committee, which contended that only older people—not more than 10 percent—would choose to return and that, once the repatriation principle had been accepted, Arab leaders would no longer resist resettlement.

The number of repatriates would be restricted to about 100,000 and the process would be stretched over a ten- to fifteen-year period, in deference to Israel's economy and security. Words like "poll," "plebiscite," and "referendum" would be avoided. U.N. offices would be opened at gasoline stations, where refugees would record their skills, training, and aspirations.

The President named Dr. Joseph E. Johnson, president of the Carnegie Endowment for International Peace, to act as mediator. Johnson's report to the Palestine Conciliation Commission revealed his sensitivity to Arab views. In his initial report, on November 14, 1961, he reviewed early history, accurately noting that the Jewish Agency had accepted partition, that the Arab Higher Committee had rejected it, and that the Arab armies had invaded Israel. When the Arabs objected, Johnson offered a new draft eleven days later, in which he deleted his earlier references to Arab negation and aggression. Instead, he wrote that "endemic Arab-Israel violence" was transformed after the expiration of the British Mandate into "organized warfare between the Arab states and the newly proclaimed state of Israel." Thus, Johnson began a mission which was doomed to failure because it raised Arab expectations while brushing aside Israeli fears.

Such fears were groundless, it was argued, because many repatriates would not remain once they realized how their city or village had changed. Israelis disagreed. They believed that repatriates would find Israel an attractive place and that Israel would not have adequate controls to guarantee her security.

Feldman carried the proposal to Ben-Gurion, along with a letter in which Kennedy wrote that the United States government would use its influence "only in support of those proposals which do not involve serious risks for Israel." Ben-Gurion told Feldman that Israel wanted a limitation on the total number to be admitted and the right to bar undesirables. There had to be an end to anti-Israel propaganda incitement, the process had to be terminated if repatriation demands exceeded 10 percent, and the Arabs had to agree to resettle the remaining 90 percent simultaneously, lest Israel's concession be overtaken by the high Arab birth rate.

Initially, they would interview 2,000 refugees, and Israel would be expected to repatriate up to 200. If that initial poll showed that more than 10 percent were opting for repatriation, the poll would be ended.

In a seven-page reply to Kennedy, Ben-Gurion warned that the plan would prove "ineffectual" and would result only in "complicating matters even more for us without any advantage accruing to the refugees themselves."

For their part, the Arabs were questioning the proposed poll because they insisted that they had the right to return to their own homeland. And would the United States drop the project after canvassing only 2,000? Moreover, they claimed both repatriation *and* compensation.

On his return to Washington, Feldman was astonished to learn that the plan had been changed during his absence and submitted to the PCC and to U.N. delegations. Some 27 phrases had been added and 37 deleted.

The revised plan, first published in *The Chicago Daily News* on October 1, enabled refugees to fill out confidential questionnaires, permitting them to opt for repatriation, or for compensation and resettlement. They could claim their property or compensation for it. Indemnities would be based on 1947–48 values with adjustments for lost interest, money depreciation, and rights in community properties, mosques, and churches. All would receive a $250 grant from a U.N. fund to which governments and the public would contribute.

Contrary to Feldman's assurances to Ben-Gurion, there would be no ceiling on the number of repatriates. All refugees would have to respect Israel's laws, but there was no requirement that they become Israeli citizens or "live at peace with their neighbors." There was no ban on hate propaganda and no way to terminate the poll. Individual Arabs rejected by Israel as security risks could appeal to an impartial U.N. body to rule whether they were treated fairly.

In his first draft, Johnson had written:

"Israel will, of necessity, always have the right to make the decision as to how many refugees can be admitted both in any given period and ultimately."

The revised draft stated:

"Establishing ceiling figures on the number of refugees who might be admitted to Israel would appear contrary to both the letter and the spirit of paragraph 11 [of the 1948 U.N. Resolution]."

Feldman protested to Rusk. Since he had been directed by the President to discuss the plan with Ben-Gurion, he thought that he should have been consulted about the proposed changes and that these should have been taken up with the President.

In a letter which Ben-Gurion authorized Harman to circulate, he wrote:

"Israel will regard this plan as a more serious danger to her existence than all the threats of the Arab dictators and kings, than all the Arab armies, than all of Nasser's missiles and his Soviet MIGs. . . . Israel will fight against the implementation down to the last man. Implementation would drown the people of Israel in blood."

Israelis were not alone. Arab leaders denounced the proposal as "a prelude to the entire liquidation of the Palestine issue in Israel's favor . . . and a devious attempt to surround the inalienable rights of the Arab nation of Palestine with equivocation, detract from them or fritter them away."

State Department officials tried to assure the Israelis that the Feldman commitment to Ben-Gurion was valid and that no one could really force a sovereign state to accept refugees who might endanger her security. They contended that they would still induce the Arabs to agree that Israel should have ample safeguards.

Meanwhile I had written a special eight-page *Near East Report* supplement on the history of the Arab refugee problem, citing the many precedents and arguments for resettlement as opposed to repatriation; a copy of it was brought to President Kennedy's attention.

In that document, I emphasized that there would have been no Arab refugees if the Arab states had not gone to war against the U.N. partition resolution and if they had resettled the Palestinian Arabs in their own vast territories, where there was room, need, and opportunity for them.

The document stressed that no refugee problem had ever been solved by repatriation and that in many conflicts there had been a population exchange. In that connection, it pointed out that as some 600,000 Arabs left Palestine, a similar number of Jews were forced to leave Arab lands. It cited the many U.S. reports, committee resolutions, and convention declarations calling for resettlement rather than repatriation and recalled the American precedent: The 13 American colonies had rejected the seven-year British pressure that they permit the return of Tories who had opposed the Revolution and who had fled to Canada.

Feldman protested at a session with Johnson and with State specialists — Assistant Secretary of State Harlan Cleveland and top Administration aides Talbot, Sisco, Bundy and Komer — but he was a minority of one. The others argued that Israel's rejection was merely a gesture that Israel could be made to accept, that negative Arab talk was merely for the record, and that the Arabs were prepared secretly to agree, although they had to oppose the plan publicly.

Johnson optimistically believed that all parties would acquiesce even without formal consent. Feldman carried the issue to Kennedy, who was not surprised. When the meeting ended, he ruled that the United States did not have much to gain by pursuing the initiative and that our country's prestige was too important to be involved in the sponsorship of a futile gesture. He preferred to see the issue returned to the PCC for burial, to be revived only if there were some hope of success.

THE BATTLE FOR WATER

In 1962, the more radical Arab states besieged Israel's water development plan with gunfire and with elaborate schemes to divert the sources of the Jordan River over the mountains and southeast to Jordan, as well as under the Lebanese mountains to the Mediterranean.

Kennedy had reviewed and approved Israel's ongoing water irrigation project, which was consistent with the Eric Johnston plan.

The Syrians were clamoring for instant war, but Nasser said that the Arabs would not be ready for four years: "I can't accept the semi-war logic. When I start a war, I take it to the only end I accept, which is decisive victory." Nevertheless, Cairo baited the Syrians, whereupon the Syrians shot at Israeli fishermen on the Sea of Galilee and on Israeli settlements at Dardara, Mishmar Hayarden, and Ein Gev, eight times between February 1 and March 7.

Israelis charged that two fishermen had been machine-gunned and that the Syrians had used armor-piercing bullets to injure them when an Israeli boat raced to their rescue. Syrians counter-charged that the Israelis had machine-gunned Syrians. U.N. observers found large holes in the Israeli police boat. The shooting was renewed on March 15 and 16. Mrs. Meir complained in vain to Secretary General U Thant and to the U.N. Truce chief, General Carl C. Van Horn. On the next day, three Israeli columns struck at Syrian gun emplacements, suffering six deaths while Syria lost 30. Both complained to the Security Council, where, on March 28, Ambassador Adlai E. Stevenson declared that there had been provocation and retaliation, both contrary to the armistice agreement. But he continued: "Whatever the facts, they do not justify the Israeli reversion to any policy of retaliation raids." An Anglo-American resolution condemned Israel and ignored her complaint. The vote was 10 to 0, with France abstaining because "the guilt was shared."

There was an uproar in Congress and in the press. A bitter Ben-Gurion denounced the resolution as an insult, warning that Israel would not permit Syrian aggression in the Galilee or yield her right to self-defense.

Ten senators telegraphed Rusk calling for negotiations, and Keating and Scott defined "even-handedness" as "the palm of the hand for the Arabs; the back of the hand for Israel." Democratic Senators Morse, Douglas, Gruening, Symington, and Humphrey joined Republican colleagues in a Floor demonstration. *The New York Times, The Herald Tribune, The Washington Post* and *The New York Post* condemned the Administration's stand.

We urged House members to sign a declaration deploring continued Arab belligerence against Israel and calling for direct negotiations. Six Democrats and six Republicans joined in co-sponsorship: Celler, Farbstein, Hays, Kelly, Multer, and Rooney—Democrats; Martin, Curtis, Fulton, Halpern, Seely-Brown, and Weis—Republicans. Scheduled for publication on Israel's 14th anniversary, the statement soon won 232 signatures—more than a majority.

Reflecting dissatisfaction with State Department policy, the declaration asserted that the issues which divided Israel and the Arab states, such as border disputes, economic development, refugee resettlement, and disarmament, could be resolved if the leaders agreed "to meet honorably in recognition of their mutual right to free existence in peace. There is no effective alternative."

The 232 representatives urged the United States to press for an Arab-Israel peace; to protest against the maintenance of belligerence, hostility, and threat; to reject all forms of aggression; and to make it clear that we do not condone war and that we persist in the search for peace.

In August 1963, the Israeli U.N. delegation complained that between December 4, 1962, and August 21, 1963, the Syrians fired 98 times at fishermen, farmers, and police. They had kidnapped three Israelis and their three Belgian guests who were boating on the Galilee. Three 19-year-old Israeli farmers from the village of Almagor had been ambushed by Syrian soldiers on August 19; two had been murdered. This time a majority of the Security Council sympathized with Israel, approving a mild Anglo-American resolution to condemn the wanton murder of the two Israeli farmers—mild because there was no explicit censure of Syria. All supported it, except the Arabs and the Soviet Union, which rescued Syria with its veto.

THE HAWK

Israel's deepest worry was the growing Arab military arsenal. Ben-Gurion met Kennedy to renew his plea for arms in 1960, before the election, and he asked for another meeting early in 1961 after Kennedy took office. The embarrassed Administration, which did not want Ben-Gurion to be the first head of state to call on the new President, preferred to doff its hat to Bourguiba of Tunisia. However, unable to resist Ben-Gurion's urgent plea, the President saw him in his Waldorf Astoria suite in New York. They talked on two different levels for some 90 minutes. Ben-Gurion kept arguing for arms to ensure Israel's security, while Kennedy kept asking what Israel could do for the Arab refugees, who, Ben-Gurion kept insisting, would undermine Israel's security. Ben-Gurion also urged Kennedy to raise the peace issue at his forthcoming meeting with Khrushchev.

The Soviet Union had always paced the Middle East arms race. Swiftly the MIG-15s were succeeded by MIG-17s, by MIG-19s, and then by MIG-21s. The arsenal also included 50 IL-28s, the same light-medium bombers which the Russians had supplied to Cuba and the removal of which Kennedy had demanded because of their grave threat to our own country. Israel had learned to live with these, and with much that was more lethal and at a much closer range.

Israelis were most alarmed by the Soviet Tupelov-16 long-range bombers which were delivered to Egypt in 1962—the first time they had been sent outside the Communist bloc and Indonesia. They could fly long distances without refueling, at 550 miles per hour, with a bomb load of 10 tons and six 23-millimeter cannon.

In May, Ben-Gurion sent two of his most articulate military experts—Shimon Peres, Deputy Defense Minister, and General Aharon Yariv, the Director of Intelligence of the Israeli Army, to explain Israel's need. I met Peres in Jerusalem that summer to hear his own cogent argument. However, I was not involved in the negotiations; I confined my efforts to the columns of the *Near East Report*.

Peres argued that at least nine countries feared Egyptian expansionism. The issue was not merely one of siding between states. One had to side between policies. Israel was a democracy; Egypt was not. Israel should be treated like other democracies. France had armed Israel and had not been injured.

Israel's air force was its defense arm against Egypt's six mechanized and armored divisions and her two-seas navy, but could Israel's planes take off rapidly enough to meet attacking forces? The real Egyptian threat was the Tupelov-16 bomber. Israel's fighter planes could not intercept them because Nasser had fast MIG-21s. The Hawk was the only effective defense against the heavy bomber.

Early in the Administration, the United States had agreed to provide Israel with an early warning system, but even with that system Israel would have only 14 minutes notice of the arrival of a MIG-21 at Tel Aviv, and 24 minutes warning of the TU-16. Egypt had 19 airports. If the TU-16s took off from a nearby field in Sinai and flew low to evade radar detection, they could devastate Israel's airfields and air force before her interceptor planes could rise to meet the threat. Suppose Egyptians destroyed Israel's airfields, making it impossible for Israelis to land? Out of action, the Israeli air force could not stop land forces and the navy from advancing from all sides. Thus, the Israelis urgently needed the Hawk, the guided missile which operates by means of a radar beam bounced against its target. Its name is an acronym—an abbreviation of Homing All-the-Way Killer.

The Israelis made an irresistible case, and Kennedy gave a landmark decision. For the first time, the United States agreed to provide Israel with arms, but they were defensive and they were not a gift.

The United States loaned Israel the $23 million needed to buy the first six batteries for a ten-year period at an interest rate of 3.5 percent. The British were annoyed because they had planned to sell Israel the Bloodhound, a comparable weapon but less effective and more expensive than the Hawk. Since Israel was not a NATO member, she had to pay for training as well as for the weapons. The Hawks and their crews did not appear publicly in Israel until the 1965 Independence Day parade.

At first the decision was tentative and conditional. Strong, veteran director of the Office of Near Eastern Affairs, went to Cairo to tell Nasser that if he would agree to slow the arms race the United States would not supply Israel with advanced weapons, but this mission failed.

The negotiations on Israel's application were entirely secret. The Israelis made no effort to stimulate pressures from Jewish organizations and

Congress. Kennedy himself made the decision, overruling the State Department. But I questioned the political manner in which he revealed his decision. Instead of an announcement to the press and to the country at large, he invited a group of Jewish leaders to break the news at a private session at the White House on September 27, 1962—a procedure which angered the press.

THE TURBULENT YEAR

Kennedy's neutralist strategy, his hope to please both sides in every troubled area, plunged him into a multitude of predicaments in the turbulent year of 1963. His pursuit of former enemies whom he sought to befriend alarmed our allies, whose fears he constantly sought to allay by strong but quiet commitments.

Golda Meir met Kennedy for some ninety minutes at Palm Beach on December 27, 1962, and she appealed for guarantees after our appalling U.N. record. She described Syrian attacks on Israel's Galilee settlements, the fear that German scientists were aiding Egypt, and the Soviet arms buildup. Kennedy was eager to explain and justify the U.S. posture.

He gave her the warmest reassurances. The U.S.-Israel relationship was special, paralleled only by the relationship we had with England. There should be no misunderstanding. If Israel were attacked, the United States would come to her aid. However, the United States wanted to be able to talk with both sides in regional conflicts—with both India and Pakistan, with both Israel and the Arab states. Kennedy did not want to give up on the refugee issue. Mrs. Meir suggested that any new discussions about refugees be held in Israel to permit Ben-Gurion's participation.

Internecine conflicts flared in Arab countries in 1962 and 1963—Kennedy's final years—and Israelis were alarmed by mounting Arab threats. They were most apprehensive because German scientists were designing rockets for Egypt. Israeli scientists charged that they planned warheads to spread radioactive waste and make Israel uninhabitable. Having itself employed German scientists, our government belittled the charges, claiming that but 15 Germans were helping Egypt to develop guidance systems for her crude rockets and that about 290 Germans and 100 other Europeans were run-of-the-mill technicians and research workers engaged in the airplane industry. Scott and five other senators appealed to Kennedy to use his good offices with European governments to discourage their scientists from developing Egypt's weapons.

Revolts in Iraq and Syria heightened the alarm. On February 8, 1963, General Abdul Karim Kassem of Iraq was overthrown by a junta of Ba'ath party officers, pan-Arab socialists headed by Abdul Karim Aref, Nasser's man in Iraq. That led to optimistic speculation that Communists would be purged.

America swiftly recognized the new regime. One month later, there was a similar revolt in Syria with pro-Nasser demonstrations in Damascus. On April 17, Syria, Iraq, and Egypt proclaimed a new United Arab Republic, with Nasser as President, Cairo as its capital, and three stars in the Egyptian flag. Their manifesto called for Palestine's liberation. Israel's U.N. delegation complained that such a declaration in a constitutional document was unprecedented and a threat to international peace and security.

Pro-Nasser demonstrators rioted in Amman and Jerusalem, demanding Hussein's abdication and Jordan's accession to the new UAR. They sewed a fourth star in the new UAR flag. Hussein ordered a curfew and sealed off the capital.

The Sixth Fleet was moved to Israel's coastline to protect Jordan as Kennedy reassured Hussein. The crisis ended on April 28, with 12 dead. The United States believed that the threat to Israel had been exaggerated.

Two days earlier, on April 26, 1963, Ben-Gurion emotionally appealed to Kennedy to join Khrushchev in a guarantee of the territorial integrity and security of every Middle East state. Kennedy doubted that he could secure Khrushchev's cooperation.

A few days later, Ben Gurion told CBS that he favored a U.S.-Israel alliance as an alternative to a Kennedy-Khrushchev pronouncement. In his reply on May 5, Kennedy reassured Ben-Gurion of U.S. concern for Israel's security and integrity. He believed that U.S. economic relations with Egypt *reduced* Soviet influence and served to restrain any Arab nation hostile to peace and U.S. interests.

On May 8, Javits called on the President to invite Britain and France and other interested nations to join in a collective defense agreement with Israel and other Middle East nations. He was joined by 16 senators. On that same day, Democratic senators sympathetic to Israel offered a resolution emphasizing the need to head off the arms race and reaffirming the Tripartite Declaration of 1950.

Meanwhile, AIPAC held its annual policy conference with a luncheon co-sponsored by the Greater Washington Jewish Community Council, marking Israel's 15th anniversary. Kuchel and Feldman were the speakers. Feldman's strong statement, which he had cleared with Kennedy, made headlines: "We are committed to the integrity of Israel. . . . Israel is here to stay and we are doing everything we can to make sure that it is so. We do not intend to sit on the sidelines if there is any threat. . . . A world which allows Israel to falter or fail could not itself survive anarchy."

On the next day, Ben-Gurion told the Knesset that the Arabs were planning attack and that he disagreed with the optimism of Western statesmen.

The President decided to reassure Israel publicly. At a press conference on May 8, he said that the balance of military power had not been changed, that there had been political changes, and that the United States supported social, economic, and political progress in the Middle East.

"We support the security of both Israel and her neighbors," he said. "We seek to limit the Near East arms race. This government has been and remains strongly opposed to the use of force or the threat of force in the Near East."

In the Knesset, Ben-Gurion declared that a U.S. attempt to limit the arms race in the Middle East could intensify the danger of war. The policy could be applied only to Israel and not to the UAR, since the United States could not halt the arms from the Communist bloc to the UAR. Again he called for joint U.S.-Soviet action to halt arms competition. "It is not Arab unity that endangers Israel; it is the dogma that Israel must be wiped out," he maintained.

Kennedy and the State Department had correctly assumed that the Egyptian-Syrian federation would not be consummated. The proposed UAR began to disintegrate in July, as Nasser denounced the "fascist government of Damascus."

Despite many differences, Kennedy was convinced that he could win and hold Nasser for the West, but he no longer had illusions about his promised peace conference. He had issued his invitation on May 11, 1961, and had received a long and negative response on August 18. Nasser could afford to reject Kennedy's peace initiative because the United States was increasing economic aid and would not permit friendship for Israel to block it. We were soon to formalize a large three-year surplus foods program for Egypt—a very substantial commitment—as well as a three-year food agreement with Israel.

Fulbright was similarly optimistic. "I only hope," he said, "that we can be sensible enough not to irritate them or to present the case falsely so as to drive them back into the Soviet orbit, thus allowing them to develop friendly relations." He thought that we should cut our aid to Israel because we had given her so much and because her standard of living was out of line with her neighbors. "You might consider helping the UAR a little more in the future," he said.

How real was Egypt's break with the Soviets? Between 1955 and March 31, 1960, Soviet loans and grants had totaled $788 million. Soviet military aid was $443 million—a total of $1.231 billion—and it was continuing.

Meanwhile, Nasser's economic policies—the virtual elimination of the private sector—had a devastating impact.

By 1962, Egypt's foreign currency reserves, dropping ever since World War II, had all but disappeared, and the Egyptian pound had fallen. Egypt was unable to meet pressing debts to Suez stockholders, and to Sudan to pay for property inundated by the Aswan Dam.

American diplomats surveyed Egypt's economy, and the United States provided Egypt with another $40 million in surplus foods. It was also agreed to lend $17 million and grant $23 million in Egyptian pounds to finance a $40-million grain storage system, an installation first recommended by Joseph during an ancient famine. In fiscal 1961, U.S. aid to Egypt, mostly in surplus foods, totaled $161 million.

The agreement to sell Egypt surplus foods for Egyptian pounds amounted to $390 million; subsequent amendments elevated the total to $431.8 million. The State Department claimed that Nasser had categorically promised not to attack Israel, that he had renounced activism, and that it was safe to involve Egypt economically with the West.

IRAN AND AFRICA

As the United States courted Egypt with its new neutralist policy, Iranians feared that Washington might cool the relationship with them established in 1953, when Mossadegh was ousted with the help of the CIA.

An Iranian intelligence chief, Teymour Bakhtiar, came to Washington in 1961, and lectured congressmen and myself on Iran's importance to the West, hoping to persuade the Kennedy Administration to maintain its traditional friendship and support. I was naturally sympathetic because Iran had a warm *de facto* relationship with Israel despite Arab protests. I commended U.S.-Iran relationships in the *Near East Report*.

In 1962, I flew to Iran and to African countries to survey Israel's far-flung technical assistance programs. African and American diplomats were grateful for Israel's innovative and down-to-earth aid. The Shah was then breaking up large estates; Iranian farmers needed to learn about cooperatives. Iran's liberal Minister of Agriculture, Hassan Arsanjani, told me that Iranians had learned more from Israel than from any other country because Israelis worked side-by-side with Iranians, in their shirtsleeves and overalls. The new Iranian cooperatives were sending leaders to Israel to learn how to run them. There were then some 65 Israelis working in Iran as schoolteachers, nurses, road builders, and agricultural experts who worked on the ground, introducing the growth of cotton, increasing the sugar beet crop, and utilizing water resources.

(Teymour Bakhtiar later defected, going over to the opposition, like his cousin Shahpour Bakhtiar, who tried to set up a new government during the 1978-1979 conflagration. Teymour was killed in Iraq where he had taken refuge.)

Everywhere in Africa I heard praise for Israel's economic and technical assistance. In Ethiopia, Emperor Haile Selassie was offering the presidency of his university to a retired Israeli army general. An Ethiopian diplomat reminded me of Theodore Herzl's promise to help liberate Africans after the Zionists had established their state.

In Ghana I learned that the donor of aid is considered to be the real beneficiary. Nkrumah had joined Nasser at Casablanca to denounce Israel, and Israel's Ambassador Michael Arnon went to the Ghanaian foreign minister to complain about Ghana's participation, in view of Israel's extensive aid program in the country. He was rebuked: "What are you complaining about? Don't we let you help us?"

AIPAC did not protest against U.S. aid to Egypt. We agreed that economic aid to the Arab people was sound, hoping that it might divert the Arabs from military adventure, but we questioned the U.S. evaluation of Nasser. We believed that a major reason for tension was Egypt's overpopulation and need for *lebensraum*.

Rival Arab leaders opposed U.S. aid to Nasser. Mecca Radio, voice of the devout Saudis, on May 21, 1962, called Nasser a "wretched little pharaoh" who had sold out to Washington. Nasser told his Arab critics that the war against Israel must wait until the Arabs were liberated and united, until reactionary kings were overthrown, and until the Arab fifth column had been eliminated.

AIPAC's 1962 policy statement endorsed economic aid to the Arab states but complained about dissipation of Arab resources on Soviet weapons.

Keating wrote to Rusk asking whether the Administration had sought or obtained any guarantees from Egypt. He argued against long-term aid commitments to Egypt until Nasser agreed not to acquire additional Soviet weapons. Dutton tried to reassure him: "Whereas we obviously do not agree with aspects of the UAR position on the question of Palestine it may be said that the UAR-Israel border has been quiescent for several years and the UAR military posture vis-à-vis Israel is essentially defensive. We have been assured on numerous occasions by UAR and other Arab officials that they do not intend to undertake aggression against Israel." (Dutton became a highly paid lobbyist for Saudi Arabia in 1975.)

Our aid to the UAR rose. By fiscal 1962 it had reached a total of $263 million. Keating complained: "The American people are getting sick and tired of giving aid to countries which use their own funds to buy arms from Russia."

In the *Near East Report* we charged that U.S. wheat shipments to Egypt were helping Nasser to acquire additional Soviet weapons, for wheat shipments enabled him to plant more cotton, which he could then trade for arms. The Department of State replied that Nasser had surplus cotton which he could not market in Europe, and that he would use it to pay for arms, whether we sent wheat or not. Critics recalled that, after World War II, Egyptians began eating wheat instead of rice. They had become short of wheat and as a result had limited the production of cotton. Now this limitation was no longer necessary because of American wheat shipments. Thanks to American generosity, the Egyptians could grow all the cotton they needed and have enough to trade for their weapons.

Nasser's intervention in the Yemen civil war and his threat to Saudi Arabia, Jordan, Israel, and the British port in Aden exposed his ambition. In a furious speech at Port Said on December 23, 1963, he pledged the liquidation of all pro-Western interests:

"Our forces in Yemen will see to it that every aggression and . . . the bases of aggression . . . run by Saudi Arabia are destroyed," he declared.

The author (right) with former Representative Thomas Morgan, Chairman of the House Foreign Affairs Committee.

Mr. Kenen with Senator Edward Kennedy at an AIPAC luncheon.

A critical moment at the U.N. in 1949: it has voted to internationalize Jerusalem.

Mr. Kenen listens as Abba Eban speaks at an AIPAC Policy Conference.

Following Israel's admission to the U.N., Israel's flag is hoisted in the circle of banners for the first time at Flushing Meadow on May 12, 1949.

Representing Israel in the Trusteeship Committee at the Fourth General Assembly of the U.N. in 1949 are (left to right) Lillian Friedman, I.L. Kenen, and Itzak Ben-Meir.

The first Israel U.N. delegation is seated, May, 1948.

Mr. Kenen and Senator Hubert H. Humphrey at an AIPAC Policy Conference.

Mr. Kenen and Bella Abzug.

The author with Representative Henry Reuss.

I) Former Secretary of State Henry Kissinger and Mr. Kenen meet at a State Department Conference.

AIPAC calls on President Eisenhower in 1953. (Mr. Kenen is located at far left.)

"The revolution in Yemen . . . will soon triumph everywhere against reactionary elements, against King Saud and King Hussein, since it was they who declared war.

"Arabs can never tolerate the existence of imperialist domination over any part of the Arabian peninsula. . . . We cannot consent to any English-made governments." Time, Nasser said, was on Egypt's side. "All is going well, reaction is collapsing . . . breathing its last breath. . . . The liberation of Yemen is a step on the road leading to the elimination of Zionism."

The State Department warned that ending aid to Egypt could have dire results, for Nasser could manufacture incidents against U.S. offices, our nationals, and our interests, including the sabotage of oil pipelines, refineries, and wells. He could provoke border raids against Israel, interfere with Israeli shipping at Aqaba, and expel UNEF from Gaza (which he later did). He could interfere with oil companies and he could enlarge Soviet influence. Suspension of aid to Egypt, they predicted, would reproduce the turmoil which had resulted from the withdrawal of the Aswan Dam offer. On the other hand, they predicted, if we increased aid and trade with Egypt, the UAR would become dependent on us for machinery, parts, and raw materials and would become so enmeshed with the West that it would not want to disengage itself. Ultimately, it would abandon its anti-Israel posture.

Nevertheless, skeptical congressmen urged amendments to deny Egypt further aid and further sales of surplus foods. Some wanted to mention Egypt by name; some wanted a mandatory ban on aid which would leave no discretion to the President; others preferred another general statement of principles.

The House Committee on Foreign Affairs approved a Farbstein amendment to bar assistance to any country which the President determined was engaging in or preparing for aggressive military efforts "against the United States or against any country receiving our aid" until the President determined that such efforts had ceased. No country was mentioned by name, but Chairman Thomas E. Morgan (D-Pennsylvania) told the House that the amendment applied to the UAR.

The Committee reported: "Consideration should be given to the withholding of economic assistance from those countries which persist in policies of belligerence and in preparation for their execution and to enter into security guarantees with those nations that will be willing to make appropriate commitments for promoting peace and stability in the area."

The House approved the Farbstein amendment without dissent. In the Senate, the same amendment was sponsored by Gruening and Javits. They were joined by Keating, Case, Williams, Ribicoff, Dodd, Morse, Young, Muskie, and Douglas. Fulbright offered a substitute that would have permitted the President to waive the prohibition if he were unable to determine from all the facts whether or not an aggression had occurred or might occur, or if the facts were determined by an appropriate international body as aggressive, or if he determined that the national security of the United States would be affected adversely.

The Senate defeated the substitute, 46 to 32, with 22 not voting.

Fulbright objected that Congress was attempting to usurp the discretion of the Executive and that "it was not merely writing foreign policy," but "seeking to tie the President's hands in the actual administration of it."

Nevertheless, on November 7, 1963, the Senate voted 65 to 13 to approve the amendment, with 17 of the 22 absentees recorded in favor. Thus, 82 of the 100 senators, including JFK's brother Edward M. Kennedy (D-Massachusetts), wanted to end the aid to Nasser policy. The angry Arab press and radio denounced "the mad policy by senators who have sold their names, country, and fame to the devil for Zionist funds" *(Al-Gomhuria)*.

Kennedy ruefully surveyed the debris of his Nasser policy at a press conference on November 14, 1963. He was sharply critical. The Senate amendment required him "to make a finding which is extremely complicated," and he did not believe that this language would strengthen our hand or our flexibility in dealing with the UAR. He went on: "In fact, it would have an opposite effect. I think it's a very dangerous, untidy world, but we're going to have to live with it; and I think one of the ways to live with it is to permit us to function." If the Administration did not function, the voters would throw it out. Kennedy asked Congress not to make it impossible to function by means of "legislative restraints and inadequate appropriations."

These words were uttered at his last White House press conference. President Johnson inherited the issue and had to deal with a similar insurrection in Congress a year later.

Chapter 18

Israel's Texas Friend

NEW MAN IN THE WHITE HOUSE

Shortly after he took office, President Johnson told a visiting Israeli diplomat: "You have lost a very great friend. But you have found a better one."

As a senator, Johnson had scored Eisenhower's threat of sanctions against Israel in 1957, had censured Nasser's blockade of the Suez Canal, and had defeated Fulbright's attempt to neutralize the United States.

As President, Johnson became the first to supply Israel with deterrent military equipment—tanks, A-4 Skyhawks, and F-4 Phantom Jets—the first to invite top Israelis for an official visit to Washington, the first to propose desalting for a water-hungry land.

Differences with the Arabs surfaced soon after Johnson became President. In January 1964, the 13 Arab states held a summit conference, at which they agreed to end disputes, to divert the sources of Israel's water, and to create a unified Arab military command—the Palestine Liberation Organization (the birth of the PLO) and the Palestine Liberation Army (the PLA).

Shortly thereafter, Deputy Under Secretary of State U. Alexis Johnson addressed the newly organized Citizens Committee on American Policy in the Middle East—a pro-Arab lobbying organization. The U.S. diplomat unwittingly provoked them, when, intending to reassure them, he said that the new Administration did not plan any fundamental policy changes. He reviewed the need for political stability, economic development, modernization, the limiting of Soviet influence, an Arab-Israeli accommodation, the continued flow of oil, and access to air and sea routes. He went on:

173

"Over the years, we have found that an essential element in a workable Near Eastern policy is to avoid taking sides in regional disputes. This does not mean that we will stand idly by if aggression is committed. Any intended victim of any would-be aggression can count on our support."

This pledge inflamed the Arabs. Typical was the comment of *Al Jihad* of Jordan: "It showed obvious haste, overt bias, and an outrageous defiance of the Arabs because it came directly after the Arab summit conference."

THE NEED FOR WATER

A major speech by the President himself was also misinterpreted as a warning. Kennedy had promised to address the annual dinner of the American Committee for the Weizmann Institute of Science, and Johnson agreed to keep this engagement. "Our own water problems in this country are not yet solved. We, like Israel, need to find cheap ways of converting salt water into fresh water," the President said. "We will better pursue our common quest for water, for water should never divide men; it should always be a force for peace. And peace is first on our agenda."

Israel had experimented with various desalting techniques: distillation — separating the salt by heating the water to steam; salt water frozen in a vacuum; electrodialysis, an electric current to eliminate the salt. Could atomic energy be produced cheaply enough to finance distillation? The joint study proposed to spend some $200 million on dual-purpose plants to develop nuclear power and to distill water. The project was to be under way by 1966, and completed by 1970. Economic feasibility would depend on interest costs. A dozen years, however, were to elapse before the joint venture, greatly revised, was to get under way.

The Arab press charged that Johnson had outdone Truman, who had recognized Israel when it was born. Beirut's *Al Nahar* protested that Johnson, "the Jew," was now recognizing Israel's "future." Arabs believed that Johnson's real purpose was to warn them to abandon their water diversion projects. Arabs had calculated that the Israelis would react militarily to such projects, and that would justify an Arab counterattack. The Israelis would then be censured as the aggressors and the Arabs would be supported by world opinion. Now, to their chagrin, the President was dismissing their projects as futile, for, even if they were successful, the United States would help to make up Israel's water deficiency.

The Israelis had hoped to complete their water carrier system by mid-1964. Our government tried by diplomacy, by guarantees, and by Johnson's speech, to discourage Arab interference. The hot-headed Syrians were clamoring for action because they wanted to embarrass Nasser, but Nasser told his fellow Arabs that Egypt would not battle Israel unless she could win the war in two hours. Otherwise Israel would win in two hours.

"Be patient," Nasser said. "We will not overbid; I am not ashamed to say that I cannot fight if I feel that I cannot. Shall I bring my country to disaster? Shall I gamble with my country? Impossible. I shall not bargain in this matter." Instead, Nasser encouraged Jordan, Syria, and Lebanon to divert the Arab tributaries of the Jordan in order to transform Israel's irrigation system into a drainage ditch, and he advocated an Egyptian-led unified command, free to cross Arab frontiers and equipped with standardized (Soviet) weapons.

A newly militant Hussein came to Washington as the officially accredited spokesman for the Arabs. He demanded new U.S. tanks and planes, threatening to turn to Moscow if the United States refused. Since Hussein had expelled the British in 1958, U.S. aid to Jordan, most of it in grants, had totaled $461 million by 1964, including $30 million in military aid. Denouncing Israel's "theft" of Arab waters, Hussein charged that Israel would curtail Jordan's water supply and render the Jordan River saline and unusable. That statement was palpably dishonest, but the State Department, characteristically, remained discreetly silent.

Hussein urged American Jews to make a deep, soul-searching and agonizing reappraisal of their support for Zionism to help solve a tragedy which threatened to engulf them. An AIPAC statement "deplored" Hussein's abuse of U.S. hospitality, "while he was a guest of the President, to malign the Zionist movement, to insult the majority of the American Jewish community, to misrepresent the facts, and to distort U.S. objectives."

In view of U.S. silence, Keating queried the Department of State and, on June 17, 1964, Dutton replied that the Israeli project was consistent with the Eric Johnston plan.

In truth, the Arab states had been favored by that water plan, which had allocated 61 percent of the Jordan-Yarmuk system to them. In the north of Israel, the rainfall averages about 40 inches a year. Down south in Beersheba, the average is about 8 inches, and at Eilat it is only about 1¼ inches a year. Accordingly, every water development plan had contemplated a water carrier from north to south. The water flows through the Arab states of Syria, Lebanon, and Jordan before it reaches Israel. Up in the northern end of the Jordan valley, the Syrians and Lebanese used very little of the Jordan water, and they were allotted the percentages they requested. Jordan needed water for all her irrigable land, estimated at 120,000 acres. Given a priority, she had been allotted all the water she could use. Israel could use what was left, which would irrigate 100,000 acres.

The Arab states had never effectively used the large amounts of water at their disposal at that time. Syria and Iraq shared the Euphrates River, with an annual flow of 25 billion cubic meters. Syria and Lebanon shared the Orontes, with an annual flow of 2.7 billion cubic meters. Lebanon also had the Litani, the Awali, and the Ibrahim. Jordan had the Yarmuk, the Arnon, and the Jabbok and shared the Jordan River with Israel. Thus Syria, Jordan,

Lebanon, and Israel had a combined water supply of 30,000 billion cubic meters. The Jordan-Yarmuk system totaled only about one billion; Israel's allocation was only 3.3 percent of the total.

U.S. diplomats did not take Arab threats seriously. They suggested that Israel appeal to the U.N. if the Arabs made trouble, and they deprecated any military response. Israelis preferred to rely on their own marksmanship. They did, and they put the Syrian tractors out of commission as soon as the Syrians started digging. Nasser refused to assist the Syrians, explaining that he would not permit the Israelis to pick the time and place for confrontation. Frustrated, the Arabs began to lose interest, and by mid-1965 the threat of war seemed to be receding.

NEW WEAPONS

Thanks to Kennedy, the Israelis had secured a defensive military weapon— the Hawk. Now they appealed to Johnson for deterrent weaponry because they could not match Arab procurement. Israel needed new bombers, tanks, and missiles which could assume the offensive; Israel feared that Egypt was acquiring ground-to-ground weapons for which she had no defense. She needed shore batteries to repel the Soviet Komar missile boats, which threatened Israel's coastline. Israelis contended that their ancient Sherman and Centurion tanks and their French AMX-13s were outclassed by the 400 to 500 T-54s which the Russians had provided to the Egyptians, Syrians, and Iraqis.

Washington insisted that Israel was exaggerating the danger because Egyptian missiles were expensive but, lacking guidance systems and nuclear warheads, inefficient and worthless. The United States did not believe that Egypt could produce nuclear warheads, while most experts felt that Israel could. If the United States or France supplied Israel with missiles, she could equip them with nuclear warheads, in which event, Washington feared, the Egyptians would acquire Soviet nuclear warheads, escorted by Soviet engineers and technicians. The United States urged Israel not to buy missiles from the French.

Kennedy had been willing to supply tanks to Israel, but in 1964 the new Administration conditioned the sale of tanks on Israel's renunciation of missiles. Israelis retorted that they could not forgo missiles because American diplomats believed that Egyptians had poor aim. Arab military strength was constantly rising. They had a three-to-one advantage, the Israelis insisted. But the State Department warned Johnson that if he were not cautious the good will won by Kennedy would soon evaporate.

Department officials worried about Hussein's threat to turn to Moscow. They argued wistfully that if only the United States had provided Nasser with weapons in 1955 he might have shunned the Soviets. Saudi Arabia wanted new U.S. fighter planes to deter Nasser; if we failed the Saudis they would turn to the British.

The United States notified Israel that it did not want to sell her tanks for a catalogue of reasons: it would weaken relations with the Arabs, undermine Hussein's stability, jeopardize the Wheelus base in Libya, and provoke Arab retaliation against U.S. oil interests. Washington conceded that Israel's armor needed modernization but urged her to buy tanks from London or Bonn at prices similar to ours, keeping the deal secret.

Feldman and Frank Sloan, Deputy Assistant Secretary of Defense, went to Jerusalem on May 17 to inform Prime Minister Levi Eshkol that Israel could get American M-48s from Germany or Centurions and Chieftains from the British. Israelis feared that the British Centurions did not match the Soviet tanks, and they could not afford the expensive Chieftains. They preferred the M-48s, which the United States was then sending to West Germany. The new transaction cost Israel between $50 and $100 million, a heavy burden, aggravated because our government was simultaneously providing Jordan with U.S. tanks without charge.

THE ESHKOL VISIT

Eshkol was the first Israeli prime minister to come to Washington on an official visit. Johnson assured him that the United States was four-square behind Israel and that "it would be wherever it was needed," that our country supported Israel's water plan, that all Arab capitals had been so notified, and that he was unconcerned about any possible Arab backlash. Our Joint Chiefs of Staff felt that Israelis were much too worried about "primitive" UAR missiles, and that if Israel obtained missiles the Arabs would link them with Israel's nuclear potential. Opposed to nuclear proliferation, the United States hoped that Israel would accept the controls of the International Atomic Energy Agency, so that we could reassure Nasser that Israel was not producing atomic weapons.

Eshkol appealed to the President to understand Israel's security concern. Nasser had a three- or four-to-one superiority in planes and armor, and a vast superiority in manpower. He conceded that Egyptian missiles might not be accurate but that the million people in the Tel Aviv area offered an easy target. He feared that Nasser intended to install hundreds of missiles. There would be none in Israel for a year or two, and Nasser might not wait.

The Israeli prime minister assured Johnson that if he could persuade Nasser to give up tanks and missiles, Israel would likewise destroy her arms. Since the Soviets had not hesitated to meet Nasser's requests openly, why should U.S. assistance to Israel be surreptitious? Public knowledge of U.S. support would serve to strengthen the U.S. commitment. Israel was not producing nuclear weapons, but Eshkol could not agree that anyone should reassure Nasser about Israel's intentions with respect to this. Nasser had tried to make Egypt a nuclear power for years; he would not be affected by Israel's intentions. The UAR, he said, was an enemy, committed to Israel's destruction.

Johnson's greeting to Eshkol was wholehearted. Their joint communiqué reiterated U.S. support for the territorial integrity and political independence of all countries in the Near East. More significant than Kennedy's promise, this was a *joint* communiqué.

In 1960, when Ben-Gurion had come here, ten Arab ambassadors had protested to Secretary Herter that his visit might injure Arab-American relations. In 1964, the Arab press attachés issued a release, declaring: "The visit of Eshkol, timed as it is before the elections, may have . . . serious implications to the future of Arab-American relations."

But it was Johnson, not Eshkol, who had "timed" the Eshkol visit. It was the President, therefore, who was now being accused by the Arabs of playing politics. A furious Johnson could talk of little else at breakfast the next morning, and he instructed Under Secretary of State George Ball to tell the Arab envoys that their conduct was "unacceptable." Leading American newspapers criticized the Arab indiscretion.

A few weeks later, Eshkol reached an arms agreement for tanks with West Germany.

NASSER'S WAR AGAINST THE WEST

On February 22, 1964, Nasser warned that American and British bases in Libya and Cyprus might be used against the Arabs if there were a clash with Israel. Within 24 hours, conservative Libya, fearing a threat to King Idris's throne, promised to terminate the U.S. base. This was a serious blow. The Wheelus base had been an ideal training field for U.S. airmen assigned to NATO because of its sky, terrain, climate, and vast open space — conditions which cannot be reproduced for maneuvers in Europe. In Cyprus, Nasser undermined NATO by providing Soviet weapons and propaganda to the militant Makarios forces. From his Yemen base Nasser spurred terrorism to oust the British from Aden. Relations between Cairo and Teheran worsened, as the Shah suspected that Arab propagandists were subverting the Arab-populated oil-rich province of Khuzistan.

Khrushchev came to Egypt in May 1964 for a 16-day visit, his first to Africa. The Soviet leader and Nasser signed a 5,000-word agreement on foreign policy issues, precipitating congressional demands for implementation of the Gruening-Javits amendment to suspend aid to Egypt. Rusk wanted to retain flexibility and Talbot assured Egypt that the United States still pursued its policy of "friendly impartiality." The United States was continuing aid to Egypt, Talbot told the House Appropriations Committee, because large numbers of people would still be there long after Nasser had gone.

Washington was disturbed by Nasser's nationalization program, and congressional revolt flared anew because of Nasser's refusal to withdraw from Yemen. This was led by Representative Oliver P. Bolton (R-Ohio), with the support of his mother, Representative Frances Bolton, who had been friendly to the Arabs in the past. Bolton pointed to the Egyptian presence in Yemen, the Nasser missile threat to Israel, and the anti-Western campaign in Libya and Cyprus. While Nasser had few defenders, Rusk again appealed to McCormack for flexibility; the Administration staved off the Bolton amendment, 117 to 113.

Nasser resumed his anti-Western attacks. Leaders of "non-aligned" states assembled in Cairo. Nasser barred President Moise Tshombe of the Congo from the conference as a "tool of imperialism," keeping him under house arrest for three days and denouncing the West for supporting him even while he smuggled arms to the Congolese rebels. When American planes flew Belgian paratroopers to rescue civilian hostages from rebel forces, the Egyptians, joining Moscow and Peking, accused America of imperialist intervention against a national liberation movement.

Nasser's fiery tirades ignited passions. On Thanksgiving Day 1964, angry students mobbed U.S. government buildings in Cairo, burning the USIA John F. Kennedy Library with its 27,000 books. Egypt failed to protect the buildings, and apologies were late and grudging.

The Egyptian National Assembly, on November 30, called for aid to the Congolese rebels and attacked the "abominable crime" committed by American and British imperialism. Stevenson defended America's rescue effort at the U.N. Security Council, declaring that he had never heard such irrational, irresponsible, insulting, and repugnant language; the four-day rescue effort had saved 2,000 lives. He accused Moscow and Peking, along with Egypt, Algeria, Ghana, Sudan, and others, of illegally supporting the rebel regime in parts of the Congo.

Ironically, Nasser was then seeking additional U.S. economic aid: $35 million more in meats, poultry, and corn. To make matters worse, Egyptian jets shot down an American plane flying for a Texas oil firm which was prospecting in Jordan. The United States protested against the murder of two civilians, but the Egyptians claimed that the pilot had failed to file a flight plan.

On December 23, Nasser made his annual speech celebrating his 1956 Port Said "victory." Contemptuous of American aid, he minimized and mocked it. "We get meat, wheat, and leftovers, not factories," and Egypt can get along without it, he said. "If the Americans think that they are giving us a little aid to dominate us and control our policy, I would like to tell them that we are sorry. Whoever does not like our conduct can go drink up the sea. If the Mediterranean is not sufficient, there is the Red Sea too. We cannot sell our independence for 30 or 40 or 50 million pounds. We cannot tolerate any pressure or accept insolent words and violence. We are a hot-tempered people."

Rusk met the press that day to protest the burning of the USIA library and the attack on the U.S. plane. Asked about food aid to Egypt, Rusk replied: "If relations are to be good, both sides must make important investments in these relationships."

Repercussions on the Hill were inevitable. On January 26, 1965, Representative Robert H. Michel (R-Illinois) proposed that none of the overall $1.6 billion appropriation for the Commodity Credit Corporation be used to finance the export of any commodity to the UAR. This was approved 204 to 177. The 128 Republicans voted solidly, while Democrats were divided between resentment of Nasser and loyalty to Johnson. The House Democratic leadership explained that it was not trying to defend aid to Egypt but was opposed to tying the hands of the President.

Within a week after Nasser had told Americans to drink the Mediterranean waters, the Administration had routinely shipped another $15 million in commodities to Egypt as part of a three-year contract, as if nothing disruptive had occurred. The Michel amendment would have halted the $37 million that was still due Egypt under the contract.

Anti-Nasser feeling was running high, but Vice President Elect Humphrey, Rusk, and Ball urged Congress to permit Johnson to send the remaining $37 million if he deemed this to be in the national interest. Johnson himself declared on February 9: "If we are to protect our vital interests in this part of the world where tensions are very high, then the President must have freedom of action. It is of course obvious that relations between the United States and the UAR must be improved. It will demand effort from both countries. I cannot predict whether improvement can be achieved."

At a reception in New York on January 31, AIPAC's Executive Committee declared that it had always favored economic aid to both Arabs and Israelis but with conditions to ensure that aid was not used to finance aggression. Our statement, which Bernstein read to New York congressmen that day, said:

"It is obvious that President Nasser has outraged the patience of the American people by policies which disparage our aid, undermine our strength, and humiliate our purpose. Accordingly, we think that the action of the House of Representatives reflects the broad national consensus that aid should not be extended to nations which insult the American people and are a menace to peace. We believe that this action can strengthen the Administration in its dealings with the Egyptian government, since it conveys most dramatically the overwhelming sentiment of the American people."

However, AIPAC had never urged mandatory bans on economic aid to any specific country, and when the President appealed to the Senate for flexibility our Committee did not oppose him. The Senate Appropriations Committee voted 17 to 6 to liberalize the House amendment, permitting the President to approve the sale if he determined it to be in the national interest. The Senate reluctantly concurred by a close vote—44 to 38. The Administration made a massive effort to win the House—241 to 165.

Aid was not immediately restored, and Egypt found it increasingly difficult to make ends meet. The Soviet bloc could not replenish Egypt's dwindling food supply; it too was suffering from food shortages and was dependent upon imports from the West. Not until the very last minute—a few hours before the June 30 deadline—did Johnson finally release the $37 million for the Egyptian economy. No more loans to Egypt were to be authorized in the 1966 fiscal program, for Congress was adamantly opposed.

BONN BECOMES INVOLVED

Israel and West Germany quarreled over three issues late in 1964: Germany was reluctant to extend the 20-year statute of limitations on new prosecutions of war criminals, due to expire on May 8, 1965; and more than 70 House members, led by Celler, petitioned the Bundestag. West Germany had not forbidden its scientists from working on Egypt's rockets and jet planes, despite unanimous appeal from Israel's Knesset, and it still withheld full diplomatic relations from Israel, although it had paid Israel more than $800 million in reparations for Nazi crimes and about $5 billion in restitution to the victims who had survived, including many who lived outside Israel. The Bonn government was embarrassed, the more so because it could not publicize and take credit for its shipment of tanks to Israel.

Still courting the new Soviet leaders, Nasser "crossed" the Berlin Wall. He invited Walter Ulbricht, the head of the East German government, to Cairo for his first journey outside the Communist world. Ulbricht was to supply Egypt with industrial equipment, worth about $78 million, in a barter deal for cotton. The West German press angrily demanded prompt enforcement of the Hallstein doctrine, which called for the severance of relations. Chancellor Ludwig Erhard warned that if Ulbricht were received in Cairo, Bonn would have to end the aid that Egypt urgently needed for industrial development. Nasser countered by exposing West Germany's arms shipments to Israel and demanding their suspension. Erhard did not need to submit, because Egypt needed Bonn's aid far more than Bonn needed Cairo. Nevertheless, he yielded to Nasser's blackmail and closed the pipeline of U.S. tanks to Israel.

In the ensuing uproar, Israel's many congressional friends protested, as did the press.

Despite Bonn's capitulation, Nasser went on to receive Ulbricht, whereupon West Germany retaliated by establishing formal diplomatic relations with Israel. Nasser urged other Arab leaders to break relations with West Germany and to recognize East Germany, but he overreached. While most were ready to break with West Germany—the exceptions were Iraq and

Yemen—they were unwilling to trail Nasser all the way to East Berlin. Tunisia's Bourguiba was indignant at Nasser's pressure to force an overt break with the West.

Bonn still would not reinstate the arms deal with Israel. Its refusal presented Johnson with a new challenge.

ARMS FOR ISRAEL AND JORDAN

In 1966, we urged Washington to abandon indirection and to provide Israel with planes and tanks openly. It was no longer a secret that the United States was shipping tanks to Jordan. That became known accidentally when the USIS indiscreetly pictured the unloading of tanks at Aqaba in its Middle East publication—intended for Arab eyes only. We reprinted the story in the *Near East Report,* and *The New York Times* picked it up from us. In addition, we reported that Jordan intended to buy $80 million worth of planes from Britain, and that there was to be a $400 million Anglo-American plane and missile transaction with Saudi Arabia.

The feverish military activity had been spurred by plans to establish a unified Arab command. Nasser preferred that Jordan deal with the Soviets so that the unified Arab armies could interchange standardized weapons. The Jordanians were claiming that the USSR could help them more, even though our economic aid to Jordan's 1.5 million people was one of our highest per capita aid programs. Saudi Arabia wanted our American jets in order to resist Cairo's threat to the Arabian peninsula.

Congress reinforced AIPAC's appeal to the President. On January 26, House members, led by Celler, wrote to the President: "Deplorably, the Arabs remain committed to destroying Israel. The U.N. has been unable to challenge this illegal posture; the Soviet Union pours new weapons into Egypt, Syria and Iraq; and our own government and the United Kingdom have recently undertaken to increase the supply of planes, tanks and missiles." Hussein, in a December 15, 1965, speech to West Bank Arabs at Jenin said: "We are getting ready for the battle . . . . We are all for Palestine, to uphold what is right and to retrieve the part lost from the dear homeland." Jordan's Premier Wasfi al-Tel, two days earlier, had declared: "Jordan has become so strong militarily that it is able to fix the date and place of the decisive battle with Israel."

These pronouncements preceded the Six-Day War, at a time when Jordan held the West Bank and East Jerusalem. Thus these boasts, whether idle or not, were calling for the liquidation of *pre-1967* Israel.

Ten days after the congressional appeal, the Administration finally confirmed that it was sending tanks to both Jordan and Israel and that it intended to provide Saudi Arabia with the Hawks.

In May, Johnson went further. The United States agreed to supply Israel

with Douglas A-4 Skyhawk tactical bombers, unlike the defensive interceptors which France had sold to Israel. These can land and take off in
short distances, but they did not reach Israel until after the Six-Day War.

ECONOMIC AID TO ISRAEL

While grant aid to Israel had ended in 1959, she was still eligible for
credits. Professor John Kenneth Galbraith, U.S. ambassador to India, had
warmly praised Israel's effective use of American aid in *Foreign Affairs*
(April 1961). Although Israel was "singularly endowed with natural resources,"
he wrote, she had the four essentials: "high literacy and a highly educated
elite, the sense and the reality of social justice, an effective government, and
a strong sense of purpose."

Eisenhower and Herter had recognized Israel's difficulties and had
increased economic credits from $57.3 million in fiscal 1960 to $84 million
in fiscal 1961. Much of this assistance, $35.4 million, was in the form of a
dollar loan from the Export-Import Bank at conventional interest rates.
More sensitive to Israel's needs, the Kennedy Administration, in its first
year, had approved a long-term development loan for $45 million with the
low interest rate of ¾ of one percent. Thus total assistance in fiscal 1962
was maintained at $82 million, under more favorable conditions.

Now, in 1963, AID and the State Department exerted pressure to reduce
aid to Israel and to terminate soft currency loans, because Israel's hard currency reserves were rising, enabling her to manage her trade deficits. However, the situation was then abnormal, because Israel had dollar proceeds
from the sale of Israel bonds, as well as German reparations and restitution.

At Feldman's request, I drafted a memorandum to the White House
showing that Israel had the highest per capita foreign currency debt in the
world, and that, while her reserves exceeded $400 million, her foreign cur-
rency obligations almost doubled that. She had to borrow to build infrastructure in order to settle people, and, regrettably, too much of her
resources had to be diverted to sterile enterprise which yielded no return,
such as weapons for defense like the Hawk, for which Israel had to borrow
$25 million. Moreover, Israel's reserves were not excessive for a country
strategically exposed to sudden attack. And Israel's growth was important
because she served as an impressive democratic showcase to the less-
developed nations of Africa.

Feldman was able to challenge the State Department's recommendations, persuading Kennedy that Israel's economy still justified loans at a
concessionary rate, and these were continued through 1963 and 1964.

A bizarre difference between Israel and the State Department arose
because of U.S. reluctance to assist in the resettlement of refugees. The
Eisenhower Administration had argued that the United States could not

underwrite immigration into Israel because the Arabs regarded Israel's expanding population as a threat to their security, but the Arabs themselves were expanding Israel's population by forcing the exodus of more than 600,000 Jews from their countries. For a number of years the United States avoided financing any projects, such as housing, to help settle immigrants. If Israel wanted to open her doors to immigrants, that was her own business as a sovereign state.

This policy was continued during the Kennedy Administration, when the State Department ruled that the Jewish Agency for Israel could not qualify as a voluntary agency for the distribution of about $60,000 worth of surplus foods for Israel because it was supporting and financing immigration into Israel. Many years later, Congress generously appropriated funds for the resettlement of Soviet Jews.

We advocated one other constructive proposal that year. For several years, our government had helped U.S. institutions abroad. The American University of Beirut was a special favorite. Grants to it beginning in 1957, totaled $33 million. In 1965, Hadassah's Medical Center in Jerusalem, which ministers to all peoples and which has extended aid and learning to many corners of Africa, asked and won a grant of three million Israeli pounds—part of the counterpart funds owned by the United States. The proposal had been approved by Chairman Morgan of the House Foreign Affairs Committee and sponsored by Senator Claiborne Pell (D-Rhode Island) and 18 colleagues in the Senate.

OUR AID TO EGYPT

Despite Nasser's anti-U.S. propaganda and his belligerence, the United States still hoped to buy his friendship.

Johnson agreed to sell Egypt $55 million in American surplus wheat, cooking oil, tobacco, and frozen chickens during the first months of 1966.

On December 10, AIPAC's Executive Committee opposed resumption of U.S. economic assistance to the UAR "until that country abandons its aggressive policies."

On October 22, 1965, Gruening, who had led the fight against aid to Egypt, told the Senate that before Egypt received further aid she should withdraw her troops from Yemen, cease her propaganda against Israel and her Arab neighbors, and negotiate peace with Israel.

In the spring, Egypt submitted new requests for $150 million in surplus foods and $100 million in development loans. In May, Moscow and Cairo attacked U.S. aid to Israel. It appeared that Nasser, as *The Economist* of May 21 noted, wanted to be able to tell America to continue drinking the Red Sea indefinitely.

It had been reported that the Administration intended to allow Nasser $55 million for surplus foods, as in the previous year, but the Administration feared another attack in Congress. In June, the House, by voice vote, re-affirmed the ban on sales to Egypt, unless the President himself determined that it was in the national interest, and that such assistance would neither directly nor indirectly assist aggressive actions by the UAR.

On July 22, Nasser marked the 14th anniversary of the Egyptian revolution with a customary harangue, charging that the United States was refusing aid unless he changed his attitude toward Israel, Saudi Arabia, and Communist China.

As 1966 ended, Egypt was in deep financial trouble. Hard currency reserves were down to $14 million, half of July's level, and among the lowest in the world. Industrial activity had dropped. The IMF had refused to lend Egypt $70 million. In November, Egypt sold $25 million of its gold cover. There were strikes and widespread labor unrest.

THE BOYCOTT

Beginning in 1951, we had fought Arab boycott and blockade. There had been favorable decisions in the U.N. Security Council and in Congress. Congress had strongly opposed the closing of the Suez Canal and had also denounced Arab efforts to discriminate against Jews. In 1965, we undertook a new initiative to challenge the growing boycott of American firms which traded with Israel.

Senator Harrison A. Williams (D-New Jersey) offered an amendment to the Export Control Act of 1949, to enable American businessmen to "oppose restrictive trade practices or boycotts fostered or imposed by foreign countries against any countries friendly with the United States." Without mentioning any specific country, the legislation called upon American businessmen to ignore questionnaires which sought information conducive to boycott practices.

Williams, who was encouraged to act by Parke W. Masters, a New Jersey member of the U.S.-Israel Chamber of Commerce, enlisted Javits and 27 co-sponsors in the Senate. There were 11 sponsors in the House. Williams' legislative aide, Woodruff M. Price, visited me to prepare Williams' opening speech. We faced a tough battle. Our own country discriminated against the Communist bloc, and American business interests generally oppose government intervention in business unless it is to prevent or secure indemnification for expropriation.

We had competent help. Susan Levine Dworkin, one of our ablest writers, prepared an elaborate *Near East Report* special supplement which indicted the boycott for its blatant discrimination, as well as for some of its absurd fantasies and inconsistencies. Yuval Elizur, a competent Israeli journalist, was a reliable information source, and Elihu Bergman, then the assistant director of the Harvard Center for Population Studies and later the executive director of Americans for Energy Independence, came to work for a nominal fee. Bergman had helped Jewish refugees to run the British blockade of Jewish Palestine in the late 1940s.

The legislation was rigidly opposed by Administration witnesses: Under Secretary Ball, Assistant Secretary Talbot, and Robert E. Giles, General Counsel for the Department of State.

Everyone deeply "deplored" the Arab boycott and no one had a kind word for it, but it was claimed that the legislation would weaken U.S. efforts to enlist other governments in our programs of "economic denial" against Communist China, Cuba, North Vietnam, and North Korea. It would challenge the Arab states to intensify their boycott; it would not end the boycott. On the contrary, failure to cooperate would hurt American business interests.

Our own best witness was the late Irving J. Fain of Providence, Rhode Island, a highly respected businessman and philanthropist who was thoroughly familiar with the issues and who wrote his own testimony.

As the legislation progressed through Congress, there were many reports of the extreme lengths to which the Arabs were willing to go. In England, in 1963, Lord Mancroft was forced to resign from the directorate of the Norwich Union and Insurance Societies because he was a British investor in Israel.

In Los Angeles, it was revealed that Republic Pictures could no longer distribute its films in some Arab countries because Victor M. Carter, one of its principal stockholders, was a former general chairman of the United Jewish Welfare Fund.

In Beirut, Andrew Goodman and Mrs. Goodman of the Bergdorf Goodman Company were confined at Beirut Airport for five hours, allegedly because of Goodman's philanthropic activities in New York.

A Yale alumnus, Lee Grigg, revealed that a phonograph record of the Yale Glee Club was held up by Beirut customs because its cover bore the Hebrew letters—a part of Yale's crest—"Urim V'tummim." The record was finally released, but only after the cover was ceremoniously burned on the lawn amid Arabic imprecations, which did not harmonize with the Wiffenpoof Song.

A Hammond map-making firm received an order for its inflatable globe; Egyptian customs officials spotted Israel on the map and snipped it out. Purchasers later complained that when they inflated the globe all the air leaked through Israel.

The boycott was far from a whimsical obsession. Many large firms shunned Israel because they feared Arab reprisal. Yet when Conrad Hilton defied their blackmail, Egypt offered no objection to the construction of a Hilton Hotel in both Tel Aviv and Cairo.

Dworkin's brilliant pamphlet was widely distributed, witnesses who had been victims of the boycott were recruited, and the legislation was well on its way early in 1965. The deadline was June 30, when the Export Control Act was scheduled to expire and was due to be extended.

Friendly congressmen energetically pushed the bill in the House Banking and Currency Committee. We lost 18 to 17 on the first Committee vote, but a number of absentees later came forward to register affirmative votes and suddenly the minority report was transformed into a majority report, an unprecedented development.

The original legislation had teeth; it *required* businessmen to refuse to reply to any boycott questionnaire. When the bill reached the Floor, however, Administration forces won an amendment. The word "require" was changed to "encourage and request" by a teller vote of 96 to 54. Thus emasculated, the bill went to the Senate, where Williams tried to reinstate the mandatory language, but he lost in Committee, 8 to 6. The Senate leadership offered a compromise to strengthen the House draft. As amended, the bill required all recipients of boycott questionnaires to report that fact to the Department of Commerce and be subject to a fine if they failed to do so.

That was the way it finally passed. It was a weak bill. More than a decade later, the boycott became a much more powerful economic weapon, bolstered by tall mountains of petrodollars.

I retired in 1975, and the battle was renewed that year by major Jewish organizations, which succeeded in winning a much stronger bill.

Chapter 19

The Road to War

ISLAMIC COALITION

We were well on the way to the 1967 Six-Day War early in 1966.

The British had announced that they would abandon their costly base in Aden by 1968, and two affluent Moslem monarchies, Iran and Saudi Arabia, were concerned over the threat to the oil-rich Persian Gulf by the aggressive Soviet-supported Arab states. King Faisal believed it imperative to forge an Islamic alliance to fill the vacuum. The cleavage between rich reactionary rulers and impoverished radicals was deepening.

On February 22, 1966, Nasser charged that Faisal was financing a Moslem Brotherhood plot against his life, as well as an Islamic coalition. He had discovered broad Brotherhood support inside Egypt, where more than 200 were facing prosecution. Moreover, all around him, left-wing dictators were disappearing from the landscape. In Ghana, Kwame Nkrumah, the *Osageyfo* (the Redeemer), whose newspaper read like the *Daily Worker*, had been overthrown. Sukarno of Indonesia and Ben Bella of Algeria were no longer on the scene.

In contrast with Nasser's acerbic threats, a mild-mannered Egyptian diplomat, Anwar Sadat, speaker of the Egyptian National Assembly, was then in Washington, speaking softly. He headed a six-man parliamentary mission and was winning friends everywhere he went, even while Nasser excoriated the United States.

Johnson was embarrassed by Nasser's outburst, for he had just entered into a new aid agreement with Egypt, and Saudi Arabia's defense minister had called on Johnson just two days before Nasser spoke.

Crusading against radicalism, Faisal toured Arab states, seeking support for the Moslem summit to be held in Mecca in April 1967, where he, along with his chief ally, the Shah of Iran, who shared his dislike of Nasser, wanted to reinterpret the Koran in the light of modern conditions. He visited Turkey, where the intrusion of religion into politics was distrusted; Mali and Guinea, two evolutionary African states; and Tunisia and Morocco. Tunisia's modern Bourguiba had little in common with the Saudis, but nevertheless he joined Faisal in a strong anti-Zionist communiqué. Royalist Morocco feared Egyptian reprisal.

Faisal came to the United States to oppose aid to Egypt. His fears had mounted because of Nasser's threat to remain in Yemen until 1968, because Kosygin supported Nasser, and because the British were abandoning Aden.

The Saudi king, as was the custom, was regally welcomed in Washington, but despite an army of PR advisers he soon blundered. At a public luncheon he was asked whether he still favored driving Israel into the sea and whether he boycotted American firms dealing with Israel. He replied:

The Jews throughout the world are supporting Israel. We regard those who provide assistance to our enemies as our own enemies. It was never our objective to exterminate Israel and drive it into the sea. We always recognized the Jews of Palestine as co-citizens of the Arabs of Palestine, but Zionism, through aggression, has taken over and occupied our country and thrown out its people. Many became refugees. Jews from outside took their place. They are aliens. By aggression, they took over land belonging to its inhabitants. It is the violation of every human right of the person to his own home.

The Saudi Arabian Information Service swiftly distributed a revised version. It changed the word "Jews" to "Zionists," and it deleted the sentence that "it was never the Arabs' intention to drive Israel into the sea," because that would provoke rebuke from other Arabs who had never abandoned that intention.

There was dead silence when Faisal finished, but the echo reached New York, where Mayor John Lindsay quickly canceled an official reception.

RATIONS FOR WARRIORS

Parallel with the arms buildup in 1966 was the radicalization of the Palestinian Arabs in the UNRWA camps, with the reprehensible collaboration of UNRWA itself, which not only permitted military training but helped to subsidize it.

Representative Peter H. B. Frelinghuysen (R-New Jersey) had protested, demanding that no U.N. funds be used to feed the families of refugees who were training for war. Congress adopted an amendment to that effect, but the U.N. evaded it by asking Arab countries to put up an additional $150,000 for the estimated cost. It was explained that UNRWA could not exclude these refugees from the rolls; their security would be imperiled if their identities were revealed.

On the other hand, a 21-year-old infiltrator, captured by the Israelis, disclosed that he had been forced to join in sabotage activities at a meeting of refugees, because he and his mother would otherwise have been deprived of their monthly rations. Thus, instead of denying rations to potential warriors, UNRWA was being used by the PLO to deny them to those who refused to enlist.

This might have been an appropriate time for the United States to suspend or to reduce its UNRWA contributions, which amounted to 70 percent of the total UNRWA budget. The "philanthropic" agency had become an instrument in the Arab political and military war against Israel.

BORDERS

The new Palestinian military units were activated. Most of the early raids had emanated from Syria, and the Jordan-Israel border had been relatively quiet. Soon after Nasser's speech, Hussein yielded to the PLO's pressure, permitting it to open offices in his country, to establish army posts on the frontier, to use Amman Radio for daily hour-long broadcasts, to assess taxes and require Jordanian employees to contribute part of their salaries, to use telephone, telegram, and mail services without cost, and to establish youth training camps.

Israel now faced guerrilla warfare on three fronts. The Jordanian border erupted on April 19, when El Fatah terrorists raided a Negev pumping station. An Israeli settler was killed and a farmhouse was blown up when a mine exploded near Masada.

Jordan's capitulation to the PLO came, coincidentally, at a time when the United States had agreed to sell it the Lockheed F-104 fighter interceptors.

Israel warned that she would hold Arab governments responsible for border raids. Israeli commandos then attacked two El Fatah bases inside Jordan, destroying 14 houses.

The major threat was on the Syrian front. On May 16, two Israeli farmers were killed by an exploding land mine at Almagor near the Syrian border. The previous week two Israelis were killed and three wounded at Dvir near the Jordanian border.

Hussein's "alliance" with Shukairy ended in June, when he barred the PLO leader from recruiting refugees in Jordan. Shukairy had disclosed that PLO members were being sent to help the Viet Cong, and Hussein accused him of "subservience to international communism."

For many months, El Fatah had been planting land mines in Israel and firing across the borders. Israel reported 10 incidents of sabotage which resulted in 16 casualties, including four deaths. Two more Israelis were killed on July 14 by a mine near Almagor.

Israeli planes strafed a Syrian anti-aircraft battery and Syrian earth-moving equipment directed at Israel's northern water supply. A Syrian MIG — one of four which rose to meet the counterattack — was downed. That was score one for the French Mirages in their first battle with Soviet MIGs. Both Syria and Israel complained to the Security Council.

Russians defended the Syrians, but America's Sisco criticized both the provocations and the reprisal. Jordan and Mali offered a one-sided resolution to censure the Israelis; it was supported by the Soviets and by Bulgaria, Nigeria, and Uganda. Nine abstained.

In mid-August, Syrian MIGs flew over Israeli territory for the first time to strafe Israeli patrol boats, which sought to rescue a patrol boat that had run aground near the eastern shore of the Sea of Galilee. Two Syrian planes were downed. Israel revealed that five Israelis had been wounded. Syrians boasted that they had killed 50 to 100 seamen and had wrecked 11 patrol boats and Israeli naval stations. On September 6, seven Israeli farm workers were wounded when a mine blew up their tractor. In October, demolition charges exploded under buildings in Jerusalem, injuring four Israelis and damaging 11 apartments. Four Israeli border police were murdered when a land mine blew up their jeep in the north, and three Israeli soldiers were ambushed and wounded in the south.

Israel refrained from retaliatory action, winning commendation in the Security Council. American and British diplomats deplored the raids and called on Syria to halt them. A majority agreed, but the Russians, unwilling to stigmatize Syria, preferred a statement which urged the parties to keep the peace and to use the local U.N. machinery.

The United States insisted on citing Syria's responsibility for terrorism and her obligation to prevent the use of her territory as a base of operation for acts violating the 1949 armistice agreement.

Ten nations, a majority, supported a mild resolution calling on Syria to prevent further border incidents. They included Nigeria, Uganda, Argentina, Uruguay, Japan, the Netherlands, New Zealand, France, the United States, and the United Kingdom. The Soviet Union rescued Syria with its veto; it was joined by Bulgaria, Jordan, and Mali; China abstained.

Just seven days later a mine exploded on a road northeast of Beersheba. An Israeli patrol lost three soldiers, and six were injured. That was the fourteenth incident on the Jordanian frontier since January. Two days later, Israeli tanks and armored units struck at the village of Es-Samu, which served as a base for terrorists in that area. Local residents were evacuated from 40 houses, which were then demolished. Israel suffered one dead and 10 wounded in a clash with Jordanian soldiers who came to defend the village; their casualties were 15 dead and 37 wounded. There were also civilian casualties—three dead and 17 injured.

On November 25, the Security Council censured Israel's attack, warning that "military reprisal cannot be tolerated and if repeated the Security Council will have to consider further and more effective steps to ensure against repetitions," a threat of sanctions. The vote was 14 to 0. New Zealand abstained.

Congressmen charged that the U.N. censure resolution was one-sided because it ignored Arab infiltration and U.N. responsibility to preserve the peace.

At a December meeting of AIPAC's Executive Committee, we attacked the resolution because it had failed to condemn provocations against Israel, and we appealed to our government to use every forum to fight for peace.

We convened an emergency mass meeting in New York at which we warned against gathering war clouds.

FALSE OPTIMISM

Alarmed over growing Arab boldness and U.N. impotence, we convened our annual policy conference in February 1967, instead of waiting for Israel's May birthday, as was our custom. At one of our sessions, four leading diplomatic correspondents participated in a symposium. All were optimistic—none shared our fears. Had we forgotten the "trip wires" about Israel—the U.N. forces which would surely prove an insurmountable obstacle? Indeed we had—and rightly so.

I was surprised to discover a much calmer view when I visited Israel in the spring of 1967. Top Israeli diplomats were confident that there would be no war. Israel's optimism was predicated on the belief that Nasser was not ready for war, largely because he was bogged down in Yemen. Moreover, it was reported, he had come to believe that his strongest weapon was demographic. He did not need to go to war against Israel because the Arab birthrate inside Israel was among the highest in the world (5.3 percent) and eventually Israel would become a binational state with an Arab majority. This theory was circulated in Israel by an American diplomat who had been stationed in Cairo and who shared this unconventional wisdom with Israeli friends while on a visit to Israel. In reaction to this intelligence, Israel's leaders began to stress stimulation of the Jewish birthrate by offering bounties to larger families and providing more adequate housing. This seemed a wishful flight from reality.

On a climactic April 7, the Israeli air force rose to silence the Syrian batteries and tanks which had been harassing Israel's northern settlements. They clashed with the Syrian air force, downing six Soviet MIGs and shaking Damascus windows and confidence.

Ten days later, Nasser sent Sidky Suleiman, his prime minister, to warn Syria that he would not assist her unless there was total aggression. Three or four weeks later there was a change. In May, Syrians told Nasser that 19 Israeli brigades were massing on the northern frontier, and the Soviets warned an Egyptian delegation in Moscow that Israel was threatening Syria. Overestimating Egyptian strength and underestimating Israel's capacity, the Soviets apparently thought there would be a short war which the Arabs would win. They assumed that the United States, immobilized by its preoccupation with Indochina, could not and would not come to Israel's assistance.

Becoming more pugnacious, Brezhnev warned the U.S. Sixth Fleet to abandon the Mediterranean. "There is no justification for the permanent presence of the U.S. Navy in the waters washing the shores of Southern Europe. The time has come to demand the removal of the U.S. Sixth Fleet," Brezhnev told Communist leaders from 24 countries in Czechoslovakia on April 24.

Syria urged Lebanon to bar the fleet from Beirut, and the U.S. AID mission was stoned and sacked by a mob in Yemen.

Chapter 20

We Travel a Lonely Road

COUNTDOWN TO WAR

Israel celebrated her nineteenth birthday on May 15, 1967.

That morning, I joined American Hadassah leaders and Senator Claiborne Pell (D-Rhode Island) in a ceremony at AID, at which officials formally approved the grant of one million Israeli pounds for Hadassah—the legislation which Pell had sponsored and which we had supported.

From there, I went to a press conference at the Israeli embassy, where Ambassador Harman described the Syrian threat. As we were leaving, Assistant Secretary of State Lucius Battle telephoned Harman to report that Egyptian troops were rolling past the U.S. embassy in Cairo, headed toward the Suez Canal.

On the next day I was in New York to make a speech on Long Island and to arrange for an AIPAC luncheon celebrating Rabbi Bernstein's sixty-fifth birthday.

On the following day, it was reported that Egyptian troops were massing in response to Syria's appeal. U.S. intelligence sources denied Syrian charges that there had been a buildup of Israeli forces, but the Soviets ignored the denial and their ambassador in Israel spurned Eshkol's invitation to visit the area and see for himself. I was then in Detroit, raising funds for AIPAC, addressing a Hadassah regional conference, and checking city desks for late dispatches.

That night there came the grim news that Nasser, baited by Syria and Jordan, had demanded withdrawal of the 3,400-man UNEF force which had been established ten years before. U Thant yielded and was strongly criticized, especially by the Canadians, who had sponsored UNEF's creation. The ouster of UNEF meant that Nasser could block Israeli shipping through the Strait of Tiran and the Gulf of Aqaba to Eilat, that the newly formed Palestine Liberation Army could now replace UNEF on the frontiers, and that terrorists would be free to infiltrate.

Harman refrained from pessimistic forecasts when I met him Friday morning. "What is needed is a clear notice to the Arab states that they must not miscalculate U.S. intentions. The U.S. commitment to preserve the peace should be reaffirmed," he said—and that was as far as he would go. Harman, I thought, was much too reticent, and I decided to alert our members. I drafted a brief message to the leadership of AIPAC and major Jewish organizations, as well as to some 75 congressmen.

"The headlines alarmingly portray the danger of a new war against Israel," I warned, and I called for telegrams to the President, the Senate, and the House appealing for "swift and positive action by the United States to prevent a catastrophe. We believe that the United States should strongly reaffirm our past commitment to oppose aggression and that efforts should be made to obtain the cooperation of the Great Powers, including the Soviet Union, which is responsible for arming the Arab states."

Ephraim Evron, Harman's minister, later told me that the United States had warned both Egypt and Syria against aggressive action and had urged Israel to take no action without consultation.

On the next day, the calls poured in from Cleveland, Boston, Canton, Pittsburgh, Atlanta, and many other cities.

On Sunday, Celler telephoned Johnson at my request. The President told him that he had been in direct contact with Nasser and had warned him that he must not think that the United States would look aside because it was involved in Vietnam. He had told Eshkol that Israel should not lose restraint, that the United States did not have to justify its position if it became involved, and that the Sixth Fleet was there and that was the restraint. He knew that the situation was very serious and he was in constant touch with the Israelis. He did not think that a public statement should be made so long as conversations went on and he assured Celler that he was in accord with our position.

On Monday, May 22, I reported to the Presidents Conference in New York and appealed for help. Upon my return to Washington on Monday night, I learned that Nasser had made an inflammatory speech to his troops in Sinai, heightening fears that war was imminent. That night I awoke Bess Dick, Celler's aide, to suggest that Celler rally support in Congress the following morning.

At midnight, Evron called to disclose that the text of Nasser's speech had been read at a dramatic session at the White House. Nasser had told his troops: "The Israel flag shall not go through the Gulf of Aqaba. Our sovereignty over the entrance to the Gulf cannot be disputed. If Israel wishes to threaten war, we will tell her 'You are welcome.'"

Later, I learned that the Senate Foreign Relations Committee was to meet Tuesday morning to hear Rusk and that senators would welcome suggestions for questions.

As our car pool drove to work from Hollin Hills, I drafted a statement for Celler, which he read on the House floor, requesting co-signers. I delivered suggestions for questions to Senator Stuart Symington (D-Missouri), another veteran friend. The Celler statement was a brief appeal to the President to speak out strongly and pledge support. It read:

> Egypt and Syria are now threatening Israel and we fear that war in the Near East is inevitable unless the United States acts firmly and vigorously to prevent it. President Nasser's speech to his troops in Sinai yesterday was in effect a declaration of war. We note with dismay that the Soviet Union is encouraging and arming Egypt and Syria in a bold move to win influence and power in the Middle East. Once again the Soviet Union appears to be testing American resolve to defend the peace.
>
> The United States Government, speaking through Presidents Truman, Eisenhower, Kennedy, and Johnson, and through the Congress of the United States, has repeatedly declared its determination to act against aggression in the Middle East.
>
> We pledge the fullest support to measures which must be taken by the Administration to make our position unmistakably clear to those who are now bent on the destruction of Israel, that we are now prepared to take whatever action may be necessary to resist aggression against Israel and to preserve the peace.
>
> We are confident that the people of the United States will support such a policy.

It should be said of Celler that he never needed prompting from us. On the contrary, we often had to restrain him. Celler's long record on Israel's Washington struggle is virtually a day-to-day chronicle of the concerns of the Jewish people of his generation.

On the Senate side, I met briefly with legislative aides to Senators Scott, Williams, and Mondale. But we were stymied in the Senate because Rusk told the Foreign Relations Committee that we must not act unilaterally and that, in effect, we must refer the problem to the U.N.

When Symington emerged from the meeting, he told us that, if he had to choose between the Far East and the Middle East, he would take the Middle East, which he regarded as far more important. But, he said, we were overcommitted in the Far East and there was nothing we could do. Lausche, Mansfield, and Fulbright insisted that we should go to the U.N.

The demand in the Senate for resort to the U.N. weakened Celler's drive in the House. Representatives Herbert Tenzer (R-New York) and Benjamin Rosenthal (D-New York) had gained 110 signatures on the Celler declaration, but some members later removed their names because Celler rejected their demand that he include a reference to the U.N.

I proposed to Scott and Javits that the GOP leadership hammer out a strong policy statement and submit it to the White House. Javits made the attempt but failed. I then asked him to urge the President to send a ship through the Strait to establish the international character of the waterway, in conformity with the Corfu decision. Javits was skeptical. He pointed out that an American ship would be permitted to transit the Strait, but there was no guarantee that an Israeli ship would be permitted to follow.

Only two senators complied with my request—Williams and Morse. The latter, a veteran constitutional lawyer, argued that the longer we delayed action, the weaker our claim would be.

In the meantime, Fenyvesi brought back a disturbing report from an Administration briefing session with editors, who had been told that in the event of war the United States would suspend aid to both sides, for it would be difficult to ascertain who was the aggressor and who was the victim. It was the traditional "evenhanded" posture which we had always resented so bitterly, and, most disturbing, it portended a diplomatic deal. Israel was being urged to rely on diplomacy rather than on weaponry, and there were rumors of an arrangement whereby Nasser would be permitted to consolidate his military advance, which would enable him to bar Israeli ships from the Straits. However, non-Israeli ships would be allowed to carry cargoes to and from Israel, and some oil tankers might be permitted passage. It was difficult to attribute such compromises to Johnson in the light of his firm stand in 1957 and again in 1960.

Israelis reminded the White House and the State Department of the 1957 commitments, the Eisenhower promise that the Canal would be kept open, and, most important, the message to Ben-Gurion acknowledging that if Israel's rights were abridged she could take action in her own defense under Article 51 of the U.N. Charter. Johnson made a strong public statement that night. He renewed the U.S. pledge to oppose aggression, both inside and outside the U.N., and in effect he asked Nasser to state his intentions. Did he intend to reinstate the blockade?

The President declared that the United States earnestly supported "all efforts in and outside the United Nations and through its appropriate organs, including the Secretary General, to reduce tensions and to restore stability." He went on to say that "the danger, and it is a grave danger, lies in some miscalculation arising from a misunderstanding of the intentions and actions of others." He referred to three "potentially explosive aspects of the present confrontation": the failure of the armistice agreements to prevent warlike acts, "the hurried withdrawal of UNEF . . . without action by either the General Assembly or the Security Council," and "the recent build-up of military forces." The President added that the "purported closing of the Gulf of Aqaba to Israeli shipping has brought a new and grave dimension to the crisis." He stressed that the Gulf was "an international waterway . . . that a blockade of Israeli shipping was illegal and potentially disastrous to the cause of peace." He reiterated that the United States "strongly opposes aggression by anyone in the area in any form, overt or clandestine."

The President criticized both U Thant and Nasser, but it was apparent that the Department of State was giving Nasser an out. Israelis were unhappy with a private letter to Eshkol in which Johnson had referred to the possibility of action through the U.N.

It was a busy week. We sent out copies of the Celler statement and renewed the call for telegrams to the President and to senators. The United Synagogue of America asked me to check the draft of an advertisement, which I edited over the telephone.

Senatorial indecision was a grave concern. We gained the impression from White House reports that the President did not feel free to act without strong congressional support. Yet from talks with senators, we inferred that the Administration was stressing diplomatic action, whereupon we appealed to our entire mailing list of 7,469 for a flood of letters and telegrams.

Three weeks earlier, on May 1, my bookkeeper had brought me the customary bad news. We were then short $4,000, but she would settle for $2,000. I did not have more than $1,500 in my checking account. I was compelled to lend AIPAC another $1,400, and I was dismayed over our inability to raise funds at a critical moment. On May 24, at 2:00 A.M., I had an inspiration.

I framed a telegram to 100 of AIPAC's strongest friends: "We are spending thousands of dollars which we do not have, on letters, telephone calls, and telegrams. We would be doing much more if we had the funds. Please help, and try to talk to your senators over Memorial Day weekend."

It worked. Within a few days, checks began to pour in from all over the country. AIPAC was able to repay me several thousands in back salary and loans. AIPAC has never been in the red since that day.

On Thursday, May 25, I met with the steering committee of the Presidents Conference in New York. They had decided to transform an annual Young Zionist salute to Israel into a massive demonstration the following Sunday. They wanted me to invite two senators to address the parade. Some were critical. Who had authorized me to edit the advertisement of the United Synagogue? Why did the Celler statement refer to the Soviet Union? Who had authorized me to appeal for a ship to go through the Canal? The committee decided to delete any such provocative language from the message it was sending to its own constituency.

In fairness, it should be noted that there was reason for the objections. Many Jewish leaders were sensitive to the Administration's criticism of their refusal to support Johnson's Vietnam policies, and in the congressional cloakrooms there were sarcastic references to the new "hawkishness" in the Middle East. "Hoves and Dawks," quipped one of our friends. Thus, my call for action was embarrassing to some of our establishment. I did not share that embarrassment. I had always favored collective security from League of Nations days, but I was also convinced that we had to be selective, and I could not accept the fallacious notion that we had to be nowhere if we could not be everywhere.

Washington Jews wanted a major demonstration and, in preparation, the Jewish Community Council invited 200 leaders to a planning session at Adas Israel Synagogue; 800 jammed the hall. Rabbi Stanley Rabinowitz called on me for an impromptu speech, in which I compared U Thant's sudden trip to Cairo with Chamberlain's flight to Hitler's Berchtesgaden not quite thirty years before. As I closed, I mentioned our need for volunteers, which brought but one question: "What's your address?"

When I arrived at the Colorado Building a short time later, the lobby and the elevators were jammed, and for days we had many bright Washingtonians in our office, clipping for scrapbooks, folding letters, stuffing envelopes, and abstracting speeches.

Israel's Eban came to Washington. En route he had seen de Gaulle, who turned against Israel because she later went to war contrary to his advice, using French Mirages to boot. De Gaulle, always dedicated to the glory of France, wanted a four-power conference to settle the crisis. He had never forgiven the United States for the deal with Admiral Darlan, and he hated the British because their sponsorship of the Arab League in 1944 had undermined French influence in Syria and Lebanon. In Washington, Eban wanted to find out what Johnson and the United States would do if Israel moved to break Nasser's new blockade and to remind the Administration of past U.S. commitments.

Since there were widespread protests against unilateral action and insistent demands for multilateral action, and since nothing could be expected from the U.N., there were hints that the White House might organize a flotilla—an international regatta—to run the blockade.

PLEA FOR ACTION

If the United States would not take unilateral action, Israel would be compelled to do so. That was the thrust of a telegram which I sent to members of the Senate, commending those who had favored action and challenging those who had preferred surrender and retreat: "We are deeply disturbed by the attitude of a number of senators who have prematurely issued statements barring unilateral action by the United States if that should become necessary." We feared that this would encourage Nasser to believe that the United States was not prepared to uphold President Johnson's reaffirmation of the solemn U.S. commitment to preserve the international character of the Strait of Tiran and to resist threatened aggression against Israel. We noted that the U.N. had never been able to cope with Nasser's defiance and aggression. "Any suggestion foreclosing complete freedom of the United States to pursue unilateral action if necessary may result in forcing Israel into taking unilateral action, standing alone in defense of her life and the rights of the international community." We believed that war could be averted if Congress could rally the American people to give complete support to any action "necessary to carry out America's commitment to oppose aggression and preserve the peace."

On that same day, Nasser declared over Cairo Radio: "We know that closing the Gulf of Aqaba might mean war with Israel. . . . We shall not back down on our rights in the Gulf of Aqaba. . . . War with Israel will not be restricted to the Egyptian frontier or the Syrian frontier. It will be total war and the objective will be to destroy Israel."

Next day there was an ominous editorial in *The Washington Post,* which has so often reflected the views of the State Department, urging "A Search for Compromise" lest we endanger Western oil interests.

There was to be an effort to persuade Israel to accept an arrangement whereby other ships would be permitted to bring her supplies but her own ships would be blocked. This would have been catastrophic, for it would have terminated Israel's expanding trade with Africa and the Orient. Moreover, on the eve of Eban's visit with the President, there was a revealing report from Canada that the United States and Canada had agreed to act jointly at the U.N., which cut the ground from under the Israelis.

My talks with friendly congressmen suggested that the President, who would not act without the support of Congress, was pushing Congress not to push him.

Two top State officials — close personal friends — who had served both in Amman and Cairo, insisted that Israel was in a good position and should not move; the Arabs had to be the aggressors. Perhaps, both agreed, Nasser might be satisfied with the victory he had already won and might withdraw.

When Eban, Harman, and Evron saw the President on Friday evening, May 26, Johnson did not tell them that they could not move ahead. He wanted time because he still wanted to establish an international fleet. There was a lengthy discussion in the presence of Secretary McNamara, Eugene and Walter Rostow, Sisco, and Battle.

LBJ kept on reading from the paper in front of him which declared that "Israel would not be alone unless she chooses to be alone." This was apparently a memorandum from Rusk, who had earlier that day received an urgent appeal from Israel, based on the conviction that the Arabs were certain to attack.

One angry Israeli diplomat, who was more outspoken than his colleagues, was upset. "Don't you know what the United States plans to do?" he asked me. He continued, "Neither do we. Probably nothing." The fact was that the President had promised nothing. It was later alleged that the

President had said "God be with you," or "God help you." Did this mean "look out" or that "God *is* with you?"

YIELDING TO U.S. PRESSURE

On Sunday word came from Israel that she would rely on diplomatic action. Eshkol confirmed this in an indecisive speech which was broadcast from Israel and which disappointed and depressed many listeners. Eshkol said that Israel had decided to continue "political action in the world arena to prompt the powers to take effective measures to ensure freedom of international shipping in the Strait of Tiran."

(Meanwhile, the mammoth parade was held in New York, but neither Robert Kennedy nor Javits was on the scene.)

Javits telephoned me from Los Angeles to express dismay over Eshkol's speech. He planned to see the President, Rusk, and Eugene Rostow the following day.

That day I heard an illustrative report of the U.N.'s subservience to the Arabs. U Thant had asked the Israeli and Egyptian missions to send urgent messages requesting their governments to take no action and promising to do everything possible to end belligerence. Thirty minutes later, U Thant told Israel's Gideon Rafael not to send the message. "I can't ask you to send it," he explained, "because the Egyptians have just rejected it and refused to send it."

Next day, I wrote a bitter editorial in the *Near East Report,* deploring Nasser's massive victory and U.S. defeat. Nasser had won "a major skirmish. . . . He is occupying a base which permits him to strangle Israel's economy and to carry his war against Israel to a conclusion. . . . Instead of direct action the Great Powers have decided to resort to the United Nations. The Government of Israel deferred to that decision yesterday. . . . Let no one minimize the implications of last week's disaster. . . . We may be approaching another Munich."

We published the editorial as an advertisement in *The New York Times* Sunday edition on June 4, when, it later turned out, Israel was a few hours from war.

Meanwhile, the Rabbinical Assembly had held an emergency meeting in Washington the previous Sunday night. Some wanted a march to the Capitol, but I discouraged a demonstration, urging them instead to make appointments to see their senators, and many spent the following day on the Hill.

History does repeat. One week before the outbreak of war—just as in 1956—Hussein made his peace with Nasser. This was another blow at Washington. The United States had given Hussein American tanks in the hope that they would help him retain his independence. Even so, some diplomats rationalized that it was better for Hussein to be shored up by an alliance with Nasser than to be overthrown by the mob. There was a persistent threat of revolt by Palestinians in Jordan who had been flaunting their weapons. As his reward, Hussein acquired an Egyptian general and an Egyptian radar station.

The speeches, editorials, and cartoons in Arab capitals became more and more hysterical and bloodthirsty. The Cairo TV broadcasts which pictured children drilling contrasted with pictures of children walking to dugouts in Israel's kibbutzim.

Javits saw Rusk and telephoned me that the United States would act in due course. The difficulty, Rusk implied, was the Senate. The more important thing was to get the Senate to agree. But who, if not Rusk and his subordinates, were encouraging Senate neutralism?

In New York, the Presidents Conference called for a mass national conference to be held in Washington on June 8. In the interim, some came to Washington on June 2 to talk with their senators. Presidents of six major Jewish organizations and their aides came away with the impression that Congress would support any program the President wanted. Senators denied reports that the Senate was holding up the President, and they blamed the Department of State. Yet, while sympathetic, most of them were noncommittal. The Vietnam debacle cast a dark and heavy shadow.

Celler and Chairman Morgan were told at the White House not to be misled by talk about the U.N. With the imminent arrival of Prime Minister Wilson, there would be a decision as to whether to send the *Intrepid*, a U.S. warship, through the Strait. A declaration had been drawn; the British and the Israelis would sign it. Celler and Morgan assured the White House that the President had support, but there was still no specific answer as to when the United States would move, if at all.

The following day, June 3, the Egyptian commander on the Sinai front, General Abdul Mortaji, proclaimed: "The eyes of the whole world are upon you in your most successful war against imperialist Israeli aggression on your fatherland, in the expectation of seeing successful results of our holy war to achieve the rights of the Arab nation. The outcome now is of tremendous historical importance to our Arab nation, and our holy war will restore the Arab rights stolen in Palestine. You will reconquer the stolen land with the help of God, the power of justice, the strength of your arms, and the unity of our faith."

On June 4, Nasser declared over Cairo Radio: "The whole Arab nation has moved. We are facing Israel in the battle and are burning with desire for it to start in order to get revenge for the 1956 treachery."

One of my calls that fateful Sunday was from Professor Milton Konvitz of Cornell, who asked me to draft an advertisement to be signed by professors. I suggested that this should be done by someone like Professor Marie Syrkin of Brandeis, and Konvitz's call to her led to the establishment of the American Professors for Peace in the Middle East under the able leadership of Professor Allen Pollack.

Chapter 21

The Great Divide

OVERNIGHT VICTORY

I woke early on Monday, June 5, and turned on the radio to discover that the war had begun. I telephoned staff and Washington representatives of other organizations to meet in our office, and three of us—Rabbi Richard Hirsch of the Union of American Hebrew Congregations, Philip Katz of B'nai B'rith, and I—went to Evron to find out what was happening.

Naturally, we wanted to know whether Israel would need U.S. help. Evron grinned broadly. "What we want," he said, "is direct negotiations." We inferred that the war was going well, although none of us dreamed that Israel's air force had already put Egypt out of the war while we slept.

In New York, the Presidents Conference held an emergency meeting, and Will Maslow of the American Jewish Congress read me the draft of a proposed statement calling for U.S. moral, material, economic, and spiritual support for Israel. I countered with the suggestion that the United States should call for direct peace negotiations, which must have sounded rather weird. I could not explain my assumption that the war had been won and that our real battle would be to win a peace.

A week earlier, Rabbi Daniel Silver of Cleveland had offered to help if we needed him. I telephoned, inviting him to come to Washington to take over. It seemed appropriate to have the son of America's most influential Zionist leader, Abba Hillel Silver, help direct our work. Several hours later, he was at my desk, handling the many telephone calls that were flooding in from the Hill and the country. His brother Raphael came to talk with Ohio senators.

Meanwhile, State Department spokesman Robert McCloskey had told the press that the United States was neutral in "word, thought and deed." Celler was one of the hundreds who lit up the White House switchboard. The statement was amended. The United States was to be "non-belligerent." In retrospect, it is evident that McCloskey was unfairly criticized, for his statement came at a moment when Johnson was using the hot line to assure the Soviets that the United States planned no intervention and trusted that they too would keep out. The McCloskey pronouncement complemented and reinforced the Johnson "non-intervention" campaign.

At the embassy, both Harman and Evron assured me that they did not need arms from the United States. I flew to New York to meet leaders of the Presidents Conference, all of whom had been invited to sit on the dais at our AIPAC luncheon in honor of Bernstein the following noon. My proposed resolution calling for direct peace talks now seemed sensible in view of the electrifying victory announcement in Israel.

Our luncheon guests included General Lucius D. Clay and Under Secretary Robert Murphy, both long-time friends of Bernstein. Murphy's speech implied that the United States must not repeat the 1957 blunder. The luncheon was a celebration, and I closed it with the deadpan announcement that Dayan had just crossed the Alps but would be too late for dessert.

In the meantime, Silver and our staff were drafting memoranda, position papers, and resolutions in preparation for the national conference which was scheduled to open Wednesday night. Some 2,000 friends from all over the country were pouring into Washington for what was to have been an urgent appeal to our government to save Israel from the threatened Arab attack but which was now transforming itself into a thanksgiving celebration.

We drew up a tentative resolution: "Don't repeat the 1957 blunder. Don't force Israel to withdraw without peace. Don't reinstate Nasser. Move for direct negotiations." Our incoming leaders were to visit the Hill Thursday, and Silver met with organization representatives to brief them while I worked with Bernstein on his speech. Our staff compiled a six-page abstract of congressional attitudes prior to the war to prepare them for their congressional visits.

Harman and I addressed organization leaders at a preparatory session. After AIPAC's Bernstein and Morris Abrams of the American Jewish Committee had made their speeches to the mass gathering, the audience broke up into small state delegations for more intensive briefing.

All day Thursday, the mobilization intended to defend Israel became a victory rally across from the White House.

Representatives and senators who had been evasive during the previous fortnight were now staunchly pro-Israel. There was mass euphoria as word spread late that day that Nasser had resigned. At that moment, our leaders were requesting an audience with Johnson, but in the meantime Julius Cahn of Vice President Humphrey's office had been calling me to arrange a meeting with Humphrey, and I rounded up the organization presidents to visit the Hill for a celebration with a veteran friend.

Humphrey confided that Rusk only that morning had praised Eban as "one of the greatest foreign ministers of our time" for his magnificent defense of Israel's action at the Security Council. I congratulated Humphrey. For the first time in years, I had heard an American leader talk about a final peace settlement.

THE STRUGGLE OVER JERUSALEM

What was most significant that day was the jubilation over the reunification of Jerusalem. There was far greater interest in the prospect of a unified Jerusalem than in the extensive territories which had been occupied by Israel's triumphant forces. What I remember most vividly about the meeting with Humphrey was the urgent appeal by our leaders, notably Dr. William Wexler, the national president of B'nai B'rith, never to permit the partition of Jerusalem now that its unity and accessibility had been restored.

This is an appropriate place to recall the struggle over Jerusalem—a major issue during the U.N. debates.

In 1947, UNSCOP and the U.N. General Assembly had proposed establishment of an international city, a *corpus separatum,* including both the Old City and the New City. The Jews had reluctantly accepted the U.N. proposal because they wanted to safeguard the entire city from war, but the Arabs, hoping to capture all of Jerusalem, had unanimously rejected the recommendation, together with the other proposals. The U.N. Trusteeship Council had defaulted and had never approved a trusteeship statute for Jerusalem after the U.S. reversal and abandonment of partition.

Jerusalem became a battleground within hours after the 1947 Assembly adjourned. King Abdullah's Arab Legion seized the Old City, where almost all the Holy Places are located, ousting its 1,300 Jewish residents and destroying the many synagogues and other institutions in the Jewish quarter. Since the entire city was an enclave in the proposed Arab state, it was surrounded and cut off from the nascent Jewish state.

The Jews of Jerusalem defended the New City, and the Jews of the coastal plain came to their rescue. They broke the blockade, brought food and water, and restored law and security. They had carved a new road through the Judean hills, establishing a land bridge between the coast and Jerusalem, lifting the siege.

They then asserted their right to knit modern Jerusalem with the state. However, aware of the sacred religious association of Jerusalem, Israelis were sensitive to the universal significance of the Old City and were willing to support some form of international safeguard for its shrines. But in view of the U.N.'s 1948 default, Israel would not agree to the transfer of the entire city to international rule, not only because Israelis constituted a large majority in Jerusalem, but also because no method had been devised to ensure an effective international regime.

To our dismay, a propaganda offensive to internationalize Jerusalem was launched in the 1949 General Assembly, resulting in a diplomatic defeat for both Israel and the United States, both on the same side in that debate. The Western states — mostly Protestant — had concluded that territorial internationalization was impractical and that the most feasible solution was to put the Holy Places — not the entire territory — under U.N. supervision. This later came to be called "functional internationalization."

The Arab states, which had unanimously opposed territorial internationalization in 1947, now reversed themselves and voted for the original concept of an international *corpus separatum.* They were joined by the Soviet bloc, which was still mechanically adhering to the 1947 partition plan, and by a number of Latin American Catholic states. As a result, the U.N. again voted for internationalization of Jerusalem late in 1949. The one significant exception was Jordan. It informed the Trusteeship Council in 1950 that it would under no circumstances accept any kind of international jurisdiction over the Old City, which it then controlled. Israel again advocated functional internationalization, and in 1950 she was commended by the U.N. Trusteeship Council for her conciliatory attitude.

Jordan remained adamant, even rejecting provisions of the 1949 armistice agreement which called for links between the Old and New Cities, accessibility to shrines, and an exchange of services. Accordingly, for a full nineteen years Jordan ruled the Old City, until her blundering involvement on Egypt's side in the Six-Day War.

Jerusalem was a unified city at last. We prayed that it might remain so. Many Americans shared our view. James Michener, author of *The Source,* advocated a unified Jerusalem in a letter to the press:

"All who love the holy city of Jerusalem will rejoice that it is again united. . . . The preposterous division that has kept it in two isolated halves has been ended, for the time being, and even though that termination came as an unexpected by-product of war, it is a happy accident which produces meritorious results for all men."

ISRAEL HAS OVERWHELMING SUPPORT

The Six-Day War strengthened U.S.-Israel relations. Overnight, there was a vast surge of identification with the victorious Israelis — 55 to 5, according to the polls — and only a minuscule percentage of the American public wanted Israel to withdraw, as the United States had mistakenly demanded in 1956.

Congressmen were greatly relieved, for in advance of Israel's decision some had feared a decisive roll call, which could have put the United States in another remote war. Many now were pleased that Israel's triumph had fortified the U.S. position countering Soviet subversion in Arab countries. An AP poll of Congress, which reached 438 of the 534 members, showed that 365 were opposed to withdrawal without peace, while some 48 had qualified answers.

We were made aware of this support when we went to dinner that Thursday night. A naval captain came over to confide that he was Jewish. The Algerian waiter was quick to disclose that he was not really an Arab; he had been born a Jew. And in Hollin Hills, our little Virginia settlement where there were very few Jewish families, there was a spontaneous house-to-house collection for the United Jewish Appeal, and just about everybody gave, except a couple of families who had relatives in Arab states.

We had confidence in our government's position. It was obvious that Johnson, who had so acidly criticized Eisenhower and Dulles for forcing Israel to return to her previous positions unconditionally in 1957, could hardly contradict himself.

Kosygin was soon to learn this when he met Johnson at the historic Glassboro confrontation, where the Soviets damned Israel as the aggressor and demanded her total withdrawal. Johnson was unwilling to reinstate the conditions which had led to the past war and which would make another inevitable. We urged our constituency to send him messages of congratulations.

Jewish communities throughout the United States came to realize that there was an effective lobbying committee in Washington, that it was right and respectable to lobby and wrong to forfeit that right, and that AIPAC merited support.

Press comment on Israel was overwhelmingly favorable. James Reston wrote in *The New York Times:* "The Israelis are now very popular in Washington. They had the courage of our convictions and they won the war we opposed." Another *Times* columnist, C. L. Sulzberger, declared: "The United States can claim no credit for Israel's swift victory, but the fact of that victory was of strategic benefit to us, although our role was confined to waffling. Despite ourselves, American prestige has risen."

I was told by the State Department that the oil lobby had gone into action only once: to urge the United States to support the Pakistani resolution to nullify Israel's unification of Jerusalem. The General Assembly vote was 90 to 0, with 20 abstentions. Rejecting ARAMCO pressure, the United States abstained.

The United States had the upper hand at the U.N. and was able to defeat Soviet attempts to brand Israel as the aggressor and to demand her total withdrawal. The Soviet-Arab axis failed, largely because many black African delegations refused to join its condemnation of Israel. A Soviet resolution to condemn Israel as the aggressor and to demand withdrawal and restitution received only four votes in the Security Council: the USSR, Bulgaria, India, and Mali. The Soviets then demanded an emergency session of the Assembly. On its eve, Johnson declared: "Certainly troops must be withdrawn, but there must also be recognized rights of national life; progress in solving the refugee problem; freedom of innocent maritime passage; limitation of the arms race; and respect for political independence and territorial integrity. But who will make this peace where all have failed for 20 years? Clearly the parties to the conflict must be the parties to the peace. Sooner or later, it is they who must make a settlement in the area."

Johnson fixed the blame for the war on Cairo: "If a single act of folly was more responsible for this explosion than any other, it was the arbitrary and dangerous announced decision that the Strait of Tiran would be closed. The rights of innocent maritime passage must be preserved for all nations."

Ambassador Arthur Goldberg replied to the Kosygin demands: "If there ever was a prescription for renewed hostilities, the Soviet resolution is that prescription." The Assembly refused to provide the two-thirds vote needed to adopt any of the controversial resolutions.

Finally, on November 22, 1967, the Security Council adopted U.N. Resolution 242, which went through only because it was ambiguous, enabling the rival parties to interpret it as they wished:

TEXT OF SECURITY COUNCIL RESOLUTION 242, NOV. 22, 1967

The Security Council,
Expressing its continuing concern with the grave situation in the Middle East,
Emphasizing the inadmissibility of the acquisition of territory by war and the need to work for a just and lasting peace in which every State in the area can live in security,
Emphasizing further that all Member States in their acceptance of the Charter of the United Nations have undertaken a commitment to act in accordance with Article 2 of the Charter,
1. *Affirms* that the fulfillment of Charter principles requires the establishment of a just and lasting peace in the Middle East which should include the application of both the following principles:
   (i) Withdrawal of Israeli armed forces from territories occupied in the recent conflict;
   (ii) Termination of all claims or states of belligerency and respect for and acknowledgement of the sovereignty, territorial integrity and political independence of every State in the area and their right to live in peace within secure and recognized boundaries free from threats or acts of force;
2. *Affirms further* the necessity
   (a) For guaranteeing the freedom of navigation through international waterways in the area;
   (b) For achieving a just settlement of the refugee problem;
   (c) For guaranteeing the territorial inviolability and political independence

of every State in the area, through measures including the establishment of demilitarized zones;

3. *Requests* the Secretary-General to designate a Special Representative to proceed to the Middle East to establish and maintain contacts with the States concerned in order to promote agreement and assist efforts to achieve a peaceful and accepted settlement in accordance with the provisions and principles in this resolution;

4. *Requests* the Secretary-General to report to the Security Council on the progress of the efforts of the Special Representative as soon as possible.

The Arabs contended that the phrase "territories" meant total withdrawal from *all* the occupied territories and that the resolution was self-implementing. No negotiations were needed, they claimed; the burden was on the Israelis to withdraw. But Israel and the United States argued that withdrawal to "secure and recognized boundaries" required negotiations between the parties. That conflict led to a long stalemate, which Ambassador Gunnar Jarring, the U.N. mediator, never could break.

Chapter 22

Erosion and Attrition

THE VANISHING VICTORY

Euphoria over Israel's spectacular victory was short-lived. We soon encountered an intensive campaign to blame Israel for the war and to deny her military aid, even though the Soviets were rapidly replenishing Egypt's devastated arsenal.

We wanted to believe that most Americans identified with Israel and now regarded her as an asset, but an articulate opposition found its voice and soon began to use it.

On the third day of the war, Ambassador Strong, who had just come back from Iraq and was unlikely to return, invited me to his State Department office. His pronouncement startled me.

"This is a terrible disaster," he declared.

"I think it is a great victory," I protested. "Why do you call it a disaster? The Israelis have defeated the Soviet-equipped Egyptians with French Mirage planes. Nasser is crushed."

"But the Soviets will pick up the pieces and get the credit and America will get all the blame."

His nightmare? The Arabs would be equipped both ideologically and militarily by the Soviets. Syria and Egypt would become more radical; they might subvert our great and good friend Saudi Arabia, and the United States might lose its oil.

I witnessed another illustration of the negative attitude of U.S. diplomats on the eve of the war when I met Richard Nolte a few days earlier at a reception given by Rodger P. Davies, Deputy Assistant Secretary of State.

Congratulating him on his new assignment as U.S. ambassador to Cairo, I expressed the hope that he could persuade Egypt that "Israel is here to stay." He replied that this was not his responsibility. It was up to Israel to do that, and, he added, Egyptians would regard him as an imperialist if he tried.

I did not share the fear that all Arab states would go to suicidal extremes. I preferred to believe that there was hope for moderation, that the peoples of the Arab and African countries would cite Israel's victory as evidence that a democratic country, where the people had a stake in their economy, could do better than military dictatorships—that free institutions and economic development offered the best future. (In those days, we were not anticipating the power of the petrodollar.)

The conspiracy theory of history was offered by Sir John Bagot (Glubb Pasha), who had trained Jordan's Arab Legion and who had been a victim of Nasser's incitement and intrigue in 1956. In an article in the *Hatchet,* the Georgetown University magazine (to which I replied) and in many speeches, Bagot speculated that the Soviets had egged Nasser on so that he would be trapped into defeat and increased dependency on Moscow. In truth, however, the Russians themselves had been routed. The leftist Arab states, which they had trained and equipped, had suffered heavy losses of materiel and manpower, and the Soviets had failed to rush to their rescue.

A veteran American diplomat, Charles W. Yost, who served in early U.N. delegations and who was named U.S. permanent representative when Nixon took office, charged that Israel was responsible for the war; she had overreacted. In articles in *Foreign Affairs* and the *Atlantic Monthly,* Yost contended that Nasser had not sought war but a face-saving diplomatic victory. Israel's warnings to Syria to desist from terrorism "may well have been the spark that ignited the long-accumulated tinder." He blamed the Israelis because in 1956 and 1957 they had insisted on "freedom of shipping, an end to the fedayeen terrorism and neutralization of the threat of attack by the joint Egypt-Syria-Jordan military command."

Like his Arabist colleagues, Yost apparently believed that Israelis should have suffered Arab terrorism in silence. He wrote of "Israel's exercises in verbal escalation" and "provocative pronouncement," and as evidence he quoted Nasser's statement that an unnamed Israeli commander threatened military operations to occupy Damascus and to overthrow the Syrian government. Yost did not reproduce the statement, despite his claim that it contributed significantly to Arab apprehensions. In Yost's view, Israelis had to forgo displays of "inflexibility and arrogance."

It is true that the Israelis warned that Syrian terrorism would lead to war, but it is disingenuous to blame the war on those who tried to sound the alarm. Lawbreakers may not be self-righteously indignant with those who summon the police to apprehend them.

Yost also opposed sending arms to Israel. The Arabs and Soviets could

not agree to end the arms race while Israelis occupied substantial Arab territories, he pointed out.

Characteristically, the Luce publications changed their position. On
June 16, 1967, immediately after the war, *Life* had written: "The Israelis
could hardly be considered unreasonable if this time they refused to withdraw until they had much firmer evidence . . . of peace. The permanent
state of war by Arab nations against Israel must be ended." But in 1968,
Life urged the President to restore U.S.-Egypt relations, to deny military
aid to Israel, and to neutralize U.S. policy. *Time* printed a Kosygin interview devoid of any reference to peace, and *Fortune* called for a reappraisal
of U.S. policy in which the author, Dan Cordtz, mentioned oil 42 times,
peace once.

Earl Bunting, former president of the National Association of Manufac-
turers (NAM), had written a letter to *The Washington Post* dated May 31,
1967, attempting to justify the Egyptian blockade of the Strait of Tiran,
but it was printed after June 5, by which time the blockade had been
broken.

Apologists for the Arabs were vocal and ubiquitous.

Rabbi Berger of the American Council for Judaism raised funds at a
Beirut dinner, where he likened Israel's nationalism to South African apartheid and told the press that no Arab government could be expected to sign a
treaty with Israel. (However, in 1968, Berger was ousted when the Council
split over whether it should confine itself to anti-Zionist campaigns in this
country or become involved in Arab-Israel issues overseas. The Council's
membership had dwindled to less than 5,000.)

John C. Campbell of the Council on Foreign Relations called for a
return of territories but added that the Arabs could not be expected to sign a
peace treaty dictated by Israel.

On the eve of Nixon's accession to the Presidency, former Governor
William Scranton of Pennsylvania returned from a Middle East tour with a
call for a "more evenhanded policy." He claimed that Egypt and Jordan
were willing to make peace and that the Egyptians seemed reasonable. Coincidentally, that statement was made even as Egypt's U.N. delegation was rejecting the U.S. peace initiative.

The State Department astonished us with a partisan pamphlet alleging
that Israelis had taken the offensive and had attacked in 1967. This was not
the view of President Johnson and most of the press. We protested, but to
no avail.

I heard the Reverend Edward L. R. Elson, former AFME chief and later
the Senate chaplain, tell a Georgetown University forum that Christians got
along better with Moslems than with Jews and that Christian–Jewish relations would suffer if Israel did not yield to the Arabs – a lament reminiscent
of the 1948 incitement.

THE THREAT OF A RADICAL SYRIA

The Israelis had been hoping that Hussein would open peace talks, but, much to their disappointment, the Jordanian monarch went to the Khartoum summit conference in August 1967, where all the Arab states—except for Syria, which had boycotted—solidly proclaimed their opposition to "peace, recognition and negotiations."

In Israel the following month I asked a top American diplomat, Heywood Stackhouse, whether any American official had ever encouraged Hussein to meet with Israel. The answer was "no." On the contrary, he told me, the State Department regarded the Khartoum conference as a victory for Saudi Arabia and a setback for the absent Syria, which had been conspicuously isolated. Apparently the United States thought it more important to check the radical Syrian infection than to promote an Arab-Israeli settlement.

The Syrians boycotted the Khartoum summit. They preferred war to talk. They snubbed U.N. Mediator Gunnar Jarring. Their Baathist regime was more narrowly based than its predecessors and had no popular backing from any social class or region. Most of its leaders belonged to the Alawi sect of Islam, which constituted only 12 percent of the population.

ATROCITY PROPAGANDA

For many months after the war, Israel's richly imaginative foes waged a propaganda offensive, charging her troops with atrocities against Arab civilians and desecration of religious shrines. These reports emanated from Beirut and other Arab capitals and were emphatically denied by Israelis, who were then trying to normalize relations by clearing away the barriers between Arab and Jew and by opening bridges and roads between Jordan, the West Bank, and Israel. The charges were swifly repudiated by official inquiry after the war.

The new Arabian Nights horror stories were rebutted by Alfred Friendly of *The Washington Post,* whose dispatches won a Pulitzer Prize. He cabled from Tel Aviv in July 1967 that no Israeli soldier had set foot in any Arab refugee camp, that "looting was minimal and rape nonexistent." "In dozens of trips to the Gaza strip and the West Bank neither I nor any reporter of my acquaintance heard of a specific instance of the brutality alleged by the Arabs," he wrote. And in a similar vein, *The Economist* of London wrote on March 30, 1968: "As occupying powers go, Israel is humane; it rules with a relatively light hand; it destroys houses or property, not people. The Palestinians who remain in the West Bank yearn to live their lives in peace. They have not, so far, openly resisted Israeli authority. Few have much affection for the Jordanian regime; few have much faith left in President Nasser."

Israeli spokesmen emphasized that Israel's soldiers had deliberately exposed themselves to needless and excessive casualties in Jerusalem by detours in order to avoid shrines and to preserve them from war damage.

James L. Merrell, editor of *World Call* — the publication of the Disciples of Christ — wrote in its December 1971 issue that "a visitor to Jerusalem soon discovers the falsity of charges made by those who fear for the future of Christian life in the city. . . . Under Jordanian control, the old sector . . . was in decay; under Israeli direction, there is a rebirth of vitality and a budding prosperity."

Six Arab religious leaders — four Christians and two Moslems — came to the United States to report on the "desecrations" and "Judaization" of Jerusalem. A Cleveland churchman, the Right Reverend John H. Burt of the Episcopal Diocese of Ohio, who had recently visited Jerusalem, told the Arabs that his perceptions were entirely different. "These gentlemen are simply out of touch with the present situation in East Jerusalem," he wrote to his Superior. "The current administration is preferred over the former ones. . . . Christians are more free than they were under the Moslem Brotherhood." And he commented: "They really want Jerusalem to be Arab."

Israelis suffered a major setback during the war when they attacked an American spy ship, the *USS Liberty,* mistaking it for an Egyptian ship. Israel apologized for the blunder and paid reparations to the bereaved families. There was criticism on Capitol Hill, but Secretary of Defense Robert S. McNamara assured the Senate Foreign Relations Committee that "the attack was not intentional."

To counter the propaganda barrage, we issued a second edition of *Myths and Facts,* reproducing the anti-Semitic cartoons and inflammatory harangues which preceded the war.

SPACE AND SECURITY

The captured territories gave Israel space and security. As one leading Israeli described it to me: "Before the war 95 percent of Israelis lived within gunshot range of the Arabs. Now 95 percent are in safe territory." Moreover, despite the expanded area, Israel's frontier lines were actually shorter because they followed normal boundaries: the Suez Canal, the Jordan River, the Golan Heights. In the Golan, they ended the Arab threat to divert water resources. At Sharm el-Sheikh, Israel could now keep the Strait of Tiran and the Suez Canal open. A unified Jerusalem had become "a mixing bowl for Jew and Arab" — to use Rodger Davies's picturesque metaphor.

Nevertheless, most Israelis were willing to trade much of the captured territory for peace. Dayan emphasized this in a television talk here late in 1968. Others, however, wanted to retain all the West Bank largely on religious grounds, for most early Jewish history was written in Samaria and

Judea. Some Israeli Foreign Ministry officials were unhappy when religious settlers proposed to restore Jewish settlements which had been destroyed near Hebron in 1948. They appealed to me to advise Eshkol to say no, but I did not feel that this was my function. Perhaps I should have, for a permissive Eshkol yielded to them.

No matter what West Bank territory would be returned to the Arabs, Israel wanted the Jordan River as the military frontier, and to establish security stations there, since many Arabs lived on the western slopes.

Most Palestinians resented Hussein because he had not helped the West Bank's economy, and some Israelis advocated establishment of a separate Arab state on the West Bank and in Gaza. Eban and many other moderates were sharply opposed. They argued that such a state might advance irredentist claims to territories which the Arabs might have claimed under the 1947 U.N. partition plan if they had not gone to war in 1948 — such as western Galilee, Jaffa, Ramleh, Lydda, and Nazareth. They pointed out that if Hussein resumed control over the West Bank, he could advance no such territorial claims, for he had no standing under the 1947 resolution.

Nasser was opposed to a separate Palestinian state. He told *Look* magazine that the Palestinians could not agree to a weak separate state because it would be under Israel's domination, and that Israel would settle only when Egypt had an effective fighting force. He had begged for Soviet officers to train Egypt's army. "I decided to bring them in and I will decide to send them out. How many? The figure 1,000 would be an exaggeration."

Looming over all else was the demographic problem. Israelis were troubled by the Arab birthrate inside Israel proper. The 120,000 Israeli Arabs had already multiplied to almost 300,000 and would double every 17 years, but by mid-1967 this 300,000 was but a small fraction of the number of Arabs on Israel's hands. In addition, there were now 600,000 on the West Bank, 70,000 in Jerusalem, and 350,000 in Gaza.

To me it seemed logical to relinquish most of the West Bank; but Gaza was a different problem, for here were 350,000 Arabs in an area which could not sustain 100,000. More serious, Gaza was close to Tel Aviv. It would be necessary to encourage Gaza Arabs to move to the West Bank, or to resettle in El Arish or other Sinai areas which could be made irrigable by the scientific development of economical desalting, or as a result of a political agreement to divert the wasting waters of the Litani River from southern Lebanon.

Apart from its proximity and density, Gaza was a menace because its people had been indoctrinated to hate Jews. At Khan Yunis I saw a shocking exhibit of children's paintings luridly forecasting the slaughter of Jews by Nasser's soldiers.

I had an acrimonious argument with a Soviet agent who visited our AIPAC office. He complained, "How can Israel retain territory which doesn't belong to it?"

I did not bother to talk about Eastern Europe. I asked whether the Russians would agree to have the Communist Chinese camped 27 miles from Moscow. He censured Israel's "blitzkrieg" and Israel's deeply resented occupation of Jersualem. "The more Israel wins this way, the more she loses," he commented.

Later, Eban reminded me that, when the Soviets objected to the presence of the Finns within 30 miles of Leningrad, the border had been amended in their favor.

ARAB INTRANSIGENCE

What Israelis thought about the future did not really matter much, for the Arabs remained intransigently opposed to any negotiations with Israel. They interpreted Security Council Resolution 242 to imply Israel's total retreat from all occupied territories, without a treaty. They would merely recognize the fact of Israel's existence—not her right to exist. Many, principally the PLO leaders, openly sought Israel's dissolution. In 1968, they adopted a covenant calling for a secular state in all of Palestine, such as exists nowhere in the Arab world. Jews who came after the Zionist "invasion"—an ambiguity, for one might read 1917 or 1948—would be forced to return from where they came. PLO slogans calling for a secular state were designed to please Western leaders who separate church and state, but this was a propaganda euphemism; all Arab states revere Islam as the state religion.

For her part, Israel was always eager for negotiations but wanted treaty commitments written in indelible, not invisible, ink. There were to be no more wishful assumptions, no more make-believe diplomacy.

The Jarring negotiations were stultified from the beginning because the Arabs wanted Israel to surrender in advance.

Arab confidence rose. The Soviets had quickly rearmed them; the French had abandoned Israel; the United States now hesitated to resume arms shipments to Israel; the admission of many new Arab, African, and Asian states to U.N. membership facilitated manipulation and logrolling by the Soviet-Arab-Afro-Asian bloc; and Arab terrorism was condoned. Arab propaganda was richly financed and was becoming more sophisticated.

The Arabs had an anti-Jewish legacy from virulent anti-Semitic sources. Despite the propaganda myth that Jews enjoyed a serene and happy life in Islamic countries, Mohammed, according to the Koran, preached anti-Semitism because Jews had resisted conversion. Islam may have been more merciful than Christianity in the Middle Ages, but there were sporadic outbreaks against Jews, who were second-class citizens and who were taxed to death in Arab countries. In modern terminology, it is easy to denounce Zionism as an agent of Western imperialism; the Arabs imbibed the allegation from Communist doctrine.

The Czars had circulated the vicious *Protocols of the Elders of Zion,* and Arabs recirculated them. Faisal of Saudi Arabia published 300,000 copies in Lebanon—where it was a best seller—about 200,000 in French for Africa, and the remainder in English, Spanish, and Arabic.

During World War II, Nasser and Sadat had collaborated with the Nazis, while the ex-Mufti had advocated Hitler's final solution from Berlin.

On June 27, 1967, the Egyptian Office of Information issued a crude anti-Semitic booklet which was called *The Ordeals of Christianity in Israel.* It was based on the *Protocols of the Elders of Zion.* The pamphlet quoted the Talmud to demonstrate that Jews "see no harm in killing, lying to, stealing from and injuring non-Jews and inflicting the severest exactions and committing the most horrible crimes against them to further their own interests." According to the booklet, the Talmud tells the Jews that they are "allowed to take the life of the best of Christians; in fact it is your duty to do so. . . . History shows that the Jews were the source of the persecution of Christians in all countries in order to satisfy their hatred against the Messiah and his disciples."

Nasser went to war in 1967, pulled by Syrian terrorists, pushed by Soviet strategists, armed by Soviet militarists, incited by Arab propagandists, and propelled, finally, by his own vaulting ambition.

According to Mohammed Hassanein Heikal, the Egyptian editor who accompanied him to Moscow in 1968, Nasser told the Russians: "Regarding political settlement and its possibilities we are not intransigent, nor do we allow ourselves to indulge in the illusion of dictating terms, but there are possible and impossible things. Giving up one inch of occupied Arab territory is impossible and I cannot do it. Accepting negotiations with Israel is impossible and I cannot do it. This is my stand."

WHAT ISRAEL SOUGHT FROM THE UNITED STATES

Confronted by Arab obduracy and renewed threat, Israel sought political and military support in Washington. Haunted by the 1956 nightmare, Israel hoped that the United States would resist Arab demands for an unconditional withdrawal. Now that the Soviets were rushing arms to Egypt, we campaigned for U.S. Phantom jets for Israel. Johnson hesitated. He believed that the French would change their minds and provide the 50 Mirage planes which Israel had purchased but which de Gaulle withheld because Israel had spurned his counsel on the eve of the Six-Day War.

Johnson not only hesitated to provide the Phantoms; he maintained a strict arms embargo against any arms to Israel for 135 days, even though the Russians were busily rebuilding Arab armies while Western diplomats were rehabilitating the Arab image.

The United States had promised in 1966 to send A4 Skyhawk bombers to Israel by December. Eshkol visited Johnson in Austin late in the year to plead his case. In their joint communiqué, LBJ agreed to keep Israel's defense capability under sympathetic consideration and review in the light of the new relevant factors, including military shipments by others to the area.

I later traveled with Eshkol and heard him outline Israel's position to overflow audiences in Toronto, Montreal, and Ottawa, and I learned that he had been disappointed by Johnson's expectation that Israel would make extensive territorial withdrawals.

In summary, I heard Eshkol say:

> Israel wants peace and will not return to "brittle arrangements." There must be no more UNEFs or armistice agreements which keep Arabs and Israelis apart. Israel will cooperate with the Jarring mission. Freedom of navigation through both Suez and Tiran is a *sine qua non*. Jerusalem is undivided, and there is free access for all faiths to all holy places. Israel will not accept past discrimination and desecration.
>
> Israel needs arms to deter Arab aggression. She does not have the bomb and will be satisfied with conventional weapons. Israel deplores Soviet arms shipments and the influx of Soviet technicians. She blames Egypt for the war, citing Egyptian mobilization, the closing of the Strait, the ousting of UNEF, and the pacts with Syria, Iraq, and Jordan. The resettlement of Arab refugees will be hastened by agreement and cooperation. Israel hopes for immigration from the Soviet Union and appeals for the immigration of young people. Israel is short of water and desalting is a must.
>
> Israel wants peace. In its absence, Israel can maintain her position.

After 135 days, the United States finally lifted the embargo on arms to Israel and five Arab non-belligerents: Lebanon, Libya, Morocco, Saudi Arabia, and Tunisia. It was indicated that Jordan would be granted arms later.

THE CAMPAIGN FOR PHANTOMS

We opened a campaign for Phantoms. Republicans took the offensive and in a 20-page report released on April 3, 1968, the Republican Coordinating Committee recommended deterrent arms for Israel to maintain the power balance. Noting that the Soviet Union had upgraded the quality of arms sent to Arab states, it rebuked the Administration for its failure to approve Israel's application.

One month later, Dirksen and Ford, the two Republican leaders, joined a GOP declaration calling for an international arms limitation agreement. In the interim, they believed, the United States should supply arms to friendly nations to maintain the balance of power and to deter war.

In mid-July Representative Lester Wolff (D-New York) and Representative Seymour Halpern (R-New York) offered a surprise amendment to the foreign aid appropriation bill *requiring* Johnson to sell to Israel not less than 50 F-4 Phantom jets. However, the amendment was defective because it used the word "shall," and the President is not obligated to take orders from Congress.

That was on a Friday afternoon. Two days later I had a reception on the terrace of my Virginia home. Ambassador Yitzhak Rabin, who had just arrived to succeed Harman, was highly pleased with the Wolff amendment, but I told him that it would have to be rewritten by the Senate into a "sense-of-Congress" declaration. Rabin objected. My other guests included three experts on the subject: Assistant Secretary of State William B. Macomber; Representative John J. Rooney (D-New York), the influential chairman of the House subcommittee on State Department appropriations; and Judge Tannenwald, who had been Harriman's counsel when he was AID Administrator. They assured Rabin that I was right, but Rabin, unfamiliar with legislative procedures, refused to believe us. It was the first of my many differences with him.

The following morning, Irving Kane, my incoming chairman, and I visited the White House to talk with Ernest Goldstein, the President's counsel. He urged us to induce the Senate to redraft the Wolff amendment so that Johnson could accept it when it reached the White House for his signature.

Senator Frank Church (D-Idaho) drafted compromise language. It was approved by both Houses and replaced the Wolff amendment. Even this was opposed by Cooper, who wanted the United States to reach an agreement with the Soviet Union on the supply of arms to Israel and the Arab states. Javits and Morse disagreed with Cooper, and Senator Clark expressed the hope that the President could quickly implement the legislation.

In a revealing sequel, Johnson announced the sale of Phantom jets to Israel when he signed the appropriations bill in October 1968. He referred to the Wolff amendment, implying that he was complying with public opinion. Once again, the Administration had permitted Congress to pressure it to do what it wanted to do. The Phantom was then the best U.S. plane made and had been sold only to Britain and Iran.

Johnson had previously deferred action on Israel's application because he had hoped to win an arms limitation agreement with the Soviet Union. He continued to press for it. He also rejected the Arab contention that no negotiations were necessary. U.N. Resolution 242, he said, was not self-executing; the parties themselves must begin the peacemaking process. Middle East leaders must exchange views on the hard issues through some agreed procedure.

On October 8, Eban had made a speech at the U.N. emphasizing Israel's readiness to talk to and through Jarring on the substantive issues. The burden of response was shifted to the Arabs. Eban called for a treaty for secure and recognized boundaries, for a pledge of mutual non-aggression, for open frontiers and free port facilities for Jordan on Israel's Mediterranean coast, for freedom of navigation, and for a conference of Middle East states to chart a five-year plan for a solution of the refugee problem. In the interim Israel would step up family unification and process hardship cases among refugees who had crossed the East Bank during the 1967 war. Christian and Moslem holy places in Jerusalem should be safeguarded by those who held them in reverence. Eban talked about the foundation of a Middle East community of sovereign states.

There was no progress. At the U.N., Egypt's Foreign Minister Mahmoud Riad insisted that the withdrawal of Israeli forces from every inch of Arab territory was an obligation that belonged to the "highest and most sacred category of international obligations." Riad likened Israel to the Nazis. His perception of "peace" was an agreement reached through Jarring, read and endorsed at the Security Council and guaranteed by the four great powers. Nothing would be signed because Israel's signature was "worthless."

Soviet Foreign Minister Andrei Gromyko referred to the Middle East as "the region directly bordering on our southern frontiers and where the situation directly affects the security of the Soviet Union." This was a creeping escalation of Soviet claims in the region. In the past, the Middle East had been merely "a region in the immediate vicinity of the Soviet Union's southern borders." The reference to the Soviet Union's security was menacing—a new threat to every state in the area.

THE CONVENTIONS

We carried our fight to the Democratic and Republican conventions. We were now authorized to speak on behalf of the Conference of Presidents of Major American Jewish Organizations, which, at the time, had 22 affiliates. Kane talked to the Republicans and Rabbi Bernstein spoke to the Democrats. They urged the parties to unite on a Middle East plank—thus to apprise the Arabs that they could expect no U.S. policy change after the November election.

The lead-off spokesman for anti-Israel forces at the GOP convention was David G. Nes, who had been the U.S. chargé d'affaires in Cairo until the outbreak of the June war. He spoke under the auspices of the American Committee for Justice in the Middle East, which circulated a memorandum attacking Zionism and Israel, and he introduced Frank C. Sakran, Executive Secretary of the American Council on the Middle East, who criticized the Administration. Nes had resigned from the State Department earlier in the year, because of its failure to react to his alarm that we were on a collision course in the Middle East. Now he seemed surprisingly unconcerned about the new Soviet rearmament and he deprecated reports that the UAR was receiving lethal weapons from the Russians.

Both parties adopted planks urging sophisticated planes for Israel. Vice President Humphrey, the Democratic party's nominee for the Presidency, sent me a telegram in Miami (while the GOP convention was in session) endorsing the shipment of supersonic planes.

The GOP platform, which was won with the assistance of Javits and Scott, disappointed the Arabs. They had hoped that the prospective end of the Johnson regime would lead to the restoration of Eisenhower-Dulles policies.

Other candidates swiftly endorsed planes to Israel: Humphrey, Eugene McCarthy, and Robert Kennedy. Senator McGovern, who announced his candidacy during the Democratic convention, made it unanimous in a letter to me strongly endorsing the sale of Phantom jets: "If the more advanced TFX, F-111, and VAX aircraft become operational, I shall support their sale if the military situation warrants it." He was opposed to any sale, loan, or gift of military equipment to nations displaying a belligerent attitude— such as Israel's neighbors.

Earlier in the year, I had been invited by the Americans for Democratic Action (ADA) to serve on their foreign affairs commission to assist in drafting a Middle East plank. In 1967, ADA had been in session in the middle of the Six-Day War, and its statement had been ambiguous and inadequate. In 1968, we were able to win a strong, comprehensive statement. The ADA urged U.S. military aid to Israel and direct Arab-Israel talks. It called for Arab recognition of the integrity and sovereignty of Israel, freedom of navigation through international waterways, secure and recognized boundaries, rehabilitation and resettlement of Arab refugees, and access for all faiths to the shrines of Jerusalem. The resolution recommended U.S.-Soviet agreements to promote disarmament and guaranteed boundaries.

I continued in the same role at many ADA conventions.

THE U.S. POSITION

While we were pleased with the improvement of the U.S. position, the United States and Israel were still a long way from complete agreement. The two positions were parallel, but not identical.

Both Israel and the United States agreed that there should not be automatic or unconditional retreat to past boundaries, that there should be freedom of navigation in international waterways, and that the parties themselves must negotiate the settlement. There agreement ended. There was no agreement between the two countries on future boundaries. If and when negotiations began, the United States would expect Israel to make substantial concessions. While the United States did not want Jerusalem to become a divided city again, our government counted on Israel to make major sacrifices to please the Moslems and Hussein. And every time Israel took any initiative, such as the erection of new housing or the demolition of dilapidated slums, a U.S. spokesman invariably expressed reservations.

Moreover, when we argued about the need for direct negotiations, our government claimed that we were preoccupied with form rather than substance, to which we retorted that U.S. solicitude with Arab reaction suggested preoccupation with face rather than with peace. We also feared that our government would be content if identical but separate documents were signed by the parties and deposited with the U.N. We were apprehensive that once negotiations began the United States would surrender to Soviet pressure, as well as to Arab demands, lest our government humiliate the Arabs. There always had been a double standard of expectations. In judging the merits of Israeli and Arab conduct, Washington expected Israel to make do with less and pay more for it.

Constantly throughout the Rusk regime, and subsequently when William Rogers was Secretary of State, the Department interpreted the 1967 resolution to please Egypt, in the never-ending effort to woo her away from the Soviet Union.

THE EPHEMERAL COMMITMENT

For years, we had been assured that the United States had a commitment to Israel's survival and that therefore Israel did not need U.S. weapons. It began in 1950 with the issuance of the Tripartite Declaration and it had been reaffirmed in the Eisenhower Doctrine in early 1957. We wanted to believe it, although in more sober moments we were fully aware that a unilateral commitment is not an enforceable treaty. Now, in August 1967, Macomber testified before the Senate Foreign Relations Committee that the United States had no obligation to come to Israel's defense under any circumstances.

Nevertheless, U.S.-Israel relations had improved as a result of Israel's victory, and even before it. Our ambassador to Israel, Walworth Barbour, assured me in Tel Aviv in March 1967 that there had been a vast improvement. Washington was no longer suspicious of Israel's motives. Israel had much greater confidence in U.S. friendship after the war. There had been disillusionment with Nasser's policies and recognition of his disposition to go to war; U.S. policies were being formulated in the White House rather than in the State Department.

At the U.N., Israel's position was impossible. There, Arab aggression was accepted as normal and righteous; Israel's reply was abnormal, evil, and inevitably censured. The U.N. was stacked; no decision was ever based on fact and equity. It was now a make-believe world—so different from the U.N. I had known in 1947 and 1948.

The Security Council was becoming more one-sided. As 1969 began, more than one-third of the new Council members had no diplomatic relations with

Israel. On any issue, Arabs could rely on seven to nine votes, as opposed to four that Israel might hope for. Two of the five permanent members—the Soviet Union and China—and four of the ten non-permanent members—Algeria, Hungary, Pakistan, and Spain—had no diplomatic relations with Israel. The situation has since worsened.

The Jarring "negotiations" were moving very slowly. Jarring made 41 visits to the three capitals—Jerusalem, Amman, and Cairo—in the first six months of circuit riding. In March 1968, Eban disclosed that Jarring had asked Israel for cooperation "on a position under which he could write to the Secretary General that the three governments had accepted the resolution as a basis for the establishment of a peaceful settlement and that accordingly they should meet under his auspices in order to achieve it."

Eban continued: "Egypt rejected the proposal with vehemence. It said that it wanted nothing to do with negotiations in any form or with any agreement, that there was nothing to negotiate or agree to and, in effect, the only thing necessary was for Israel to get up and go away. In other words, would we please get into a position in which they could destroy us in the next attempt."

HUSSEIN'S BLUNDER

An inexplicable mystery of the 1967 war was Hussein's costly intervention. There had been no need for him to enter, and he paid for his folly. One week before the war, as in 1956, he went to Cairo and signed a new pact with Nasser, and when war began he plunged in, despite appeals from Israel, the U.N., and the United States to remain on the sidelines.

In Jerusalem, a few weeks after the war, Arthur Lourie of Israel's Foreign Ministry told me how he had sent a formal appeal, conveyed by General Odd Bull of the U.N., urging Hussein to remain out of the conflict. Lourie exhibited the reply—a plateful of bullets that had crashed through his windows, which overlooked the Old City. More than 1,000 buildings in the New City were hit in the ensuing 36 hours. Presumably, Hussein moved because he did not know that Israel had already won the war against Egypt. He had been deceived by Cairo Radio's fabricated victories.

His decision had also violated a pledge to the United States; for when Washington agreed to send tanks to Jordan, he had promised that they would not cross the Jordan River into the West Bank. But Hussein's American M-48 tanks went into action, and many were captured by the Israelis. One Israeli diplomat later sadly commented that the Israelis had blundered when they had opposed the transfer of a better grade tank to Jordan. It would have cost much less to upgrade those than the ones they had captured.

Shortly before the war, apprehensive lest Hussein be overthrown by mutinous troops after their humiliation by Israeli soldiers at Es-Samu, the

United States had loaned him several F-104 planes. However, the United States did not want any American involvement in the war; our planes and mechanics were swiftly flown out of the area.

Hussein came to Washington to ask for additional arms. We heard him at the National Press Club, where he acknowledged that he had knowingly collaborated with Nasser in the Big Lie that Americans had helped the Israeli air force attack the Egyptian planes – an incendiary accusation that might have provoked World War III. Why had he entered the war? Because if he remained aloof, he might be abandoned if he needed aid in the future.

Did Hussein really want the West Bank back? He had never done much for it when he had ruled the area. He had restricted investment; his major contribution was to improve, with U.S. aid, the highway to Jerusalem to encourage tourism. Hussein might have established his throne and capital in Jerusalem, but it was only in the last year of his rule there that he rented a villa in the city.

There was a gulf between the educated and cultured Palestinians and the Bedouins. The influx of Palestinians into Jordan during and after the Six-Day War enabled them to assume a dominant role in the country. While Israel was ready to accept the return to the West Bank of many who had fled, a surprisingly small number accepted the offer, perhaps because they thought they could do better in the more prosperous East Bank, perhaps because they feared becoming embroiled in another war. Besides, Israel's unprecedented open bridges policy enabled many from Jordan, Lebanon, and the Persian Gulf to visit the West Bank, Jerusalem, and all of Israel whenever they chose to do so. About 15,000 Arabs visited Israel that first summer; the number rose to 500,000 in a few years.

Nasser was less frank than Hussein when *Look* asked him about the Big Lie. Were faulty information and misunderstandings responsible for his accusation? Nasser's answer to *Look* was: "You could say so, yes." But this "retraction" was beamed toward the West. The Arab press report was different. *Al Ahram,* quoting Nasser, said: "You may say so, but others may say something else."

NIXON'S VIEW

In April, we invited all presidential candidates to offer us their views on the Middle East for publication in a special issue of the *Near East Report*.

Richard Nixon was the first to respond, on April 22, with a very strong statement, which he reaffirmed in a speech to B'nai B'rith on September 8 and in a meeting with the Conference of Presidents of Major American Jewish Organizations on October 21.

He stressed arms superiority for Israel in order to deter Arab militants, the first presidential aspirant to do so; preventive diplomacy to warn the

Soviet Union that we would resist Soviet expansionism; diplomatic initiatives to promote an Arab-Israel peace; and aid to the Arab states to combat hunger and disease. He warned that the Russians had been the principal beneficiaries of the post-war truce, that they had naval bases, that the number of Soviet vessels in the Mediterranean had more than quadrupled, from 11 to nearly 50, and that for the first time in 60 years Soviet ships had moved into the Persian Gulf.

Why are we for Israel? Because, Nixon answered, we believe in the self-determination of nations; we oppose aggression in every form; Israel is threatened by Soviet imperialism; and its example offers long-range hope to the Middle East. Furthermore, he continued, Americans admire a people "who can scratch a desert and produce a garden." Israelis have shown qualities with which Americans identify: "patriotism, idealism, and a passion for freedom." America is not about to abandon Israel. We recognize her predicament. Israel's enemies can afford to fight a war and lose and come back to fight again. Israel cannot afford to lose once. America knows that and is "determined that Israel is here in the family of nations to stay."

Recalling that statement, I find it easier to accept Ambassador Keating's disclosure to me in Israel in the summer of 1974. Nixon had told him that it was he who had made the fateful decision to speed and enlarge the historic military airlift to Israel in October 1973. "Send 50, send 100 planes," he had said.

The earlier Nixon had not been all that friendly. He was not one of the 36 senators who sponsored aid to Israel in 1951. On November 2, 1956, Vice-President Nixon had defended the Eisenhower-Dulles opposition to the British-French-Israeli move into Sinai. At Hershey, Pennsylvania, he had said that while this country cherished the friendship of all three, "force is wrong when it is used by our enemies and it is just as wrong when it is used by our friends. For the first time in history, we have shown independence of Anglo-French policies toward Asia and Africa, which seemed to us to reflect the colonial tradition. That declaration of independence has had an electrifying effect throughout the world."

Later, however, it was reported that Nixon joined Knowland and Johnson in criticism of the Administration's threat of sanctions against Israel. But in 1963 Nixon visited Cairo and criticized the United States for withdrawing aid from the Aswan Dam project and for providing Israel with the Hawk anti-aircraft missile.

The Arab Information Service disseminated newspaper interviews in which Nixon was quoted as complimenting Nasser, praising UAR progress in education, and urging U.S.-UAR cooperation for development. In a speech to the Arab Socialist Union on September 14, Nasser was critical of Nixon's pro-Israel statements: "He heard our views from me, Dr. Fawzi, and the officials here. When he came here, we honored him and assigned him a special plane. He went to Aswan and saw the High Dam. He came back and met with me. He said he was sorry that the United States had withdrawn its offer to finance the High Dam. Naturally, he says something here and when he goes back he says something else."

On the eve of Nixon's inauguration, AIPAC sent an appeal to him to make it clear beyond any doubt that the United States would take firm action to resist any aggression against Israel and would reject any pressures by the Soviet Union and the Arab states designed to force Israel to withdraw from occupied territories without an Arab-Israeli agreement. AIPAC also called on the new Administration to provide Israel with deterrent strength and to encourage Israel and the Arab states to negotiate peace agreements.

THE POSTURE OF THE CHURCH

Elson, never our friend, had complained that Christians had been indifferent, that there was too much silence and inaction in American life, remoteness as well as alienation. I heard Jewish leaders voice a similar complaint — that many of the Christian clergy were apathetic and neutral, if not pro-Arab; they could not understand the relationship of American Jews to Israel. I learned very early that the people in the pews were much closer to Zion than the preachers in the pulpits. Were Christian missionaries and their church property hostages in the Arab world? Certainly the public opinion polls had always resulted in large pro-Israel majorities.

It was gratifying to have the support of men like Sir Basil H. Liddell Hart, world-famous military authority, who wrote in *Encounter* in February 1968 that Israel should stay put until Arab leaders agreed to cooperate with her, and that she should remain in control of almost all the area she had conquered.

The beloved Martin Luther King, Jr. did much to help combat the pernicious anti-Israel propaganda which insidiously enticed blacks to align themselves with the Arabs. He spoke out, ten days before he was murdered, before the annual convention of the Rabbinical Assembly. On the Middle East crisis, he said:

> The response of some of the so-called young militants does not represent the position of the vast majority of Negroes. There are some who are color-consumed and they see a kind of mystique in blackness or in being colored, and anything non-colored is condemned. We do not follow that course . . . .
> Peace for Israel means security, and we must stand with all our might to protect her right to exist, its territorial integrity and the right to use whatever sea lanes it needs. Israel is one of the great outposts of democracy in the world, and a marvelous example of what can be done, how desert land can be transformed into an oasis of brotherhood and democracy. Peace for Israel means security, and that security must be a reality.

The American Professors for Peace in the Middle East, an inter-faith group of some 10,000 academicians, issued a 50-page report in which they said that the Arabs will make peace with Israel provided there is no Israel with which to make peace. Four representatives had met with key figures in Jordan and Egypt. They were Professors David S. Landes of Harvard; Herbert Stroup, who had served with the National and World Council of Churches; Allen Pollack of the University of Pittsburgh's history department; and Dr. Albert B. Sabin, the renowned medical scientist.

In a message to AIPAC that year, Johnson declared: "Your continuing support of efforts to assure stability, peace and progress in the Middle East deserves the gratitude of all men of good will everywhere. . . . Your own deliberations are a significant contribution to that cause and I wish you the utmost success."

At the end of 1968, Kane and I called on Assistant Secretary Parker Hart, who told us that there was a new U.S. initiative. On the next day, a dispatch from Paris outlined the proposal. The United States was advocating the complete withdrawal of Israeli forces from Sinai and replacement at Sharm el-Sheikh by a U.N. force, an end to the state of war, an East-West agreement to restrict arms, freedom of navigation, and a signed peace. Although the proposal went far to meet Arab demands, Nasser told the Arab Socialist Union that he rejected it.

Mrs. Meir told her audience at a Washington dinner sponsored by the Israel Bond organization that Israel would not again entrust her security to a new UNEF in the light of the 1967 experience.

At the U.N., Egypt was said to be ready to end the state of belligerence if Israel withdrew from Sinai and announced her readiness to return all other occupied territories, but would not sign a peace treaty. In Stockholm, Egypt's Riad visited Jarring and talked softly to the peace-loving Scandinavians. He said that the Egyptians were for peace, but not for peace treaties. Thus he was acknowledging the fact of Israel's existence, but not her right to exist.

THE GROWTH OF TERRORISM

Early in the post-war period, terrorists began to take over in Jordan, renewing their border warfare on the Israel-Jordan frontier and in Jerusalem. Plastic mines, shaped like buttons, were scattered in Jerusalem's streets, endangering pedestrians and shattering hands, feet, and limbs.

In reaction to mounting terrorism, on March 20, 1968, Israelis attacked Karameh, a refugee camp which had been transformed into an El Fatah base by some 1,000 terrorists from Syria who were on the refugee rolls, and who had been supplied with rations, housing, school, and health facilities. Unfortunately for the Israelis, Karameh was honeycombed with tunnels and bunkers and was ready for the attack. Arabs claimed that Israel suffered heavy casualties.

Responding to Jordan's demand, the Security Council unanimously condemned Israel's military action and threatened further steps to ensure against repetition.

Shortly thereafter, Jordan received 16 Starfighter planes and 100 Patton tanks from the United States.

By November, Jordan had accorded the terrorists legal sanction and agreed to respect their right to attack Israel; they promised not to undermine Hussein's authority. There were restrictions: the terrorists were required to use Jordanian license plates, and they were not permitted to recruit regular army men.

In November 1968, 12 people were killed and more than 50 hospitalized when explosives in a parked car were set off in a crowded Jerusalem market.

On October 26, Egyptian artillery had gunned down 13 Israelis who were playing soccer near the Canal. Five days later, helicopter-borne Israeli commandos crossed the Red Sea, went 130 miles inland, and blew up two bridges and a Soviet-built power relay station on the Nile, 150 miles from the Aswan Dam.

In July 1968, Palestinian terrorists hijacked an El Al Israel plane with 38 passengers and 10 crewmen on a flight from Rome to Tel Aviv. They landed in Algeria.

The three Palestinians spurned U Thant's appeal to release the plane. The 20 non-Israeli passengers were allowed to leave the day after the hijacking—10 Israeli women and children five days later. Algeria gave no indication as to what it intended to do with the five Israeli male passengers and the seven Israeli crewmen. Algeria kept the Israelis for 39 days, yielding up its prisoners to avert a boycott of airline pilots. Israel ultimately released 16 convicted Arab infiltrators—the first and only time that Israelis made a deal with terrorists, trading their prisoners for the lives of the Israelis, until 1979, when they exchanged 76 Arabs for one Israeli prisoner of war.

The Arabs also persisted in their boycott against Jews.

Saudi Arabia had accepted the appointment of a British ambassador to Jedda named Horace Phillips, an Arabist who was head of chancery for three years. Although Phillips was not a practicing Jew and his children had been baptized, the Saudis revoked their consent after the *Jewish Chronicle* of London revealed his Jewish background. The British press condemned the Saudi move as racist.

In contrast, Johnson had named Supreme Court Associate Justice Goldberg as our ambassador to the U.N. in 1965, to succeed Adlai Stevenson. In effect, Johnson told the Arab League that Zionists would not be disqualified from speaking for the United States and that the Arabs would have to deal with them. A few weeks before Goldberg was appointed, he accepted my invitation to make a speech to a national AIPAC policy conference and he associated himself with the historic pro-Zionist declaration made by Justice Louis D. Brandeis just fifty years before.

Goldberg came under attack because of that speech. After listening to a long harangue by Saudi Arabia's Baroody on Zionism and the influence of American Jews on American political leaders, Goldberg offered this comment:

> I merely would point out that the public policy of the United States, including its foreign policy, is determined by our people at large, through a democratically elected President and Congress and by no other means. We are proud of this and we would have it no other way, and reject aspersions on the undivided loyalty to our country of all citizens, regardless of their origins. To the people of the United States, the true test of the American is this: that he is one who does not conceal but affirms his origin, who is proud of it whatever it may be, and who recognizes that in the plurality of American life is our strength and the source of the freedom that we so proudly profess in the world.

Goldberg was the U.S. spokesman during the 1967 debates. *The Washington Post* later disclosed that many Arab diplomats privately acknowledged that Goldberg had been scrupulously fair.

Chapter 23

The Rogers Plan

NIXON TRIES FOR PEACE

Like every new President, Nixon undertook an initiative to promote a settlement. He proposed to try every option: talks with the Arabs and Israelis, then with the Soviet Union, after which the Big Two would offer their views to Britain and France. The four would transmit them to Jarring for submission to the parties.

We doubted that the Great Powers could ever agree, and we worried that any Great Power agreement would mean appeasement of the Arabs and erosion of Israel's security. A special *Near East Report* supplement recalled the Soviet-American push against Israel in 1957 and warned against a repetition of that blunder.

Nixon was under pressure. The Soviet Union demanded a victory for Nasser. France wanted recognition as a Big Power, as well as an opportunity to regain Arab good will. Oil men feared for their rich concessions. And Nixon wanted to strengthen NATO.

After Israel had refused to heed de Gaulle's advice in 1967, he had halted export of military equipment to Israel, including the 50 Mirage planes which Israel had paid for. With the exception of Communist and Gaullist publications, the French press criticized de Gaulle's anti-Israel policy. *Le Monde* branded it cynical and fraudulent. *L'Aurore* attacked it as a "stab in the back." "We are all Jews," a Catholic editorial writer commented in *Combat*.

However, the Soviets and the Americans agreed that action was imperative because of surging terrorism and retaliation.

THE RISE OF TERROR

The terrorist contagion spread in an environment which refused to quarantine it.

Five months after the Palestine Liberation Front had hijacked an Israeli plane to Algiers, terrorists attacked the same plane at Athens, killing an Israeli U.N. official, Leon Shirdan, and crippling a stewardess.

A few days later, on December 28, Israel retaliated when her soldiers, carried by helicopters, smashed 13 planes at the Beirut airport after warning passengers and crews to leave the field. No one was injured. On December 31, the Security Council condemned Israel and threatened sanctions, even though it had ignored a dynamite explosion which had blown 12 people to their deaths in Jersualem a few weeks before.

Israel's U.N. Ambassador Yosef Tekoah told the Security Council that Beirut sanctioned an El Fatah office, that there had been 22 terrorist raids from Lebanon in five months, and that Premier Abdullah Yaffi had described terrorist operations as "sacred" and "legal."

Kane and I telegraphed Rusk, charging that the United States had become partisan, less than evenhanded, and insensitive to the plight of Israel's people; 14 senators and 63 representatives signed statements of protest which had been initiated by Javits and Mondale in the Senate and by Celler in the House.

Rusk told the press that he did not favor an imposed peace; the countries themselves must find the solution. Arabs must restrain terrorism; Israelis must restrain retaliation.

The New York Times condemned Israel, but *The Washington Post* sarcastically chided the Great Powers for their double standard and even rebuked its former editor, J. R. Wiggins, who was then serving as the U.S. ambassador to the U.N.

THE HANGINGS IN IRAQ

On January 27, 1969, Iraq's military junta, headed by Major General Hassan Bakr, flexed its muscles by hanging 14 men—nine Jews, four Moslems, and one Christian—who were accused of spying for Israel. The defense counsel had weakly appealed for clemency. Some 500,000 men, women, and children responded to the invitation by Baghdad Radio to "come and enjoy the feast," and they danced happily past the scaffold in "Liberation Square."

Baghdad Radio scolded fellow Arabs for failing to support this outrage, although Yasir Arafat had welcomed it. Baghdad justified the crime by reminding the world that Jews had killed Christ. Our new Secretary of State, William P. Rogers, condemned the hangings in his first policy statement. If nothing else, the savage deed mocked El Fatah's October pretense that Iraqi Jews were eager to return home from Israel in order to make room for Arab repatriation.

Both Jordan and Lebanon were knuckling under to the terrorists. Arafat was welcomed in Hussein's palace—a surrender which Hussein was to regret in 1970. In Lebanon, Premier Rashid Karami was forced to resign after 17 people were killed in two days of rioting.

Congressmen protested against aiding countries which harbor terrorists.

On February 18, an El-Al plane was machine-gunned and bombed at Zurich airport by three terrorists, one of whom was killed by an Israeli security guard. One crew member died of his wounds. Six days later, two Hebrew University students were killed when a bomb exploded in a Jerusalem supermarket; eight other shoppers were wounded. On the same day, Israeli planes bombed El Fatah camps near Damascus in reply to 12 terrorist incidents in the Golan Heights.

The weak regime in Syria was swept away by Defense Minister Hafez Assad, who promised to help the terrorists. Unlike his many predecessors, the skillful Assad contrived to retain power for many years.

BACK TO THE TALKS

An optimistic Nixon told the press on March 4 that he hoped a four-power recommendation might bring both sides to the conference table. He gave assurances that the four powers would not impose a settlement.

After talks with Nixon and Rogers, Eban confidently told the National Press Club that he had observed no erosion in the U.S. position, but he cautioned against Great Power involvement.

In Egypt, Nasser hurled threats to please Egyptians, while he disarmed Western correspondents. He promised *Newsweek* that he would accept a non-belligerence declaration, reciting the five points of Resolution 242. None of this was translated for the home folks; twenty-five of his thirty-five answers were rewritten in an Arabic version.

In a January 20 speech, Nasser had again reaffirmed that Egypt could accept the U.N. resolution "to eliminate the consequences of the June aggression" but that Palestinians were entitled to reject the resolution "because it is inadequate for determining the Palestinian fate."

As with *Newsweek,* Nasser also had a cheerful talk with *Time* on May 16. Nasser said that he would accept the reality of Israel "if there is a humanitarian solution." The Cairo translation was limited to a 119-word denunciation of Israel's "aggression."

In Cairo, Egypt's Foreign Minister Riad told *Al Ahram* that the Arab objective was the liberation of Palestine and not merely the liberation of Sinai. He believed that all diplomatic efforts would fail because Israel was "expansionist."

Growing more militant, Nasser had assured the 1,700 members of the Arab Socialist Union that Egypt would bomb and shell Israeli civilian centers. He described artillery exchanges across the Suez Canal as war. World opinion, he explained, responded only to pressure and "explosive situations." He warned the Big Four that their attitude in the current talks would determine their future relations with the Arabs for many years. He insisted that Egypt had not lost the war in 1967, since the air force had been knocked out before Egypt had time to enter it.

As Nasser spoke, Rogers indicated to the Senate Commitee on Foreign Relations that the United States favored return of most of the lands which Israel had occupied in 1967, except Jerusalem. On April 7, Rogers again told the press that he was opposed to an imposed settlement, but he went on to suggest that world opinion would achieve it.

THE WAR OF ATTRITION

On May 1, Nasser opened his war of attrition to pressure the Big Four, and the Suez clashes increased in number, intensity, and casualties. He declared: "Our armed forces have begun to implement their plan . . . to destroy the Bar Lev Line. Israel must withdraw from occupied territory or there will be continued fighting."

Our annual AIPAC conference was scheduled to open April 23 — Israel's 21st birthday. Prior to that two-day meeting, I suggested to Celler and to Scott and Ribicoff that they circulate a declaration calling for direct negotiations, opposing "any attempt by outside powers to impose half-way measures not conducive to a permanent peace," and opposing "all pressures upon Israel to withdraw prematurely and unconditionally from any of the territories which Israel now administers." The statement was based on the one I had promoted in 1962. It also deplored "one-sided U.N. resolutions which ignore Arab violations of the cease-fire and which censure Israel's reply and counteraction."

Celler read the text at an AIPAC luncheon on the Hill. By that time, the signers included 227 members of the Senate and House. In response to constituency appeals, the total subsequently rose to 70 senators and 282 members of the House — 352 in all. We later reproduced the statement in advertisements in *The New York Times* and *The Washington Post*.

The Administration was gaining support from big business. "What's at stake in the Middle East, specifically, is money — a lot of it," one read in the *Wall Street Journal*. To deepen our concern, Sisco disclosed that the Administration was again supporting the 1961 Joseph E. Johnson plan, which would have permitted Arab refugees to opt for repatriation to Israel or for resettlement and compensation.

HUSSEIN IN WASHINGTON

The ever popular Hussein came to Washington in April to win anti-aircraft guns, communications equipment, and other items for his arsenal. He was to get 18 Starfighters in June, and he wanted another 18, although he lacked trained Jordanian pilots to fly them home.

As usual, Hussein talked softly. He was for a just and lasting peace. He would not mention Israel by name. He would accept the pre-1967 borders, although a few days before both he and Nasser had spoken to Jarring of the earlier boundary lines that had been recommended in the 1947 partition resolution (which Jordan's Abdullah had wiped out by invading, seizing, and annexing the West Bank). Hussein favored free navigation through the Suez Canal, but two days later Cairo repudiated his claim to speak for both Egypt and Jordan, asserting that the Suez Canal would be open to Israel only after the refugee problem had been solved. Even as Hussein arrived, terrorists based in Jordan's Aqaba fired rockets at Israel's Eilat.

In his book, *My War with Israel,* Hussein contended that Nasser did not intend or want war in 1967 but that his brinksmanship had made war inevitable when he ousted UNEF. Hussein had believed Nasser's lie that Americans had intervened to help Israel. How else could one explain all those enemy planes after Nasser's claim that he had destroyed the Israeli Air Force? He also revealed that "Nasser never called on us. It was we who called on him."

In June the Big Two talks suffered a setback. The U.S.-Soviet talks had focused on an Egyptian-Israeli settlement which provided for Israel's withdrawals in the Sinai. Fearing a U.S. attempt to divide the Arabs, Nasser again insisted on an all-embracing settlement which would include Jerusalem, Gaza, the Golan Heights, and the West Bank. Gromyko obligingly joined Nasser in a communiqué voicing that demand. The talks were obviously assymetrical. Gromyko was serving as Nasser's advocate, while Israel had no similar support from the United States.

For its part, the United States had hoped to defer Israeli-Jordanian talks until after a settlement with Egypt, inasmuch as the Soviets had no authority to speak for Jordan.

The Soviets and Americans were far apart on many points, as were Americans and Israelis. The United States continued to favor Israel's withdrawal from Sinai and Sharm el-Sheikh, while Israel wanted continued access to that critical navigation base.

Egypt wanted to reoccupy Gaza. The United States was considering either its accession to Jordan or its control by the U.N.

While the United States favored return of the West Bank to Jordan, with minor border rectifications, it did not want to restore the ugly barricades in Jerusalem. It sought some recognition of Hussein's rights there, however.

Russians and Americans both advocated demilitarized zones, with UNEF on both sides of the lines; Israelis were opposed. The United States wanted

Security Council supervision; the Soviets believed that the respective parties should have the power to exclude UNEF after five years.

The Soviets wanted representation for all political and geographic groups, a demand which implied the presence of Communist troops. The Israelis naturally objected.

The United States thought of a contractual peace obligating the parties to each other, but it rejected Israel's insistence on a *de jure* peace leading to diplomatic, cultural, and economic relations. The Soviet concept was a reciprocally binding accord on the implementation of Resolution 242, the documents to be signed separately and filed with the Security Council.

The United States wanted the Suez Canal opened for all, but the Russians wanted it to be governed by the Constantinople Convention, which the Egyptians had invoked in the past to bar Israeli ships on security grounds. Americans favored repatriation of a limited number of Arab refugees, while the Russians opposed any limitations. Americans wanted the parties to negotiate a final settlement through Jarring. The Russians wanted the Big Four to do it all, inasmuch as the Khartoum formula forbade negotiations.

A vigorous critic of the Administration's role in Vietnam, Fulbright introduced legislation to the effect that a national commitment to a foreign power requires affirmative action by both Congress and the Executive Branch through a treaty, convention, or other legislative instrumentality. Fulbright opposed commitments which were merely based on declarations by the Executive. The Senate agreed. The report prepared by the Senate Committee on Foreign Relations cited the many commitments made to Israel by the Executive which had never been ratified by the Senate: Truman's 1948 declaration of support; the 1950 Tripartite Declaration pledging opposition to the violation of Middle East frontiers; the Eisenhower Doctrine in 1957; the 1957 Dulles assertion that the Gulf of Aqaba was an international waterway; the 1963 Kennedy press conference promising American opposition to any aggression in the Middle East; Johnson's 1964 statement indicating support for the territorial integrity and independence of all Middle Eastern countries.

Incessant warfare across the Suez Canal took a heavy toll in late summer. In addition, bombs exploded in an Israeli pavilion at a trade fair in Izmir, Turkey; in the Zim Israel Navigation Company office in London; in Israeli embassies in The Hague and Bonn; and at the Brussel's El Al office. Iraq executed 15 more alleged spies for "Israel and the United States." Terrorists hijacked an Israel-bound TWA plane, diverting it to Damascus. After releasing the passengers from the plane and exploding the cockpit, Syria held two prominent Israeli passengers, one of them a Hebrew University professor, Shlomo Samueloff, for 98 days. The two terrorists were freed.

Most alarming was the fire in the Al Aksa Mosque in Jerusalem, which ignited hysterical cries in Arab countries for a *jihad,* a holy war, against Israel. It was denounced as a plot to destroy the Mosque and to restore the

Temple. The turmoil was reminiscent of the Reichstag fire in 1933. Twenty-four hours later, however, it was established that the fire was set by an Australian Christian fundamentalist, Michael Denis Rohan, who had slipped into the Mosque because of the negligence of Arab guards. Rohan was found insane by the court.

Never abashed, Nasser now insisted that this was a Jewish conspiracy to incite Moslems against Christians. In further aggression against the truth, the Beirut *Daily Star* published a 1,300-word article on August 29, written by Sami Hadawi for the Institute for Palestine Studies. He quoted a *Time* article of June 30, 1967, to prove that the fire was linked with Jewish plans to rebuild the Temple, which was purported to say: "The Temple must be reconstructed on its original site; this could only be done by demolishing Islam's sacred Dome of the Rock."

In fact, this was a scandalous and mischievous misquotation, as we soon learned by checking the original article. Hadawi had deliberately twisted the quotation, which had explained that the Temple could not be rebuilt without demolishing the Rock, and *Time* continued: "Despite their enmity with Arab nations, devout Jews would be reluctant to destroy the shrine of another faith" — a statement which Hadawi omitted to quote.

Despite rising U.S.-Israeli tension, Golda Meir's visit to Washington in late September evoked an extraordinary exchange of compliments between her and Nixon.

At a White House dinner on September 25, 127 guests heard Nixon describe Israel's people as "brave and courageous." He praised their assistance program to other countries and observed that, despite their immense military burden, "they had made the land bloom" — to which Mrs. Meir responded that she would assure Israel's people that they had a great and dear friend who would "help us overcome many difficulties. They must not become cynical or give up hope." I later told the President and Rogers that it was a pity that no one had thought to call for UJA contributions after those cordial toasts.

A few days later in Los Angeles, I heard Mrs. Meir tell her audiences that the Hebrew language had a word for one who listens and another one for one who absorbs. She had told Nixon that he not only listened but also shared what she was saying. "We discussed Israel's problems as though they were our common problems."

Customarily, Arabs always try to undercut a visiting Israeli with advertisements, press conferences, and a "peace" offensive. On the day Mrs. Meir arrived, *The Washington Post* carried an advertisement published by the American Council on the Middle East which urged rejection of Israel's aid requests. At the U.N., Egypt's Riad told the press that if Israel renounced expansionism, negotiations could be possible. This sanguinary prophecy was later disavowed by a Cairo declaration barring talks and treaties.

The West suffered a heavy blow in Libya that same month, when an unknown Army officer, Muammar Qaddafi, overthrew the aging King Idris.

Worried about our base at Wheelus Field and Libya's gushing oil wells, the State Department recognized the new regime within six days, although it conceded that it did not know who its leaders were. They turned out to be a never-ending threat to stability—to Egypt, to Israel, to Sudan—and, worst of all, they lionized terrorists and gave them sanctuary.

From time to time, Israel tried to demonstrate Nasser's vulnerability to discourage him from pressing his war. Aggression could not escape reaction. Israel had suffered 21 fatal casualties in August, and so, before dawn on September 9, Israeli tanks, armored units, and naval commandos swept across the Canal, rolling 40 miles down the coast in a ten-hour raid in which they destroyed all installations. An Egyptian spokesman dismissed the raid as theatrical rather than military and the Egyptian press charged CIA-Israel collaboration.

Nasser told the Egyptian parliament that "Americans are fighting behind the Israeli personnel and the planes that are being used against us."

"Nasser is mistaken in describing the United States as an enemy of Egypt," Rogers struck back next day. He described the Nasser speech as a "setback in efforts to find a political solution."

The bloody civil war which devastated Lebanon in 1976 and 1977 had its beginning in 1969, when the Lebanese army had tried to prevent a Yasir Arafat take-over. A cease-fire negotiated by Nasser in Cairo gave the terrorists sanction to operate against Israel from Lebanon. They swiftly seized control of 14 of the 15 UNRWA camps. Israel's Ambassador Tekoah urged UNRWA to withhold assistance from these new terrorist bases. The House Committee on Foreign Affairs drafted an amendment to the foreign aid bill barring the use of U.S. contributions to UNRWA for Arab refugees involved in terrorism.

To put new pressure on Washington, the Arabs scheduled a summit conference in Rabat, Morocco, for December 20 and planted rumors that they might withdraw their acceptance of Resolution 242.

Nasser charged that the United States was trying to block the summit, and an Egyptian parliament resolution blamed the United States for the failure of the peace efforts. It indicted the United States as an enemy because it provided arms to Israel and permitted U.S. citizens to volunteer in Israel's army, and because, it charged, the Israelis had participated in Anglo-American naval maneuvers.

In order to blunt the Rabat meeting, Rogers outlined the U.S. position on an Egyptian-Israeli "peace" on December 9 and offered proposals for a Jordanian-Israeli agreement to the Big Four nine days later. This was the "Rogers Plan."

Israelis charged that there was little left to negotiate, for the United States wanted Israel's withdrawal from virtually all the occupied territories. For Jerusalem, the United States proposed some form of binational regime, permitting both Jordan and Israel to participate in the civic, economic, and religious life of the Old City. Gaza, presumably, would go to Jordan, and the United States upheld the unconditional right of the Arab refugees to choose between repatriation and resettlement under the supervision of an international commission. Israel would have to accept a fixed annual quota.

Reflecting their special interest, leading American oil men and financiers were in Washington on that same day to meet Nixon and his National Security Adviser, Dr. Henry A. Kissinger. They were David Rockefeller, president of Chase Manhattan Bank; John J. McCloy, former president of the World Bank; and former Secretary of the Treasury Robert B. Anderson.

Israel's rejection was sweeping. Mrs. Meir reacted bitterly on December 22. "We didn't survive three wars in order to commit suicide so that the Russians can celebrate a victory for Nasser. That isn't what we are here for and what thousands have died for. Nobody in the world can make us accept it. What can happen is that life can be made very difficult for us."

Fulbright scolded "an unseemly attack," pointing out that the United States permitted Israel to raise funds in this country. He praised the plan as a "balanced and sensible approach to the interests of the United States and of peace."

Some 1,400 leading American Jews from 31 states descended on Washington on January 25 and 26 to voice their protest. In preparation for their visit, we published an updated *Myths and Facts* and arranged appointments with 250 members of the Senate and House.

Jews were not alone. On December 22, Richard Cardinal Cushing of Boston urged the Administration to insist on direct negotiations and warned that the Big Four initiative could end in calamity. President George Meany of the AFL-CIO called on the Administration to provide arms to Israel and denounced appeasement of Soviet and Arab dictators.

The Washington-briefed press was impressed. *The New York Times* on December 11 described the Rogers plan as "a clear call to reason and fair play." It suggested that Israel's withdrawal in exchange for "Arab acceptance of a permanent peace based on binding agreements" would be "a fair exchange." Next day, *The Times* was pleased that Rogers had not called for Israel's retreat from Golan and suggested that Nasser should drop his demand if he really wanted a settlement: "How can anybody—including the other Arab states—sensibly call for the restoration of a situation on the old Syria-Israel border that threatened not only the security of Israel but the peace of the entire region?"

The Washington Post seemed satisfied with the Rogers plan. "What could be more unexceptional," the *Post* asked, referring to Israel's withdrawal, "if her territorial integrity is assured" in accordance with Resolution 242? *The Washington Star* understood Israel's rejection: "They still insist, and with ample reason, there must be direct negotiations . . . if there is ever to be a trustworthy peace."

Many other papers, remote from State Department influence, were disenchanted and supported Israel's position. The *Atlanta Constitution* said that the Administration proposal was "doomed." The *Dayton Daily News* declared that the oil interests had prompted a spur-of-the-moment whim which would cause harm. The *Lubbock Avalanche Journal* called Mrs. Meir a realist. The *San Jose Mercury* said that the Administration was blundering. The *Richmond News Leader* called the U.S. plan a pro-Arab product written in Amman. The *Chattanooga Free Press* insisted that the best way to avoid another war was to keep Israel strong. The *New York Post* warned against diplomatic isolation of Israel, a long war of attrition, or a new conflagration, and the *Miami Herald* wrote that Israel's security involved U.S. national interests ten times more clearly than did Vietnam.

Sensitive to the indignant protests, Nixon sent a reassuring message to the Jewish leaders: "The United States stands by its friends. Israel is one of its friends." He went on to say that peace could be achieved only through negotiations and that the United States would not attempt to impose it. The United States was prepared to provide the arms that Israel might need. The question on the agenda was whether the Administration would continue sending Phantoms to Israel when the initial agreement was fulfilled. A few days later, the President told the press that he would announce a decision on Israel's pending arms request in thirty-one days.

The Cairo press angrily protested that Nixon's statement was "the most hostile yet," but U.S. officials assured Cairo diplomats and press that there had been no basic change in U.S. policy.

Simultaneously, Celler and Senators Joseph D. Tydings (D-Maryland) and Clifford P. Case (R-New Jersey) circulated a new round robin which called for direct negotiations, but, unlike the 1969 declaration, it also included a call for arms for Israel lest her foes believe that she might be left defenseless in the face of Soviet arms. Constituents encouraged their congressmen to sign the declaration and, as in 1969, 70 members of the Senate (but not the same 70) agreed, as did 280 members of the House.

Apart from that, 84 Republicans and four Democrats endorsed a separate resolution calling for direct negotiations. It was initiated by Representative Philip M. Crane (R-Illinois); 64 Democrats signed a similar statement drafted by the veteran Representative Claude Pepper (D-Florida).

Leading sympathizers of the Arab cause were also active that day, calling on Under Secretary of State Elliot L. Richardson to warn that arms sales to Israel obstructed peace. They included Dr. John H. Davis, who, when he headed UNRWA, encouraged Palestinian Arabs to oppose the Jewish state, as well as Dr. Daniel Bliss, president of American Middle East Rehabilitation, Inc.; Dr. Alfred Carleton, president of AFME; Dr. Robert Crawford, vice-president of the American University of Beirut; Dr. Thomas Mallison, professor of law at George Washington University; Dr. Frank Maria, chairman of the Department of Near East and Arab Refugee Affairs of the Christian Antiochian Orthodox Archdiocese of New York and North America; and John Richardson, executive director of ANERA.

"The key to peace in the Middle East is appropriate rectification of the injustices committed against the people of Palestine when Israel was created," Davis said.

Twelve days later, leaders of Egypt, Jordan, Syria, Iraq, and the Sudan met in Cairo to threaten that American oil companies would be nationalized if Israel received more Phantom jets. Nasser charged that the new American proposals were less satisfactory than those that Rusk had offered in 1968.

Congressmen received a 20,000-word memorandum from the Friends Committee on National Legislation (the Quakers), who had questioned aid to Israel in 1951. It criticized Israel's demand for direct negotiations and her preoccupation with "security" as contrasted with the Arab preoccupation with "justice." Accepting most Arab demands, it urged that all occupied territories except the Jewish part of the Old City be placed under U.N. trusteeship, with U.N. forces in demilitarized zones. Israel, the Quakers said, was the product of Western "political cynicism," and the Six-Day War resulted from false moves, inflammatory speeches, and threats from both sides. They lauded Arab terrorists as "resistance forces." There were curious misstatements. They claimed, inaccurately, that Israel had not accepted the 1947 U.N. proposal for Jerusalem and Resolution 242 in 1967.

Later, Dr. Landrum Bolling, who had edited the Quaker peace plan, told Pauline Frederick over NBC that the Senate declaration reflected that body's "bankruptcy." Responding to my appeal for a reply, NBC invited an answer by Scott and Javits.

One of our most inveterate Senate critics was Mark Hatfield (R-Oregon), who filled 17 pages of the Congressional Record to argue that, instead of trying to maintain the military balance, the United States should give more funds to Arab refugees.

The Democratic Policy Council, on February 9, urged face-to-face negotiations. It called on the Administration to reduce the arms flow, but stipulated that in the meantime the United States must correct or prevent an arms imbalance that could threaten Israel's existence or provoke hostilities.

Gerald Ford was worried about planes to Libya. He told the B'nai Zion annual Award Dinner: "I cannot imagine why Libya, with an army far smaller than the New York City Police Department, needs over 100 of the latest French Mirage fighter bombers or hundreds of British Chieftain tanks."

President Pompidou was rudely received when he arrived in Washington and other cities because of the planes he had provided to Libya. When he addressed Congress, he was astonished by the age level of the members. Many had boycotted the session, and McCormack had to round up youthful pages to sit in their places. AIPAC was in no way responsible for the discourtesy. I was in Florida during his visit and counseled our staff to refrain from any anti-Pompidou action.

Meanwhile, Israel continued her military successes. As 1969 ended, five gunboats, which had been built for Israel but embargoed by the French, were spirited away from Cherbourg to Haifa by the Israelis. Most French-men applauded, the polls showed. Soon after, Israeli commandos seized a million dollar seven-ton radar station across the Gulf of Suez. They removed it with blow torches and airlifted it to Israel by helicopter. Responding to terrorist attacks from Jordan, Israelis blocked Jordan's East Bank irrigation canal. When Lebanese-based terrorists kidnapped a 50-year-old watchman in Metulla, Israeli commandos captured 21 persons, including 10 soldiers.

Israel's jet planes flew low over Cairo and Damascus, attacking military installations, but, in a deplorable blunder, they bombed a scrap metal fac-tory at Abu Za'abel; Egypt charged that 70 workmen were killed and many more wounded.

Israel's bombing raids were intended to cripple Egyptian supply bases, in order to relieve Egyptian pressure on Israel's Suez Canal line, for Nasser had intensified his attacks, inflicting many casualties.

Kosygin warned Washington, London, and Paris that unless Israel stopped the bombing the Soviet Union would increase its supplies to Egypt. Meanwhile, the United States was still deferring action on Israel's request for additional arms, hoping that the Soviets would curtail shipments to Cairo and Damascus.

Arab terrorism grew more daring and brutal. A 31-year-old Israeli was killed and 10 other passengers were injured at Munich on February 10, when two Jordanians and an Egyptian tried to hijack an El Al plane. How-ever, Mordechai Ben Ari, El Al's president, disclosed that, despite five inci-dents in 30 months, passenger traffic on El Al planes was growing. He ap-pealed for international action to ensure that hijackers were extradited to countries whose planes they attacked.

An Israel-bound Swiss airliner, carrying 47 passengers, crew, and time bombs in its mail sacks, was blown out of the sky on February 21, 1970. An Austrian plane escaped a similar tragedy. The General Command of the Popular Front for the Liberation of Palestine claimed credit, but later dis-claimed it as world revulsion rose. The Arabs charged that Israelis them-selves had plotted the bombings to discredit the Arabs, but two Jordanians were arrested because they had purchased barometers which were used to detonate the time bombs. In Palm Beach, I pointed to the outrage as a deci-sive point in a debate with an Arab spokesman.

Shortly after the bombings, a bus carrying Americans on a Holy Land tour was ambushed near Hebron, and one of Ford's constituents, the wife of a Baptist minister, was killed. Two other women were injured.

A few months later, both Nixon and Kissinger made new and impressive policy statements while on the West Coast. In a television interview on July 1, Nixon warned that the Middle East danger exceeded that of Vietnam because it could lead to a Big Power collision. It was in the U.S. interest to maintain Israel's strength in order to deter her neighbors. He branded both Egypt and Syria as aggressive, differentiating between them and Israel by pointing out that the Arab states wanted to drive Israel into the sea but that Israelis had no such intentions against their adversaries. Most importantly, Nixon called for defensible frontiers, which seemed to imply abandonment of the Rogers plan. So we always wanted to believe.

Kissinger, briefing the press as a senior American spokesman, astonished the Department of State when he said that it would be necessary to expel the Russians from the Middle East. On the very next day, Kane and I were with Sisco, who was obviously startled by the Kissinger announcement. The State Department had been less critical of the Soviets. Its spokesman had maintained that Moscow was limiting involvement of its pilots to defensive action. Yet the Russians were busily installing missile sites along the Suez Canal, manned by military and civilian personnel, whose total number in Egypt *Newsweek* later estimated at 28,000.

On July 30, Soviet pilots sought, unsuccessfully, to intercept Israel's air force, losing four planes. Nixon warned against the presence of Soviet military advisers in the Middle East at a press conference 20 days later.

We made the most of Nixon's use of the phrase "defensible borders." Later, in 1972, we encouraged all the Democratic candidates for the presidency to endorse that concept and we successfully urged its inclusion in the Democratic platform. Ironically, although it was Nixon's own language, we could not persuade the Republican platform committee to accept it. The Democratic platform again referred to defensible borders in 1976, and so did its nominee, Jimmy Carter, who, unfortunately, later qualified it by distinguishing between the permanent frontiers and provisional defense lines.

In the meantime, it became evident that the military sales aid bill would be blocked in Congress because of the Cooper-Church amendment barring arms sales. Accordingly, Senator Henry M. Jackson (D-Washington), one of Israel's staunchest supporters, offered an unprecedented amendment to the Defense Procurement Act, authorizing the President "to transfer to Israel by sale, credit sale, or guarantee such aircraft and equipment appropriate to use, maintain, and protect such aircraft as may be necessary to counteract any past, present, or future increased military assistance provided by other countries to the Middle East." The amendment called for transfer out of America's own military supplies to Israel.

This was a highly unorthodox measure, since it bypassed the Senate Committee on Foreign Relations, and Fulbright opposed it. His amendment to postpone action until the foreign aid bill had been disposed of was defeated 87 to 7. The six senators who joined him were Hatfield, Mansfield, Church, Cooper, Allen J. Ellender (D-Louisiana), and John Williams (D-Delaware). Church's vote haunted him in subsequent campaigns, but his position was not unnatural, since he was a member of the Foreign Relations Committee as well as the author of the Cooper-Church amendment. At the same time, he was one of Israel's best friends.

Later, after relations with Israel were reconciled, Secretary of Defense Laird strongly endorsed the Jackson amendment. The amount in the Military Sales Act would have been inadequate even if it had been voted, he said, and if the effective date on the Jackson amendment were tied to final action on the military sales legislation, the delay would block "maintenance of the military balance in the Middle East."

WE LOBBY FOR DESALTING AND AID

While our attention was riveted on the Big Power talks, we lobbied that summer of 1969 for three projects: a desalting program in Israel, and grants to two major American-supported institutions, Hadassah Hospital and the Graduate School of the Weizmann Institute of Science.

President Johnson had advocated a desalting project early in 1964, and there were many feasibility studies. Just before leaving office, Johnson recommended a proposal submitted by George Woods, the former president of the World Bank. It called for a U.S.-Israel partnership in a prototype desalting plant, producing 40 million gallons a day and generating 450 megawatts of power. The United States would pay half the construction and operation costs for five years, but not more than $40 million. The major burden would be assumed by Israel—an estimated $100 million, including the cost of electric power generation and distribution.

Ignoring Johnson's recommendation, Nixon made no provision for it in his budget. I asked two members of the House Committee on Foreign Affairs, Rosenthal and Frelinghuysen, to co-sponsor an authorizing amendment to the Foreign Assistance Act. Chairman Morgan arranged for a hearing, and two noted experts testified. They were Dr. Abel Wolman of Baltimore, one of America's top water experts, who had chaired the U.S. National Water Resources Board as well as a board of consultants on water problems in Israel, and Dr. Philip Sporn, a distinguished authority on power, who had served the United States in many capacities, in addition to service as chairman of the Israel Sea Water Conversion Commission.

They told the Committee that Israel was the most water conscious country in the world and the best place for a breakthrough. Israel had a complete inventory of her resources, know-how, and technological experience. A U.S.-Israel partnership would be helpful to both countries as well as to many developing countries which needed new techniques to combat hunger.

The House Committee approved the amendment, and the House voted approval late in November. The State Department announced opposition "because of budgetary restraints and the need to test available but unproven new technology in this country before using it in a large-scale plant overseas." Apparently the Department of Interior wanted to develop its own program.

The White House recommended delay to permit review of a new engineering survey. It questioned whether the proposal represented an optimum in so far as the research and development plans of the Department of Interior were concerned. Was it up-to-date? Could there be a corresponding gesture to friendly Arab countries, "hopefully to alleviate the refugee problem?" — obviously advice from State.

There was a setback in the Senate, where Gaylord Nelson (D-Wisconsin) and 21 co-sponsors offered similar legislation. The grant was transformed into a loan, but, in conference, the grant was restored. However, the amount was cut from $40 million to $20 million. The money remained unused for more than seven years. Meanwhile, there had been an encouraging breakthrough in Israel: the use of horizontal aluminum tubes to prevent corrosion.

In June 1975, the United States and Israel finally signed an agreement to build a 10-million-gallon-a-day dual purpose power-generating/desalting plant at Ashdod over a four-and-a-half-year period, financed by a $20 million U.S. grant and a $35 million Israeli investment.

There was little opposition to the requests for Hadassah, whose appeal was presented by Mrs. Faye Schenk, its president, and sponsored by Representative Donald Fraser (D-Minnesota) and Senator Pell; or for the Weizmann Institute, whose spokesman was Dr. Albert Sabin. Hadassah was asking for a grant of $1 million a year for five years, as part of a $12 million expansion program, including the reconstruction and re-equipment of the Hadassah Hospital on Mt. Scopus, closed by the 1948 war and now free once again, and an Oncology Institute for treatment and research. Fraser succeeded in winning the $5 million without delay. Johnson had recommended a $3 million grant for the Weizmann Institute, which had been established at Rehovoth by Dr. Weizmann in 1934. Both institutions had been hit by Israel's need to divert so much of its resources to defense. The United States had always provided aid to Arab-based institutions: $9.6 million to the American University in Cairo and $55.7 million to the American University of Beirut in the previous decade.

Chapter 24

The Violent and Violated Truce

THE U.S. TRUCE

Deeply alarmed over the fierce battles on the Suez front, the United States sought a cease-fire and stand-still agreement so that Jarring could proceed with his mission. Under the terms of the U.S. proposal, the parties would be forbidden to use the cease-fire to improve their military positions. The Israelis had a number of objections, including the provision for a 90-day truce—a deadline whose misuse facilitated periodic threats. Israel feared that the Egyptians would violate the truce to install new missiles in prohibited zones close to the Canal.

Nixon sought to reassure them in a televised Los Angeles press conference on July 30, 1970: "Some concern has been expressed by Israeli government officials that if they agreed to a cease-fire they would run the risk of having a military buildup occur during the cease-fire. We, and others, have attempted to assure them that that would not be the case. If there is a cease-fire . . . a condition . . . would be a military standstill during that period." Thus assured, Israel accepted the cease-fire on July 31.

The agreement provided that "both sides will refrain from changing the military status quo within zones extending 50 kilometers to the east and west of the cease-fire line." Activities within the zones would be limited to the maintenance of existing installations and to the rotation and supply of forces.

The standstill went into effect on August 7, but the Soviet Union and Egypt swiftly moved SA-2 and SA-3 missiles into the prohibited 32-mile zone west of the Canal.

245

The next issue of the *Near East Report* predicted: "The Egyptians and the Russians may be in a position to claim mastery of the skies over the Suez Canal. They may move to span the waterway, to smash Israel's Bar Lev Line, and roll tanks across the Sinai desert." The 1970 prophecy was tragically confirmed in 1973 at a cost of many Israeli lives. [There was a similar threat in 1981, when Syria installed Soviet missiles in Lebanon, menacing Israel's northern defense line.]

We protested the violation. At first the United States was unwilling to acknowledge it or to take action. The Department of State seemed to be more annoyed with Israel for disclosing the breach than with Egypt for committing it; Department officials deplored publication of the complaint, speculating that the Egyptians and the Soviets had begun to install the missiles before the truce and continued for only a short period thereafter. Four weeks elapsed before the State Department acknowledged Egypt's violation with the disclosure that American diplomats had raised the issue both in Cairo and Moscow.

In October, Israel's Yariv revealed that the Egyptians had 40 to 50 missile sites in the 30-mile zone west of the Suez, with some 600 missile launchers, compared with 16 such sites before the standstill. In the 60-mile zone, he claimed, there were now 30 to 40 missile sites, compared with only one before the standstill. He estimated that one-third of the missile sites were SA-3s manned by some 3,000 Russians. Egypt, aided by the Soviets, now had the most massive anti-aircraft system in the world.

The Washington Post declared on August 14: "It is up to the United States to satisfy Israel's understandable apprehension about being let down by the United States for Washington's own convenience."

Mrs. Meir came to the U.S. on September 18 to meet Nixon — to clarify misunderstandings and to end the arms stalemate. For their part, Nixon and Rogers visited the Sixth Fleet in the Mediterranean, implying U.S. readiness to strengthen it. Mrs. Meir was still refusing to rejoin the Jarring talks unless the illegal missiles were removed, but there was scant hope of that, and Israel agreed to resume the negotiations as the Administration sold her 18 Phantom jet planes as well as an undisclosed number of Skyhawks — fewer than Israel had requested — and M-60 tanks.

Congressmen reported that public opinion favored renewed support for Israel. Representative John Rhodes (R-Arizona) polled his constituents: "Do you think the United States should try to maintain the balance of power in the Middle East by providing military equipment to Israel when necessary?" Of the 45,192 respondents 58% said yes, 23.8% said no, and 15.5% were undecided.

Similarly, Representative Thomas M. Rees (D-California) found that 58% supported the sale of supersonic jets to Israel, 23.7% believed that the United States should refuse to send arms to either side, and 7% favored only non-military aid to Israel.

Riad defiantly told Cairo TV: "We shall not withdraw a single missile. Indeed, if we can double that number we shall do so. Indeed, if we had more missiles we would move them forward to increase our forces and defensive ability in the Canal area."

THE RISE OF TERROR

Terrorism rose to a climax in September 1970, when the PFLP hijacked three planes, forcing 400 passengers to land in the Jordanian desert. A TWA flight, with 145 passengers, was hijacked en route from Frankfurt to New York. A Swissair plane was carrying 155 persons from Zurich to New York. A BOAC jet, with 117 passengers, was on the way from Bahrein to London. A fourth plane, a Pan American 747, flying from Amsterdam to New York, was forced to land in Beirut, loaded with explosives, and then flown to Cairo, where it was blown up two minutes after 173 persons disembarked.

Terrorists failed in an attempt to seize an El Al plane flying from Amsterdam to New York. The plane's security guards killed a hijacker, a U.S. citizen, in a gun battle, while the passengers overwhelmed his 24-year-old accomplice, Leila Khaled. She was delivered to British authorities in London, who later released her

A spokesman for the terrorists had the temerity to inform Damascus Radio that El Al's use of armed guards violated international law. The terrorists demanded that the Swiss, German, and British governments free seven terrorists who had been imprisoned for earlier crimes against civilians. An RAF plane flew them out after the three governments capitulated.

However, Israel refused demands that she exchange Arab prisoners for American and Israeli hostages. The Arabs insisted on referring to American Jews as Israelis.

After releasing all but 55 hostages, the terrorists said that they would release the balance only if Israel yielded terrorists held in Israel. On the next day, Israelis seized 450 suspected terrorist sympathizers in the West Bank and Gaza, but then cleared and released 75. Five Arabs were deported to Jordan. There were rumors that Israel might ask the death penalty for five terrorists who were then facing trial for murder in Israel, but Israel released the last of the 450 and, after a long ordeal, the PFLP released the remaining American hostages.

Throughout this outrage, Hussein was contemptuously ignored, almost as if he did not exist, even as the terrorists operated on Jordanian soil. The terrorists were now entrenched in Amman and other cities, while some 15,000 Iraqi soldiers were still stationed in Jordan—a further threat to Hussein's regime.

THE TERRORISTS TAKE OVER JORDAN

As in Lebanon, terrorists had tried to dominate Jordan. Yielding to their pressure, Hussein had told the press on June 17 that he would no longer respect the U.N. cease-fire agreement unless Israel agreed to withdraw completely from the occupied territories. "To hell with the November 22 resolution," he said.

Sisco and his top aide, Alfred L. Atherton, had been touring the Middle East in April, and the newly appointed U.S. ambassador, Harrison Symmes, urged them to bypass Amman because just three days before their scheduled arrival terrorists had laid siege to the U.S. embassy and had burned down a U.S. library. Sisco accepted Symmes' advice, and an indignant Jordan demanded Symmes' recall. Symmes, a friendly State Department official, was my neighbor, and before he left for Amman I gave a farewell reception for him at my home.

In September, terrorists attempted to take command in Jordan, and the country was plunged into a bloody civil war. Another American diplomat, Major Robert P. Perry, a 34-year-old assistant army attaché, was slain by terrorists whose bullets pierced the door of his house as he was negotiating safe conduct for his family. Jordanian police were helpless spectators.

Hussein had wanted the Palestinians to fight Israel rather than Jordan. But thanks to his permissiveness, the Palestinians were gaining ascendancy. When he ultimately decided to put a stop to it, the ensuing conflict between Hussein's army and the terrorists took an estimated 15,000 lives.

Threatening to intervene on behalf of El Fatah, the Syrians then moved toward Jordan's northern frontier. Israel rolled tanks into the Golan Heights to deter them. Israel and the United States were conserting action. An American warship headed for Haifa to signal American support. The Syrian tanks turned around and rolled back.

Months later, in his State of the World message on February 25, Nixon described the Syrian intervention in the Jordanian civil war as "the greatest threat to world peace" since the Administration had taken office. The bloody clash came to be known as "Black September," and some 14 months later, Arab terrorists avenged their defeat by assassinating Wasfi al-Tal, Jordan's 51-year-old prime minister, in the lobby of the Sheraton Hotel in Cairo, where he was heading Jordan's delegation to an Arab League Defense Council.

Once again, Hussein owed his survival to Israel. During the 1958 revolt in Iraq, Syria had shut her air corridors, barring fuel oil for Jordan. Hussein had been rejected when he appealed for oil supplies from Saudi Arabia. The United States then secured Israel's permission for overflights to provide Jordan with the needed oil. There were threats from Moscow, but Israel ignored them, and Hussein later bitterly wrote in his autobiography that, while an Arab nation refused, an enemy agreed to support him—a humiliating episode.

Terrorism, we have learned, does not always cause revulsion. It often evokes acceptance, tolerance, and even sympathy and support. Veteran pro-Arab Americans now began to talk about a Palestinian entity in the West Bank, independent of Jordan. I heard Badeau, our former ambassador to Cairo, call for recognition of the Palestinian "entity," when he and I appeared before the House Committee on Foreign Affairs on July 22, 1970.

I testified that the United States had provided billions in military and economic aid to many other countries, but none had ever faced the dire threat which the Soviet Union posed to Israel. I pointed out that the United States had never extended grant military aid to Israel and that grant economic aid to Israel had ended almost a decade earlier. I urged economic and military assistance to ease Israel's heavy economic burden and to put the Soviet Union and the Arab states on notice that the United States supported Israel's struggle for peace.

There were many opposition witnesses; when one of them argued that Phantom Jets were not a defensive weapon, I pointed out that the Israelis were outgunned on the Canal and had to use planes to silence the guns which were used against them. The Soviet Union and the Egyptians might claim that their missiles on the Canal were defensive, "but if those missiles enabled them to activate their air force and to cross the Suez with their tanks [as they did three years later], then those missiles are an accessory to aggression."

Later, during the mass hijackings, former Ambassador Nolte contributed an article to *The New York Times* in which he suggested a Palestinian state including the West Bank, Gaza, and East Jerusalem.

A State Department spokesman, John King, observed on October 15 that the Palestinians would have to be a "partner" to the peace and "their legitimate interests and aspirations" would have to be considered in such a peace settlement. Thus, the Department reacted to pressures for recognition of the Palestinian cause. A Department official recalled that the Balfour Declaration, which recognized a homeland for the Jewish people, did not explicitly specify a "state." Hussein himself noted these new pressures when he told an Istanbul daily that he might establish a federation with the Palestinians.

But what of the Palestinians themselves?

On November 13, Yasir Arafat told *Al-Musawwar,* a Cairo magazine, that he opposed a separate state: "Tell the West Bank inhabitants that if anyone raises his voice calling for the establishment of a feeble state we will cut off his head," he threatened. The terrorist daily *El-Fatah* denounced a "plot to create a Palestinian state on the West Bank to wipe out the Palestinian revolution" and warned that any advocate would be tried before a Palestinian revolutionary court as a traitor.

In December, in a speech before the National Press Club, Hussein insisted that the Palestinians would always vote to remain "in the Jordanian family."

In September, the Middle East Institute sponsored a seminar on the "Palestinian entity" entitled "Violence and Dialogue in the Middle East." I was invited to speak on Jewish refugees. I quoted from the official memorandum which the Jewish Agency had filed with the Anglo-American Committee of Inquiry in 1946 and with UNSCOP in 1947, in which the Agency accurately predicted that virtually all Jews in Arab countries would have no option but to emigrate as soon as the Jewish state was established. There had been a foreseeable population exchange. My statement, based on official documents and vindicated by events, was booed by pro-Arabs in the audience.

AIPAC was always deeply concerned but could do very little about the catastrophic fate of Jews in Arab lands, who became the victims of the xenophobia which also hit other minorities, such as the Greeks of Egypt.

The Middle East Institute subsequently circulated a summary of the seminar speeches. My statement was accurately paraphrased, but my name was deleted.

I kept very busy traveling, talking, and writing in 1970. Badeau and I addressed legislative assistants at a dinner sponsored by the Georgetown Center for Strategic and International Studies. I also was invited to participate in a confrontation sponsored by the American Enterprise Institute. That conservative organization scheduled two veteran anti-Zionists: Christopher Mayhew, a former member of the British Parliament, and Elmer Berger. I nominated Professor Pollack, who led the American Professors for Peace in the Middle East. Peter Lisagor, a *Chicago Daily News* correspondent, was moderator.

The AEI had an elaborate format. Each participant had to contribute a lengthy article stating his position. Then, at a dinner at the Madison Hotel, each was to present a condensation. There would be questions from a select audience consisting of an equal number of partisans for Israel and partisans for the Arab states—some 50 in all.

A small book was published and hour-long video tapes were distributed to television stations as a public service. On the surface, there seemed to be nothing partisan about the arrangement. Each side was to nominate the persons whom it wished to have in the audience, but I did not realize how the program might be distorted to favor the Arab side until I watched the television report. All the friendly and leading questions that were submitted to the pro-Arab speakers, enabling them to respond effectively and vigorously, were broadcast in the question and answer period. In contrast, the program featured the aggressive questions that put Pollack and myself on the defensive.

However, we made some debating points. Mayhew quoted a moving passage from "Return Ticket," written by an Arab poet, Nasr al-Din al-Nashashibi, in which the father tells his son that they will return to the holiness and beauties of Palestine. I called attention to his failure to read the next paragraphs, in which the father assures his son that they will return "to smash with axes, guns, hands, fingernails, and teeth."

I reminded Mayhew that he had been elected to Parliament in 1944 on a Labor Party platform, written by Hugh Dalton, which had strongly advocated an Arab-Jewish population exchange.

Some eight years later, William J. Baroody, head of AEI, assured me that my suspicion about a one-sided broadcast was subjective and unjustified.

The New York Times described the pro-Israel lobby, featuring Max Fisher, a Detroit industrialist who was active in Republican politics. There were pictures of Rabin, the Jordanian ambassador, and of me. This was the first of many similar newspaper and magazine articles.

I now made a major decision for the *Near East Report*. We had won second-class mailing privileges in 1969, but because the *Near East Report* was a bi-weekly, mail delivery was tardy and irregular, and many readers complained. The solution was to transform it into a weekly, and that began on October 28. In 1970, for the first time during my Washington work, the press took note of my existence.

Chapter 25

Sadat Trades Allies?

EGYPT'S NEW LEADER

"There is no hope for an Arab-Israel peace as long as Nasser rules Egypt," I said on September 28, 1970, at a luncheon at the National Institute of Health. As I drove back to my office, I heard the astonishing report of Nasser's sudden death.

We now speculated that Egyptians, who had paid heavily to feed Nasser's imperialistic bid for prestige and glory, might turn inward and abandon pan-Arabism. Having little in common with the Arabs of the desert, they might become Egyptians once again, remove the Syrian star from Nasser's obsolete flag, and change the name of the United Arab Republic back to Egypt.

Nasser's successor was Anwar Sadat, who had been vice-president and who had won so many friends here in 1966; but, despite our wishful thinking, Sadat was still Moscow's man. He gave no indication at that time that he would break with the Soviets and change allies and policies. In one of his first speeches, he declared that "Israel has imposed the first electronic war in history on us and we are preparing for it." He denounced the United States for exploiting Nasser's death to use "pressure and threat" to weaken Egypt.

Sadat called 1971 the Year of Decision, and he began it by threatening an "all-out war in which everybody must take part" if a timetable for Israel's withdrawal were not agreed to. Egypt, he said, would not extend the cease-fire which was due to expire on February 4. He later agreed to 30 days grace.

Acknowledging Soviet support, Sadat inadvertently revealed to a Cairo audience that Russians were manning Egyptian missile sites and that six

Russians had been killed in an Israeli air raid near Cairo. However, the Middle East News Agency issued an "urgent" and "corrected" version of the speech which eliminated the references to Soviet casualties. Sadat then said: "No Russian missile man is on the Canal. . . . We have our men manning these missiles on the Canal. . . . Do you think I am going to stand with folded arms? Or am I going to ask for help from whatever source I can have?" Sadat said that the coming "total war" will take place "in the fields, the factories, the hinterland—throughout the Republic. . . . We consider it a thousand times more honorable to die standing proudly than to live kneeling." Egypt was training at least 5,000 pilots to overcome Israel's air supremacy, and he expected war after five years because "Israel wants the land from the Nile to the Euphrates."

In year-end interviews and speeches, Sadat insisted that "what has been taken by force must be restored only by force; we have no alternative." Egypt was prepared for an "all-out battle." Egypt could not be treated like a defeated, backward nation. No one in the Arab world would agree to the surrender of one inch of Arab land. "Don't ask me to make diplomatic relations with them. . . . Never! Never! Never! This is something no one can decide. Our people here will crush anyone who would decide this! Leave it to the coming generations to decide that. Not me!"

The missiles had cost Egypt $96 million. The missile pads had been built by Egyptian manpower, planning, and engineering, and, thanks to the Russians, Egypt was ready for another war. "The Soviet Union gives us everything . . . we ask for, very sincerely." On January 4, Sadat acknowledged and justified Russian operation of the missile sites: "Our sons needed eight months to be trained . . . Nasser then asked that Soviet missiles be accompanied by Soviet soldiers until our sons were trained."

ADMINISTRATION REACTION

The Administration was "not encouraged" by Cairo's pronouncements, Rogers told CBS, but he added that Sadat had stated maximum positions to a domestic audience in advance of the negotiations.

The Rogers plan, requiring Israel to make unrealistic territorial concessions, was glaringly one-sided and, because it undermined Israel's negotiating capacity and inflated Arab expectations that the United States would dictate a settlement, it made negotiations with Israel unnecessary. It was familiar U.S. strategy to lure the Arabs away from the Soviets. Israel would again have to pay the price for Cold War competition.

Our fears had been partly allayed by Nixon's reassuring reaction to our 1970 demonstration and by his subsequent call for "defensible" borders, as well as by the arms agreements with Israel. We did not anticipate that the worst was yet to come, after the United States had persuaded Israel to rejoin the Jarring peace initiative late in December 1970. We were skeptical that Jarring could win a compromise, for Sadat had constantly reiterated his maximal position—Israel's total withdrawal without negotiation and peace. We did not suspect that Jarring would endorse Sadat's extreme stand, that Nixon would back him, and that Israel would be harshly denounced as the intransigent foe of peace. Once the United States had sponsored the Rogers plan, it could not expect the Arabs to settle for less.

Jarring had undertaken his mediation in early 1968. Israel then called for direct negotiations with Egypt and with Jordan, but both Arab states scorned discussions until Israel had retreated to pre-war boundaries. Israel then agreed to indirect negotiations under Jarring's auspices on condition that they would lead, eventually, to a directly negotiated agreement. While Egypt was not averse to indirect negotiations, she demanded that Israel declare her readiness to implement Resolution 242 as Egypt interpreted it. The talks were discontinued in April 1969 because Jarring was frustrated. U Thant called on him to resume in August 1970, after the U.S. standstill agreement, but the truce violations aborted the contemplated talks.

After Mrs. Meir agreed to reenter the talks later that year, she invited Jarring to Israel to inform him that the extent of Israel's territorial withdrawal would be determined by the extent of the Arab states' readiness to negotiate a genuine peace. Spurning negotiations, Arabs insisted that the Big Four implement U.N. Resolution 242 in lieu of peace treaties.

The ensuing Jarring initiative was a non-starter because Sadat was demanding Israel's total capitulation; whereas Israel, much to the Administration's annoyance, had categorically spelled out her refusal to withdraw completely to the pre-1967 borders. Sadat told the Palestine National Council on February 28 that Egypt would seek a political settlement but not a separate peace. "There is but one solution—an Arab solution. We have rejected an Egyptian solution, which was always open to us."

Eight days earlier, the Central Committee of the PLO had rejected a separate Palestinian state on the West Bank and Gaza because it "would be an Israeli colony . . . and would enable Zionism to evacuate occupied Palestinian lands of its Arab population." In January 1971, the Jordanian parliament voted 40 to 1 against establishment of a West Bank Palestinian state.

Pressed to outline Israel's perceptions of the peace settlement, Mrs. Meir was constrained to draw a map for *The London Times*. She emphasized that Israel would not surrender Sharm el-Sheikh and the Golan Heights. Sinai would have to be demilitarized, and a mixed force, including Israeli and perhaps some Egyptian troops, would guarantee demilitarization of Sinai. A united Jerusalem would remain part of Israel, with continued Moslem access to the Holy Places. Israel's borders with Jordan would be negotiated. Arab troops should not be permitted to cross the Jordan River. She barred Egypt's return to Gaza, and proposed that Israel provide a port linked by a corridor with Jordan. Israeli compensation and international funds would spur industrialization of Jordan and the West Bank.

The interview led to revolt and secession in the Knesset on March 16. The Begin-led Gahal group, a combination of Herut and Liberal party members, opposed yielding any territory; 20 Gahal members walked out, and 12 members abstained on a vote of confidence. Mrs. Meir retained but 62 of the 120 members.

On the same day, Rogers told the press that the United States was talking about "a contractual agreement entered into by the parties with reciprocally binding commitments, signed, sealed, and delivered; with full agreement of all concerned that belligerency will cease; that they will live in peace with each other; and that they will not intefere with each other's internal affairs. Provisions would be made for security, with an international force consisting of those nations that are willing to participate, and who may participate because the parties are prepared to accept it. There would be an understanding that they will continue for a definite period of time, probably with options to renew, so that it can't be removed unilaterally, which would mean that if the United States participated it would not remove its forces except by agreement."

Assistant Secretary of State Joseph Sisco wrote to me in a similar vein, complaining that the *Near East Report* was unfair in comparing the current U.S. initiative with the unconditional roll-back of Israeli forces dictated by the Eisenhower-Dulles regime.

He insisted that there should be no return to past conditions, that there must be a "settlement which replaces armistice with peace based on direct and reciprocal commitments of the parties to each other . . . recognizes Israel's borders and its sovereignty . . . terminates all claims of belligerency . . . and includes security arrangements that are inherently durable." The United States had never interpreted the Security Council resolution to mean Israel's total withdrawal. "In our judgment," Sisco wrote, the resolution "neither endorsed nor barred the 1967 lines as the 'secure and recognized' final borders called for in that resolution. We recognize that in some instances the possibility must be kept open for changes in the pre-June 1967 armistice lines where a return to those lines would leave elements of the conflict unresolved."

Mrs. Meir was critical of the Rogers proposal for international guarantees:

We cannot rely only on a written treaty but mainly on secure borders. We cannot trust what Rogers offers us, even if he does so with the best of intentions. There are some points beyond which a nation cannot go. We do not know how much it will cost, but a people must stand up for itself. This is not the border of the USA but of the Jewish people. Why should we be the ones to serve as guinea pigs for borders? . . . Why should we be the only country in the world that agrees to become a protectorate surrounded by a framework peopled by

Americans, Russians, Yugoslavs and Indians? . . . Some say it is bad for our image if we stand firm. What did Czechoslovakia lack in the way of a good image, yet Soviet tanks rode into Prague?

The Big Four had in fact been discussing guarantees, but there were some important differences: the United States and Britain wanted the U.N. Secretary General to control the proposed international force, while the Soviets and France preferred that the Security Council have charge.

On March 25, *The Washington Post* carried an editorial cautioning against "guaranteeing an intrinsically unstable situation . . . a settlement imposed by the Great Powers rather than negotiated by the local parties." *The Post* said: "Not without reason" Egypt has "evidently concluded that the United States is so intent on quickly tying up the Mideast package with a Big Two ribbon that Egypt does not have to negotiate a settlement; it need merely sit tight while Washington imposes the so-called Rogers plan on Israel." Such a settlement "would be a great mistake," because "it is bound to be second-rate; it would not involve a real commitment by either Egypt or Israel. . . . Negotiations are the horse; guarantees are the cart."

The Administration overreached as it fought hard to sell its plan. Thus, on March 2, there was an extraordinary and highly inappropriate USIA briefing for the foreign press. A former U.S. ambassador and Middle East specialist, who insisted on remaining anonymous, called for Israel's total withdrawal and accused Israel of stalling because it hoped that the 1972 election would put a Democrat in the White House. Mystified reporters questioned the propriety of that performance.

In the Senate, Israel was supported by Javits, Ribicoff, Jackson, Birch Bayh (D-Indiana), and Humphrey. Scott suggested that Israel lease Sharm el-Sheikh for 99 years—which would be consistent with Egypt's sovereignty.

Ribicoff noted that Egypt's U.N. representative had refused to accept Israel's February 26 communication from Jarring, because it was headed "From the Government of Israel."

Fulbright defended Rogers, charging that Israel was dreaming up the threat of Soviet expansionism in the Middle East in order to win U.S. support. "I perceive in this some of the same old Communist-baiting humbuggery that certain other small countries have used to manipulate the United States . . . . When it comes to anti-communism . . . the United States is highly susceptible, rather like a drug addict, and the world is full of ideological 'pushers,'" he said at Yale University early in April.

While Fulbright did not command many votes in the Senate, he had broad public influence because of his criticism of U.S. policy in Indochina, and his views had particular appeal to youth leaders who opposed the over-extension of U.S. power. We thought it most important to emphasize the vast difference between Vietnam and the Middle East and to persuade liberals and radicals who were opposed to our involvement in Southeast Asia that we should not automatically and mechanically oppose U.S. support for Israel in her struggle to defend herself.

McGOVERN'S VIEW

The logical man to do this was George McGovern, the senator from isolationist South Dakota, who was already a front runner for the Democratic nomination for the presidency. I had always considered McGovern, a former history professor, to be a friend of Israel. Eban and I met with him in 1957 soon after his election to the Senate, and he recalled that he had been a member of the pro-Zionist American Christian Palestine Committee.

In 1970, however, he had delivered an unfortunate speech in the Senate, which was designed to reconcile his support of Israel with the negative views of those who uncritically opposed all U.S. arms shipments to other countries. He advocated negotiations between Israel and the Arab states, opposed imposition by outside parties, and called for military assistance to Israel as he had in the past. He qualified his advocacy of Phantom jets by urging that the planes should not be used for forays over Arab territory. Such a U.S. declaration would signal America's intention to seek some Israeli restraint and would restore U.S. credibility in Arab eyes. The Arabs would then reciprocate by ending the formal state of war.

We disagreed because the Phantoms were making deep penetration raids to destroy the Soviet missile sites, which were then being installed in preparation for an assault across the Suez. If Israel could not use the jet planes as a deterrent, they would have little value. A few of us lunched with McGovern and his aides within a week after he made that statement on the Hill to explain why we thought that this was a mistake.

Early in 1971, I met McGovern at a Sunday brunch at the home of Hobart Rowen, financial editor of *The Washington Post,* whose son James had married McGovern's daughter Susan. He told me that he was troubled by heckling he had encountered on college campuses from anti-war students. I suggested that the potential leader of the Democratic party had a major responsibility to differentiate between Vietnam and the Middle East and to prevent his party from becoming isolationist. I invited him to make a strong speech to that effect at the forthcoming AIPAC policy conference. He readily agreed.

He warned young Americans to distinguish between Vietnam and the Middle East. "One of the most pathetic symptoms of national frustration" over the Vietnam war, he told our audience, was "disillusionment." He warned that this could result "either in a total rejection of international responsibility or in a severe impairment of judgment and a doctrinaire grasping at every political position which bears the revolutionary label. . . . How have even the most revolutionary of our youth missed the impact of the monumental struggle for liberation and self-determination which the Israelis waged 23 years ago against British troops — a struggle which enabled tens of thousands of survivors of the Nazi Holocaust to find refuge?"

At that same conference, Senator Robert Dole (R-Kansas), chairman of the Republican National Committee, again called for "firm and unyielding" American support for Israel.

Representative Carl Albert (D-Oklahoma), the Speaker; the two Floor Leaders, Representatives Hale Boggs (D-Louisiana) and Ford, and Senators Scott and Jackson also addressed our delegates at an AIPAC luncheon on the Hill. Ford, soon to be in the White House, said that he rejected "any diplomatic concept that would force our friends, the Israelis, to negotiate with the United States rather than Egypt on the territorial question," and he warned against "unwitting collaboration with Moscow in imposing a settlement."

In early April, Israel's Labor Party called for substantial, but not total, border changes in a peace settlement and rejected any substitute arrangements and guarantees. A *Time* Louis Harris poll found that 90 percent of Jewish Israelis approved the incorporation of Jerusalem, 86 percent favored absorption of the Golan Heights, 72 percent supported the retention of Sharm el-Sheikh, and 49 percent were for keeping the Gaza strip. Some 73 percent believed that Israel should return some of the occupied territories, but only four percent said all occupied territories should be returned.

THE INTERIM AGREEMENT

The Jarring talks were stillborn because they were crudely one-sided and clumsily counterproductive. By mid-March, the principals were considering a fall-back alternative to negotiate an interim agreement to clear and open the Suez Canal. Both Israel and Egypt appeared ready to consider it, but once again they were far apart and the gap could not be bridged. Israelis were proposing that both Israel and Egypt thin out their troops on both banks of the Canal, that missiles be withdrawn from the Canal zone, that the Canal be opened and operated by Egyptian civilians, and that Israeli ships be permitted to transit it. The Israelis believed that reopening of the Canal would test Egypt's intentions. If Egyptian civilians in many thousands were to return to Canal cities, this would end the shooting and signify readiness for peace. Thus it would pay Israelis to give up "a piece of territory for a piece of peace," as Rabin formulated it. Europe would also gain because that would reduce the transit cost of oil.

Egypt was demanding much more than Israel was willing to give by insisting on a military crossing of the Canal. Having been stung by the missile doublecross less than a year before, Israelis were strongly opposed because it would negate Israel's demand for demilitarization of all Sinai.

Israelis wanted to know what kind of American support would be forth-coming if Egypt violated the agreement and her forces crossed the Canal. It was reported that the United States would give Israel political support, but there was no promise of direct military intervention. The United States would uphold Israel's right to act under Article 51 of the U.N. Charter and could veto any anti-Israel resolution in the Security Council.

On his way to a SEATO conference late in April, Rogers planned to stop off for meetings with Arab and Israeli leaders to press for the interim agree-ment. Prior to Rogers's arrival in Cairo, Sadat delivered an uncompromis-ing May Day speech at Helwan, killing hope for any kind of agreement, interim or final. He demanded pressure on Israel to force complete withdrawal from all territories.

Rogers secured no concessions from Sadat. Egyptians were disappointed because Rogers had brought no concessions from Israel despite their convic-tion that the United States could deliver Israel. Sadat later maintained that Rogers had expressed satisfaction with Egypt's position and had asked nothing further from him. As for any interim agreement, Egypt was insist-ing that Israel withdraw 115 miles back to El Arish. With characteristic asymmetry, Egypt wanted her soldiers to cross the Canal but would not per-mit Israeli ships to transit it. Israel's interim withdrawal would have to be linked with her total withdrawal within six months.

Rogers's visit to Israel was discordant. Apparently overly optimistic that he could win Knesset members, he asked for a meeting with Israel's Foreign Affairs Committee, a return favor inasmuch as Eban had recently met with a large number of senators. Rogers clashed with Knesset members, espe-cially with Menachem Begin, the veteran Herut leader, who was opposed to any Israeli withdrawal.

Israelis hoped that Rogers would fly over the Golan Heights, so that he could see how the escarpment dominated Israel's settlements in the Galilee and forbade territorial concessions. He refused to do so. He flew to Sharm el-Sheikh in his own plane but was careful not to overfly any of the land that Israel had occupied during the war. He removed the Israeli flag from his car when he drove into the Old City.

He visited Ben-Gurion before he called on Mrs. Meir. The aged Israeli leader had broken with Israeli public opinion by advocating the return of the occupied territories, with the exception of Jerusalem, in exchange for a peace treaty. The visit to Israel did yield a minor result. Dayan told Sisco that Israel would agree to permit Egyptian policemen and civilians—but not soldiers—to cross the Canal, a concession which Sisco promptly transmitted to Cairo.

THE SOVIET LEASH

While Rogers pursued Sadat, the Soviets kept a vigilant watch lest Nasser's successor snap the Moscow leash. On January 15, 1971, on the anniversary of

Nasser's 53rd birthday, President Podgorny arrived to open the Aswan Dam, for which Moscow had loaned $300 million, and to offer help in the development of nuclear power.

The Soviets were increasingly suspicious of the new diplomatic intimacy between the United States and Egypt—as reflected by Sadat's cordial welcome to Rogers and U.S. readiness to applaud Egypt and to alienate Israel. Inside Egypt, Nasser's former associate, Ali Sabry, and his colleagues were regarded as pro-Soviet and critical of Sadat's pro-U.S. orientation. Shortly after Rogers left Cairo, Sadat launched his first major purge of opposition leadership, jailing or dismissing some 300 officials, including Sabry, six cabinet ministers, four of the eight members of the Arab Socialist Union politburo, 17 members of parliament, and many ex-Nasserites. Sadat claimed that he had averted a coup and had installed his own men in charge of the army, information, and police.

Podgorny and Sadat signed a new Soviet-Egyptian treaty of friendship in which Moscow reasserted its hegemony. This was the first such Soviet treaty with any country outside the Soviet bloc. Whether Sadat liked it or not, Podgorny was telling Egypt that she was not a free spirit. Perhaps Soviet leaders were trying to reassure skeptics in Moscow who were asking hard questions: Had they wasted billions in rubles, arms, and training on an unfaithful Egyptian leader who seemed ready to defect to Wall Street and the Potomac? Podgorny's demonstration of continuing Soviet power should reassure Soviet leaders that Moscow had lost nothing and was still in charge of the most influential Arab country and that it had military, economic, and propaganda bases from which to challenge the West in the Mediterranean, the Persian Gulf, and the Indian Ocean.

The treaty forged strong links. Article 8 obligated the Soviet Union to arm and train Egypt so that she could "eliminate the consequences of aggression," a euphemistic code phrase for the defeat of Israel.

Courted by both Moscow and Washington, Sadat grew more demanding. Nine days before the pact, on May 20, Sadat declared: "If the United States wants peace, then it must squeeze Israel." He continued: "Israel's position does not matter to us. What matters is the attitude of the United States." Sadat would rather fill the Canal with sand than yield to Israel's terms, and his soldiers were eager to resume battle. "I can hardly hold them back," he said.

On June 10, 12 days after the new treaty, Sadat declared that the Soviet pact would increase Egypt's capability to liberate Israeli-held territories, and he promised never to relinquish Soviet friendship. He wished the pact were of 30 years' duration instead of 15. Again he predicted that the battle would end, one way or another, in the year 1971.

Even if there were "peace," Sadat still barred any normal relationship with Israel. He said, "The Zionist invasion will last our generation and that of our children. Israeli aggression will remain even after we complete the liberation of our land. It is like a sword above our neck." *The New York Times* now concluded that Sadat had killed the Rogers initiative and the Jarring mission "with one reckless blow."

On the next day, there was chilling evidence of Israel's persisting peril at sea. A speedboat fired bazooka rockets at an Israeli-chartered oil tanker, the *Coral Sea,* near the Bab el Mandeb Straits between the South Yemen Republic and Somalia, 1,300 miles from Eilat, but failed to sink it. The tanker, flying the Liberian flag, was carrying 78,000 tons of oil from Iran; part of its crew was from Israel. In Beirut, the PFLP claimed credit. For Israelis this was the hardest blow to their shipping in the Red Sea since Nasser's closing of the Strait of Tiran in 1967. Rogers called it "a very serious matter . . . which deserves the condemnation of responsible nations."

In 1969, editor Hassanein Heikal had called the Red Sea an Arab lake and had predicted that "an Arab naval command of the Red Sea would ultimately challenge Israeli shipping."

On the anniversary of the Naguib-Nasser-Sadat revolution, Sadat warned that Egypt would sacrifice one million soldiers and revoke her acceptance of Resolution 242 if 1971 ended without a decision.

That ultimatum doomed an impending Sisco trip to Israel, during which the American diplomat had hoped to negotiate a new Suez compromise. Sadat himself had queried that Sisco initiative late in June. The Egyptian foreign ministry leaked a story to columnist Joseph Kraft that a U.S. diplomat, Donald Bergus, the U.S. chargé d'affaires in Cairo, had submitted a memorandum to Riad on May 23 which called for an Israeli withdrawal halfway across Sinai, the presence of Egyptian troops in part of the evacuated territory, and the interposition of U.N. forces between Egyptians and Israelis.

Was this an official map or a "phantom" memorandum (as it came to be called) by the chief of our Cairo mission? No matter what it was, its result was to stiffen Cairo's demands. I later invited Bergus to relate his version to an AIPAC conference breakfast, which he freely did, confident that no copies would be leaked, as had been the case in Cairo.

Sadat was again threatening war in order to pressure the United States, which, in September, he had accused of deception. He was demanding that the United States withhold further jets from Israel and that the Security Council denounce Israel. The Soviet Union called on all states to insist that Israel yield. The Soviets wanted a four-power statement interpreting the November 22 resolution to mean Israel's withdrawal from *all* occupied territories. Obviously, the United States could not agree.

There was an unending forensic battle at the U.N. between two ambassadors—the Soviet Union's Malik and Israel's Tekoah. Malik branded Israel's "Hitlerian tactics" as "nefarious." He denounced banditry, enslavement, pillage, violence, and racism. Tekoah replied that the Arab minority in Jerusalem possessed all the rights that Jews in the Soviet Union were denied. The Moslems of Jerusalem, numbering less than 70,000, had 53 Arab schools, 36 mosques, and 11 prayer rooms—while the one-half million Jews in Moscow had one rabbi, one synagogue, two small houses of worship, and not a single Jewish school.

Chapter 26

We Strengthen Israel

We won both military and economic aid for Israel in 1971. Our friends in both Houses opened a campaign to resume military assistance to Israel. At the same time, on another front, and for the first time since 1959, we succeeded in winning restoration of economic assistance, which Israel urgently needed because of her escalating debt.

ARMS

We had assumed that the U.S. arms flow to Israel would continue through 1971, without interruption, but the Administration, responsive to Egyptian pressure, had deferred a new decision, hoping to maintain credibility with Cairo and fearing Sadat's reaction.

Senator Jackson renewed his campaign for additional arms in December 1970. A member of the Senate Committee on Armed Services, he warned that peace in the Middle East was threatened by the aggressive ambition of the Soviet Union, "which transcends the tragic conflict between Arabs and Israelis and indeed is based upon its exploitation."

Jackson's report likened Soviet foreign policy to that of "a burglar who walks down a hotel corridor trying the handles of all the doors. When he finds one unlocked, in he goes." Noting Soviet deployment of SA missiles, he estimated that Israel's arms requirements for the coming year would at least equal the $500 million credit voted in 1970.

According to the Swedish International Peace Research Institute, Arab arms procurement had tripled since 1969. The 13 Arab countries had spent

$2.43 billion in 1969. Egypt topped the list with an outlay of $982 million, while Israel's expenditures totaled $790 million. The Administration intended to reduce military sales and credits for Israel to $300 million in fiscal 1972 under the Military Sales Act, which provided for conventional interest rates, rather than under Jackson's amendment to the Defense Procurement Act, which permitted lower interest rates.

Egypt disclosed that her defense expenditures for the fiscal year beginning July 1 would total $1.56 billion—11 percent more than the previous year, and 24 percent of the budget.

As in 1970, most Americans strongly favored continued military support for Israel. Representative Albert W. Johnson (R-Pennsylvania) asked his constituents whether the United States should supply Israel with enough aircraft and supplies to replace combat losses and maintain the military balance: 70.3% said yes; 22.7% said no; and 7% did not respond. This question received the highest percentage of yes votes of any of Johnson's 18 questions.

The Military Sales Act was in jeopardy because of Senate-House differences, and Jackson again offered an amendment to the Defense Department appropriation bill to sell $500 million worth of aircraft to Israel, half of it earmarked for Phantom jets. It was adopted by 82 to 14 in November.

Just before the vote, eight senators called on Rogers to urge him to change course and permit Israel to have the Phantom jets without further delay. They were Kennedy, Gale McGee (D-Wyoming), Ribicoff, Symington, Edward Brooke (R-Massachusetts), Dole, Charles Percy (R-Illinois), and Javits. A decision was urgent, for Sadat had angrily terminated the protracted negotiation, blaming the United States and again threatening war. Fulbright and Senator Henry Bellmon (R-Oklahoma) charged that the amendment would interfere with a settlement.

Jackson warned that Egyptians were training 100,000 troops for an invasion in November or December. He described access ramps to facilitate pontoon bridges and the transfer of Egypt's surface-to-air missiles to the Canal. The 1973 experience later confirmed Jackson's account, and it is possible that Sadat might have moved at that time had the Pakistan-India war not distracted the Soviets.

Early in October, Congress pressed the Administration for an immediate and positive response to Israel's plane request. As in June 1970, a resolution was circulated in the Senate by six Republicans and six Democrats, rapidly gaining 78 sponsors. We nominated the list, which included Symington, McGee, Kennedy, Ribicoff, Jackson, Scott, Javits, Brooke, Dole, Percy, Gurney (R-Florida), and Herman Talmadge (D-Georgia). A similar resolution was introduced in the House by Albert, Ford, and Celler; 272 representatives followed suit.

After a two-hour private meeting with Mrs. Meir in December, the White House announced that the President had recognized that Israeli forces must maintain a long-term program of modernization and that the United States would participate in this process.

Once again the Egyptian foreign ministry attempted to capture the headlines away from Mrs. Meir by professing an intense desire for peace. Operating from the U.N. in New York, Riad mounted the barricades over CBS's "Face the Nation" to protest against Rogers's failure to deliver Israel. Asked whether that would justify Sadat's threats to wage war, Riad vigorously denied that Sadat meant what he seemed to be saying: "No, no, no— we have never said that. Because war can't be declared like that, because we are already at war, it's a war declared by Israel," Riad protested. "What we want is not war. I hate to use this word because war means destruction, means killing, killing of our boys and also of the boys of the Israelis. We want to avoid that. All that we want is to liberate our territories." It is just that if peace efforts fail, Riad said, the Egyptians will have "no choice but to do our best to liberate our territories." The Palestinians intended to return to Israel to live at peace with the Christians and Jews, he added. Israel will not agree, he said, because "she does not permit any Christians or Moslems to live there." That was an astonishing revelation, inasmuch as Christians and Moslems then approximated 12% of Israel's citizenry, as compared with the minuscule percentage of Jews in Arab lands.

ECONOMIC AID

1971 marked the twentieth anniversary of my arrival in Washington, and the first effort to secure Israel's inclusion in the foreign assistance program. That year we won an additional grant of $50 million in economic aid. Now, twenty years later, we repeated that effort and, by an odd coincidence, for the same amount.

In 1970, Israel appealed for the resumption of economic aid, because she had to divert so much of her economic resources to military procurement and the amortization of a mounting foreign currency debt. The Administration rejected the application. In 1971, we initiated the effort on the Hill and I met with Chairman Morgan of the House Committee on Foreign Affairs.

The Administration had proposed to grant $731.5 million in military assistance, but none of that was for Israel, although there was materiel, advice, and training for Iran, Greece, Jordan, Saudi Arabia, and Turkey. The Administration intended $300 million in military sales for Israel, but none of that was a grant. The legislation also contemplated $778 million in supporting assistance for friendly countries that had heavy defense burdens or extraordinary economic or political problems. "If there is one country which qualifies under that definition, it is Israel," we wrote.

We stressed that the United States had never granted Israel arms, that grant economic aid to Israel had ended more than ten years before, that

U.S. economic aid had consisted largely of loans, more than half of which had been repaid, and that Israel had used all these funds for purchases in the United States.

Israel's economic statistics were disheartening. The 1971 current account deficit would be $1.4 billion—$100 million more than the 1970 deficit. The foreign currency debt totalled $3.4 billion—$500 million more than the previous year. The defense budget was $1.925 billion, out of a total budget of $3.780 billion.

Exports were $725 million in 1970 and were expected to rise to $850 million in 1971. Imports, not including armaments, were rising from $1.4 billion to $1.6 billion. Imports for defense were estimated at $850 million.

Debt service would be $500 million in 1971, and would rise to $550 million in 1972—double the amount needed five years ago, the year before the Six-Day War.

Each Israeli man, woman, and child now owed $1,100 in foreign currency, twice as much as in 1967—by far the highest of any people anywhere—as had been the case for many years.

The Administration opposed Israel's request. Letters from the State Department referred to her rapid economic growth, and her high economic self-sufficiency. Her high per capita GNP had qualified her for graduation from the aid club.

The State Department's attitude encouraged critics like Fulbright, Hatfield, Nes, and others to oppose Israel's request. In a sweeping disregard for the differences between grants and loans, as well as between U.S. government aid and private Jewish philanthropy, they vastly exaggerated the amount of aid Israel had received. For example, it was unfair to include the sales of Israel bonds as "aid," while ignoring that the U.S. Treasury actually profited from taxes paid on interest.

They argued that per capita aid to Israel exceeded aid to other countries, but their calculations were distorted and inaccurate. Thus Hatfield claimed that the United States had poured more into Israel than into Vietnam—an absurdity which failed to include the massive U.S. military contribution to the Vietnam war.

The *Near East Report* published an analysis entitled "The Malicious Attack on Aid to Israel," which Representative William S. Broomfield (R-Michigan) inserted in the Congressional Record on July 16.

Morgan told me that the House Committee would not vote on an additional sum for Israel. However, it would make no cuts in the Administration's proposed supporting assistance program, and that would leave enough money in the House authorization to finance an $85 million grant for Israel.

The House approved a two-year foreign aid authorization of $6.9 billion in economic and military assistance on August 3, by a vote of 200 to 192. Committee members took the Floor to write a clear legislative record in support of the aid for Israel. Morgan explained that he had not offered an amendment to cut some $85 million from the supporting assistance authorization because he knew that this would be adequate to take care of Israel's application. He was joined by Bingham, Fraser, Fulton, and Representative Wilbur Mills (D-Arkansas), the chairman of the powerful House Ways and Means Committee.

Could we win the Senate Committee on Foreign Relations? I feared that Fulbright would never permit his Committee to recommend the grant for Israel. I urged Javits to write to Rogers. If he were writing the Senate Committee report, he stated, he would recommend the inclusion of a $200 million grant for Israel, the amount that Israel had originally requested. Then, with his characteristic flair for action, Javits enrolled 10 of the 16 members of the Senate Committee as co-signers, which showed that we now had a clear majority on the Committee and that Fulbright was in the minority. The 10 signers included Sparkman, Symington, Pell, McGee, Muskie, Case, Javits, Scott, James Pearson (R-Kansas), and William Spong (D-Virginia).

We now feared that the Appropriations Committees would not include the appropriation unless the authorization bill explicitly provided an amount earmarked for Israel. The Senate Committee was then in session, marking up the bill, and I was unable to see Javits personally. I sent him a note explaining why it was urgent to write the sum of $85 million into the legislation. I was then on the eve of a flight to London and Israel, and was most happy to read a paragraph in the London press next morning reporting that Javits had succeeded.

Later, when the legislation came up in the Senate, Scott told his colleagues that he, Jackson, Dole, and Tunney (D-California) had called on Rogers to win assurances that the money would not be impounded or delayed and that the full $85 million would be granted to Israel. As it turned out, however, the sum for Israel was cut to $50 million when the Appropriations Committees voted on it.

PROPAGANDA

Capitol Hill was the one battlefront where we maintained friendship. Elsewhere Arabs gained in influence and power because of their numbers, their wealth, and their reckless perversion of the truth. We were in retreat on the fields of propaganda and diplomacy.

At the U.N., the manipulation of Arab, Moslem, Soviet, and Afro-Asian blocs stultified the General Assembly, enabling them to falsify records and reports and to win adoption of resolutions which commended aggression and censured defense, which condoned terror and betrayed its victims, and which defied equity and truth. U.N. roll-calls were lock-step performances.

A special U.N. committee, consisting of Yugoslavia, Ceylon, and Somalia, offered hearsay evidence of many alleged Israeli crimes against Arabs in occupied territories. Diplomats listened to invectives such as "diabolical," "refined torture," "apartheid" and "genocide." Zionism was coupled with Nazism, and Herzl's "Jewish State" with "Mein Kampf."

Suddenly, a Catholic Costa Rican delegate, Father Benjamin Nunez, challenged the false testimony, recounting his own experience as ambassador to Israel. He offered a glowing description of progress and serenity in Israel, and he wished that all military occupations were like this one.

Even so, the U.N. committee condemned Israel's policy, 53 to 20, with 46 abstentions. The resolution admonished Israel to refrain from confiscation, annexation, torture, and collective punishment.

The World Health Organization, meeting in Geneva on May 18, accused Israel of preventing distribution of medicine by the International Committee of the Red Cross. It threatened to suspend Israel's WHO voting rights and services. The vote was 41 to 2 (the United States and Israel) with 53 abstentions. The very next day, the ICRC announced in Geneva that "it is completely untrue to assert that we have been barred from this distribution work by Israeli authorities." The spokesman added: "We have several times made distributions in the Gaza strip, the Sinai area and Jordan, for example, and as recently as February 17 to 50,000 Bedouin in Sinai."

A U.N. special committee investigating Israeli practices in occupied territories heard Arab witnesses in Jordan during the first fortnight in July. Ironically, even as diplomats listened in Amman to reports of terror in Israel, embattled Arab terrorists were fleeing from Hussein's Amman to seek sanctuary in Israeli-controlled areas.

Terrorists were not the only Arabs entering Israel at the time. Thanks to Israel's open bridges policy, thousands from all Arab countries were free to enter the West Bank, to visit Jerusalem and the Mediterranean coast. In 1968, there had been 17,000 visitors. The number grew to 23,000 in 1969, to 54,000 in 1970, and by September to 100,000.

Arab visitors found their kin working in Israel for three and four times their previous wage. Army camps were being converted to small villages, with utilities, parks, and playgrounds. Always apprehensive that Jordan might blight the West Bank's new prosperity by barring its crops and forcing it to compete with the Israelis, Israel introduced new crops in the West Bank to encourage exports to Europe and thus complement, rather than compete with, Israeli agriculture.

Although the Jarring initiative had long been stalemated and Egypt had summarily terminated the interim agreement talks, the General Assembly adopted a resolution on December 13, 1971, urging resumption of the Jarring talks, praising Egypt for her positive replies, and calling on Israel to respond favorably. The vote was 79 to 7, with 36 abstentions. Six Latin American countries voted with Israel.

Charles Yost discussed conflicting interpretations of Resolution 242 in *Life* magazine. Did it mean withdrawal from all or only some of the occupied territories? Abandoning the U.S. position, Yost said, "Which interpretation one chooses is immaterial." To Yost, perhaps. But it could mean life or death for Israel's people.

Hardliners blamed Israel for Arab suffering at a rally in the National Cathedral in January 1971. Elson presided. The speakers included Dr. Davis, head of American Near East Refugee Aid, Inc., and former Commissioner General of UNRWA, and Mayhew, my one-time adversary.

As usual, Mayhew quoted sad and sentimental Arab poetry, but carefully edited out embarrassing passages which threatened bloody vengeance, as he had in his debate with me the previous fall. The speakers that night talked only of the Arab refugees. Outside, on a bitterly cold night, Washington Zionists distributed a hastily printed six-page excerpt from the *Near East Report* entitled "Two Refugee Problems."

Chapter 27

An End to Carrot and Stick

THE U.S. AND ISRAEL AGREE

Odd-numbered years are pro-Arab; even-numbered are pro-Israel. The contrast in U.S. policy between 1971 and 1972 confirms that axiom.

The cynical may contend that politicians sacrifice the national interest in pursuit of votes and campaign contributions. That is how pro-Arabs have long rationalized American policy. But 2.7 percent of the American people do not have all that influence. The truth is that democratic Israel's survival has always concerned the majority of thoughtful Americans.

As 1972 began, Nixon declared that the Soviet Union had been sending significant arms shipments to the UAR and that the United States had to consider Israel's requests for planes in order to see that the balance did not shift.

Moreover, the House Foreign Affairs Committee recommended the constant and long-range supply of arms to maintain "Israel's deterrent capabilities and the balance of power."

The Administration abandoned pressures on Israel to surrender to Sadat's demands.

Assured of a steady supply of U.S. Phantoms, which were superior to the Mirage, the Israelis relinquished their demand that France deliver the 50 Mirage planes which Israel had purchased before the Six-Day War, and which France had refused to deliver because Israel had spurned de Gaulle's advice in 1967 not to move.

Earlier, Sadat had won the promise of new Soviet planes and missiles, menacing Israeli cities and their civilians.

Nixon told Congress that the Russians were to blame for prolonging the conflict, for upsetting negotiations, and for the arms race.

Rogers now began to stress direct negotiations. Other rival nations were talking to each other. Why not the Arabs and Israelis? he asked. And once again, presidential candidates and political parties competed in their affirmations of friendship and support for Israel.

Avoiding any divisive endorsement of candidates, we offered our platform planks and decried any partisan effort to inject Israel into national or local campaigns.

In 1972, the GOP was determined to make inroads and to win Jews away from their traditional Democratic alignment, which dated back to Roosevelt and the New Deal.

Nixon was vulnerable to criticism because he had pressed Israel on the territorial issue and had employed the carrot and stick on arms and economic aid. However, these issues had been resolved by 1972. Moreover, Nixon could exploit divisions inside the Democratic party. McGovern's 1970 speech continued to dog him, and those who favored a strong defense posture accused McGovern of dovishness; but McGovern had responded to my 1971 appeal that he differentiate between Vietnam and the Middle East. I insisted that McGovern was a friend of Israel, that both parties and all candidates supported aid to Israel, and that Israel must not be an issue in the campaign. "Vote for the candidate who you think is best for America," I told many audiences.

As in 1968, a special issue of the *Near East Report* gave the records and attitudes of all the candidates: "The statements of the major candidates reveal substantial agreement. They favored Arab-Israel talks leading to an agreed settlement, and all are opposed to a makeshift or imposed peace. They agree that Israel should be strengthened militarily to enable her to deter attack. They also favor economic aid to Israel. They believe there should be some boundary adjustment. They also favor a unified administration of Jerusalem. They support efforts to ameliorate the plight of Soviet Jewry—including assistance to help Israel absorb Soviet refugees."

That special *Near East Report* issue came under attack. McGovern was then far in the lead for the Democratic presidential nomination and, as the convention neared, Humphrey forces scored his record on Israel and defense, quoting his unfortunate 1970 speech. The two crossed swords in California, and we printed both Humphrey's charges and McGovern's replies in our special supplement. Humphrey then rebuked me, charging that I was endorsing his foe despite his own long record of friendship and support for Israel. He circulated copies of his letter to a number of Jewish leaders, who called to warn me that I should not become partisan, which in fact was the last thing I wanted to be.

I wrote to Humphrey to protest. I pointed out that our views were necessarily different because we had different vantage points. As a candidate seeking preferment, he would naturally emphasize differences between himself and his rivals. As an advocate seeking to win endorsement of our views by all, I would emphasize agreements.

The Israeli embassy came under criticism because Ambassador Rabin had made an ambiguous statement praising deeds rather than talk. That was widely interpreted as a pro-Nixon statement, and Mrs. Meir was constrained to assure Ribicoff in June that "Israel's policy—past, present and future—is never to involve itself in the domestic politics of any country." Rabin said that in his statement he had expressed his "gratitude to all U.S. presidents who had demonstrated by deeds their positive attitude toward Israel" and added that there was no change in Israel's policy of "non-interference in the internal affairs of any country."

Immediately after the Six-Day War, Richard Stearns, a young student, had joined in an advertisement which called for substantial territorial withdrawal by Israel. Now, six years later, Stearns was active in McGovern's pre-convention campaign, and he was attacked in advertisements and columns for his 1967 posture. He wrote me a letter in which he declared that he now supported Israel, that he agreed with McGovern's position, and that he had managed a Floor fight in favor of a Jackson amendment to strengthen the Middle East plank in the Democratic platform. I printed Stearns's letter. Some thought that I had gone out of my way to clear Stearns, and I again came under attack; but I was pleased later when Stearns went before the Watergate inquiry to testify about dirty tricks—"guilt by association"—such as the anti-McGovern smears, and he commended my effort to keep the record straight.

Both parties adopted strong Middle East planks—the strongest we had ever won. Invariably, the party out of power is free to make a forceful statement and, paradoxically, the Democratic platform borrowed from statements which had been made by Nixon and Ford.

In 1970, Nixon had called for defensible borders. In 1972, following Humphrey's lead, Ford and Robert Griffin (R-Michigan) had urged that the United States recognize Jerusalem as Israel's capital. All Democratic candidates for the presidency endorsed both concepts, and so did the Democratic platform; but I could evoke no similar enthusiasm when I submitted them to the GOP, because the Department of State always looks over the shoulder of platform committees and strives to defend the Administration from criticism and attack.

Occasionally, we polled congressional candidates. Our custom was to mail out the texts of the national convention platforms and to invite reactions from the candidates. The purpose was to win readership for the platform planks and to stimulate candidates to endorse and quote them.

Political leaders may be influenced by constituency; they in turn are in a position to inform constituency and thus help crystallize public opinion. Our cause was helped by speeches, resolutions, and platforms because of their educational impact, which could be translated into action.

SADAT'S PERSISTENT THREAT

As 1972 began, Sadat was still threatening war, while Israel was asking for negotiations. The Israelis kept pressing for peace. Deplorably, the world was more impressed by the threat of violence.

The New York Times, on December 27, blamed Egyptians for the impasse because their demand for a military crossing of the Suez Canal undermined prospects for a full settlement. *The Times* called on Egypt to accept demilitarization on Sinai and to assure free navigation.

In Moscow, Sadat joined the Soviets in a communiqué emphasizing a political settlement rather than war. Ignoring the U.S. initiative for negotiations, they called for a resumption of the Jarring mission, which was so loaded against Israel. Nixon accused the Soviets of exploiting Sadat's dependence on them to gain naval and air facilities.

Sadat had to explain why the "year of decision"—1971—had ended without his oft-threatened attack. In a 70-minute address on February 16, he charged that the United States had obstructed all progress toward peace. He explained that the Soviet Union had been preoccupied with the Indian subcontinent because of the Indo-Pakistan war. Sadat said that the United States had suffered a defeat in that conflict and might dash into a more foolish course because of its "readiness for rashness and folly." In addition, the United States was augmenting Israel's strength with Phantoms and Skyhawks.

Late in April, another joint Soviet-Egyptian communiqué hinted at a new war with the declaration that "the Arab states have every reason to use other means [besides a political settlement] to regain captured Arab lands." Once again, Sadat announced a deadline. Within the year, he would "liberate our land" and "defeat Israel's arrogance." Then came an unforgettable denunciation of Israel, in which he quoted Mohammed's imprecations against the Jews: "They are talking about direct negotiations. They were the neighbors of Mohammed . . . in Medina. They were his neighbors and he negotiated and concluded a treaty with them. But they eventually proved to be a mean, traitorous, conspiratorial, and treacherous people when they allied with his enemies to strike at him in Medina and from within. The most splendid thing our Prophet Mohammed . . . did was to evict them from the Arabian peninsula. We will never negotiate with them directly. We know our history and we know their history with our Prophet."

SADAT BREAKS WITH MOSCOW

Dramatic confirmation of Kissinger's 1970 prediction came in mid-July when Sadat sent Soviet military advisers home. Egyptian military hawks complained that the Soviets had been blocking a new war with Israel. Sadat was an angry man. The Soviet experts had irritated Egyptian officers and the Soviet Union had withheld equipment. However, Sadat insisted that Egypt would continue to receive defensive weapons and that the USSR would continue to monitor the U.S. Sixth Fleet.

Since the Russians were leaving, Sadat felt that the United States should reward him by delivering Israel. On September 28, he rejected a Rogers proposal for direct negotiations or, failing that, for close proximity talks which might lead to the opening of the Canal. Israelis were not disturbed by Sadat's threats. Rabin told AIPAC delegates in May 1972 that Israel's post-1967 cease-fire lines were the best that could be drawn for the defense of Israel. He declared that the Egyptians and Russians realized that the Egyptians were incapable of resuming hostilities, "nor could they achieve anything significant if they tried."

AIPAC's thirteenth policy conference was held, as usual, on Israel's birthday, and this year it marked my thirtieth year in the service of the American Jewish community. Eban flew from Israel to celebrate the occasion. Earlier, the *National Journal* had carried a special 16-page article by Andrew Glass featuring the work of the Jewish lobby.

In September, the United States and Israel established a U.S.-Israel Binational Science Foundation to support non-military scientific research. Israel would contribute 30 million Israeli pounds; the United States would contribute an equal amount. Israel would make this possible by prepaying $30 million in loans owed to the United States in the future. Interest on the money would finance continuation of significant pioneering projects, mainly in health.

Earlier, on March 15, 1972, Hussein announced his own plan for a semi-autonomous Arab state on the West Bank to be linked with Jordan in a United Arab Kingdom. Amman would be the overall capital, and Jerusalem would be the capital of "Palestine." Evidently, Hussein was trying to regain the friendship of West Bank leaders who had been alienated during his pre-1967 regime and who had been critical of the 1970 bloodbath in Amman. As a result of that struggle, Kuwait and Libya had ceased to contribute to the $105 million annual subsidy promised after 1967.

Hussein's proposal was scathingly attacked by the PLO and by the Arab states as "liquidationist," a "minefield," "defeatist," and CIA-inspired. The "moderate" Sadat broke off diplomatic relations, denouncing the plan as "an imperialist plot." Qaddafi threatened to topple the "lackey" regime. Only Saudi Arabia had continued its $40 million subvention. The United States helped Jordan with a $35 million supporting assistance grant in 1971. Now the Administration was proposing to increase it to $40 million, along with $45 million in grant military aid. Since the beginning of aid, Jordan had received $83.3 million in military grants through fiscal 1971, while Israel had received none. Economic grants to Jordan totaled $585 million, compared to $370.2 million for Israel. Most aid to Israel had been on a loan basis.

Later, in November, Hussein told *Le Monde* that he was ready to negotiate peace with Israel, but he demanded her total withdrawal, and Jordanian
sovereignty over the Old City. Mrs. Meir welcomed a courageous and revolutionary step and said that she would go to Amman to sign a peace with
Hussein but warned that Hussein could not expect to go to war twice, lose
each time, and still regain his former situation.

TERRORISM

Israelis made it a principle to reject deals with terrorists. They successfully maintained that policy in May, 1972, when four armed hijackers landed
a Sabena plane in Lod, threatening to blow up the plane, 87 passengers, and
10 crewmen if Israel refused to free 100 terrorist prisoners. After a 21-hour
ordeal, Israeli "repairmen" forced the plane's emergency door, killed two
terrorists and captured two female terrorists. In that same month terrorism
came to a gruesome climax. Civilian travelers arriving from Rome were
slaughtered on May 30 by three Japanese terrorists as they disembarked
from their Air France plane at Lod airport. The three had been permitted to
board the plane in Rome with weapons in their uninspected baggage. The
dead included 16 Puerto Ricans, six on their first pilgrimage, three Americans, six Israelis, and two of the Japanese. More than 70 were injured. The
Japanese, members of the Sikigun (Red Army), had been trained in Beirut
by the PFLP, the radical wing of the terrorist movement. The lone Japanese
survivor was sentenced to life imprisonment.

There was universal revulsion. Hussein called it a "sick crime . . . contrary to the true spirit of the Palestinian people." The Egyptian premier,
Aziz Sidky, observed that the operation "shows that we can win victory in
the battle with Israel," and two major Egyptian dailies and Radio Cairo
were similarly gratified.

Three months later, there was another outrage—the slaughter of Israel's
athletes at the Olympic games in Munich. Two had been slain and nine held
hostage by eight Arab terrorists when they battered into the team's dormi-
tory. The terrorists, members of Black September, a militant arm of El
Fatah, demanded that Israel release 200 of their imprisoned comrades.
After a long and terrifying deadlock—even while the games were permitted
to continue—the nine Israeli athletes, five terrorists, and a German police-
man were killed in a shootout near a waiting Lufthansa plane which the terrorists had expected to board for an Arab airport.

Sidky refused to cooperate with the West German government's appeal
that Egypt assure release of the hostages if they and their captors were
flown to Cairo. Again, Hussein, unique among his people, denounced a
"despicable crime" against humanity, the Palestinian people, and "real"
Arabs. Later, in October, West Germany permitted the three imprisoned

terrorists to go free, after Black September terrorists hijacked and threatened to blow up a Lufthansa airliner.

Nixon cabled Mrs. Meir, deploring the "senseless tragedy" as a "hideous perversion of the Olympic spirit." Congress adopted resolutions sponsored by Mansfield, Scott, and Celler calling for ostracism of nations which provide sanctuary for terrorists.

There was an unprecedented sequel. Soon after Munich, Israeli planes attacked terrorist bases in Syria and Lebanon. The Security Council debated a resolution calling on the parties to cease all military action. Britain, France, Italy, and Belgium offered amendments deploring all acts of terror, but the Soviet Union and Communist China vetoed them. Whereupon the United States cast a veto, for the first time on a Middle East issue, while 13 other U.N. members voted yes, and Panama abstained.

Letter bombs, posted by Black September, were next. Israel's agricultural attaché in London, Ami Schorry, was killed in September when a parcel mailed from Amsterdam exploded on its arrival at Israel's embassy. A few days later, letter bombs mailed from Holland, Italy, Malaysia, and Germany to Israeli diplomats and Jewish leaders, as well as to Jordanians, were intercepted in many cities.

The terrorists, unable to mount a war of "liberation" inside Israel or the occupied territories, were waging war from a convenient distance. By this time, few Jews were left in Arab countries. The Chief Rabbi of Egypt, Haim Douek, managed to escape from Cairo, and in Paris he disclosed that he had been forced to tell journalists that no Jews had been arrested after the Six-Day War. There had been 80,000 Jews in Cairo before 1948 but there were now only 450 to 500. The 5,000 Jews left in Syria—one-third of the prewar Jewish population—were victims of ugly intimidation and harassment.

PROPAGANDA

The never-ending propaganda war, twisting aggressor and victim, continued unabated.

At the Capitol, three senators, Philip Hart (D-Michigan), Harold Hughes (D-Iowa), and Margaret Chase Smith (R-Maine), protested against the use of their names by propagandist Alfred Lilienthal, who had published an advertisement implying that they had opposed U.S. support for Israel.

Arab press and leadership continued to exploit the infamous *Protocols of the Elders of Zion. Al Akhbar,* an Egyptian daily, told its readers that rabbis use Christian flesh and blood to prepare matzoth for Passover. King Faisal of Saudi Arabia made the same accusation at a conference of Arab foreign ministers, David Hirst wrote in the *Manchester Guardian* in April. An Egyptian had remonstrated with Faisal "with the daring proposition that Jews do after all belong to the human race."

Arabs were courting the blacks. On March 12, the National Black Political Convention, meeting in Gary, Indiana, urged suspension of aid to Israel, and that it be "dismantled." The Black Caucus of 13 congressmen was embarrassed. Mayor Richard Hatcher of Gary called it a most unfortunate resolution, adopted at a time when few people were on the convention floor. Representatives Charles Diggs (D-Michigan) and William Clay (D-Missouri) invited my reaction, and the congressmen then issued a strong statement commending Israel's aid to Black African countries. Mayor William S. Hart of East Orange, New Jersey, urged black elected officials to repudiate the Gary resolution, and Bayard Rustin wrote in *ADA World* that Arabs in Israel enjoyed more freedom than Arabs in Arab lands. The NAACP withdrew from the coalition, declaring that a one-sided condemnation of Israel was as "unjustified" as to condemn all of today's Arabs simply because of their long history as the chief traders of black African slaves.

Once again, Dean Francis B. Sayre used the Washington Cathedral pulpit to denounce Israel's administration of Jerusalem as an example of the "moral tragedy of mankind." The "oppressed" had become the "oppressors." Arabs were deprived of their patrimony and imprisoned without charge. *The Washington Post* editorially denounced Sayre's sermon as "unfortunate . . . deplorable . . . intemperate . . . and unjust." It pointed out that freedom of religion and open access were better protected than at any time in memory. It quoted Sayre: "Now the Jews have it all. But even as they praise their God for the smile of fortune, they begin almost simultaneously to put Him to death." *The Post* wrote: "The words run painfully close to a very old, familiar line of bigotry . . . the gun is loaded."

The U.N. persisted in its slavish support for the Arab states. On June 26, the Security Council again censured Israel for reprisals against terrorist positions in Lebanon, but the Council ignored the provocative attacks against Israel's civilians.

GENOCIDE CONVENTION

One of our failures was in the long, vain struggle to win ratification of the U.N. convention outlawing genocide. Deplorably, the United States failed to ratify a number of U.N. conventions because southern conservatives feared that they would permit international intrusion into our domestic affairs.

Most significant was the genocide convention which was put on the U.N. agenda by a Jewish professor, Dr. Raphael Lemkin. Thanks to his perseverance, the U.N. approved it in Paris on December 9, 1948, 55 to 0. I had worked with him in Paris, and after his decisive victory I urged newspapermen to interview him and to give him credit. Many have mistakenly believed that he was motivated by the Nazi Holocaust. In fact, he had initiated his campaign before World War II, in a reaction to the genocidal slaughter of Christian Assyrians in Iraq in August 1933. Lemkin, who was a member of the League of Nations legal committee, tried unsuccessfully to induce the League to declare the destruction of racial and religious "collectivities" a crime under the law of nations.

Coincidentally, Hitler seized power in that same year. Lemkin came to the United States to teach at Duke and Yale universities. He compiled evidence for the Nuremberg trials. Later, he passionately and successfully lobbied at the U.N. He died in 1959, deeply disappointed because the U.S. Senate had failed to ratify.

By 1971, 75 governments had ratified the convention, including the Soviet Union, Israel, and most of the Arab states (with the exception of Sudan, which was waging a genocidal war against southern blacks in that year). Opposition in our own country had begun to recede, and the Nixon administration urged Senate ratification. On March 30, 1971, the Senate Committee on Foreign Relations voted 10 to 4 for ratification, but despite the fact that a majority of the Senate petitioned for Floor action, ratification was blocked in 1971 and 1972 by southern conservatives.

Chapter 28

Soviet Jews

AN EARLY CONCERN

We were deeply concerned about Jews in the Soviet Union. In an earlier chapter, I recalled our reaction to the vicious Soviet anti-Semitism in the early 1950s: the show trials in Czechoslovakia and the Stalinist fabrication of the Jewish doctors' plot against Communist leaders.

At that time, we were not thinking about emigration of Jews from the Soviet Union. We hoped that Jews would be permitted to practice their religion and to develop their culture like other nationality groups, but Soviet Jews were victims of the worst discrimination and prejudice, apparently because the Soviet Union was determined to wipe out their past and destroy their future.

Jews were unique among the other nationalities of the USSR because, lacking a territorial base, they could not develop their ethnic personality. They were a disembodied ghost people. Jewish literature and theater were suppressed. Soviet Jews were bewildered. Identified as members of the Jewish nationality in their passports, they became aware of its meaning only when they encountered anti-Semitism.

When Anastas Mikoyan visited Washington early in January 1959, I printed a two-page article on Soviet anti-Semitism in the *Near East Report* and sent it to Senate leaders requesting them to raise the issue with Mikoyan if and when they met him here.

In September 1963, Ribicoff and 63 colleagues introduced a resolution urging that Soviet Jews be allowed the free exercise of their religion and the pursuit of their culture. The Senate Foreign Relations Committee held hearings eleven months later. Hopkins, the veteran pro-Arab lobbyist, argued that Christians and Moslems also suffered discrimination and that the resolution should refer to all three faiths.

Fulbright offered an amendment which would merely condemn religious persecution per se. He was defeated 68 to 1. When it reached the House side, the State Department contended that it would be "counterproductive" to name any country or religious group. The resolution went to conference, and Fulbright prevailed, watering down the resolution to a meaningless generality: The United States believed in freedom of religion for all peoples and condemned persecution because of religion. All should be permitted the free exercise of religion and the pursuit of culture.

Early in 1965, Ribicoff and his colleagues reintroduced their original resolution. At first the State Department was negative. Later, Assistant Secretary Douglas MacArthur II wrote to Fulbright that Russian Jews "suffer not only from the severe restriction imposed on all religions, but also from additional restrictions, which make it impossible for them to enjoy their cultural and community life."

The new resolutions were sponsored by 70 senators and 140 House members. Again the House created difficulties, thanks largely to Representative Edna Kelly. The new House version deleted references to Jews from the enacting clause, and, going further, broadened and diffused the target. It insisted on indicting "the governments of Eastern Europe." But some Eastern European countries did respect Jewish religious freedom and cultural pursuits, and it was manifestly unjust to lump them with the Soviet Union.

We preferred to let the proposal die. In 1966, I suggested to Ribicoff that he send a message to the American Jewish Conference on Soviet Jewry, which was then holding a conference in Philadelphia. Sixty-nine senators joined Ribicoff in that message, calling on the Soviet Union to allow its three million Jews to live creatively and in dignity as Jews. The statement made banner headlines and later was printed as a full-page advertisement in *The New York Times,* with 90 signers. In the House, Representative Jonathan Bingham (D-New York) initiated a similar declaration signed by well over 300 representatives. These advertisements made no reference to emigration.

News of Israel's 1967 victory had awakened Soviet Jews, many of whom had never known about Israel or what it meant to be a Jew. They now learned from foreign radio broadcasts. Now, more sensitive to the anti-Semitism which barred their admission into Soviet society, some began to study Hebrew secretly, preparing for the day when they might escape the Communist yoke and emigrate to Israel.

Earlier, in April 1967, Bingham had sponsored a statement which was signed by 300 House members from all states, attacking the suppression of Jewish spiritual and cultural life in the Soviet Union, and urging that Jews be permitted to join their relatives. That was the first explicit reference to emigration.

Five years later, in April 1972, the House voted 359 to 2 in favor of a resolution calling on the Soviet Union to permit the free expression of ideas, the exercise of religion, and the right of emigration. It was sponsored by O'Neill and John Anderson (R-Illinois), and by 12 of the 14 members of the Subcommittee on Europe of the House Foreign Affairs Committee. Nixon was then about to meet with Soviet officials and he was asked to raise the question.

THE NEW ALIYAH

There was a trickle of emigration in 1967 and 1968, and astonished Israelis welcomed a new, unprecedented Aliyah. The number increased slowly, for many were denied emigration because they were alleged to be security risks.

Stung by criticism in *Al Anwar,* a Beirut newspaper, the Soviets broadcast in September 1973: "After all, only 42,000 Jews have left the Soviet Union for Israel, but about 800,000 have left the Arab countries for Israel."

The plight of Soviet Jews was dramatized in June 1970, when Soviet police charged 31 Jews with conspiracy to hijack a 12-passenger Soviet plane to Sweden in an effort to reach Israel. Just before their December 15 trial, 2,000 people protested at an interfaith demonstration in Washington Cathedral, under the auspices of the American Jewish Conference on Soviet Jewry and the Washington Jewish Community Council.

The court sentenced two of the accused, Mark Dymshitz and Edward Kuznetsov, to death by firing squad. A former military officer, Wolf Zalmanson, was sentenced by a military tribunal, which might also impose a death sentence. In May 1971, nine Leningrad Jews were sentenced to one to ten years in strict-regime prison camps. There were also trials in Riga, in Vilna, and in other cities. State Department spokesman Charles W. Bray branded secret trials as "abhorrent . . . depredations of fundamental human rights."

The harsh sentences evoked worldwide protest from religious leaders, including Pope Paul VI, from congressmen, major newspapers, dock workers who boycotted Soviet cargoes, and even from Communist parties in Western countries. National Jewish leaders came to Washington to appeal to Nixon and Rogers for U.S. intercession.

Massively sponsored resolutions were introduced in both houses of Congress, but before they were put to a vote the Soviet Supreme Court commuted the death sentences to fifteen years of hard labor, which could mean slow death, for rations would be reduced and mail and packages would be cut off.

Yet, surprisingly, the Soviets were permitting an increase in emigration. In 1970, only 1,000 were allowed to leave. In January and February 1971, the number was only 200. In March there were 1,000; in April there were 1,300. By November, it was estimated that 80,000 Soviet Jews had filed applications at the Dutch embassy, which then represented Israel in the Soviet Union.

In November 1971, many witnesses told the Subcommittee on Europe of the House Committee on Foreign Affairs that Soviet Jews were living in terror. However, Deputy Assistant Secretary of State for European Affairs Richard T. Davies testified that "all Soviet citizens, not just Jews, suffer from the Soviet government's policy of militant atheism and its refusal to consider emigration as a right rather than a rare privilege." He said one had to draw a line "between loyal Jews at home and Zionists abroad." He insisted that Jews were still the best educated Soviet minority but that there were now ceilings on their educational aspirations. Skilled Jews who dared to apply were denied visas for five years on security grounds, discharged from employment, humiliated before their fellow employees, and sentenced to the purgatory of isolation.

Soviet emigration, continuing at the high rate prevailing in late 1971, totaled 13,000 as compared with 1,000 in 1970, and reached 31,700 in 1972.

Why was the Soviet Union letting Jews go? This was not a gesture of friendship toward Israel and Jews. Discrimination and repression persisted. There were some explanations. Many Jews who sought visas were unassimilable Oriental residents of Georgia and Bukhara who had never given up their age-long prayer for Zion. Similarly difficult to absorb were thousands of Jews who had lived in Baltic and former Rumanian territories up until 1939 and had been exposed to other Jews, to Judaism, and to Zionism. Hence, unlike Jews in Moscow, Leningrad, and other "old" parts of the USSR, who had no such memories, they could not be considered reliable Communists.

The Soviets feared that other nationality groups might try to emulate the Jewish emigration, but the Soviets could argue that the Jews were unique because they had no national territory of their own inside the Soviet Union, and therefore might be allowed to emigrate to a national homeland elsewhere.

One odd theoretical explanation of Soviet conduct was the experience at the end of World War II, when Stalin suddenly agreed to let Polish refugees flood back into Poland, which was ill-equipped to absorb them. Perhaps the Soviets thought that Israel might likewise be overwhelmed and that disillusioned Soviet Jews would return to discredit Zionism once and for all. Fortunately, if that was a Soviet objective, a friendly U.S. Congress helped to circumvent it.

CONGRESS AIDS SOVIET JEWS

Senator Muskie, a presidential candidate, initiated a move for U.S. financial help to Soviet Jews in December 1971.

"The main burden of relocating and absorbing Soviet Jews necessarily falls on Israel. . . . None but the Israelis can build the homes, teach the language, find the jobs, and otherwise pay the social costs. . . . But there is a financial cost as well. . . . I believe we must help," he said. He pointed out that since World War II the U.S. contribution in refugee assistance exceeded $2.8 billion, including close to $600 million for Cuban refugees; $237 million to the International Refugee Organization (IRO); about $85 million for Koreans; and more than $500 million for Arab refugees.

Some Israeli diplomats were troubled. In 1971, they had argued the case for supporting assistance, and they hoped that the $50 million grant would be renewed in 1972. They feared that this might be jeopardized by Muskie's appeal for an additional, separate fund for Soviet Jews. I saw no conflict. Funds for refugees could be legislated as an amendment to the Department of State budget and could be administered by the State Department rather than by the Agency for International Development (AID). The authorization for supporting assistance would be an amendment to the 1972 Foreign Assistance Act. Thus, the two proposals would be considered by separate committees and would travel on separate tracks.

Muskie's office asked for my opinion, and I suggested that he sponsor a request for $85 million, the amount the House committee had recommended for supporting assistance in 1971. The legislation was co-sponsored by Ribicoff, Javits, and Richard Schweiker (R-Pennsylvania), and our office and constituency helped to secure 46 co-sponsors. Bingham and Halpern submitted a similar proposal supported by 67 House members.

In the House, the project was sympathetically received both by Morgan and by Ohio's Hays, chairman of the subcommittee dealing with the State Department's budget. Morgan announced support at an AIPAC policy conference luncheon in the Rayburn Building in April. There were two images of Israel, he said: the Israel which defended herself, and the Israel which freely opened her doors to refugees. Both Israels deserved support. However, he told the congressmen, it would be up to AIPAC to win the House Appropriations Committee. Speaker Albert rose to promise that he would relieve us of that responsibility.

In the meantime, the Administration had revised its negative attitude toward Israel's request for supporting assistance, and in 1972, on its own initiative, it sponsored a $50 million grant for that purpose. But in its justification, it declared that the money should also be used to meet the growing burden arising from Soviet immigration and that additional funds for Soviet Jews would not be needed. So Sisco testified.

We submitted our own testimony to the Senate and House Committees. We estimated that immigration would approximate 30,000 from the Soviet Union, in addition to another 40,000 from other parts of the world, a total of 70,000 in 12 months.

The Jewish Agency had a global budget of $775 million. Of this sum,

$200 million would be needed to resettle Soviet Jews and another $260 million for the remainder. The government of Israel would contribute $240 million for refugee absorption. Thus the overall total would be slightly more than $1 billion. In addition to food and temporary shelter, Israel needed to establish new communities, schools, hospitals, dormitories, roads, and religious and cultural centers. The government also had to create employment opportunities.

Small tradesmen needed vocational training and instruction in Hebrew. Professionals, including doctors and engineers, needed more up-to-date instruction. Some new immigrants presented psychological problems because, as former wards of the Soviets, they had to learn how to fend for themselves to secure education, employment, and housing and to pursue cultural activities.

The House and Senate approved the $50 million appropriation for supporting assistance, as well as the $85 million authorization for Soviet Jews. However, the amount for Soviet Jewry was cut to $50 million by the Appropriations Committees.

In March, I received a congratulatory message from the late Louis A. Pincus, head of the Jewish Agency: "Now that the fifty million has at last been finalized, I would like just shortly to express my appreciation for the part you played in it. I have no doubt that without your action nothing probably would have come of it. This, amongst your other achievements, will be recollected not only because it is money but it was in assistance of the historic event of Soviet Jewry's Aliyah."

The Soviets struck at visa applicants in August 1972, when they imposed a schedule of exit fees ranging from $5,000 to $27,000, depending on the extent of the applicant's education, presumably to reimburse the government for its costs. That explanation was untenable, because the fees were five times higher than educational costs. Soviet citizens, theoretically, were entitled to free education, and applicants who earned 200 to 300 rubles a month would have to work many lifetimes to save the exorbitant amounts— 15,000 to 20,000 rubles—which the government demanded.

Even as the Soviet's new ransom plan went into effect, it was revealed that Professor Benjamin Levich, a noted physicist, had been denied the right to leave for a post at Tel Aviv University. It was estimated that the Levich family would have to pay more than $100,000 in exit fees. (Five years later, British scientists planned to honor Levich at Oxford, but the Soviets still refused to permit him to travel—until 1979 when Senator Kennedy interceded with Brezhnev on Levich's behalf.)

The Soviet Union was now accused of grinding Jews into commodities to be traded for a huge ransom to be paid by world Jewry. Congressmen talked of striking back at inhumane Soviet trade practices by opposing economic concessions. They included Ribicoff, chairman of the Subcommittee on International Trade of the Senate Finance Committee; Hale Boggs,

House Democratic Floor Leader; and Senators Javits, Humphrey, Bayh, Mondale, Schweiker, and many others.

Many proposals were being circulated, and there was an obvious need to achieve unified action. I suggested to Amitay, then Ribicoff's aide, that he invite legislative assistants from both Houses to arrive at a consensus. Jerry Goodman of the National Conference on Soviet Jewry and Yehudah Hellman of the Conference of Presidents came from New York. It was at this meeting in the Capitol that Richard Perle, Jackson's aide, proposed the amendment to deny most-favored-nation status to a nation which denies its citizens the right or opportunity to emigrate and which imposes more than nominal exit fees. A day or two later, Jackson addressed a Washington meeting of the National Conference on Soviet Jewry, which promptly endorsed his proposal. Both Javits and Humphrey had different approaches but responded to our appeal that they join forces with Jackson. That led to a campaign for additional sponsors, which our constituency helped to win. At the end of three weeks, there were 76 co-sponsors from all but five states—Oklahoma, Montana, Nebraska, Utah, and Vermont.

On October 18, the United States and the Soviet Union signed the new trade agreement to grant the Soviet Union most-favored-nation status. The Soviets agreed to pay $722 million to the United States in settlement of its $11.1 billion World War II lend-lease debt—6.5 cents on the dollar. Export Import Bank credits would be extended to the Soviet Union to finance purchases here, and Soviet goods would enter U.S. markets at the lowest tariff.

As if in celebration of the new agreement to soften congressional opposition, the Soviets simultaneously permitted 175 Jewish families to emigrate without paying substantial education taxes. Veteran Jewish activists were still denied the right to leave. Later, the Soviets allowed exemptions for older people and percentage reductions based on the years of work service. In February of 1973, they formerly published a ransom tax decree but disclosed that it would not be put into effect because of the exemptions. Jackson commented: "We are going to put the Jackson amendment on the books but in the hope that it won't apply to the Soviet Union because they will be in compliance with the free emigration provisions."

Paralleling Jackson's initiative, Representative Charles Vanik (D-Ohio) introduced a similar proposal in the House, and soon he had 121 co-sponsors. We were elated by the progress in the Senate but we realized that the measure had to originate in the House and win the approval of the House Ways and Means Committee before it could be taken up in the Senate, because it was proposed to offer it as an amendment to the Trade Reform Act, which was pending before that Committee. Accordingly, we needed all the House sponsors we could get.

Mark Talisman, Vanik's aide, assured me that he needed our help. We then wrote to 1,000 local and national leaders asking them to enlist co-sponsors. We soon had 190. At that point, on Friday afternoon, Talisman called to say that Vanik had urged Wilbur Mills, Chairman of the House Ways and Means Committee, to become the number one sponsor on the House side. We called an old friend, Phillip Back, in Little Rock. On Monday morning, February 6, he telephoned me to say that Mills had agreed. From that time on, there was no stopping the amendment in the House. The number of co-sponsors climbed to 288. All 16 members of the Black Caucus were on the list.

Mills's accession was most significant. Up to that time, neither the Administration nor the Russians had taken the bill seriously, believing it to be a demonstration fated to die in Committee, but Mills was a sincere and ardent supporter. In September of 1973, he said that he did not favor expanding trade relations with the Soviet Union if the price was to be paid with the martyrdom of men of genius like Solzhenitsyn and Sakharov. "One cannot work to liberalize the movement of goods in the world market place if the doors are to be slammed shut upon what Justice Holmes called the 'market place of ideas,'" he said.

Throughout 1973, all Jewish organizations helped to win support. AIPAC's Ken Wollack spearheaded the effort to win the House Committee members.

The Soviet Union made no secret of its resentment, although its criticism was directed mostly against the Stevenson amendment, which barred much-needed credits.

The measure was scheduled to come up for a Committee vote in October 1973. On the fifth day of the Yom Kippur War, a Wednesday, we feared that the Soviet Union might now join Egypt and Syria, with men as well as weapons, in a crushing attack on Israel. Israel's life now seemed to hang in the balance. I talked with Talisman that day and suggested that Vanik might propose a brief delay in Committee action. But the Committee was not in a mood to consider postponement.

Big business, eager for new trade opportunities in the Soviet Union, campaigned against the amendment. Donald M. Kendall of Pepsi Cola and chairman of the Emergency Committee on American Trade (ECAT), which had negotiated a multi-million-dollar deal with the Soviet Union, urged his organization members to telephone or telegraph each member of the House Ways and Means Committee.

Fulbright told the American Bankers Association that the Jackson amendment was a call to renew the Cold War. Leonid Brezhnev came to lobby Congress and claimed that 95 percent of the Jews had been permitted to leave. He used a 60,000 figure, which was an obvious exaggeration. If, in fact, that number had been permitted to go, why were the Soviets objecting to the legislation, since they would have been in compliance with it?

The Nixon Administration appealed for delay. Rogers had insisted that quiet diplomacy was the appropriate course and that congressional action would be counterproductive. His successor, Dr. Kissinger, urged Jewish leadership to support an amendment which would eliminate the paragraph dealing with trade restrictions (Title IV). Eight of us—leaders of the national organizations—met in New York to discuss the Kissinger request. I was opposed to delay, arguing that the Administration would be in a much stronger position to deal with the Soviets if the bill went over to the House without any weakening amendments. When Jewish leaders met with Jackson to discuss the Kissinger proposal, he rebuked them sharply in a rough and widely publicized encounter. Counting on my support, Jackson had invited me to attend, but I was testifying at that hour in support of the Administration's request for the $2.2 billion authorization for Israel.

The trade bill was approved in the House 272 to 140 on December 11, 1973. An amendment to delete Title IV, as urged by the Administration, was defeated by a similar vote. Action was deferred in the Senate while Kissinger, Jackson, Ribicoff, and Javits negotiated a compromise. That was spelled out in a Kissinger-Jackson exchange of letters in October 1974; and on December 13, Jackson offered an amendment which permitted the President to waive the trade restrictions for an 18-month period, providing he could certify to Congress that Soviet emigration practices would conform with the letter exchange. At the end of 18 months, Congress and the Administration would review Soviet emigration to determine whether the waiver should continue. On December 3, Kissinger had told the Senate Finance Committee that the Administration had assurances on emigration from Soviet diplomats and that these had been confirmed at the Brezhnev-Ford summit at Vladivostok in November. The Senate voted approval, 77 to 4.

Two weeks later, *Tass* published an October 26 letter in which Gromyko had told Kissinger that the letter exchange created a "distorted impression" of the Soviet position; he rejected Soviet assurances of any specified increase in future emigration.

On January 14, Kissinger disclosed that the Soviet Union could not "accept a trading relationship based on the legislation recently enacted in this country" and that it was renouncing the 1972 U.S.-USSR trade agreement.

However, it was widely believed that the Soviets were mostly interested in securing credits; they were angered by the Stevenson amendment, which limited Eximbank credits to $300 million over a four-year period even if the Soviets complied with the emigration provisions in the Jackson-Kissinger letter. Presumably, too, the Soviet renunciation of the trade agreement was an attempt to bring pressure on Congress to modify both the Jackson and Stevenson amendments and to persuade American public opinion that the amendments were counterproductive. The Soviets slashed emigration totals and intensified harassment of dissidents and would-be emigrants.

I never accepted the argument that the Jackson amendment should be reconsidered and modified, for that would have been vindication and victory for the Soviets, who would have further hardened opposition to any relaxation of policy.

Chapter 29

Complacency

We were optimistic as 1973 began. The ill-fated Rusk-Rogers-Jarring-Nixon plan had been shelved, or so we wanted to believe. Israel was permitted to buy the planes and arms she needed. U.S. influence in the Middle East seemed to be growing. Sudan and North Yemen had moved to restore diplomatic relations with the United States. Washington had "interest sections" in Egypt and Iraq, and Algeria was eager to sell natural gas to the United States. Most influential Middle East countries appeared to be in the American orbit.

Our optimism was dampened by awareness that the Arabs had two devastating weapons: terror and oil. Radicals had not hesitated to wield the first; conservatives were now threatening to invoke the second. Terrorism was never a weapon against Israel's army; it was aimed at her civilians. Nevertheless, it was able to intimidate the world community, paralyze legitimate response, corrupt the United Nations, isolate Israel by alienating her friends, pressure and alarm conservative Arab leaders, and incite radical discontent and revolt.

Oil threats were nothing new. "They like to beat the oil drums," I had told the press at the U.N. in 1948. Now they beat louder and faster and demanded a higher price for their menacing music. They had threatened American oil interests again in 1956 and 1967, but the West was then independent enough to meet and overcome vague and disunited gestures.

Throughout 1972 and 1973, there had been an astonishing escalation in Arab oil power. By that time, the United States had become a net importer of petroleum and could no longer hold oil prices down. The Organization of Petroleum Exporting Countries (OPEC), established in 1960, came into its own. The oil producing countries could raise oil prices at will and force the major international oil companies to serve as their agents in the collection of taxes from the industrial world. They could impose their terms on the oil distributors, refiners, and marketers who bargained for preferred access, and they could deploy their enormous wealth to purchase power wherever they pleased—in governments, counting houses, land, and industry. Confronted with this threat to their independence, Western nations supinely failed to impose discipline in order to restrict surging energy demands, to expand their own energy production, and to develop alternative sources.

Terrorism could extort subsidies from the oil plutocracy and dictate their foreign policy. Saudi Arabia was the most vulnerable target. Always fearful of the envious underprivileged and their threats to pipelines and palaces, the Saudis felt that they had no alternative but to pay protection money. Twice in 1973 King Faisal was handed bloody warnings. The first blow came on March 2, when the El Fatah striking force, Black September, invaded the Saudi embassy at Khartoum, executing the new U.S. ambassador, Cleo A. Noel, Jr., the retiring U.S. chargé d'affaires, George C. Moore, and a Belgian diplomat, Guy Eid. Later that year, three Palestinians stormed the Saudi embassy in Paris, seizing five hostages and demanding the release of Palestinian terrorists held by Jordan.

In a subsequent humiliation of the oil oligarchy on December 21, 1975, Black September had the effrontery to invade and extort tribute from an OPEC conference in Vienna.

A Treasury ruling made decades ago permitted oil companies to treat their royalty payments to overseas governments as tax credits rather than as expense—as deductions from taxes, rather than as deductions from revenues. As a result of that privilege, which they had won in the 1940s, they paid little or no taxes to the U.S. government. The practice rewarded investments abroad, contributed enormously to Saudi development, and was partly to blame for the failure to build refineries and adequate distribution facilities in this country.

I could not understand why our government should have waived antitrust laws to permit the oil companies to bargain as one—and thus surrender to OPEC. The United States was the architect of its own subsequent impoverishment. It should have forced the Arab governments to compete for markets as they nationalized the oil companies. I questioned depletion allowances which subsidized oil exploration both here and abroad. I never could see why those who drew on our country's underground wealth should have been so enriched.

A perennial optimist, I never feared that the American people, resenting blackmail, would surrender to Arab oil pressures at Israel's expense. I urged our government to declare that the United States would not permit the price or the availability of oil to influence Middle East policy. I hoped to win such an assurance at our annual AIPAC policy conference in May 1973.

We invited Charles Di Bona, Special Consultant to the President on Energy, to brief and reassure AIPAC delegates at our briefing session at the State Department on May 8. He accepted our invitation but later declined because I had written him that I expected him to debunk the propaganda which had been printed on February 15 in *Forbes Magazine:* "That day seems sure to come when American politicians will face a hard choice between the pressing need for Saudi oil and the Jewish vote." At the last minute, I persuaded him to address us, after I assured him that he could say what he pleased. Di Bona later became the president of the American Petroleum Institute.

Much later, in 1973, Mike Wallace of CBS invited me to participate in "60-Minutes." He suggested that I express fear that the energy crisis might undermine the future of Israel and the American Jewish community, but I had no such fear. I insisted that the American people were too intelligent to hold Jews responsible for Arab impositions and extortions. Wallace was disappointed, but shortly before the program went on the air a CBS poll vindicated my contention that most Americans blamed the energy crisis on the Administration and Congress, on the oil companies, and on the Arabs. Few blamed Jews, and I never saw one of those elusive bumper stickers inciting folks to "Burn Jews, Not Oil."

AIPAC's annual statement of policy urged effective measures to meet anticipated energy shortages. We noted the "reckless and irresponsible" propaganda drive to link the oil crisis with the Arab-Israel conflict. We declared: "Surrender to demagogic demands at Israel's expense will neither guarantee oil shipments from the Arab world nor safeguard foreign investments nor allay the adverse economic effects of U.S. dependence on Arab oil." A solution required joint economic planning with other oil-importing countries, drastic energy conservation, increased utilization of our own resources, and rapid development of alternative sources.

I frequently met with Mike Ameen, who was ARAMCO's Washington representative and whom I respected for his frankness and availability. On May 4, he had dramatic news for me. He told me that King Faisal had urged ARAMCO to work for a change in U.S. policy. The day before, Faisal had told Frank Jungers, president of ARAMCO, that he was "not able to stand alone much longer as America's friend." It would be more and more difficult to hold off on the tide of opinion "that was now running so heavily against America."

Faisal told Jungers that "a simple disavowal of Israeli policies and action by the U.S. government would go a long way toward quieting the current anti-American feeling." He urged American businesses to make their thoughts and actions felt.

Faisal's attitude was ambivalent. Indebted to the United States for defense and to American oil companies for massive oil revenues, he hesitated to threaten an oil embargo. Saudi Arabia, with vast oil resources, was not anxious to hoard oil underground until another generation's research and initiative made it worthless.

ARAMCO had invested some $700 million the previous year to increase Saudi production to nine million barrels a day in order to meet America's growing energy consumption. (Saudi output had been 4.9 million a day in 1971.) The eventual goal was 20 million barrels a day. Now Faisal, although baited by other Arabs, preferred to threaten a production cut rather than a complete cut-off. His many statements revealed his indecision.

In 1972, Egypt's Sadat had urged Arab countries to wield oil politically and warned that "U.S. interests in the Middle East are in for a long, hot autumn." Faisal told *Al Mussawar,* an Egyptian weekly, that withholding oil would impair the economies of the Arab countries and prevent them from supporting Arab "steadfastness." Moreover, Saudi Arabia wanted a stake in the United States. At the Middle East Institute in Washington, Oil Minister Sheikh Ahmed Zaki Yamani proposed that Saudi Arabia be permitted a share of marketing and refining operations in exchange for a guaranteed supply of oil. Arab threats were counterproductive. Leading American newspapers warned against capitulation.

The Washington Post declared: "It is to yield to hysteria to take such threats as Saudi Arabia's literally . . . Washington remains its principal arms supplier, its only great power patron. Dependence works both ways. Perspective and a sense of history, not a panicky reaction to the energy crisis, should guide American policy."

The Wall Street Journal said: "If the United States ever does suggest that it will bend its Middle East policy for the sake of oil, American policy would quickly find itself under intensified pressures and increasingly dangerous threats from all quarters. Given one breakthrough, this dam will burst."

Soon after the Faisal-Jungers May 3 talk, there were disconcerting indications of U.S. efforts to placate Faisal. The oil companies began to lobby for a change in U.S. policy. Faisal had also communicated his displeasure to American diplomats, and he had an impact. This was evident on May 7, during the AIPAC policy conference which celebrated Israel's twenty-fifth anniversary, when we heard an unprecedented clash between Sisco and Israel's new ambassador, Simcha Dinitz. In a carefully prepared speech, Sisco blamed both sides for the prolongation of the Arab-Israel conflict, in what seemed to be a signal to the Arabs that an "even-handed" United States was changing its image if not its policy.

He spoke of lost opportunities. "It is time for the parties to begin to choose options, to establish priorities, to decide what is most important and what it will cost, and to decide whether it is worth the price," he said. However, we welcomed some of Sisco's comments, such as his declaration that outside powers could play a responsible role in encouraging the parties to get a negotiating process started but could not be a part of the process itself. "When they seek to substitute their views for the positions of the parties directly concerned or openly advocate the positions of one party, they do not further progress. They inhibit it."

Dinitz, as was his custom, had a spirited response. ". . . If I stand before you . . . a representative of a country still . . . without peace, it is not due to a lack of effort on our part. For 25 years we have extended our hand of friendship to our Arab neighbors and pleaded for peace . . . . No opportunity for peace was ever missed by Israel . . . . Real peace can never be achieved either by surrendering to blackmail or by satisfying frustrations."

I had invited the laconic Walworth Barbour, who had been the most popular American ambassador to Israel, to come from Massachusetts to sit on the dais, promising him that he would not have to make a speech. He was happy to be remembered, and he later rewarded me with a new definition of AIPAC. "It airs differences in order to reconcile them," he wrote.

We might have known that war was imminent if we had paid more attention to what Sadat was saying. In April, Sadat had warned of war, but his periodic threats, unfulfilled so often, were no longer taken seriously. He had told *Newsweek* Editor Arnaud de Borchgrave: "Everything in this country is now being mobilized in earnest for the resumption of the battle, which is now inevitable." He disclosed that the Russians were providing Egypt with "everything that was possible for them to supply [a fact which U.S. and Israel Intelligence had observed] and I am now quite satisfied."

ARMS FOR SAUDIS

Within days after the Sisco-Dinitz clash, there was further evidence of a U.S. policy shift. It became known that the United States was negotiating the sale of $1 billion in weapons—including Phantom jets—to Saudi Arabia, on top of a $600 million Navy training program, and $600 million in weapons to Kuwait. The State Department contended that both countries were vulnerable to a radical Soviet-armed Iraq. Trading guns for oil helps to buy friends, to bolster the U.S. balance of payments, to sustain the defense establishment, and to ensure an uninterrupted supply of oil.

The United States had been selling Saudi Arabia arms since the early 1950s, but the total had been kept a classified secret for many years.

Saudi purchases between 1950 and 1972 totaled $435 million. U.S. military credit sales came to an additional $257 million. Between 1973 and 1976, U.S. military commitments to Saudi Arabia soared to $1.042 billion, while Saudi Arabia's total military purchases from all sources exceeded $12 billion.

We sent a memorandum to the Administration and to Congress, charging that Saudi Arabia would be enabled to bomb Israel's cities, to interrupt Israel's navigation lines in the Gulf of Aqaba, and to transfer the Phantoms to Egypt. We reviewed the past inexplicable arms largesse to the Arab states. We recalled the 1954 opposition to the U.S.-financed arms gift to Iraq, pointing out that the weapons had been inherited by a left-wing regime in the Kassem coup four years later. Violating commitments, Jordan had rolled American tanks against Israel in 1967. Courted by all sides, Egypt might now be able to get arms from the Russians, the British, the French (via Libya), and from the Americans (via Saudi Arabia).

Sisco insisted that weapons for Saudi Arabia must not be regarded as a knee-jerk reaction to oil. The proposed sales had been envisaged long ago because the British were abandoning the Persian Gulf, an area remote from the Arab-Israel conflict. He believed that the sales would stimulate cooperation between Iran and Saudi Arabia, "the two major elements of stability in the area." He noted that both their rivals, Iraq and South Yemen, were getting MIG-21s from the Soviets. Secretary Rogers told the House Foreign Affairs Committee that Saudi Arabia could not practically transfer the planes to a third party because it would be dependent on American spare parts, maintenance, and trained personnel.

At Sisco's request, the *Near East Report* published his reply to our memorandum. He pointed out that an Iraq-Kuwait border skirmish on March 20 and a South Yemen MIG aircraft attack on a Saudi Arabian border outpost two days later "illustrate the reality of the threats that presently exist to the Arabian states." The sale would not shift the balance against Israel, and the United States would vigorously enforce the obligation against transferring the equipment to a third party, he insisted. Both states, Saudi Arabia and Kuwait, were strong and stable, had a close friendship with the United States, and could make a positive contribution to an atmosphere conducive to Middle East peace.

Late in June, we learned that Saudi Arabia was to get 24 to 30 Phantoms over a two-year period. There would be no deliveries before 1975 and no transfers to third parties. There would be no Phantoms for Kuwait. By the time the Phantoms reached Saudi Arabia, there would be new planes— the F-14s and F-15s. This report proved to be premature and academic. The Phantom deal was dropped because there had been so much opposition.

The proposal, however, had a salutary side effect; it prompted the Senate, by a vote of 44 to 43, to adopt a major amendment to the Military Sales Act sponsored by Nelson and five Democratic colleagues. This gave Congress the right to veto major arms sales—$25 million for any single sale to one country or cumulative sales of more than $50 million. A Senate-House conference committee later killed the proposal, but it was finally adopted in 1974.

A Jackson-Ribicoff amendment to terminate shipments of sophisticated weapons or spare parts to countries which transfer them to third countries was adopted by a voice vote and later broadened to prohibit transfer of training.

Arab leaders were displeased by the controversy, and Faisal warned that continued cooperation with the United States would be difficult unless the United States corrected its anti-Arab policy.

Kuwait's Defense and Interior Minister Sheikh Sabah Abdullah rejected any arms deal which included restrictions on their use. "We are free to use our arms when and where we want," he defiantly declared.

The New York Times, on July 7, ridiculed the argument that if we did not sell arms to the Saudis someone else would: "The same argument could be made by a debt-ridden dope pusher." To the contention that we would gain influence, *The Times* asked: "Has nothing been learned from the Soviet experience in Egypt?"

The Administration's aid program for 1973 was a further indication of diminishing support. In 1972, we had won $50 million in supporting assistance for Israel and $50 million to help her resettle Soviet Jews.

We were jolted when the Administration now proposed to cut the supporting assistance figure for Israel to $25 million, even while it was boosting the authorization for Jordan from $50 million to $65 million. In addition, Jordan was to receive $39.5 million in grant military assistance. The United States promised to help modernize Hussein's force with two squadrons of F-5 supersonic jet fighters. Israel's military needs were to be met by $300 million in military credits — not grants.

We urged restoration of the $50 million in supporting assistance for Israel, and the House Committee on Foreign Affairs voted 17 to 0 for an amendment to that effect, sponsored by Representatives Fraser and John Buchanan (R-Alabama). The Senate Committee concurred.

As in previous years, we did not oppose the appropriations for Jordan. Fulbright, favoring loans rather than grants, proposed to cut the grant for Jordan down to $20 million, but his Senate Foreign Relations Committee boosted it to $35 million. On the Senate floor, Javits and McGee moved to raise the figure to the $65 million recommended by the Administration, and this was approved 65 to 28 over Fulbright's objection.

We encountered opposition to a proposal to provide $36.5 million to help Israel resettle Soviet Jews. Although both Houses approved the authorization, the Senate Finance Committee eliminated the grant from the appropriation bill, and we lobbied for restoration. Senator Hiram Fong (R-Hawaii) offered the amendment, which was adopted 60 to 26, whereupon Abourezk urged a similar amount for Arab refugees, and that was agreed to.

I became AIPAC's chairman that spring. Irving Kane had decided to retire and I asked the Executive Committee to permit me to fill the post for the next 18 months until my scheduled retirement, to make way for Amitay, who was to become Executive Director at the end of 1974.

On the day of my election, we discovered that we were at war with oil companies that had opened their lobbying campaign. On June 24, the Mobil Oil Company, an ARAMCO partner, published an advertisement in *The*

New York Times entitled "U.S. Stake in the Middle East I," which urged the United States and the Soviet Union to "insist" on an Arab-Israel peace guaranteed by the Great Powers.

I circulated a statement to our constituency questioning the propriety of the advertisement, and letters poured into Mobil. I was frustrated by the Jewish Telegraph Agency, when I asked them to publish my statement. "The way to reply to an advertisement is to publish one yourself," I was told. There were to have been a series of advertisements, but that was the first and last of Mobil's. Soon thereafter, along with American Jewish Committee leaders, I was invited to lunch with William Tavoulareas, Mobil's president, who claimed that he had not intended to call for an imposed settlement. That, we pointed out, was the import of the word "insist." The meeting was pleasant, but, at the end, Tavoulareas warned that our future was unpleasantly uncertain.

On July 26, one month later, Standard Oil of California (SOCAL) reported in a letter to its stockholders and employees a growing feeling in the Arab world that the United States had "turned its back on the Arab people," that Americans did not properly regard the national interests of the Arab states, their important contributions to civilization, or their efforts to achieve political stability and to develop sound and modern economic structures. This was at a time when the Arab states, because of their vast reserves of crude oil, were becoming increasingly important to the Western world. SOCAL's plea: "There must be understanding . . . of the aspirations of the Arab people and more positive support of their efforts towards peace in the Middle East."

We urged our constituency to protest this attempt to mobilize a lobby against Israel for profit. Our memorandum emphasized that oil from the Persian Gulf and other Arab sources accounted for only seven percent of the current total U.S. crude consumption and that this figure would not need to increase substantially if our country developed alternative sources and eliminated wasteful consumption. We noted that the large oil companies had acquiesced to OPEC's price boosts beginning in 1970 at immense cost to the American consumer, facilitating the international squeeze on crude oil supplies and the evolution of OPEC into a powerful cartel.

Financial hardship had not forced SOCAL to become the Arab mouthpiece. SOCAL had record-breaking profits, $6.45 a share in 1972, and earnings were rising to dazzling heights—almost $10 a share in 1973 (before a stock split), the highest in a decade. And we could not agree that U.S. policy had favored Israel over the Arabs.

In San Francisco, Otto N. Miller, Board Chairman of SOCAL, wrote to Richard M. Kaplan, Chairman of the San Francisco Jewish Community Relations Council, explaining that his reference to the "legitimate interests of all the peoples of the Middle East" included the "legitimate interests of Israel and its people."

Ed Sanders, chairman of the Jewish Community Council in Los Angeles, invited me to his community, where irate leaders were demanding that we initiate a boycott of SOCAL. But I cautioned that a desultory demonstration would be weak and ineffective.

In an editorial on August 9, *The Washington Star* decried the SOCAL letter but pointed out that there was a powerful pro-Israel lobby. To equate the pro-Israel lobby with SOCAL was an absurd compliment. SOCAL had immense resources to disseminate its views to 262,000 stockholders and 41,496 employees, and it could deduct the expense of its advertisements in computing its taxes. AIPAC's minuscule budget was raised the hard way— from citizens' contributions which were not deductible from income tax. Motivations also differed. SOCAL was lobbying to secure investments and profits. AIPAC was lobbying to secure the survival of a people.

On September 10, Miller elaborated in a new letter: "Some people . . . thought I meant to imply . . . that peace and stability . . . could be established without regard to the existence of Israel or its legitimate interests. This is simply not true and no such implication can or should be read into what I have said."

In September, the third ARAMCO partner, Maurice Granville, Chairman of Texaco, told the Independent National Gas Association that the United States should "feel concern when those who have been so close to us urge us to review our policies. When such long-time friends assert that we are not being fair and evenhanded, it seems only sensible to pause and examine the actions about which they express concern."

Early that month, Faisal told NBC that America's "complete support for Zionism against the Arabs would make it extremely difficult to supply it." Its failure to change policy would "place us in an untenable position in the Arab world and vis-à-vis the countries which Zionism seeks to destroy." Faisal told *Newsweek* that the United States must abstain from "biased attitudes" and unlimited aid to Israel. That had increased Israel's "arrogance" had led her to reject peace and to insist on the retention of war gains.

There were contradictory voices in our own government. Sisco declared over Israeli television that the United States had important political, economic and strategic interests in the entire area and that there was "increasing concern in our country over the energy question. I believe it is foolhardy to believe that this is not a factor."

Nixon told the press on September 8 that it would be "highly inappropriate" to suggest that we are going to relate our policy toward Israel, "to whose independence the United States was dedicated," to what happens on Arab oil. "We are keenly aware that no nation . . . must be at the mercy of another nation by having its energy supply suddenly cut off."

We also faced a propaganda barrage. Organized in 1972, the National Association of Arab Americans was seeking to involve Arab Americans more actively. One of its leaders, Washington lawyer Richard C. Shadyac, said: "We do not seek the destruction of Israel. But . . . there should be an evenhanded policy. . . . The energy problem and the trade deficit are of prime concern to Americans and . . . the United States now is not acting in its best interests."

The partnership of oil and terror enabled Arabs to entice and to intimidate Israel's friends. They began in March 1972, when Uganda's President Idi Amin transferred allegiance to a fellow madman, Libya's Muammar Qaddafi, who offered him aid after Israel had rebuffed his request for $10 million in weapons and Phantom jets to invade Tanzania.

Three poor sub-Saharan nations, in the shadow of strong Arab neighbors, were next. Chad, Niger, and Mali abandoned Israel, which had helped them to establish youth training farms and had participated in their development projects. Libya had promised Chad $97 million in loans. Congo Brazzaville followed. The four were hailed, on January 6, 1973, by the Kuwait National Assembly and promised an economic mission. Israel, which had ties with 31 African governments in 1972, had only five diplomatic missions at the year's end.

The year was a blood-stained calendar of terror. Late in 1972, four Black September terrorists—so named because that was the month in which Jordan crushed the Palestinian terrorists in 1970—stormed the Israel embassy in Thailand and held hostages for 19 hours as they demanded release of 36 Palestinians from Israeli jails. The Thai government forced their surrender and shipment back to Cairo.

The ghastly Khartoum massacre of diplomats had a bitter echo 20 days later in a symposium at the Georgetown University Center for Strategic and International Studies in which I participated, along with Ambassador Armin Meyer, coordinator of the U.S. anti-terrorist campaign, and other scholars and journalists. Professor Michael Hudson, then of Johns Hopkins University's School of Advanced International Studies (SAIS), charged that America lost the two diplomats because it had failed to insist on the Rogers plan.

An audience of legislative aides and some on the dais assailed Hudson for blaming Israel for every Middle East setback, even as Hitler had blamed Jews for Versailles.

Later, arraigned in Khartoum, the eight Black September terrorists claimed credit while spectators applauded: "We are very proud of what we have done." Two weeks later, Ambassador William B. Macomber, Jr. reacted angrily when I quoted Hudson to him. Only one Arab diplomat, an Egyptian, had been at Macomber's plane when he returned the bodies of the two diplomats to their widows. "We have killed your two guys. Now you had better take us seriously," the PLO seemed to be saying. So Macomber characterized their ultimatum, which Washington could never accept.

Meanwhile, Black September crossed into the United States. On March 7, on the eve of Mrs. Meir's arrival, someone planted bombs in parked cars near El Al freight terminals at Kennedy Airport and at two mid-Manhattan Israeli bank offices. Demolition squads arrived in time.

It appeared that no terrorist could ever be punished—unless he was captured by Israelis. Terrorists were guaranteed freedom to act as they pleased, because any government which tried to hold them would be targeted for a new outrage. Wasfi al-Tal's murderers were released by Cairo. England, West Germany, and Switzerland released seven terrorists during the 1970 mass hijacking. West Germany paid $5 million to ransom a Lufthansa plane. The three terrorists who had been jailed after the Munich Olympic massacre were lionized as heroes when Libya welcomed them. Terrorism spread: an explosion on an Israel-bound passenger ship, a letter bomb in Singapore, and a murder in Cyprus. On April 9, Arab terrorists bombed the home of Israel's Ambassador Rachamin Timor in Cyprus, but they failed to hijack an Israeli Arkia plane. Two of them were killed, five were captured, and two escaped.

Within 12 hours Israel retaliated in a pinpoint commando raid against Beirut terrorist headquarters, workshops, and garages, killing three top leaders in their apartments. Ignoring Arab provocation in Cyprus, the Security Council approved an Anglo-French resolution condemning Israel 11 to 0. The United States abstained but managed to delete a threat of sanctions and to include a reference to all acts of violence. Newspaper editorials were praising Israel's stunningly effective blow against terrorist leaders. Arafat charged that Ambassador Meyer had coordinated intelligence with Israel, and Rogers summoned Arab envoys to reject the falsehood.

Terrorists neared my home on June 30, when they ambushed and murdered Colonel Yosef Alon, Israel's air and naval attaché who had helped to procure Phantom jets, as he parked his car in his Chevy Chase garage. That called for new security devices at our homes and offices. His assailant was never caught.

Twenty-six American citizens, mostly of Greek origin, who were waiting to board a New York-bound TWA plane, were among the 55 wounded when two Black September terrorists hurled grenades and fired machine guns in the Athens airport on August 5. They killed four. Later they had missed their intended victims: Israel-bound planes and passengers who were already aloft.

Silent on that tragedy, the Security Council unanimously condemned Israel a few days later because she intercepted a Baghdad-bound Lebanese airliner over Beirut in the mistaken belief that the Number One PFLP terrorist, George Habash, was aboard. Passengers were served refreshments; no one was hurt.

The year ended in gory climax. Five Palestinian terrorists sprayed the customs inspection area at Rome. They hurled fire bombs and grenades, incinerating a Pan Am plane and burning 28 passengers to death, including 14 ARAMCO employees and four Moroccans. They hijacked a Lufthansa plane to Athens, killing some Italian police and the co-pilot on the way. They flew to Kuwait, where the PLO negotiated for their release.

How did the Soviets react to terrorists? Despite Munich, they royally welcomed Arafat at their World University Games in Moscow in August, while Israeli journalists were denied visas, Israeli athletes were heckled, and Soviet Jewish ticket holders were arrested.

That summer, Sadat provoked both the PLO and Hussein when he urged establishment of an independent Palestinian state based on the partition resolution—the state which would have come alive in 1948 if Egypt had not invaded Palestine in a campaign to liquidate Israel and to seize Jerusalem. The PLO protested, insisting on its struggle to liberate all "Palestinian" soil—including Israel—while Hussein reasserted his claim to the West Bank.

At the U.N., the United States vetoed a maneuver to gut Resolution 242. Eight Security Council members introduced a resolution condemning Israel for rejecting Jarring's 1971 demands. Thirteen voted in favor. China abstained, claiming the resolution was not strong enough. Guinea, India, Indonesia, Sudan, the Soviet Union, Yugoslavia and China had no diplomatic relations with Israel. Reluctant to veto, the United States had worked for acceptable compromises, but Egypt had refused.

We should have taken heed when Hussein went to Cairo to meet Sadat and Assad in September. Twice before, in 1956 and 1967, Hussein had made a pilgrimage to Cairo on the eve of war. This time they agreed that he would pin down Israel's forces on her eastern frontier. It was a signal of the impending strike but we—and Israel—failed to recognize it.

Chapter 30

The Yom Kippur War

THE FOURTH TIME

I was confident that the Arab attack on October 6 would be swiftly repelled. I had visited the Bar Lev Line with a group of UJA leaders the year before, and I thought the line was impregnable. I could not suspect that morning that a mere handful of 400 to 500 Israelis were facing an Egyptian host who were pouring across pontoon bridges under cover of missiles illegally emplaced during Rogers' "cease-fire." Shortly after noon, a confident young embassy official telephoned me to say that the Syrians had been stopped on the Golan Heights and that Israelis would soon mop up the small Egyptian force at the Canal.

I invited some 30 Washington Jewish leaders and friendly legislative aides to meet in my office Sunday morning. We decided to urge Congress to adopt a resolution promising Israel support in negotiations for peace. We drafted the text along with a telegram urging senators to vote for it.

Both texts stressed that Egypt and Syria had started the war, spurning Kissinger's embryonic peace initiative. Our new Secretary of State had been in New York during his first fortnight, sounding out Arab diplomats at the U.N.

On Monday morning I brought my draft to Scott's office. He had always worked closely with me since the 1956–1957 crisis, but I failed to realize that, as the GOP Senate leader, he would check with the Department of State. Moreover, I later learned that he had an agreement to consult with Senate Democratic leader Mansfield on all foreign policy issues.

Arab aggression was palpable, while Israel had refrained from a preemptive strike, but the State Department always avoided fixing responsibility for aggression and preferred to take refuge in the euphemism "war broke out." My draft was side-tracked, and neither Scott nor Kissinger could tell me who was responsible when I questioned them later. The two Floor Leaders substituted an innocuous resolution which evoked scant enthusiasm on the Senate Floor and attracted few co-sponsors. My telegram recalled past Arab aggression, terrorism, and the threat to divert oil supplies. It urged support for Israel's resistance to aggression and her struggle for negotiations for a genuine peace. The noncommittal Scott-Mansfield resolution deplored the outbreak and urged a cease-fire and the return of the parties to their previous positions.

Kissinger had many critical questions to ponder. Arab diplomats who had talked with him about peace in the previous fortnight had been, to say the least, dissembling and insincere. Was his own peace initiative dead? What would the Russians do? Was this the end of détente? Were we headed for a Big Power confrontation? Could the new conflict open a new Arab-U.S. relationship? Could we avoid an oil embargo?

On Monday night, October 8, I heard Kissinger warn the Russians in an address to 3,500 people attending *Pacem in Terris,* sponsored in Washington by the Fund for the Republic: "We shall resist aggressive foreign policies. Détente cannot survive irresponsibility in any area, including the Middle East."

My telegrams were not wasted. Although the Senate did not consider my draft resolution, many members expressed support for Israel. Scott said: "It is clear that Israel was attacked on a High Holy Day just as we were attacked at Pearl Harbor on a Sunday many years ago. The action by the aggressors was ill-advised."

Characteristically, Fulbright was quick to attack us. During a CBS "Face the Nation" interview on the day after the war began, he charged: "Israelis control the policy in the Congress. The emotional and political ties are too strong. On every test, on everything the Israelis are interested in, in the Senate the Israelis have 75 to 80 votes."

CBS interviewer George Herman jolted Fulbright: "It is a fairly serious charge to say that your colleagues in the Senate—some 70 of them—are controlled by a power group rather than by their own vision of what they think are proper principles of freedom and right." Fulbright retreated just a little: "They have been persuaded that this is in our interest. I don't know these niceties of semantics, perhaps I could withdraw it and rephrase it. It still comes out with the fact that influence is dominant." Senator Griffin, who was on "Meet the Press" (NBC) the same day, said that Fulbright's statement was "unfortunate" and would not help Congress play a meaningful role. There were many pro-Israel statements in the Senate by Kennedy, McGovern, Mondale, Percy, Pell, Tunney, and others.

We had no conception of Israel's needs at that time. Our confidence in a swift victory was buoyed by a Monday night broadcast in Israel which failed to report her reverses on both fronts. It was not until late Tuesday that

Dinitz publicly revealed the gravity of Israel's need for weapons—although he did not call for public action—at a hastily convened leadership meeting which AIPAC helped to organize at the request of the Conference of Presidents of Major American Jewish Organizations.

Kennedy and Schweiker brought assurances of support, and I reported that our setback in the Senate did not truly reflect the views of Congress, but was a diplomatic evasion. Later that evening, Rabbi Israel Miller of New York and I addressed an overflow mass meeting at the Ohr Kodesh synagogue in Chevy Chase. Israel now faced two weapons, I said: the loaded gun and the empty gas tank. The huge Arab military preponderance now sadly confirmed our contention that Israel had never received adequate military aid. The war would have a shattering effect on Israel's economy. and Israel would need massive support.

A few days before the Arabs attacked, Mrs. Meir had asked the United States to accelerate shipment of the 48 Phantom jets negotiated during her March visit and which had been scheduled for delivery over a four-year span. Her request was a reaction to the huge Soviet supply of jets, tanks, missiles, and bridge-crossing equipment to Egypt and Syria. On Sunday, October 7, she renewed that request.

Washington hesitated because Kissinger was still hoping that the Soviets would remain on the sidelines. But now, on Monday, Israel was asking for ammunition and spare parts, offering to carry them in her own planes. On that day, Dinitz was told that Nixon had agreed to replace Israel's losses. The United States was offering two planes, but Mrs. Meir telephoned Dinitz that Israel's losses were heavy, and Dinitz stressed the urgency of her message. The embassy was acting on the diplomatic level and did not want a public campaign.

By Tuesday, Israel had lost 15 Phantoms and 45 A-4 Skyhawks and was pleading for replacements and electronic jamming equipment. Late in the day, Dinitz was assured that Israel's request would be met. However, the United States was rationing its assistance, hopeful that the Soviets would stay out and fearful that overt U.S. aid would precipitate an oil embargo.

By Wednesday, huge Soviet Antonov 22s were beginning a massive airlift to Egypt and Syria, and there was no longer any excuse for delay. Israel had stopped the Syrians in the north, but it could not repel the Egyptians without additional supplies. But then I was assured by the embassy that 20 planes would be chartered; presumably, the crisis was over.

In the meantime, friendly senators and their aides were impatiently delaying circulation and introduction of resolutions calling for swift action. It now seemed as if they might not be needed. At a meeting of Jewish leaders in New York that morning, I was opposed to a major public campaign for arms because I had been led to believe by the embassy that it would not be necessary.

Expectation and disappointment alternated on those three tense days.

Each morning—Tuesday, Wednesday, and Thursday—seemed to start with promise, to be followed within a few hours by setback. On Thursday morning, Dinitz told me that Israelis were getting missiles which were being rushed in disguised Israeli planes. They had been promised planes and tanks, but they feared they might not arrive in time. Our office requested Senate members of the Armed Services and Appropriations committees to urge action on Israel's appeal. We then believed that civilian officials in the Pentagon were the stumbling block. McGee, who called the Pentagon at my request, was told that the charter planes were not available because their owners feared terrorism. It was also explained that funds had not been appropriated. That second excuse was patently evasive because appropriations did not need to be voted for 120 days.

On Friday, the United States finally agreed to use its own military planes, and the delivery rate was expedited because of Israel's urgent need. It was Nixon himself who broke the log jam. So I was told by U.S. Ambassador Keating at lunch in his embassy home at Herzliya in 1974. Nixon had told him: "They [the Pentagon] said, 'We're sending planes at the rate of one and a half a day.' I said, 'Send 50, send 100.'"

The final decision came Friday night, but in the last hours Kissinger tried to reach an agreement on a cease-fire which might have made the airlift unnecessary. By that time, the Egyptians were well established on the east bank of the Canal, while Israelis had advanced into Syria. Kissinger then hoped that both sides would agree to a cease-fire in place. Although somewhat reluctant, Mrs. Meir was willing, I was told; but she declined to confirm that to me when I met her in Israel in 1974. However, Sadat, who stood to gain much, rejected the proposal. He was confident of a decisive victory.

On Saturday afternoon, the huge C-5s and C-130s were on their way.

WHO WAS TO BLAME?

I am often asked who was responsible for the delay. Was it Kissinger or was it Defense Secretary Schlesinger? I have little personal evidence to contribute to that debate. Eban briefed me in New York Saturday night. He had been in Kissinger's office that morning, and he had been impressed as the Secretary, speaking in the President's name, transmitted Nixon's orders to speed the airlift and to prevent sabotage. That afternoon, Kissinger had called Eban to say that there were 67 planes in the air. Again, when I met him in Israel in 1974, Eban scoffed at suggestions that Kissinger had staged a theatrical performance when he cast Schlesinger, rather than himself, as the obstacle. And again, in 1977, Eban reaffirmed his view that the account in the Kalb brothers' book exonerating Kissinger was accurate. A few days after the airlift began, Dinitz frankly blamed Pentagon civilians and frankly described them as non-cooperative.

At first, I suspected that military men were unwilling to empty their own arsenals, but I later learned that General George S. Brown was ready and eager to speed the airlift long before it began and that no one worked more enthusiastically than he. That high praise came from Israeli airmen, even though Brown came under fire a year later for his grotesque parroting of the hate propaganda that Jews dominated the media in the United States.

I tend to believe the Eban-Dinitz-Kalb version. When I later testified for the $2.2 billion emergency appropriation for Israel, I was aware of the enthusiastic testimony of Deputy Secretary of State Kenneth Rush, which contrasted with the less than passionate advocacy of Deputy Secretary of Defense William P. Clements, Jr., who had been the head of Sedco, one of America's largest oil drilling companies, and who resumed as Sedco's chairman in January 1977.

The airlift had a profound impact on war-ravaged Israel. The first plane brought blankets for soldiers on the Golan Heights. People craned their necks as they counted the huge cargo planes which arrived at 15-minute intervals. Every time one passed overhead, some would fearfully say: "That must be the last." The airlift enabled Israel to take the offensive with confidence that she would not run out of ammunition or friends.

In 1967, the Soviets had remained aloof, later bringing their weapons into Egypt and Syria to rehabilitate and restore the defeated Arabs. In 1973, the Soviets knew long in advance when the Arabs would strike and they were confident of victory. They rushed deliveries on the eve of the war, and two days before the attack they evacuated their civilians from Damascus and Cairo.

Despite this record of deceit, Kissinger still hoped for détente. He had Nixon send a message to Brezhnev stressing their 1972 and 1973 promises "to do everything in their power so that conflicts or situations would not arise to increase international tension." Yet two days later, following a meeting between Algerian President Houari Boumedienne and Soviet leaders, there was a joint communiqué in which the Soviets promised to "assist in every way possible in the liberation of all Arab territories occupied by Israel." In Lebanon, the Soviet ambassador declared that Syria would receive arms, enabling her to take the offensive.

On October 9, the French radio quoted Brezhnev's message to Boumedienne urging Arab states to aid Syria and Egypt. "There must be fraternal Arab solidarity today, more than ever; Syria and Egypt must not remain alone in their fight against a treacherous enemy."

The Soviet airlift became massive on October 10, and five days later, when State Department spokesman McCloskey confirmed that the U.S. airlift was on the way to Israel, he estimated that the Soviets had already sent 4,000 tons of equipment on 280 flights to Egypt and Syria.

Most shocking of all was the refusal of European governments to assist the U.S. airlift. Portugal's Azores provided the life-saving station. Far from neutral passivity, NATO countries were actually critical of the American diversion of weapons to Israel, for it cut into what they seemed to regard as a monopoly.

In a sarcastic editorial on November 3, "The Day of the Ostriches," *The Economist* attacked Europe's attitude, pointing out that West Europeans needed the United States to provide the "counterweight" against Soviet power and failed to understand the connection between that and what was happening in the Mediterranean. "They would not help the United States to do for someone else what they want it to do for them." Europe had failed to see where its own interest lay.

McCloskey observed that maintenance of the military balance and the establishment of a durable peace in the Middle East was as much in the interest of West Germany and other NATO allies as in the interest of the United States and the world at large.

As the airlift began, Israel's friends circulated the congressional resolutions which had been held back, in the hope that the Administration would act. This was not an anticlimactic gesture, for they served a significant purpose—to encourage the Administration to continue to strengthen Israel, and, in effect, to ask for the $2.2 billion arms authorization which Nixon proposed on October 14.

The resolutions were sponsored in the Senate by Humphrey and Jackson, who were joined by 10 co-sponsors, and in the House by Democratic Floor Leader O'Neill. He had no Republican counterpart, because at that moment there was no Republican Floor Leader. Ford had just been nominated for the Vice Presidency to succeed Spiro Agnew. Much to my surprise, Ford took the trouble to telephone me to express regret that he could not be a co-sponsor as had been his custom. Ford had always been a staunch friend of Israel throughout his congressional career.

Both texts were much stronger than the ill-fated Mansfield-Scott resolution, for, like my original draft, they noted that the "armed forces of Egypt and Syria launched an unprovoked attack against Israel, shattering the 1967 cease-fire."

Our office began calling constituents to encourage their congressmen to co-sponsor, and when the resolutions were introduced (on October 18 in the Senate, and October 23 in the House), the sponsors included 68 senators and 260 representatives. Others added their names, bringing the total to 71 senators and 269 representatives. Several congressmen later became uneasy because Nixon's appropriation request unleashed a flood of critical mail from isolationists who feared U.S. intervention and involvement. Pro-Israel mail began to taper off slightly after the Kissinger alert to counter the threat of Soviet intervention. Three representatives asked us to delete their names from an AIPAC advertisement in *The New York Times* which reproduced the texts and the list of sponsors.

I was dismayed by the apathy, if not hostility, of Christian friends. On

October 22, I was invited to the Washington Hebrew Congregation to meet Christian ministers whom Rabbi Joshua Haberman had invited for a briefing. There were more rabbis present than ministers.

Two days later, Amitay, Edelsberg, and I were invited by Bookbinder to brief representatives of civic organizations. Once again we were disappointed by the small turnout and were shocked by a Unitarian minister who observed that the only Arabs who might agree to Jews living in the West Bank would be "Uncle Toms."

McGovern told me that nationwide mail was running 50-50, but mail from his own state was about 95 percent negative, which doubtless reflected Abourezk's complaints that the United States was neglecting South Dakota's needs for hospitals and for relief for flood victims.

In reaction to the protests, McGovern was joining with Hatfield in an amendment forbidding the dispatch of U.S. troops without congressional consent. He agreed to drop it, after I argued that it would signal the Soviets that they had a green light to attack Israel without fear of swift U.S. reaction. Kissinger himself had warned against it.

Nixon told Congress that the $2.2 billion for Israel was needed to "prevent the emergence of a substantial imbalance resulting from large-scale resupply of Syria and Egypt by the Soviet Union. The magnitude of the current conflict, coupled with the sale of Soviet supply activities, has created needs which exceed Israel's capacity to continue with cash and credit purchases. The alternative . . . is for us to supply Israel with grant military assistance."

The White House disclosed that during the first 12 days the United States had airlifted $825 million in air-to-air and air-to-ground missiles, artillery, fighter aircraft, crew-served and individual weapons, as well as replacement of tanks, aircraft, radios, and other military equipment lost in battle.

This was the first time in Israel's 25 years that the United States was providing her with arms as a gift. Israel had always had to buy arms and, although such purchases were often financed by low interest loans, the effect was to boost her extraordinary foreign currency debt.

There were voices of dissent. Representative James P. Johnson (R-Colorado) described military aid to Israel as "an act of war" against the Arabs. Representative Richard T. Hanna (D-California) claimed that the Administration did not have a "balanced view." Representative Paul Findley (R-Illinois) charged that Israel had steadfastly refused to return occupied territories and had moved Israeli settlers into "oil-rich Arab lands."

Senator McClure said that our government had mistakenly given Israelis the impression that a total commitment from the United States made her invincible, with no reason to negotiate. He introduced his own resolution, similar to the pro-Israel proposal but substituting Vietnam for Israel. Representative Stephen D. Simms (R-Idaho), in like vein, denounced "hypocrites" who opposed the war in Vietnam but had jumped to aid Israel.

Hatfield warned that the President's request would "up the ante in this deadly arms race. . . . Saber rattling of this magnitude taunts the Russians into showing that they can top the United States."

OUR APPEAL FOR AID

I testified before the Senate Appropriations Subcommittee on Foreign Operations to describe the disastrous effect of the war and worldwide inflation on Israel. I was authorized to speak for all the organizations in the Presidents Conference.

I called it a war for the liquidation of the Jewish state. If Arab armies had reached the pre-June 1967 armistice lines, or had started their offensive from those lines, Israel would have been overwhelmed. All major powers had, at one time or another, provided weapons to Israel's hostile neighbors. In the last fateful 30 days, Israelis had to face Soviet MIG-21s, SA-3s, SA-6s, SA-7s, the Frog surface-to-surface missiles, French Mirage planes, British Hunter jets and Centurion tanks, and even some tanks furnished by the United States. Some Arab states and guerrillas had received military aid from Communist China.

Between 1946 and 1972, the United States had distributed $55 billion in grant military assistance throughout the world—but none of it to Israel. Washington had sent $324 million in military aid to nine Arab states and an additional $34 million to Jordan in 1973. U.S. grant economic assistance to the Arab states had far exceeded that given to Israel during this period. Communist countries had poured huge quantities of weapons at cut-rate prices into Egypt, Iraq, Syria, and six other Arab states—conservatively estimated at more than $6 billion.

Our government had recently agreed to wipe out the Soviets' $11 billion debt owed for lend-lease in World War II for $722 million—a tiny fraction of what this terrible war, subsidized and sustained by the Soviet Union, would cost Israel, the Arab states, the United States, and other countries whose economies had been disrupted.

Israel's tremendous defense expenditure equalled 26 percent of her GNP in 1972 and would approximate 40 percent in 1973. Israel's external debt had soared: from $2.1 billion in 1970 to $4.5 billion by October 6, 1973. As 1973 began, her per capita foreign currency debt was $1,300. External debt service cost Israel $532 million in 1971; $687 million in 1972; $705 million in 1973; and would rise to $790 million in 1974. If Israel had to go further into debt for the additional weapons she was now acquiring, her debt service would rise to about $940 million, or even to $1.1 billion, depending on the interest she would have to pay.

Israel had to mobilize 30 percent of her labor force. Transportation had to be diverted. Tourism had fallen, and exports had been curtailed. Her growth rate, which had averaged 9.9 percent over the years, would be drastically reduced.

Both Humphrey and Javits testified for the $2.2 billion. For the State Department, Rush noted that 70 percent of the Senate and 60 percent of the House had sponsored the resolutions and that emergency appropriations for Israel fell "within the broad framework of our policy objectives in the Middle East."

For Defense, Clements estimated that the Soviet air and sea lifts exceeded 100,000 tons and that anywhere between 25 to 90 Soviet planes had landed in Arab countries every 24 hours since October 6. He confirmed the reports that North Korean pilots were flying Syrian MIGs, that Soviet personnel were manning SA missile sites, and that Pakistani troops were training in the area.

While I was a lone citizen testifying for the authorization, there was a substantial pro-Arab demonstration. Nineteen pro-Arab organizations signed a telegram calling on Congress not to vote for arms and advisers for Israel but to turn its attention to the needs of Americans at home. The Middle East needs peace with justice, not Phantoms, they said, and the U.S. Congress, not Israel, should decide how U.S. tax dollars are spent. The organizations were from Atlanta, Berkeley, Boston, Cleveland, Columbus, Detroit, Durham, and New York. The Committee for New Alternatives in the Middle East—an anti-Zionist group with some Jewish members—was listed, but it later repudiated the use of its name.

Two Washington professors, Alan R. Taylor and John Ruedy, representing the Middle East Affairs Council, declared: "No minority group can be allowed to endow American policy with parochial vision."

Dr. Peter S. Tanous, head of the newly organized National Association of Arab Americans, warned that the U.S. position threatened détente with the USSR and isolated the United States from the world community. He said that all the Arabs asked in exchange for oil was fairness. "If we are cold this winter it will be because we have turned our backs on the Arabs' plea for peace with justice in the Middle East." And he insisted: "We must respect the right of Arab producers to exercise leverage in behalf of their own interests."

Several weeks later—I was then in Los Angeles at an AIPAC fundraising meeting—Rabbi Bernstein took my place to testify before the Senate Foreign Relations Committee. Fulbright was presiding, and an audience of pro-Arabs had turned up, apparently anticipating an angry crossfire between Fulbright and myself. They were disappointed. Fulbright did go out of his way to recall Bernstein and to cross-examine him about our lobby, but he scored no points, for Bernstein was always a doubty protagonist of the right to lobby and to be heard.

Six pro-Arab spokesmen testified before the Committee against the $2.2 billion package that day. In addition to Taylor and Ruedy, they included

Dr. Faiz Abu-Jaber of the Arab American Association of Syracuse, N.Y.; Dr. John H. Davis of the American Near East Refugee Aid; Alfred Lilienthal of Middle East Perspective; and David G. Nes representing the American Committee for Justice in the Middle East.

Israelis changed the tide of war in fierce tank battles on both fronts. They had pushed across the Suez, establishing a substantial bridgehead on the western bank, and they had neared Damascus.

An apprehensive Kosygin flew to Cairo on October 16 and found Sadat unaware of the danger which Soviet intelligence had comprehended. Still convinced that he was ahead, Sadat had declared that day that Egypt would fight until she had recovered the lost territories, and until "the legitimate rights of the Palestinian people had been restored." He would accept a cease-fire only after Israel had withdrawn to the pre-June 5, 1967 lines.

On the same day, Assad told Radio Damascus that Syrian forces would recover the occupied territory and continue until "all the land is liberated."

The Soviets had opposed a cease-fire as long as they believed that the Arabs were winning. Now, on October 19, Kosygin summoned Kissinger to Moscow. He arrived on the 20th, the day that Saudi Arabia began the oil embargo. Two days later, the Moscow talks led to Security Council Resolution 338, which provided for a cease-fire in place and negotiations to implement 242:

> The Security Council calls on all parties to the present fighting to cease all firing and terminate all military activity immediately—no later than 12 hours after the movement of the adoption of this decision in the positions they now occupy;
> Calls on the parties concerned to start immediately after the cease-fire the implementation of Security Council Resolution 242 in all of its parts;
> And decides that immediately and concurrently with the cease-fire, negotiations start between the parties concerned under appropriate auspices aimed at establishing a just and durable peace in the Middle East.

In Washington, Dinitz warmly praised the text as a revolutionary breakthrough. Ever since 1967, Arab leaders had contended that Resolution 242 was self-implementing and that there was no need to negotiate with Israel. Now, for the first time, in Resolution 338, the Security Council was calling for negotiations.

Despite the cease-fire, shooting continued. The Israeli Army had consolidated their hold on the southern road, cutting off Egypt's Third Army of 19,000.

The Soviets then opened a diplomatic offensive to force Israel to withdraw to the October 22 lines, but no one knew precisely where those lines had been; and the Israelis had no desire to return to the earlier lines because their own forces could then be cut off and encircled by a revived Third Army.

By this time, Israel had seized 475 square miles of territory on the west bank of the Canal and controlled the supply lines to Egyptian troop concentrations in central and south Sinai about 40 miles from Cairo. Sadat's forces now faced the nightmare of dwindling food, fuel, and ammunition. To the north, Israelis held some 300 square miles beyond the Golan Heights about 20 miles from Damascus.

On October 24, encouraged by the Soviets, Sadat demanded establishment of a joint Soviet-American peacekeeping force. The United States was opposed. There were reports that seven Soviet divisions totaling 50,000 troops were on the alert, with some 85 Soviet ships aswarm in the Mediterranean. That evening, Ambassador Dobrynin transmitted a stiff note in which Brezhnev, denouncing Israel as a violator of the cease-fire, insisted on Soviet and American contingents.

In 1956, Bulganin had rattled rockets in his ultimatum to Britain, France, and Israel to end the Suez war, then warning that the Soviets were "determined to crush the aggressors and restore peace in the Middle East through the use of force."

In 1967, after the Syrian rout, Kosygin opened the hot line to warn Johnson that the USSR would take necessary action, including military, unless Israel unconditionally halted operations.

In 1973, Brezhnev warned: "I will say it straight, that if you find it impossible to act together with us in this matter we should be faced with the necessity urgently to consider the question of taking appropriate steps unilaterally. Israel cannot be allowed to get away with the violations."

Kissinger tried to calm the Russians. "We do not consider ourselves in a confrontation with the Soviet Union," he said. "It is inconceivable that the forces of the Great Powers should be introduced in the numbers that would be necessary to overpower the participants."

The U.S. reply to Brezhnev was to alert U.S. forces around the world. The United States denied that Israel was violating the cease-fire and insisted that there was no need to send Soviet or American forces. Nixon urged that U.N. observer and peacekeeping forces of non-veto or non-nuclear countries be sent. The crisis ended.

Kissinger then became embroiled with the Israelis on two issues. He was demanding that Israel permit a truck convoy to carry humanitarian supplies to beleagured Suez, or else suffer a diminution of U.S. aid. Before securing a commitment from Israel, Kissinger had promised Sadat to open the road; Nixon and Kissinger became furious when Israel offered reservations.

While some Israelis would have preferred to force the Third Army's surrender, their leadership recognized that she had little to gain from imposing her will. To humiliate the Egyptians would mean no hope for dialogue. If Sadat had been overthrown at that time, Israel would have had no one to talk to.

However, Israel wanted to control the convoy route and did remain in control, with U.N. observation check points. Israel was demanding an exchange of prisoners. She feared for the safety of those who were in the hands of Egypt and was especially concerned for those in the hands of the Syrians. In violation of the Geneva Convention, Egypt was refusing to permit Red Cross visits to Israeli wounded. Syria refused even to provide a list of prisoners.

The United States persuaded Egypt to abandon her impractical demand for Israel's withdrawal back to the October 22 lines, but Sadat would not accept Mrs. Meir's proposal that both armies withdraw to their pre-war positions. Sadat said he would never agree to withdraw from the east bank. Kissinger supported Sadat's stand, much to Israel's resentment, but he insisted that Egypt meet with Israel and exchange prisoners.

The Israelis had been denouncing the Arabs for their failure to liberate POWs in compliance with the Geneva Convention, and they were also demanding an end to the blockade which Egypt had instituted at the Bab el-Mandeb Straits, at the southern end of the Red Sea.

It was finally agreed that the prisoner exchange would proceed as soon as U.N. check points were established. Egypt released 238 Israelis; Israel gave back some 8,000 Egyptians.

Under the initial disengagement agreement, Israel was to withdraw from both banks of the Canal. She would pull back 20 miles into the Sinai, an area to be divided into three zones. About 7,000 Egyptian troops would be stationed in the zone adjacent to the Canal, while an equal number of Israelis would remain in the eastern zone. U.N. forces would be stationed in the buffer zone.

THE OIL EMBARGO

Meanwhile, Arab oil-producing states had embargoed all oil shipments to the United States and had boosted prices to record levels, while European and Asian customers, notably France, England, and Japan, were promised undiminished shipments. Thus American oil companies who had opposed the airlift to Israel were compelled to serve as enforcement agents of a boycott against their own government and collectors of a war tax.

Cries for retaliation rose from all sides. Maritime unions threatened to stop shipments of wheat to the Soviet Union unless the Soviets ended their huge arms airlift to the Arabs.

The Washington Post, on October 20, editorialized: "One sees the curious spectacle of Mr. Nixon encouraging Congress to give Moscow trade benefits and Moscow encouraging the Arabs to wield oil as a weapon against the United States on the very same day. . . . Who would object, for instance, if, while the Soviet supply airlift continued, [President Nixon] suspended exports of grain?"

Many called to ask why the United States did not stop the flow of exports to the Arab boycotters. The *Near East Report* pointed out that food flowed freely. It noted that Egypt and Kuwait were members of GATT, the General Agreement on Tariffs and Trade, and that Algeria, Bahrein, and Qatar were de facto members. According to Article 11, "no prohibitions or restrictions other than duties, taxes or other charges . . . shall be instituted or maintained by any contracting party on the importation of any product or on the exportation or sale for export of any product destined for the territory of another contracting party."

In addition, the United States had a treaty of friendship with Saudi Arabia going back to 1933 and a similar treaty of friendship with Iraq going back to 1940. Discriminatory boycotts, we suggested, violated the spirit, if not the letter, of these treaties.

In 1970, a U.N. General Assembly resolution on friendly relations and cooperation among states had declared: "No state may use or encourage the use of economic, political, or any other type of measures to coerce another state in order to obtain from it the subordination of the exercise of its sovereign rights and to secure from it advantage of any kind."

Senator Strom Thurmond (R-North Carolina) introduced a Senate bill to prohibit export of agricultural grain "to any nation reducing for political purposes the quantity of oil normally exported to the United States or nationalizing any U.S. properties." In the House, Representative William A. Barrett (D-Pennsylvania) offered a sense-of-the-House resolution proposing that the President proportionately curtail exports of goods, materials, and technology to any nation restricting the flow of oil to the United States.

A Department of Agriculture survey showed that Saudi Arabia was 100 percent dependent on imports for both wheat and other grains; Kuwait was 100 percent dependent on imported feed grains; and Iraq was 38 percent dependent on wheat imports. Egypt, Jordan, Lebanon, and Syria also needed imported food stuffs.

The Shah of Iran chided the Arabs: "Oil is like bread. You cannot cut it off during a time of peace. Why do you want to look as if you want the world to starve?"

Kissinger reacted to the oil embargo in Peking in November. The United States had supported Israel because of emotional ties, because of her democratic tradition, because Israel was a going concern, and because of U.S. opposition to domination by force. "It is not possible for us to be swayed in the major orientation of our policy by the temporary monopoly position enjoyed by a few nations," he said. In another statement, Kissinger warned: "If pressures continue unreasonably and indefinitely, then the United States will have to consider what countermeasures it may have to take."

At a regional AIPAC conference in which we participated earlier in San Francisco, Rodger P. Davies, who was assassinated in Cyprus nine months later, had noted that all U.S. and Israeli assessments had erred in the belief that the military buildup prior to the war "did not presage hostilities. We were wrong."

Many leading American economists and diplomats warned against surrender to oil blackmail, including Paul A. Samuelson, John Kenneth Galbraith, and George Kennan.

The New York Times declared that blackmail could not be permitted to dictate the American response. Once met, "blackmail demands have a way of growing next time around in oil negotiations, no less than in aerial terrorism."

THE MOOD IN ISRAEL

In November, I flew to Israel with leaders of the Presidents Conference. In the United States we had celebrated an extraordinary victory. In Israel there was resentment and bitterness. Most of all, Israelis were mourning the slaughter and maiming of so many young men. Israel intelligence had failed, and the government had been ill-prepared and slow to resist the Arab attack. Israel had refrained from a preemptive strike in deference to world opinion. Yet Israelis now stood virtually alone and, while they appreciated the size and significance of the massive U.S. airlift, they resented the fact that the United States, as so often since 1948, had prevented them from winning the final decisive and unconditional victory. Israel, they had learned from long experience, could always win wars on the battlefield, with considerable cost, but she was always defeated on the diplomatic front. As a consequence, she had never won the peace and had always been compelled to fight again.

There was a revealing press conference upon our arrival. The Israeli press always exaggerated the power of the American Jewish community, and their questions implied suspicion that we had been held back by the Israeli government. Why had we not taken on Japan, which had barred air traffic with Israel. What were we doing to fight the energy crisis? Manifestly, Israelis were looking for scapegoats.

In my talks, I deprecated the view that America was not with Israel, as a disservice to Israel's own welfare. I listed the many negative issues and forces we faced in the struggle for American opinion: oil, détente, U.N., NATO, Arabists, anti-foreign aid, disengagement, isolationism, Indochina, and the New Left—a depressing list.

I was startled by the widespread animosity toward Kissinger. At one meeting with the editors of Israel's five major newspapers, I pointed out that Kissinger, after helping Israel to maintain the balance of strength, had moved to establish the balance of influence. We had always argued that, if the United States strengthened Israel, it would gain the respect of the Arabs, who would come to understand that the United States—and not the Soviet Union—had influence in Israel and could exercise leadership. The United

States was now *persona grata* with both sides and in a strong position to promote a settlement.

I reviewed the records of ten Secretaries of State: Hull, Stettinius Byrnes, Marshall, Acheson, Dulles, Herter, Rusk, and Rogers. In my opinion, Kissinger was a more understanding friend than any of his predecessors. I doubted whether I persuaded anyone.

About 3:00 A.M. on the morning of Saturday, December 1, my last day in Israel, Wollack telephoned that the special $2.2 billion authorization for Israel was in trouble. There had been a move to slash $500 million. He insisted on my immediate return. In fact, I was already packed.

When I arrived in Washington on Monday, December 3, I drafted a long, emotional telegram, describing the forlorn and lonely bitterness in Israel and the urgent need to restore confidence and morale. I appealed to all members of the Foreign Affairs and Appropriations committees to vote the full $2.2 billion.

The following morning, December 4, the Chairman of the Foreign Operations Subcommittee, Representative Otto Passman (D-Louisiana), seconded by Representative Silvio O. Conte (R-Massachusetts), moved to recommend inclusion of the $500 million. The full Committee concurred.

The House Foreign Affairs Committee voted approval 32 to 1. It rejected a Findley amendment, 30 to 5, to the effect that the purpose of the legislation was to support implementation of Resolutions 242 and 338. And, by a vote of 15 to 5, the Committee defeated an amendment offered by Representative Lee Hamilton (D-Indiana) to slash the request by $500 million.

Later, some columnists and news magazines gave me credit for the result, but I always suspected that Kissinger, who had breakfasted with Passman that morning, was more persuasive than I. Five years later when I traveled in the White House delegation to attend Golda Meir's funeral, I asked Kissinger whether he indeed had met with Passman and deserved the credit. He generously assured me that he would be glad to share it with me. In that same talk, Kissinger emphatically rejected a widely held suspicion that he wanted neither side to win when the war began. "In any conflict between U.S. and Soviet weapons, U.S. weapons must prevail," he told me.

The Senate Committee on Foreign Relations approved the $2.2 billion authorization, 15 to 2. Mansfield and Fulbright voted no. The Senate accepted an amendment by Humphrey to provide that $1.5 billion of the $2.2 could be allocated as grant military aid for Israel.

Fulbright offered a series of amendments which were defeated:

- Not more than $1.2 billion should be furnished Israel until the President had found that Israel was taking appropriate steps to comply with 242. That was tabled 62 to 12.
- This action should not be construed as a U.S. commitment to Israel for her defense, 49 to 25.

- Nothing should be expended until all funds previously appropriated and impounded for domestic needs had been released, 62 to 12.

The final Senate vote on the bill was 66 to 9. That brought a rebuke from Fulbright: "I do believe that the Senate has taken leave of its senses. . . . [This is] the ultimate in irrationality."

The nine nays were Abourezk, Burdick, Curtis, Fannin, Fulbright, Hansen, Helms, Scott (Va.), and Mansfield.

THE SEVEN-TO-ONE-MAJORITY

The House, on December 11, 1973 voted 364 to 52. Findley, who supported the bill, again proposed that the legislation was intended to support U.N. Resolutions 242 and 338. That was defeated 334 to 82.

Oddly, the 7 to 1 vote—both in the Senate and House—confirmed the ratio of public support for Israel revealed in public opinion polls.

A Gallup poll showed that 47 percent of those polled were with Israel; 6 percent with the Arabs; 22 percent favored neither; and 25 percent had no opinion.

A Harris poll disclosed that a large majority—68 to 10—believed that the Arabs still wanted to destroy Israel. An overwhelming majority supported U.S. arms shipments to Israel; 63 to 15 ruled that Nixon and Kissinger were "right to send arms to Israel and then to get together with the Russians to work out a cease-fire."

In that same Harris poll, a two to one majority voted against the statement: "We need Arab oil for our gasoline shortage here at home; so we had better find ways to get along with the Arabs, even if that means supporting Israel less."

The hope for genuine peace negotiations at Geneva receded, as Arabs kept insisting that Israel was in violation of 242 and that the burden rested on her.

Former Ambassador Arthur J. Goldberg, one of the draftsmen of the U.N. resolutions, and Professor Eugene Rostow, who had been Under Secretary of State, drew on their personal experience to refute the Arab contention.

Arab leaders struck a devastating blow at the peace when they met in the seventh summit conference at Algiers on November 26 to 28. They called for a full Israeli withdrawal, the Arabization of Jerusalem, greater ties with black Africa, oil embargoes against colonial Portugal, Rhodesia, and South Africa, and a new system of allocating oil to "friends, neutrals and enemies." Most irresponsible and dangerous was a decision to recognize the PLO's Yasir Arafat as the sole representative of the Palestinian people. They rebuffed Hussein, who had boycotted the summit because Arafat had been accorded head of state status.

Chapter 31

My Final Year

REVERSION

After the massive 1973 airlift, the United States reverted to its pre-war posture as it resumed courtship of the Arab states in two areas: the aid program and the amoral reaction to Arab terrorism.

As I began my final year as AIPAC's chairman, we seemed to be back where we had begun, struggling to overcome the Administration's traditional preoccupation — concern lest the Arab states, and particularly Egypt, should align themselves with the Soviets in the Cold War.

Inside Israel there was deep introspection, as her people sought to fix responsibility for complacent blunders. They began to fear that time was not on their side, as they had led themselves to believe, and, as an inevitable reaction, there was uncertainty about the future and inability to chart a confident course of action.

Inside the Arab states there were high expectations of future triumph. They held the conviction that the United States would champion their cause and pressure Israel to make major concessions, if not total surrender, leading to her ultimate dissolution.

In the United States, we feared a repetition of the erosion of public support we had witnessed and deplored in 1957 and 1968, when the euphoria that accompanied Israel's spectacular victories had begun to vanish.

AID

When Congress approved the $2.2 billion appropriation for the airlift in 1973, it intended $1.5 billion for grants, the balance to be in credits at

316

concessionary rates. Late in April, there was a major blow. The Administration announced that it would provide only $1 billion in grants. O'Neill protested. He told AIPAC's fifteenth annual policy conference that he hoped the Administration would grant the full amount because of Israel's urgent needs.

There was further erosion—a congressional move to charge Israel an additional sum for the weapons because it was estimated that it would cost more to replace them in Defense procurement stocks. The Senate Armed Services Committee fixed the replacement cost at $155.8 million. The House estimated $140.3 million. Congressmen protested that it was unfair to require the Israelis to pay new model prices for the old models they had received the previous year.

Another blow was the program for fiscal 1975. The Administration resumed its pre-war custom, budgeting $300 million in military credits and $50 million for supporting assistance for Israel. Pursuing its courtship of the Arab states, the Administration carmarked $250 million in supporting assistance for Egypt; $77.5 million in supporting assistance, $100 million in military grants, and $30 million in military credit sales for Jordan. The Administration indicated that it might allocate $100 million for Syria.

The decision to reduce assistance to Israel contrasted with the generous program for the Arab states. The Administration proposed $430 million in military and economic grants to six Arab countries. The Arab states to receive grant military aid included Jordan, Tunisia, Morocco, Saudi Arabia, Lebanon, and Sudan.

Coincidentally, the Administration's $250 million offer in grant supporting assistance to Egypt was precisely the amount which Israel had requested, and which the Administration had rejected early in the year.

Humphrey threatened to oppose the amount for Egypt unless there were assurances that all nations, including Israel, were permitted freedom of passage through the Suez Canal.

We decided to urge increases for Israel. We proposed that the bill include $250 million in supporting assistance for Israel, and that $100 million of the $300 million arms authorization be in the form of grants.

I testified before the Senate Appropriations Committee, submitting an elaborate memorandum in which I quoted a *New York Times* editorial to the effect that Congress and the Executive Branch would do well "to stay flexible in meeting this country's long standing interest in preserving Israel's economic and military strength. Unlike the Arabs, Israel has no other major source of investment and economic aid." I also informed Congress that our proposal had the support of the Conference of Presidents of Major American Jewish Organizations, which now included 32.

We hoped that the Administration would boost the amount of grant military aid to Israel and authorize the full $1.5 billion voted in 1973. It was our understanding that the $2.2 billion was to be spread over a three-year period: $800 million for the arms which Israel received during the war, $800 million in the current year, and $600 million in 1975. We told the Committee that Israel's arms procurement requests already exceeded $3 billion, that agreements already signed approximated $1.2 billion, that agreements approximating $1 billion were awaiting signature, and that the remainder were in various stages of negotiation. "This means that Israel must continue to go more deeply into debt to pay for her survival unless Congress approves additional grant assistance."

We submitted these arguments:

1. The war did not end on October 22. It had continued for more than seven months. Despite the U.N. cease-fire, incessant shooting had violated Israel's cease-fire lines in a costly war of attrition.
2. Israel suffered heavy losses in manpower and materiel. Her economy was shaken by the war and its prolongation and by worldwide inflation.
3. Israelis were paying heavy taxes and loans to maintain their security and to amortize the heaviest per capita external debt burden of any people on earth.
4. The military balance was beginning to tilt dangerously against Israel, partly because of Soviet shipments and partly because of the ominous proliferation of arms in the Persian Gulf.
5. A drastic contraction of American aid for Israel, coinciding with a substantial expansion of U.S. aid for the Arab states, could have a psychological impact on public opinion in the region, impeding progress toward a settlement.

I submitted statistical data on Israel's mounting debt to buttress our case:

Total Debt (in billions):		Foreign Debt (in billions):	
1972	$ 7.9	1972	$4.1
1973	$ 9.0	1973	$5.0
1974	$10.5 (estimate)	1974	$5.8 (estimate)
1975	$12.0 (estimate)	1975	$6.8 (estimate)

Per Capita Foreign Debt:		Debt Service (in millions):	
1972	$1,275	1972	$ 663
1973	$1,510	1973	$ 710
1974	$1,680 (estimate)	1974	$ 790 (estimate)
1975	$1,940 (estimate)	1975	$1,080 (estimate)

Meanwhile, Congress was becoming more sensitive to Israel's financial plight. A joint conference committee of the House and Senate Armed Services Committees agreed that Israel need not pay the $140 million for the cost of replacing the weapons received in October.

On the eve of my testimony, I appealed to the Department of State that it tell the Committees that it sympathized with our proposals, but a high ranking diplomat politely declined to take any initiative. "We much prefer to be raped," he explained—a six-word epigram which telescoped U.S. policy for many years, such as President Johnson's readiness to provide Phantom jets for Israel if only Congress would take the initiative.

I was worried about the prospect of a clash with Fulbright, but, much to my relief, I found Humphrey in the Chair. Since he would have made a much more eloquent witness, I told him that I would be willing to yield my time to him, but he carefully kept his distance from advocacy. The Administration opposed Humphrey's amendment to block aid to Egypt. Kissinger told Congress that strings on aid to Egypt might jeopardize progress toward peace.

There was now evidence that the Administration was taking a more realistic look at Israel's defense needs. Kissinger told the Senate Foreign Relations Committee that the United States planned a multi-year arms process for Israel, which would terminate the annual bargaining.

There was further progress when the Administration finally released the $500 million grant it had withheld. Simultaneously, the Israeli government was imposing $1 billion in additional taxes on her people: increases in import surcharges, compulsory loans, and real estate and automobile taxes.

Our proposals to boost the aid allocations for Israel won overwhelming support in the House Foreign Affairs Committee, which voted 24 to 4 for an amendment submitted by Representatives Dante Fascell (D-Florida) and Buchanan to increase the amount of supporting assistance to $250 million. Representative Charles Wilson (D-Texas) submitted the amendment that $100 million of the military credits be a grant; it was approved 26 to 1.

Strongly supporting Kissinger's view, the Committee defeated amendments to cut the amount for Egypt. The Committee believed that closer U.S.-Egyptian relations would benefit Israel, and some members observed that reconstruction of cities along the Suez Canal would be an investment in peace. But the Committee had reservations about aid to Syria and voted to deny the contemplated $100 million for that country.

Egypt complained about congressional delay on the $250 million supporting assistance grant intended for her. The U.S. ambassador in Cairo, Herman F. Eilts, cabled the Department that delay would be "a blow between the eyes" for Sadat, who had been assuring his people that substantial U.S. foreign aid and private investments would lift the depressed Egyptian economy. To prod Washington, Sadat told NBC's Barbara Walters that he was sending his foreign minister, Ismail Fahmi, to Moscow on October 15 to negotiate resumption of Soviet arms shipments.

The Senate Foreign Relations Committee approved our requests but the continuing deterioration in Israel's economy impelled it to boost the amount that we had recommended. The Committee had reported that Israel's foreign currency reserves, which had totaled $1.7 billion in January, had dropped to $930 million by October and were now declining at a rate of more than $100 million a month. The Committee estimated that Israel's current deficit had risen from $1.1 billion in 1972 to $2.5 billion in 1973 and that it would exceed $3.7 billion by the end of the year, while Israelis were paying the highest per capita taxes in the world, contributing more than 65 percent of the GNP to the treasury. Israel's foreign currency debt was expected to total $6.1 billion by the end of 1974. The Senate voted that the amount for grant economic assistance be fixed at $339.5 million. In December, after long delay, the Senate and House Conference Committee finally fixed the amount in supporting assistance for Israel at $324.5 million.

PROPAGANDA

As 1974 began, we were confronted by widespread propaganda. Israel and her American Jewish supporters would be the scapegoats of the energy crisis. I had refused to accept that thesis when Mike Wallace interviewed me on "60-Minutes," and public opinion polls upheld my view. "The Advocates," a public television program, showed that nine out of ten Americans opposed any pressure on Israel to withdraw from occupied territories in exchange for American security guarantees to Israel.

Part of the CBS broadcast originated at a breakfast at my home, the initial meeting of a new "Truth Squad" proposed by Hyman Bookbinder of the American Jewish Committee to counter Arab propaganda. Throughout the following year the squad, consisting of Washington representatives of national Jewish organizations, sought to refute pro-Arab propaganda and to combat inaccuracy. We urged the media to take a second look at their coverage and opinions.

While we met frequently with correspondents and columnists, we utilized what became known as "The Monitor" column in the *Near East Report* to clarify controversial issues and to expose negative propaganda. An early target was Dr. Clovis Maksoud, a 46-year-old Lebanese Christian propagandist who represented the PLO and had come to the United States to interpret the Arab cause. In advance of his first press conference, we circulated many of his earlier statements which showed that he had championed the extremist PLO position. Many newspapermen in Washington and other cities were well briefed prior to his 90-day tour of the United States.

We frequently clashed with Fulbright, who disseminated the calumny that Israel's friends were raising funds everywhere to defeat his renomination in the Arkansas primary in 1973. There was no basis for these reports. We pointed out that the Jewish population of Arkansas, estimated at 2,750, was a tiny fraction of the state's 1,923,295, and could hardly influence the outcome. As for out-of-state contributions, *The Wall Street Journal* reported that Governor Dale Bumpers, Fulbright's opponent, "denies receiving any such contributions and swears he will take only small out-of-state contributions from personal friends and previous donors." Ironically, it was Fulbright — not Bumpers — who received substantial out-of-state contributions from American Jews and Arabs.

Bumpers defeated Fulbright by a two-to-one majority. Over ABC's "Issues and Answers," he disagreed with Fulbright, and favored sending arms to Israel, declaring that any peace settlement must include secure and defensible borders for Israel.

Later in the year, we were dismayed by a rash of press comment implying that Israel might be blamed for any failure in the peace negotiations. The pendulum was swinging away from Israel, as it had after the initial rapture over her victories had faded in 1957 and 1967.

We wrote many columns about "The Mini-War Against Israel" waged by columnists Evans and Novak. Their tendentious attacks reached a climax in September when they claimed that Israel had made "an incredible secret request for $4 billion a year in U.S. arms." Evans attributed this incredible exposé to a briefing which Kissinger had allegedly given to major American industrialists early in the month. When Fulbright asked about Evans's remark, Kissinger declared that Evans had confused Israel's total arms budget with the amount she sought from the United States, a figure estimated at $1.5 billion. Despite Kissinger's statement and the publicity which we gave it, Evans refused to correct his misstatement for many weeks, and it required an avalanche of letters to local newspapers which carried the Evans-Novak column to force Evans to retract.

There was widespread indignation when General Brown told a Duke University audience that the Jewish lobby was strong because Jews owned the banks and newspapers. He concluded that if the American people are the victims of another oil embargo they will "get tough-minded enough to set down the Jewish influence in this country and break that lobby." Representatives of major Jewish organizations protested to Defense Secretary Schlesinger, who told us that Brown deeply regretted his remarks as "both unfortunate and ill-considered."

There was a reversal of scapegoats. Oil men who had hoped that Israel and her friends would become the scapegoats of the oil embargo became the targets themselves. Congress was angered by the disclosure that ARAMCO and Gulf Oil had been prohibited from delivering Saudi and Kuwaiti oil to U.S. military forces during the October war. During Senate hearings, Jackson contended that the oil companies had been disloyal. *Business Week* carried a report that Faisal had ordered ARAMCO "to cut off the supply of products derived from Saudi oil." As a result, the endangered U.S. Sixth and Seventh Fleets were forced to curtail normal sea and air operations.

These charges were later elaborated during testimony and memoranda made public by the Senate Foreign Relations Subcommittee on

Multi-National Corporations. Church, chairman of the Subcommittee, portrayed the oil companies as hostages of the Saudis, operating at their beck and call. Testimony showed that ARAMCO supplied the Saudis with information about indirect shipments of Saudi oil to the U.S. military from other sources, thus enabling the Saudis to reduce oil shipments to those destinations.

The U.S. Ambassador to Saudi Arabia, James Akins, had telegraphed ARAMCO, urging the company to make it clear to our government that the Arabs would not lift their restrictions unless the political struggle was settled in a manner satisfactory to them.

On another front, Representative Clarence D. Long (D-Maryland) issued an extensive study of the "invisible" foreign aid benefits which oil companies derived from the ruling which permitted them to treat the royalties paid to Arab governments as taxes that could be credited against their U.S. taxes. Long, a leader in the House Appropriations Subcommittee on Foreign Operations and an economist, estimated that these tax credits totaled $7.025 billion between 1968 and 1973. To that sum he added U.S. arms supplies, economic assistance, and the U.S. share of multi-lateral aid programs to the 11 Arab states which had participated in the October war. That figure came to $1.927 billion, making a grand total of $8.952 billion. He noted that Soviet military and economic assistance amounted to $3.707 billion, which showed that American aid was 2.4 times that of Russian aid. If our tax policy had been different, he contended, we could have encouraged development of domestic resources to avert dependence on imported oil.

TERRORISM

In 1974, Arab terrorists intensified an unrelenting war against Israel and its supporters. On the eve of the New Year, a Jewish philanthropist, Joseph Edward Sieff, president of London's Marks and Spencer Department Stores, was shot and critically wounded by an intruder who invaded his bedroom. The PFLP promptly claimed credit for the attack, carried out, we learned later, by the notorious "Carlos."

Throughout the year, the U.N., as usual, ignored Arab provocations and censured Israel for her retaliations. In 1972, the United States had vetoed these prejudicial inequities; but in 1974 it passively abstained.

In February, an Islamic conference at Lahore sought to mobilize the Moslem world to support the PLO's claim to represent the Palestinians. Thus the PLO, which always called for a secular state in Palestine, hypocritically sought and was accorded religious sponsorship.

On January 17, after one week of Kissinger's intensive shuttle diplomacy, Egypt and Israel reached a landmark disengagement agreement providing for an Israeli pull-back 15 miles along the El Arish road, 20 miles down the Sharm el-Sheikh road, south of Suez, and back to the Gidi and Mitla passes 14 to 20 miles east of the Canal. Egyptian forces east of the Canal were to be limited to 7,000 men, 30 tanks, and six artillery batteries, and there were to be limited Egyptian and Israeli police forces on either side of a U.N. peace-keeping force of 7,000 men.

In a public opinion poll 60 percent of the Israelis approved the pact, but Menachem Begin's Likud bloc denounced it as "betrayal and surrender." Begin had gained strength in the elections held the day before 1974 began, at the expense of the ruling Ma'arach (Alignment) of Golda Meir, a casualty of the Yom Kippur War. Begin now warned that Egypt could restore the Third Army to its full military strength and that Egypt now controlled both sides of the Canal and was in a position to liquidate Israel in stages. Ironically, Begin agreed in 1977 to give up all Sinai to Egypt in exchange for peace.

Sadat now demanded disengagement between Israel and Syria as the next step. He described Egypt and Syria as a single country with a single front under one commander-in-chief.

After difficult negotiations with other parties, Mrs. Meir was finally sworn in for another term in early March. She promised not to return to the 1967 lines because they were never recognized boundaries and were not defensible. Israel was opposed to representation of Palestinian terrorists at any Geneva conference. Most important, she promised that Israel would not withdraw from territory on the West Bank without holding new elections if one of the coalition partners requested them.

Mrs. Meir did not remain in office long. The Agranat Commission, investigating responsibility for Israel's mistakes in evaluating the situation and for blunders in the first days of the Yom Kippur War, cleared both Mrs. Meir and Dayan, but she was criticized for not having conferred with her Cabinet about Egypt's war preparations until just before the war began. The clearing of Dayan was most unpopular.

Citing her age and disunity in her coalition, Mrs. Meir resigned on April 10 and Itzhak Rabin became Israel's fifth Prime Minister, narrowly defeating Shimon Peres by a vote of 298 to 254. He won a slim vote of confidence, 61 to 51, with five abstentions.

Meanwhile, Kissinger won a disengagement agreement between Syria and Israel, although Syria repeatedly barred direct negotiations and peace. Rabin told the Knesset that the next stage on the road to peace would be between Israel and Egypt.

In order to disrupt any new negotiations, the PFLP General Command, the most extreme offshoot of the PFLP, committed the worst terrorist outrage in Israel since the massacre at Lod airport in 1972. School children were the target of terrorists who entered the northern town of Kiryat Shemona in April. They attempted to capture a school on the outskirts, but the pupils were at home because of the Passover holiday. Frustrated, the invaders moved into the ground floor of an apartment building, spraying the area with machine-gun fire. Hurling hand grenades, they went from apartment to apartment, throwing children from third-story windows, sniping at anyone moving below, and slaughtering 18 men, women, and children. The PFLP General Command was headed by a former Syrian army officer, Ahmed Jibril, who broke away from George Habash's PFLP in mid-1968, with an estimated 1,000 followers. Arab radios described the killing of 18 "Zionist soldiers" and the wounding of 16 others. Inevitably, the Israeli army moved against six Lebanese villages which had harbored terrorists. They warned civilians before dynamiting some 20 houses and arresting 10 suspected collaborators. Two civilians died—a woman and a child.

The State Department condemned the Kiryat Shemona raid as the "brutal and senseless slaughter of innocent civilians, particularly the murder of women and children, as we deplore and condemn all terrorism in any area." But at the U.N., Lebanon charged Israel with aggression, contending that the terrorists had not crossed the border, while Egypt's Fahmi blamed Israel for escalating the fighting.

Syria's war of attrition, which continued while the disengagement negotiations were under way, was ignored by the U.N. Security Council, which adopted a resolution censuring Israel but refrained from condemnation of the Kiryat Shemona massacre. Much to our dismay, the United States—in a retreat to pre-1972 expediency—voted for that resolution, even though the Council, by a vote of 7 to 6 (with the Soviet Union and Byelorussia abstaining), had rejected a U.S. amendment to include condemnation of the Kiryat Shemona outrage. Many congressmen criticized the U.S. failure to veto the resolution, which was adopted 13 to 0.

Coincidentally, the State Department's tendency to withdraw to the sidelines was further revealed when it wrote a letter to an Israeli describing the fate of Syrian Jewry as an "internal affair" of the Syrian government. That response caused a furor in Israel, and a Department spokesman assured the *Near East Report* that this unfortunate phrase was not Department policy. He insisted that the Department was concerned about the fate of the Jewish community in Syria but preferred to use the diplomatic approach as the most effective way to deal with it.

Encouraged by the U.N.'s exercise in appeasement and the U.S. failure to veto, another terrorist splinter group, the PDFLP (Popular Democratic Front for the Liberation of Palestine), struck swiftly and brutally in a massacre at Ma'alot. Three Arab terrorists invaded a high school, holding nearly 100 children as hostages for the release of 26 terrorist prisoners. The Israelis, after negotiations had collapsed, moved to rescue the children, killing two of the terrorists. A third, although wounded, machine-gunned the children.

Hours before the massacre, while the children were still alive, Congress adopted resolutions sponsored by 51 senators and 324 representatives, calling upon the Security Council to condemn the act of violence and urging governments who harbor groups and individuals "to take appropriate action to rid their countries of those who subvert the peace through terrorism and senseless violence."

The Senate text was softened at the request of the State Department, in order to secure the unanimous consent needed for immediate adoption. Deleted was a specific reference to "Arab terrorists," and the clause "governments who harbor these groups and individuals" was changed to "the countries where these groups and individuals are found." A paragraph requesting the U.S. ambassador to the U.N. to take appropriate action before that body to introduce a Security Council resolution condemning "this brutal act of violence" was likewise deleted.

The PFLP General Command struck again a few days before President Nixon arrived in Egypt. Four terrorists attacked Kibbutz Shamir, killing three women. They had intended to toss grenades and explosives into the kibbutz dining hall where 470 were eating breakfast, but they themselves were killed in a shoot-out. "This is how every Arab should receive Nixon," said an organization spokesman.

A few days later, three Palestinian terrorists murdered a mother, her two children, and an Israeli soldier and wounded eight other Israelis in an apartment house in Nahariya. The trio, who had come from Lebanon by boat, were killed by Israeli troops.

There was speculation that the United States might recognize a "moderate" Arab leadership which would acknowledge Israel's right to exist, settling for a demilitarized Palestinian state on the West Bank with ties to Jordan and with Sadat-Faisal support.

However, the PLO-led Palestine National Council adopted a new ten-point program on June 8, reaffirming its major objective and pledging to struggle, by all means, to "liberate the Palestinian land" and to establish "a national independent and fighting authority on every part of it"—a threat to both Israel and Jordan.

There was a difference of opinion in Israel on how to deal with the PLO. In mid-July, Information Minister Aharon Yariv declared that Israel would be willing to meet with the PLO, if it would first recognize Israel's existence and agree to end its terrorist attacks. But the next day Prime Minister Rabin insisted that Israel would not recognize the Palestine entity and that the Palestinian problem could be solved through talks with Jordan.

Late in July, Hussein and Sadat joined in a communiqué to the effect that the PLO does not represent Palestinians living in Jordan, only those living outside the Hashemite Kingdom. It noted that an Israeli-Jordanian disengagement agreement was the "first step toward a peaceful and just solution."

The Israeli Cabinet declared that Israel would work toward a peace agreement with Jordan and that such an agreement would be "founded on the existence of two independent states only—Israel, with united Jerusalem as her capital, and a Jordanian-Palestinian-Arab state east of Israel with borders to be determined in negotiations between Israel and Jordan." The Cabinet endorsed a Rabin statement that "Israel will not conduct negotiations with terrorist organizations whose aim is the destruction of the state of Israel."

At this stage, the United States and Israel seemed to agree. Kissinger had told a Senate committee that the Palestinian problem should be solved within the context of Israeli-Jordanian negotiations and that after Israel and Jordan had worked out an agreement it would be up to Jordan to reach a settlement with the Palestinians over the future administration of the West Bank. Israeli Foreign Minister Allon had discussed these issues with Kissinger.

In August the Egyptians changed their minds, as Egypt's Fahmi espoused a hard line one day after he had been warmly received by President Ford. On NBC's "Today" show Fahmi declared that Israel had to recognize the PLO as the representative of the Palestinians and withdraw completely from all occupied territories before there could be peace in the Middle East and that the PLO, not Jordan, was the legitimate spokesman for West Bank Palestinians. The only reason that Egypt would permit Jordan to negotiate with Israel over the West Bank was "for the sake of convincing Israelis to withdraw from occupied territory." Should the West Bank be returned to Jordan, it would be merely as a temporary "trust," just as Gaza was ruled by Egypt after the 1949 armistice.

Hussein, who also was then in Washington, disagreed, telling the press that he would not impose PLO control on the West Bank Palestinians. They were Jordanian citizens who had "partaken fully in the political life of the country."

In August, I flew to Israel to talk with leaders about the next step in the negotiations. I tended to agree with Kissinger that an attempt should be made to urge a disengagement agreement between Israel and Jordan in order to arrest Arafat's bid for credentials.

Kissinger had summoned Rabin to Washington, and when I arrived I found that Israelis were deeply troubled because Kissinger had not asked Rabin if he wanted to be invited at that time; thus they feared that Kissinger intended to exert pressures on Israel. Rabin was then reluctant to proceed with the strategy which Kissinger had proposed.

Greeted at the airport by press and television crews who could talk of nothing else, I ventured the opinion that the invitation to Rabin reflected Kissinger's desire to keep the momentum going. Since he had talked with the Egyptians and the Jordanians and was about to talk with the Saudis and the Syrians, he would naturally want to see Rabin as quickly as he could. The press was skeptical because Kissinger was still a scapegoat for Israel's 1973 setbacks.

I found both Eban and Allon in accord with Kissinger's view. Allon had his own plan for an agreement which would permit Israel to establish security bases at both ends of the Jordan River. But when I asked Allon why he hesitated to press his proposal, he reminded me of Mrs. Meir's promise that

Israel would not withdraw from any West Bank territory without holding new elections should one of the coalition partners in her government request them. When I suggested to Allon that Israel might now agree to go to the public, he expressed fear that the government could not then win a mandate. It had not been in office long enough and had not resolved economic problems which had alienated the electorate.

I raised another issue with Israeli leaders: newspaper reports of new huge arms agreements between Israel and the United States. I had been convinced that these were exaggerated, largely because of comments by Israeli officials themselves. I told Dan Margalit, correspondent for *Haaretz,* that members of Congress were alienated by these reports and that Israelis should not contribute to the misunderstanding. His article precipitated action by Rabin, who instructed his Israeli officials to desist.

Late in September Sadat further dimmed hopes for peace by ruling out a unilateral Egyptian declaration of non-belligerency with Israel in exchange for a total Israeli pull-back from the Sinai. He told Barbara Walters that Israel must first withdraw from all occupied territories, including Jerusalem, and that the Palestinian question must be solved. "I can't make a separate peace," he declared.

Allon charged that the new Cairo position was aimed at "legitimitization of terrorist activities." Rabin declared, "Those who directed acts of murder cannot be a partner for peace talks."

At the U.N., the PLO was invited to participate in plenary sessions by a vote of 105 to 4. The four negative votes included the United States, Israel, Bolivia, and the Dominican Republic. There were 20 abstentions and nine absent. Humphrey, Javits, Case, and McGee had telegraphed Ford urging that the U.S. delegation vote against the resolution. The Department of State agreed.

Never before had the U.N. permitted a non-governmental agency to address the Assembly. It had now set a precedent, opening the door for any subversive or terrorist group. The PLO would use U.N. recognition to prevent any Arab state from negotiating a settlement with Israel. The U.N. victory was repeated at Rabat, where 20 Arab League countries voted to authorize the PLO to represent the Palestinians and to inherit any West Bank areas that Israel might yield.

Hussein fought a last ditch battle at Rabat, but the PLO victory was inevitable after the amoral decision of the General Assembly.

The *Near East Report* carried a 12-page article describing the evolution of the PLO, the attitudes of its component groups, its record of bloodshed, its objectives, its covenant, and its ten points for war. We noted that the Soviet Union "had won a victory with an assist from wealthy and pro-Western Saudi Arabia."

Arafat triumphantly proclaimed that he would soon form a provisional government-in-exile as the first step toward establishing PLO sovereignty over the West Bank and Gaza. This mini-state would become the nucleus for a much larger Palestinian state encompassing all of Israel. However, because of divisions in the PLO, Arafat could not create a provisional government-in-exile, because such a government must delineate the territories which it assumes to govern. Were Arafat to limit himself to the West Bank in order to justify his claim to moderation, he would immediately be the target of the more radical factions under the PLO umbrella.

At the General Assembly in mid-November, Arafat's 90-minute harangue won a minute-long standing ovation. His major objective was the liquidation of the Jewish state, which he described as the "Zionist entity."

"I have come bearing an olive branch and a freedom fighter's gun. Do not let the olive branch fall from my hand," Arafat triumphantly proclaimed. However, he came to the U.N. bearing only a holster and pistol—the olive branch was invisible.

The General Assembly adopted a resolution 89 to 8, with 37 abstentions and 4 not present, reaffirming "the inalienable rights of the Palestinians." It failed to mention the rights of Israel.

The Assembly adopted a second resolution—95 in favor, 17 opposed, 19 abstentions, and 7 not present—according the PLO "Observer Status" at the General Assembly and other U.N. bodies.

Soon after Arafat's U.N. speech, three PDFLP terrorists entered an apartment building in the northern Israeli town of Beit Shean. They machine-gunned two men and a woman, who died instantly, while a fourth died after jumping from a third floor window. Twenty-three were injured. Demanding the release of 14 jailed terrorists, they held some 75 men, women, and children for three hours. Israeli security forces, who rushed the building, killed all three terrorists.

Following that massacre, U.S. Ambassador John Scali, addressing the General Assembly, strongly denounced terrorism and Arafat's attempt to draw an analogy between PLO terrorists and George Washington. "If there were instances during the American Revolution when innocent people suffered," Scali declared, "there was no instance where the revolutionary leadership boasted or condoned such crimes."

The eight nations opposing the U.N. resolution on "Palestinian rights" included Bolivia, Chile, Costa Rica, Iceland, Israel, Nicaragua, Norway, and the United States. The 37 who abstained included European and other Western democracies.

The reaction of Congress, the American people, and the American press was an almost universal condemnation of the U.N. action as a repetition of Munich which could lead to the disintegration of the U.N. General Assembly, not unlike the League of Nations. "The League of Nations was powerless then; the U.N. General Assembly is disintegrating now. It is the Coliseum, not the Forum," Eric Sevareid, the CBS commentator, observed.

So Israel became the pariah, the scapegoat of the Third World.

Chapter 32

Conclusion

My "retirement" began in December 1974.

After discontinuing my lobbying activities, I headed a "Truth Squad," focusing on the media and writing a "Monitor" column in the *Near East Report,* which was circulated to many Jewish weeklies without charge. I wrote for *The Jerusalem Post* and the London *Jewish Chronicle.* I gave many interviews to scholars, students, and correspondents and spoke for the United Jewish Appeal and Israel Bonds. I made trips to Israel, Oxford, London, and Europe.

In London, in 1975, I urged parliamentarians and journalists to support Ambassador Daniel P. Moynihan's vigorous resistance to Yasir Arafat's siege of the U.N.

During 1976, I was skeptical of Candidate Carter's virtually total identification with Israel. My doubts were confirmed after he became President and began to speak of a Palestinian "homeland" and to qualify the concept of "defensible borders." I strongly favored bilateral negotiations and opposed Carter's advocacy of the "comprehensive" settlement, which, like the negotiations at Lausanne in 1950, would enable extremists to veto any solution short of Israel's total capitulation, if not dissolution.

I was invited to testify before the Senate Foreign Relations Committee on October 3, 1977, two days after Carter's startling agreement to permit the Soviet Union to resume a role in the peacemaking process at a Geneva conference.

In 1978, Israel's thirtieth year, I visited Israel twice, once under the flag of Israel and once under the flag of the United States.

In April, the Israel government invited me to her celebration—despite

329

my long identification with the views of the Labor party and my opposition to the Begin government's policies with respect to Samaria and Judea. At that time I found Israelis deeply troubled by the U.S. decision to send F-15 planes to Saudi Arabia.

In December, the White House invited me to join the official U.S. delegation to the funeral of Golda Meir. On that visit I found Israelis apprehensive that the United States was preparing to renew pressures on Israel. There was a grotesque imbalance. Israel was asked to make vast concessions to pay for peace, while Egypt was to be richly rewarded for abandoning war.

Far from even-handed, the Carter Administration constantly charged that Israel's settlements on the West Bank were illegal and an obstacle to the peace. It was ready to arm the Arab states despite congressional protest. Notwithstanding its commitments to U.N. Resolutions 242 and 338 requiring Israel's foes to recognize her right to exist, the Administration seemed to be courting the PLO. When Ambassador Andrew Young was forced to resign because of his contact with the PLO, black leaders blamed American Jews for his plight. Carter was slow to exonerate them from responsibility. The deepening black-Jewish rift alarmed and embittered American Jews.

Although Begin was the author of an autonomy plan for the inhabitants of Judea and Samaria, the Carter Administration blamed Israel for rejecting the demands of West Bank Arabs for legislative authority, which would have inevitably led to a separate Palestinian state.

Israelis and American Jews were resentful when the U.S. delegation to the U.N. voted for a resolution censuring Israel for insisting on sovereignty in all of Jerusalem, a reiteration of Israel's stand in 1967, when her armies liberated East Jerusalem from Jordanian occupation. The stormy reaction led the White House to repudiate this vote.

Then, as always, incessant Arab violence inside Israel was condoned by the U.N. while Israel's response was condemned.

In 1979 and 1980, Israel was a state besieged—threatened by a plutocratic cartel preoccupied with profit rather than peace, by power-hungry communists and fascists, and by venomous anti-Semites. As so often in the past, Jews in Israel and around the world were menaced by intolerant forces that had decried Jewish existence for centuries. They have renewed the call for a holy war, emboldened by the weakness and disunity of the democratic world.

We American Jews share Israel's danger. We have learned that what happens to Jews anywhere affects Jews everywhere, for we are an interdependent people. We witnessed anti-Semitic incitement in many lands as Hitler rose to power in the 1930s. We remember Fritz Kuhn's Nazi Bund, the Pelley Silver Shirts, Gerald L. K. Smith, the Ku Klux Klan, and the frenetic outbursts of Father Coughlin.

And it was happening again: in Iran, where Jews became hostages in a tinder box, fearing denunciation by a maniacal ayatollah; in Ethiopia, where

Jews were caught in crossfire; in Syria, where they were trapped between the violent Assad government and the militant Moslem Brotherhood; in Poland, where Jews were scapegoats for social unrest; and in the Soviet Union, which was slashing Jewish emigration. Anti-Semitic terrorists declared war against the Jews in France. Ironically, that land gave birth to contemporary Zionism—founded by Theodor Herzl, who had been shocked by the infamous Dreyfus trial. Elements who conspired to entrap Dreyfus were alive—and vile again.

In 1947, we won an uphill battle for partition. But our foes moved to scrap the plan and to establish a U.N. trusteeship. We defeated them, but Israel's enemies never abandoned their struggle. They were still determined to treat Israel as a U.N. chattel, to be supervised and circumscribed by U.N. instruments.

Thus the U.N. had become a mosque, sounding the call to deny Israel sovereignty and survival—to treat her as a pariah, to deny her legitimacy, while Islam trumpeted the ancient shibboleth for Israel's disappearance.

The oft-quoted George Santayana warned us that those who forget history are condemned to relive it. We could freely discuss and debate the policies of the United States and Israel and the disagreements that divided us. But that could not divert us from the dangers that confronted Israel and Jewish communities everywhere. We had to close ranks—for we were on the front line, the defense line—in Washington.

On March 26, 1980, we celebrated the signing of the Egyptian-Israeli peace treaty. Its most dramatic feature was the promise to normalize relations—economic and cultural—and to promote the free movement of people, transport, communications, and knowledge. But there has been very little progress. Israeli tourists flooded into Cairo; a handful of Egyptians came to Israel. Egyptian exports—handicrafts and finished goods—amounted to a minuscule fraction of Israel's exports of agricultural and chemical goods.

Israel publicly blamed Egypt. Manifestly, Sadat still feared reprisals from the Arab rejection front and denunciation from bitter military men who could not forgive him for signing a peace treaty with Israel.

The first to make peace, Sadat has yielded to his enemies as he demands that Israel grant self-determination to Arabs on the West Bank, as he calls on Arafat to set up a provisional government-in-exile, as he fails to discourage the Europeans from their pro-PLO initiative.

Most depressing, the Cairo press from time to time disseminates anti-Semitic propaganda reminiscent of the *Elders of Zion*. And some speculate that an anti-Sadat military coup would be directed against all collaborators with Israel.

Throughout 1980, the Carter Administration tried to reassure Israel's American friends of U.S. support. For the first time in many years, there was a substantial defection from the Democratic party. This was not easy for many American Jews who feared that Ronald Reagan would sponsor measures favoring the wealthy and curtailing benefits for the disadvantaged. Some Jews voted for John Anderson, who had expressed support for Israel when he came to Congress in 1961 and who had been a leader in the struggle in support of Soviet Jewry.

During the campaign, all three candidates pledged support for Israel. Reagan left no doubts. He denounced the PLO as a terrorist organization. He described Israel as an asset. He disagreed with the Carter Administration's efforts to characterize Israeli settlements as illegal. And he was quick to reaffirm his position after the election.

Israel's American friends were also encouraged by the support of the new Secretary of State, General Alexander Haig, and the new U.S. Ambassador to the U.N., Jeane Kirkpatrick.

The Reagan Administration has identified with Israel's war against terrorism and does not censure her when she reacts to it. It is determined to challenge Soviet expansionism. That is consistent with Israel's view that the Soviets are the major force arming her foes with sophisticated weapons and malignant propaganda.

History recalls that the recrudescence of the Cold War could mean the cold shoulder for Israel. Thus, in 1951, we had to lobby on the Hill for aid because the Truman Administration feared that the Arab states would align themselves with the Soviets if the United States extended aid to Israel.

And in 1954, the Eisenhower Administration sent arms to Iraq, denying them to Israel because of the illusion that it could organize the Baghdad Pact "Alliance" — Turkey, Iraq, Iran, and Pakistan — to contain the Soviet Union. The Reagan Administration is now embarked on a similar initiative, but it does not exclude Israel because it recognizes that Israel is a strategic asset — the strongest anti-Communist regime in the Middle East. It is difficult to see how Israel's potential contribution can be ignored as it was in the early 1950s. But will the Saudis accede to such a bizarre partnership, even as they sound the call for a holy war? And if they do not, do we still sell them devastating weapons, like the AWACS, which can give effect to their calls for Israel's destruction? Does Saudi Arabia continue to dominate U.S. policy?

Israel was our forgotten ally in our early struggle against Nazism, fascism, and communism. She continues to be in the vanguard of democracy in the Middle East. President Reagan and Congress have it in their power to recognize and secure Israel's right to survival and peace.

Index

Abdullah, King, 9, 46, 54, 59, 79, 205, 234
Abdullah, Sheikh Sabah, 294
Abell, Maxwell, 102–103
Abourezk, Sen. James, 118-119, 294, 315
Abrams, Morris, 204
Abu-Jaber, Dr. Faiz, 309
Acheson, Dean, 67, 82–83, 93, 96, 314
Action Committee on American-Arab Relations, 116
Adams, Pres. John, 7
Adelson, Dorothy, 37
Adler, Warren, 69
AFL-CIO, 238
Agency for International Development (AID), 283
Agnew, Vice Pres. Spiro, 305
Agron, Gershon, 21
Aiken, Sen. George D., 151
Akins, James, 322
Albert, Rep. Carl, 258, 264, 283
Allon, Yigal, 326–327
Alon, Col. Yosef, 298
Ameen, Mike, 290
American Christian Palestine Committee (ACPC), 70, 78, 124, 141, 257

American Committee for Justice in the Middle East, 220, 309
American Council for Judaism (ACJ), 11, 16–17, 22–23, 39, 87, 89, 90, 108, 124, 212
American Council on the Middle East, 220, 236
American Emergency Committee for Zionist Affairs (AECZA), 6, 10, 12–14
American Friends of the Middle East (AFME), 87, 115–116, 123, 141, 143, 212, 239
American Friends Service Committee, 74
American Jewish Committee, 11, 12–13, 16, 17, 20, 24, 29, 30, 49, 69, 102, 134, 204, 295, 320
American Jewish Conference, 6, 10, 11–13, 14–15, 16, 20, 22, 24, 27–30, 32–33, 37, 39, 48–49, 99, 112; Palestine Commission of, 15, 17; Rescue Commission of, 14–15
American Jewish Conference on Soviet Jewry, 280–281
American Jewish Congress, 12, 16, 24, 29, 146, 203
American League for a Free Palestine, 17

American Middle East Rehabilitation, Inc., 239
American Near East Refugee Aid, Inc. (ANERA), 118, 269, 309
American Palestine Committee, 9, 10, 11, 18
American Professors for Peace in the Middle East, 202, 226–227, 250
American Veterans Committee, 74
American Zionist Committee for Public Affairs (AZCPA), 107-109
American Zionist Council (AZC), 68, 69, 80, 82, 89, 91, 95, 97, 106–107, 109, 111
American Zionist Emergency Council (AZEC), 14, 16, 17, 20, 23, 24, 68, 69, 118
Americans for Democratic Action (ADA), 221
Americans for Energy Independence, 186
Amin, Idi, 297
Amitay, Morris J., 113, 285, 294, 306
Ammerman, Dr. Harvey, 55
Anderson, Rep. John, 281, 332
Anderson, Robert B., 238
ANERA, 239
The Anglo-American Committee of Inquiry, 32, 34–36, 250
Anti-Defamation League (ADL), 69, 70
Arab American Association, 309
Arab League, 37, 39, 47, 57, 64, 94, 123, 199, 228, 248, 327
Arafat, Yasir, 25, 116, 231–232, 237, 249, 298–299, 315, 326–329, 331
Ardalan, Ali, 44
Aref, Abdul Karim, 166
Arnon, Michael, 169
Arsanjani, Hassan, 169
Arvey, Col. Jacob, 155
Assad, Hafez, 232, 299, 309, 331
Association of Arab-American University Graduates (AAUG), 118
Atherton, Alfred L., 248
Atkinson, Henry A., 76
Attlee, Clement, 34, 35–36
Austin, Sen. Warren, 24, 51, 56
Back, Phillip, 286

Backer, George, 68
Badeau, John, 117, 249–250
Baehr, Harry, 71
Baehr, Rev. Karl, 70, 141
Bagot, Sir John. *See* Pasha, Glubb
Bain, Beatrice (Bebe), 5, 6
Bakhtiar, Shahpour, 169
Bakhtiar, Teymour, 169
Bakke, Allan, 116
Bakr, Gen. Hassan, 231
Balaban, Barney, 69
Ball, George, 178, 180, 186
Barbour, Walworth, 222, 292
Barkley, Sen. Alben W., 17
Barnes, George, 38, 61, 105
Baroody, Joseph, 118, 229
Baroody, William J., 251
Barr, Joseph, 69
Barrett, Rep. William A., 81, 312
Battle, Lucius, 194, 200
Bayh, Sen. Birch, 256, 285
Begin, Prime Minister Menachem, 4, 17, 33, 255, 259, 323, 330
Bella, Ben, 188
Bellmon, Sen. Henry, 264
Ben Ari, Mordechai, 241
Ben-Gurion, David, 11, 32, 39, 70, 72, 73, 79, 81, 86, 90, 110, 132–133, 137, 160–168, 178, 197, 259
Ben Zvi, Izhak, 43
Bennike, Vagn, 101, 103
Benton, Sen. William, 72, 79
Berger, Rabbi Elmer, 11, 22, 117, 212, 250
Bergman, Elihu, 185–186
Bergson, Peter. *See* Kook, Hillel
Bergus, Donald, 261
Bernadotte, Count Folke, 58–62, 64, 96
Bernstein, Rabbi Philip S., 29, 43, 107, 111, 116, 139, 180, 194, 204, 220, 308
Bevin, Ernest, 35–37, 40, 42, 50, 59, 63
Bingham, Rep. Jonathan, 267, 280, 283
Bisgyer, Maurice, 13, 27
Black, Eugene, 148
Blackstone, Rev. William E., 8
Blaustein, Jacob, 30
Bliss, Dr. Daniel, 239
Blitzer, Wolf, 112

Bloom, William, 70
B'nai B'rith, 11, 16, 49, 69, 102, 108, 155, 203, 205, 224
B'nai Zion, 155, 240
Board of Deputies of British Jews, 21, 31
Boggs, Rep. Hale, 258, 284
Bolling, Dr. Landrum, 240
Bolton, Rep. Frances P., 69, 75, 98, 179
Bolton, Rep. Oliver P., 179
Bonner, Rep. H. C., 76, 79
Bookbinder, Hyman, 306, 320
Borah, Sen. William E., 9
Boughton, James, 108
Boukstein, Maurice, 109
Boumedienne, Pres. Houari, 304
Bourguiba, Pres. Habib, 164, 182, 189
Brandeis, Justice Louis D., 9, 228
Bray, Charles W., 281
Brewster, Sen. Owen, 73, 78–79, 88
Brezhnev, Leonid, 193, 284, 286–287, 304, 310
Bridges, Sen. Styles, 79, 102, 135
Brilej, Dr. José, 44
Brody, David, 69
Brooke, Sen. Edward, 264
Broomfield, Rep. William S., 266
Brown, Rep. Clarence J., Sr., 69
Brown, Gen. George S., 304, 321
Brown, Matthew, 102–103
Buchanan, Rep. John, 294, 319
Bulganin, Premier Nikolai, 132–133, 310
Bull, Gen. Odd, 223
Bumpers, Sen. Dale, 321
Bunche, Ralph, 41, 61, 63–65, 73, 100–101, 122, 157
Bundy, McGeorge, 162
Bunting, Earl, 212
Burdick, Sen. Quentin, 315
Burleson, Rep. Omar, 84
Burt, Rev. John H., 214
Byrnes, James, 314
Byroade, Henry, 93, 96, 108, 111, 114, 123–124

Cadogan, Sir Alexander, 50, 56, 61
Cahn, Julius, 204
Calmenson, Jesse, 13
Campbell, John C., 212

Canadian Jewish Congress, 21
Carleton, Dr. Alfred, 239
"Carlos," 322
Carter, Pres. Jimmy, 4, 24, 65, 112, 242, 329–332
Carter, Victor M., 186
Case, Sen. Clifford P., 239, 267, 327
Case, Sen Francis, 151, 171
Catholic Near East Welfare Association, 74
Celler, Rep. Emanuel, 27, 72, 81, 89, 134, 163, 181, 182, 195–196, 198, 202, 204, 231, 233, 239, 264, 276
Central Committee of the Liberated Jews of Europe, 28–29
Chamberlain, Neville, 34, 199
Chamoun, Pres. Camille, 138
Chatham, Rep. Thurmond, 86
Chesney, Esther, 112
Chiang Kai-shek, 53
Chiperfield, Rep. Robert B., 98
Church, Sen. Frank, 113, 219, 242, 322
Churchill, Winston, 9, 34, 110
Citizens Committee on American Policy in the Near East (CITCOM), 116, 173
The Clapp mission, 157
Clark, Sen. Joseph, 141, 219
Clay, Gen. Lucius D., 204
Clay, Rep. William, 277
Clements, William P., Jr., 304, 308
Cleveland, Harlan, 162
Clifford, Clark, 54, 68
Cohen, Ben, 48
Cohen, Marcus, 69
Cohn, Dr. Josef, 69
Comay, Michael, 32, 37
Commager, Henry Steele, 142
The Committee for a Jewish Army, 17
The Committee for Justice and Peace in the Holy Land, 114
The Committee for New Alternatives in the Middle East, 308
Compton, Rep. Renulf, 17
Conference of Presidents of Major American Jewish Organizations (Presidents Conference), 111–112, 132, 195, 198, 202–204, 220, 224, 285, 302, 307, 313, 317

Connally, Sen. Tom, 71, 78–79
Conte, Rep. Silvio O., 314
Cooley, Rep. H. D., 75–76, 79–80
Cooper, Sen. John Sherman, 146, 150–151, 219, 242
Cordtz, Dan, 212
Coughlin, Father Charles, 330
Council of Jewish Federations and Welfare Funds, 111–112
Council on Foreign Relations, 212
Crane, Rep. Philip M., 239
Crawford, Dr. Robert, 239
Curtis, Rep. Charles, 163
Curtis, Vice Pres. Charles, 9
Curtis, Rep. Charles, 163
Cushing, Cardinal Richard, 238

Dalton, Hugh, 251
Daniels, Jonathan, 68
Darlan, Admiral, 199
Davies, Richard T., 282
Davies, Rodger P., 210, 214, 312
Davis, Dr. John H., 118, 239–240, 269, 309
Davis, John W., 68
Davis, Leonard J., 112
Davis, Monnett B., 81
Dayan, Moshe, 204, 214, 259, 323
de Borchgrave, Arnaud, 292
Decter, Moshe, 113
de Gaulle, Charles, 199, 217, 230, 270
Democratic Policy Council, 240
Dewey, Gov. Thomas E., 36, 61
DiBona, Charles, 290
Dick, Bess, 72, 195
Diggs, Rep. Charles, 277
Dillon, C. Douglas, 144, 148, 153
Dine, Thomas A., 113
Dinitz, Simcha, 291–292, 302–304, 309
Dirksen, Sen. Everett, 78, 151–152, 218
Dobrynin, Anatoly, 310
Dodd, Sen. Thomas, 171
Dole, Sen. Robert, 258, 264, 267
Donnelly, Dixon, 116
Douek, Rabbi Haim, 276
Douglas, Sen. Paul H., 70, 71, 72, 74, 77–79, 89, 135, 141, 146, 150–153, 163, 171

Dreyfus, Alfred, 8, 331
Duce, James Terry, 51
Dulles, John Foster, 60, 87–88, 92–94, 96, 98–99, 100–101, 102–103, 106, 111, 123, 125–130, 134–135, 143, 145, 154, 155, 157, 207, 221, 225, 235, 255, 314
Dunn, Leo, 112
Dutton, Frederick, 120, 170, 175
Dworkin, Susan Levine, 112, 185–186
Dymshitz, Mark, 281

Eban, Abba, 33, 37, 40, 42, 52, 53, 54, 56, 64, 67–68, 71, 72, 74, 77, 84, 90, 95, 103–104, 136, 199–200, 205, 215–216, 219–220, 223, 232, 257, 259, 274, 303–304, 326
Eddy, William A., 114
Edelsberg, Herman, 69, 306
Edson, Peter, 22–23
Eichelberger, Clark M., 51
Eid, Guy, 289
Eilts, Herman F., 319
Eisendrath, Dr. Maurice, 15, 49
Eisenhower, Pres. Dwight D., 27, 81, 89, 90–91, 92, 95, 97, 106, 122, 127, 132, 134–135, 137–139, 143, 145, 152, 154, 156, 173, 183, 196–197, 207, 221–222, 225, 235, 255, 332
Eisenhower, Milton, 68
Elath, Eliahu, 21, 23, 37
Elizur, Yuval, 185
Ellender, Sen. Allen J., 242
Elson, Rev. Edward L. R., 143, 212, 226, 269
Emergency Committee to Save the Jews of Europe, 17
Emerson, Sir Herbert, 31–32
Epstein, Eliahu. *See* Elath, Eliahu
Erhard, Chancellor Ludwig, 181
Eshkol, Prime Minister Levi, 177–178, 194–195, 198, 201, 215, 217–218
Ethridge, Mark, 68
Evans, Jane, 13
Evans and Novak, 321
Evron, Ephraim, 195, 200, 203–204

Fabregat, Enrique, 41

Fahmi, Ismail, 319, 324, 326
Fain, Irving J., 186
Faisal, King, 4, 9, 141, 188-189, 217, 276, 289-291, 293, 296, 321, 325
Fannin, Sen. Paul J., 315
Farbstein, Rep. Leonard, 149, 163, 171
Farley, James, 76
Farouk, King, 93
Fascell, Rep. Dante, 319
Fawzi, Dr. Mahmound Bey, 225
Fein, Rep. Sidney, 81
Feinberg, Abraham J., 71, 89, 155
Feldman, Myer, 115, 155, 160-162, 167, 177, 183
Fenyvesi, Charles, 112, 197
Ferguson, Sen. Homer, 79, 98, 102
Field, Marshall, 68
Findley, Rep. Paul, 306, 314-315
Finletter, Thomas E., 145
Fisher, Max, 251
Flaiszir, Dr. J. C. *See* Talmon, Jacob
Flanders, Sen. Ralph E., 140-141
Fong, Sen. Hiram, 294
Ford, Pres. Gerald, 124, 218, 240-241, 258, 264, 272, 287, 305, 326-327
Forman, Judge Philip, 30
Forrestal, James, 49, 114
Frankfurter, Justice Felix, 9, 142
Fraser, Rep. Donald, 244, 267, 294
Fraser, Peter, 23
Frederick, Pauline, 240
Frelinghuysen, Rep. Peter H. B., 189, 243
Friendly, Alfred, 213
Friends Committee on National Legislation, 240
Frisch, Daniel, 110
Fugate, Rep. Thomas, 81
Fulbright, Sen. J. W., 109, 120, 141, 143, 146, 149-153, 155-158, 168, 171-173, 196, 235, 238, 242, 256, 264, 266, 267, 280, 286, 294, 301, 308, 314-315, 319-321
Fulton, Rep. James G., 75-76, 126, 144, 163, 267

Galbraith, Prof. John Kenneth, 183, 313

Gardiner, Arthur Z., 82, 84-85, 97, 99
Gehrig, Benjamin, 23
Gelber, Lionel, 37
George, David Lloyd, 99
George, Sen. Walter F., 71
Ghori, Emile, 39
Giles, Robert E., 186
Gillette, Sen. Guy M., 71, 79, 98
Ginsberg, Paul, 89
Glass, Andrew, 274
Gold, Rabbi Wolf, 37
Goldberg, Abraham, 9
Goldberg, Arthur J., 208, 228-229, 315
Goldmann, Nahum, 12, 22-24, 30, 37, 68, 111
Goldstein, Abe, 71
Goldstein, Ernest, 219
Goldstein, Rabbi Israel, 16, 21
Goodman, Mr. and Mrs. Andrew, 186
Goodman, Jerry, 285
Goodrich, Nathaniel, 134
Gordon, Matthew, 38, 61
Gore, Rep. Albert, 79-80
Grady-Morrison plan, 36
Granados, Jorge Garcia, 41, 47, 55
Granville, Maurice, 296
Green, Sen. Theodore F., 143
Greenberg, Chaim, 15, 37
Griffin, Sen. Robert, 272, 301
Grigg, Lee, 186
Grinberg, Dr. Zalman, 28-29
Gromyko, Andrei, 39, 220, 234, 287
Gronich, Fred, 70
Grossman, Meir, 14, 27
Grossman, Rita. *See* Lefkort, Rita
Gruber, Ruth, 42
Gruening, Sen. Ernest, 151, 163, 171, 178, 184
Gurfein, Murray, 68
Gurney, Sen. Edward J., 264

Habash, George, 298, 324
Haberman, Rabbi Joshua, 306
Hadassah, 5, 10, 37, 69, 102, 111, 150, 184, 194, 244
Hadawi, Sami, 236
Haig, Gen. Alexander M., 332
Hall, Leonard, 81

Hallstein doctrine, 181
Halpern, Prof. Benjamin, 15
Halpern, Rep. Seymour, 163, 218, 283
Halprin, Rose, 37, 54, 102–103
Hamilton, Rep. Lee, 314
Hammarskjold, Dag, 133, 148, 153
Handler, Prof. Milton, 15
Hanna, Rep. Richard T., 306
Hansen, Sen. Clifford, 315
Harman, Avraham, 156, 161, 194–195, 200, 204, 219
Harriman, Averell, 219
Harris, Louis, 258, 315
Harrison, Pres. Benjamin, 8
Harrison, Earl G., 27–28
Hart, Sir Basil H. Liddell, 226
Hart, Merwin K., 87
Hart, Parker, 114, 227
Hart, Sen. Philip, 276
Hart, Mayor William S., 277
Hatcher, Mayor Richard, 277
Hatfield, Sen. Mark, 240, 242, 266, 306–307
Hayes, Helen, 159
Hays, Rep. Brooks, 71, 89, 159
Hays, Rep. Wayne, 149, 163, 283
Healy, Timothy, 118
Hebrew Committee of National Liberation, 17, 39
Heikal, Mohammed Hassanein, 217, 261
Hellman, Yehudah, 285
Helms, Sen. Jesse, 315
Henderson, Loy, 38, 48, 51, 114
Hendrickson, Sen. Robert, 79
Herman, George, 301
Hershman, Ruth, 112
Herter, Christian A., 76, 80, 87, 141, 178, 183, 314
Herzl, Theodor, 8, 156, 169, 268, 331
Hickenlooper, Sen. Bourke B., 151
Hilldring, Gen. John H., 29, 48
Hilton, Conrad, 186
Hirsch, Rabbi Richard, 203
Hirst, David, 276
Hitler, Adolf, 4, 9, 10, 11, 12, 20, 25, 26, 35, 39, 45, 57, 94, 131, 141, 199, 217, 261, 278, 297, 330
Hobby, Oveta Culp, 71

Holland, Sen. Spessard L., 79
Hollister, Atty. John B., 88
Holmes, Justice Oliver Wendell, 286
Hood, John D., 43, 45
Hope, Rep. Clifford R., 75
Hopkins, Rev. Garland Evans, 116, 280
Horowitz, David, 40, 42
Howard, Bushrod, 115
Howard, Prof. Harry, 117
Hudson, Prof. Michael, 117, 297
Hughes, Sen. Harold, 276
Hull, Cordell, 13, 314
Humphrey, Vice President Hubert H., 79, 80, 91, 98, 127–128, 135, 141–142, 144, 146, 149, 153, 163, 189, 256, 271–272, 285, 305, 308, 314, 317, 319, 327
Huss, Pete, 54
Hussein, King, 15, 139–140, 167, 171, 175–177, 182, 190, 201–202, 213, 215, 221, 223–224, 228, 232, 234, 247–249, 268, 274–275, 294, 299, 315, 325–327
Husseini, Hadj el-min, 39, 41, 46
Husseini, Jamal, 46, 53
Hutchinson, Elmo, 115, 123

Idis, King, 139, 178, 236
Intergovernmental Committee on Refugees, 31–32
International Refugee Organization (IRO), 283
Ives, Sen. Irving M., 78–79, 87–88, 90–91, 102, 134

Jabotinsky, Vladimir (Ze'v), 14
Jackson, Sen. Henry, 112, 242–243, 256, 258, 263–264, 267, 272, 285–287, 293, 305, 321
Jackson-Vanik Amendment, 3
Jacobi, Lou, 70
Jacobson, Eddie, 75
Jamali, Fadhil-al, 46, 123
Jarring, Gunnar, 209, 213, 216, 218–220, 223, 227, 230, 234–235, 245–246, 254, 256, 258, 261, 268, 273, 288, 299
Javits, Ida Littman, 81
Javits, Sen. Jacob K., 71–75, 77, 81, 86–87, 90, 96–97, 99, 102–103, 134, 141,

146, 149-150, 153, 167, 171, 178, 185, 197, 201-202, 219, 221, 231, 240, 256, 264, 267, 283, 285, 287, 294, 308, 327
Jewish Agency for Palestine, 6, 10-12, 16, 22-23, 29, 32, 36-38, 40, 42, 43, 44, 46, 49, 50, 52, 54, 70, 109, 160, 184, 250, 283-284
Jewish Community Council (JCC) (Cleveland), 14
JCC (D.C.), 199, 281
JCC (Los Angeles), 296
Jewish Community Relations Committee (JCRC) (San Francisco), 295
Jewish Labor Committee, 13
Jewish National Assembly, 17
Jewish Telegraphic Agency, 295
Jewish War Veterans (JWV), 69, 89
Jibril, Ahmed, 324
Johnson, Rep. Albert W., 264
Johnson, Herschel, 47
Johnson, Rep. James P., 306
Johnson, Dr. Joseph E., 159, 160-162, 233
Johnson, Pres. Lyndon B., 71, 92, 134-137, 141, 142, 151-153, 155, 172-174, 176-178, 180-182, 184-185, 188, 195-202, 204, 207-208, 212, 217-219, 221, 225, 227, 228, 235, 243, 244, 310, 319
Johnson, U. Alexis, 173
Johnston, Eric, 104-105, 157, 163, 175
Joint Distribution Committee (JDC), 27, 29, 30, 74, 95
Joubran, Salim, 52
Judd, Rep. Walter H., 75, 76, 80, 86, 91
Jungers, Frank, 290-291

Kahane, Menachem, 37
Kalb, Bernard, 303-304
Kalb, Marvin, 303-304
Kallen, Horace, 9
Kampelman, Max, 80
Kane, Irving, 111-112, 219-220, 227, 231, 242, 294
Kanias, Susan, and family, 101
Kaplan, Richard B., 295
Karami, Premier Rashid, 231
Kassem, Gen. Abdul Karim, 166
Katz, Philip, 203

Katzen, Bernard, 102
Keane, Rose, 71
Keating, Sen. Kenneth B., 81, 126, 150-153, 163, 170, 171, 175, 225, 303
Kelly, Rep. Edna, 84, 163, 280
Kendall, Donald M., 286
Kenen, Peter, 5
Kenen, Regina (Mrs. Peter), 5
Kennan, George, 313
Kennedy, Sen Edward, 172, 264, 284, 301-302
Kennedy, Pres. John F., 73, 76, 77, 86, 104, 120, 135, 142, 146, 151, 155-156, 158, 160-169, 172, 174, 176, 178, 179, 183-184, 196, 235
Kennedy, Joseph, 155
Kennedy, Sen. Robert, 116, 156, 201, 221
Keren, Moshe, 69
Kersten, Rep. Charles L., 76
Khaled, Leila, 247
Khan, Sir Muhammed Zafrulla, 47
Khrushchev, Nikita, 164, 167, 178
King, John, 249
King, Martin Luther, Jr., 226
King, Sen. William H., 9
Kirchwey, Freda, 39
Kirkpatrick, Jeane, 332
Kirshblum, Rabbi Max, 37
Kissinger, Dr. Henry A., 238, 241-242, 273, 286-287, 300-306, 309-315, 319, 321-323, 326
Klein, Abraham, 21
Klutznick, Philip, 49, 102, 155
Knowland, Sen. William F., 134-135, 141, 142, 225
Kohanski, Dr. Alexander, 15
Kollek, Mayor Teddy, 68
Komer, Robert, 162
Konvitz, Prof. Milton, 202
Kook, Hillel, 17, 22, 39, 71
Kosygin, Aleksei, 189, 207-208, 212, 241, 309-310
Kraft, Joseph, 261
Kretzmann, Edward M. J., 141
Kuchel, Sen. Thomas, 151, 167
Kuhn, Fritz, 330
Ku Klux Klan, 330
Kuznetsov, Edward, 281

LaGuardia, Mayor Fiorello, 81
Laird, Melvin, 243
Landes, Prof. David S., 227
Lansing, Robert, 99
Lasker, Albert, 68
Lausche, Sen. Frank, 151, 196
Lazarus, Fred, Jr., 69
Lefkort, Rita Grossman, 67-68, 70, 79, 112
Lehman, Sen. Herbert, 28-29, 78-79, 89, 96, 145
Lemkin, Dr. Raphael, 277-278
Lesser, Allen, 108
Levich, Prof. Benjamin, 284
Levinthal, Rabbi B. L., 16
Levinthal, Judge Louis E., 13
Levy, Mrs. Adele, 90
Lie, Gen. Trygve, 50, 57
Lilienthal, Alfred, 276, 309
Lindsay, Mayor John, 189
Lippmann, Walter, 129, 132
Lipsky, Louis, 9, 12, 14, 16, 21, 23, 37, 49, 67-69, 70, 74, 77, 82, 89, 91, 93, 102-103, 107, 124
Lisagor, Peter, 250
Lodge-Fish Resolution, 9, 17
Lodge, Sen. Henry C., Jr., 77, 86, 90, 135, 136, 156
Long, Breckenridge, 15
Long, Rep. Clarence D., 322
Long, Sen. Russell B., 79
Lourie, Arthur, 21, 37, 53, 54, 63, 64, 223
Lovett, Robert, 48, 54
Lowdermilk, Dr. Walter C., 99
Luce Publications, 212
Ludwin, Ruth, 70

MacArthur, Gen. Douglas, 88
MacArthur, Douglas, II, 280
Macomber, William B., Jr., 219, 222, 297
Magnes, Dr. Judah, 40
Magnuson, Sen. Warren G., 53, 71, 73
Majali, Gen. Hafiz, 140
Majali, Hazza el, 140
Maksoud, Dr. Clovis, 320
Malik, Charles, 138, 261

Mallison, Dr. Thomas, 239
Mancroft, Lord, 186
Mansfield, Sen. Mike, 151, 196, 242, 276, 300-301, 305, 314-315
Marcus, Mickey, 70
Margalit, Dan, 327
Margolin, Olya, 69
Maria, Dr. Frank, 239
Marja, Fern, 37
Marshall, Gen. George C., 18, 37, 45-46, 50, 53, 54, 59, 61, 314
Martin, Rep. Joseph W., 17, 71, 81, 87, 163
Masaryk, Pres. Jan, 3, 23
Maslow, Will, 203
Masters, Parke W., 185
May, Steve, 150
Mayhew, Christopher, 117, 250-251, 269
McCarthy, Sen. Eugene, 221
McCarthy, Sen. Joseph, 71
McCloskey, Robert, 204, 304-305
McCloy, John J., 238
McClure, Sen. James A., 118, 306
McCulloch, Frank, 71, 77, 150, 152
McFarland, Sen. Ernest W., 79
McGee, Sen. Gale, 264, 267, 294, 303, 327
McGhee, George, 72, 73, 78
McGovern, Sen. George, 112, 221, 257, 271-272, 301, 306
McKellar, Sen. Kenneth, 79
McMahon, Monsignor Thomas J., 74
McNamara, Robert S., 200, 214
McNarney, Gen. Joseph T., 29-30
McNary, Sen. Charles L., 10
Meany, George, 238
Mehdi, Dr. Mohammed, 116
Meir, Prime Minister Golda, 42, 43, 51, 136, 158, 163, 166, 227, 236, 238-239, 246, 254-255, 259, 264-265, 272, 275-276, 297, 302-303, 311, 314, 323, 326, 330
Merrell, James L., 214
Meyer, Armin, 297-298
Michel, Rep. Robert H., 180
Michener, James, 206
Middle East Affairs Council, 308

Mikoyan, Anastas, 279
Millenson, Roy, 72
Miller, Rabbi Irving, 14
Miller, Rabbi Israel, 302
Miller, Otto N., 295–296
Mills, Sheldon, 141
Mills, Rep. Wilbur, 267, 286
Minor, Harold B., 114, 141
Mondale, Vice- Pres. Walter, 196, 231
  285, 301
Monsky, Henry, 11, 16, 21, 22, 23, 35,
  36, 37, 49
Montgomery, Gen. Bernard, 84
Moody, Sen. Blair, 79
Moore, George C., 289
Moore, Wiley, 71
Morano, Rep. Albert P., 126
Morgan, Lt. Gen. Sir Frederick S., 28
Morgan, Rep. Thomas E., 171, 184, 202,
  243, 265–267, 283
Morse, Sen. Wayne, 70, 78–79, 128–129,
  142, 144–146, 149–150, 153, 163, 171,
  197, 219
Mortaji, Gen. Abdul, 202
Moslem Brotherhood, 331
Mossadegh, Premier Mohammed, 115,
  169
Moubarak, Archbishop Ignatius, 118
Moynihan, Sen. Daniel Patrick, 329
Mufti (of Jerusalem). *See* Husseini,
  Hadj el-min
Multer, Rep. Abraham, 163
Murphy, Charles S., 89
Murphy, Robert, 107, 204
Murray, Wallace, 114
Muskie, Sen. Edward, 171, 267, 282–283
Mussolini, Benito, 57
NAACP, 277
Nadich, Rabbi Judah, 90
Naguib, Gen. Mohammed, 93–94, 96,
  261
Nagy, Premier Imre, 133
Nardi, Shulamith, 72
Nasr al-Din al-Nashashibi, 250
Nasser, Gamal Abdel, 4, 60, 94, 104,
  116, 117, 123, 125–126, 129, 131–132,
  136, 138–139, 143, 148, 150, 153–155,
  157, 161, 163, 165–182, 184–185,
188–190, 192–202, 204, 210–211, 213,
  215, 217, 222–225, 227, 230, 232–234,
  236–238, 240–242, 252–253, 259–261
Nathan, Robert R., 74
National Association of Arab Americans
  (NAAA), 118, 119, 296, 308
National Conference on Soviet Jewry,
  285
National Council of Churches, 227
National Council of the Churches of
  Christ, 74
National Council of Jewish Women, 13,
  69
National Jewish Community Relations
  Advisory Council (NJCRAC), 102,
  112
Nelson, Donald, 68
Nelson, Sen. Gaylord, 244, 293
Nes, David G., 117, 220, 266, 309
Neturei Karta, 8, 15
Neuberger, Sen. Richard, 141
Neumann, Dr. Emanuel, 37, 99
Newspaper Enterprise Association, 23
Niebuhr, Reinhold, 76
Nixon, Pres. Richard M., 88–89, 156,
  211–212, 224–226, 230, 232, 236, 238–
  239, 241, 243, 245, 246, 248, 253–254,
  270–273, 276, 278, 281, 286, 288, 296,
  302–306, 310, 311, 315, 325
Nkrumah, Kwame, 169, 188
Noah, Major Mordechai Manuel, 7–8
Noel, Cleo A., Jr., 289
Nolte, Richard, 210, 249
Novins, Louis, 69, 70
Nunez, Father Benjamin, 268

Oakes, John, 71
Oftedal, Mathilde, 30
O'Hara, Rep. Barrett, 149
O'Neill, Rep. Thomas, 281, 305, 317
OPEC, 288–289, 295
Organization of Arab Students, 116
O'Toole, Rep. Donald, 76, 81

Pahlavi, Shah Mohammed Reza, 169,
  178, 189, 312
Palestine Conciliation Commission
  (PCC), 62, 64–65, 157, 160–162

Palestine Liberation Organization (PLO), 4, 118-119, 120, 136, 173, 190, 216, 254, 274, 299, 320, 322, 325-328, 330-332
Palestine National Council (PNC), 254
Palestine Partition Commission (PPC), 50-51
Pasha, Azzam, 51, 57
Pasha, Glubb, 126, 140, 211
Passman, Rep. Otto, 314
Paul VI, Pope, 281
Pearson, Drew, 12
Pearson, Sen. James, 267
Pearson, Lester, 132
Pehle, John, 15
Pell, Sen. Claiborne, 184, 194, 244, 267, 301
Pelley Silver Shirts, 330
Pepper, Rep. Claude, 239
Percy, Sen. Charles, 264, 301
Peres, Shimon, 165, 323
Perle, Richard, 285
Perlov, Marian, 70
Perry, Major Robert P., 248
PFLP, 241, 247, 261, 275, 298, 322-325
Phillips, Horace, 228
Pickett, Clarence, 74
Pike, Bishop James, 135
Pincus, Louis A., 284
Plimpton, Francis T. P., 159
Poage, Rep. William R., 76, 79
Podgorny, Pres. Nikolai, 260
Poling, Daniel, 76
Pollack, Prof. Allen, 202, 227, 250
Pompidou, Pres. Georges, 240
Pool, Mrs. David de Sola, 16
Popular Democratic Front for the Liberation of Palestine (PDFLP), 324, 328
Porter, Paul, 68
Price, Woodruff M., 185
Proskauer, Judge Joseph, 13, 20
Proxmire, Sen. William, 141

Qaddafi, Muammar, 118, 236, 274, 297

Rabb, Max, 90
Rabbinical Assembly, 201, 226

Rabin, Prime Minister Yitzhak, 219, 251, 258, 272, 274, 323, 325-327
Rabinowitz, Rabbi Stanley, 199
Radwan, Rep. Edward, 126
Rafael, Gideon, 201
Raginsky, Anna, 5
Rahman, Sir Abdur, 44
Rand, Justice I. C., 40
Rankin, Rep. John, 29
Reagan, Pres. Ronald, 331-332
Reedy, George, 134, 135, 151
Rees, Rep. Thomas M., 246
Reichert, Rabbi Irving F., 23
Reid, Ogden, 141-142
Reston, James, 207
Reuss, Rep. Henry, 145
Rhodes, Rep. John, 246
Riad, Mahmoud, 220, 227, 232, 236, 247, 261, 265
Ribicoff, Sen. Abraham D., 71, 77, 81, 113, 171, 233, 256, 264, 272, 279, 280, 283-285, 287, 293
Richards, Rep. James, 139
Richardson, Elliot L., 239
Richardson, John P., 118, 239
Rifai, Samir el, 140
Rifkind, Judge Simon, 28-29, 68
Riley, Gen. William, 60, 100
Robinson, Dr. Jacob, 21
Rockefeller, David, 238
Rockefeller, John D., 8
Rockefeller, William, 8
Rogers, William P., 222, 231-233, 236-238, 242, 246, 253-256, 259-261, 264-265, 267, 271, 274, 281, 286, 288, 293, 297-298, 300, 314
Rohan, Michael Denis, 236
Rooney, Rep. John J., 163, 219
Roosevelt, Mrs. Eleanor, 48
Roosevelt, Pres. Franklin D., 10, 12, 14, 18-19, 20, 34, 68, 271
Roosevelt, Rep. Franklin D., Jr., 75, 76
Roosevelt, Rep. James, 149
Roper, Elmo, 35
Rosenbaum, Aaron, 112
Rosenman, Judge Samuel, 68, 69
Rosenthal, Rep. Benjamin, 196, 243
Rosenwald, Julius, 90

Rosenwald, Lessing, 11, 90, 102
Rosenwald, William, 90, 102–103
Ross, Thomas B., 115
Rostow, Eugene V., 24, 200–201, 315
Rostow, Walter, 200
Rothenberg, Judge Morris, 16
Rowen, Hobart, 257
Rowen, James, 257
Rowen, Susan McGovern, 257
Ruedy, Prof. John, 117, 308
Rush, Kenneth, 304, 308
Rusk, Dean, 50, 51, 53–54, 114, 156, 158, 161, 163, 170, 178–180, 196, 200–202, 205, 222, 231, 240, 314
Russell, Francis, 20
Russell, Sen. Richard B., 71, 79, 89
Rustin, Bayard, 277

Sabath, Rep. Adolph, 29
Sabin, Dr. Albert B., 227, 244
Sabry, Ali, 260
Sachar, Abram, 49
Sadat, Pres. Anwar, 4, 65, 188, 217, 252–254, 259–261, 263–265, 270, 273–274, 291–292, 299, 303, 309–311, 319, 323, 325, 327, 331
Sadd, David J., 118
Said, Nuri-es, 46
Sakharov, Andrei, 286
Sakran, Frank C., 220
Salpeter, Eliahu, 106
Saltonstall, Sen. Leverett, 77, 78, 135, 141
Samueloff, Prof. Shlomo, 235
Samuelson, Paul A., 313
Sanders, Edward, 112, 296
Sanders, Rabbi Ira, 71
Sandstrom, Chief Justice Emil, 40
Santayana, George, 331
Saud, Ibn, 36, 54, 115
Saud, King, 124, 145, 171
Sayre, Dean Francis B., 277
Scali, John, 328
Schaffner, Herbert H., 89
Schenk, Mrs. Faye, 244
Schlesinger, James, 303, 321
Schorry, Ali, 276
Schwartz, Dr. Joseph, 74

Schweiker, Sen. Richard, 283, 285, 302
Scott, Rep. Hugh, 126, 134, 163, 166, 196–197, 221, 233, 240, 256, 258, 264, 267, 276, 300–301, 305
Scott, Sen. William L., 315
Scranton, Gov. William, 212
Seely-Brown, Rep. Horace, 163
Seidel, Dr. Herman, 9
Selassie, Emperor Haile, 169
Sevareid, Eric, 328
Shadyac, Richard C., 118, 296
Shah of Iran. *See* Pahlavi, Shah Mohammed Reza
Sharabi, Prof. Hisham, 118
Sharett, Moshe (also known as Shertok), 32, 37, 39, 47, 52–53, 55, 64, 68, 79, 81, 107, 126
Sharett, Mrs. Moshe, 42
Shiloah, Reuven, 21, 37, 106–107
Shirdan, Leon, 231
Shone, Sir Terence, 63
Shriver, Sargent, 158
Shukairy, Ahmed, 190
Shulman, Herman, 14
Shultz, Lillie, 13, 39
Sidky, Aziz, 275
Sieff, Joseph Edward, 322
Silber, Tina, 112
Silver, Abba Hillel, 9, 13, 14, 15, 18, 23, 37, 38, 39, 51, 54, 70, 71, 91, 103, 122, 203
Silver, Rabbi Daniel, 203–204
Silver, Raphael, 203
Simms, Rep. Stephen D., 306
Sirhan, Sirhan, 116
Sisco, Joseph, 162, 191, 200, 233, 242, 248, 255, 259, 261, 283, 291–293, 296
Slansky, Rudolph, 94
Sloan, Frank, 177
Smathers, Gen. George A., 79
Smith, Sen. Alexander, 84
Smith, Gerald L. K., 330
Smith, Rep. Lawrence, 53
Smith, Sen. Margaret Chase, 276
Smith-Prouty Report, 153
Smith, Walter Bedell, 123, 127
Smith, Sen. William, 79
Smuts, Jan, 39

Solzhenitsyn, Aleksandr, 286
Sparkman, Sen. John, 70, 127, 134, 142, 150, 267
Spong, Sen. William, 267
Sporn, Dr. Philip, 243
Stackhouse, Heywood, 213
Stalin, Joseph, 94, 279, 282
Stassen, Cmdr. Harold, 22, 71, 76, 96–98
Stearns, Richard, 272
Stettinius, Edward, Jr., 314
Stevenson, Gov. Adlai E., 90, 163, 179, 228, 286–287
Stimson, Henry, 18
Stone, Dewey, 107, 155
Stone, Elihu, 9, 69, 71
Strong, Robert, 115, 165, 210
Stroup, Prof. Herbert, 227
Sukarno, Achmend, 188
Suleiman, Sidky, 193
Sulzberger, C. L., 207
Swanson, Sen. Claude A., 9
Swig, Ben, 22
Symington, Sen. Stuart, 141, 163, 196, 264, 267
Symmes, Harrison, 248
Syrkin, Prof. Marie, 202
Szold, Henrietta, 5

Taft, Sen. Robert A., 17, 18, 70, 71, 74, 77–79, 87–89, 153
Talbot, Phillips, 158, 162, 178, 186
Talisman, Mark, 285–286
Talle, Rep. Henry O., 76
Talmadge, Sen. Herman, 264
Talmon, Jacob, 31
Tannenwald, Judge Theodore, 219
Tanous, Dr. Peter S., 118, 308
Taube, Bernice, 6
Tavoulareas, William, 295
Taylor, Prof. Alan R., 117, 308
Taylor, Telford, 68
Tekoah, Yosef, 231, 237, 261
Tenzer, Rep. Herbert, 196
Thant, U, 163, 194, 198–199, 201, 228
Thompson, Dorothy, 72, 87, 115
Thurmond, Sen. Strom, 312
Tigay, Alan M., 113
Timor, Rachamin, 298

Toff, Moshe, 37, 40, 42
Toomin, Philip, 87, 89
Tourover, Denise, 69
Trager, Bernard H., 102
Truman, Pres. Harry, 2, 7, 19, 24, 27, 28, 34–39, 45–46, 48, 51, 53–57, 60–63, 67, 71, 75, 87–88, 91, 92, 145, 174, 196, 235, 332
Tshombe, Pres. Moise, 179
Tunney, Sen. John, 267, 301
Twain, Mark, 142
Tydings, Sen. Joseph D., 239

Ulbrich, Walter, 181
U.N. Emergency Force (UNEF), 132–133, 136, 140, 157, 171, 194–195, 197, 218, 227, 234–235
Unger, Rabbi Jerome, 69
Union of American Hebrew Congregations, 15, 49, 203
United Jewish Appeal (UJA), 66, 90, 96, 111, 140–141, 207, 236, 300, 329
United Jewish Welfare Fund, 186
United Synagogue of America, 102, 198
UNRRA, 27, 28, 30, 35
UNRWA, 73, 101, 118, 157, 189, 190, 237, 239, 269
UNSCOP, 40–47, 51, 55, 57, 118, 205, 250
UNTSO, 157
Usher, Arsene Assouan, 159

Va'ad Le'umi, 43, 52
Vandenberg, Sen. Arthur, 90
Van Horn, Gen. Carl C., 163
Vanik Amendment. See Jackson-Vanik Amendment
Vanik, Rep. Charles, 285–286
Van Kirk, Dr. Walter, 74, 78
Voss, Carl Hermann, 51, 76
Voyrs, John M., 69, 76

Wadsworth, George, 46
Wagner, Sen. Robert F., 10, 17, 18
Wallace, Mike, 290, 320
Walters, Barbara, 319, 327
Warren, George, 15
Wasfi al-Tel, Premier, 182, 248, 298

Washington, Pres. George, 39, 328
Weinberg, Lawrence, 112
Weis, Rep. Jessica, 163
Weisgal, Meyer, 12, 13, 21
Weizman, Ezer, 63
Weizmann, Dr. Chaim, 11, 40, 43, 51, 54, 57, 62, 69, 244
Welles, Sumner, 12
Wexler, Dr. William, 205
White, Lee, 150
White, Sen. Wallace H., Jr., 17
Wiggins, J. R., 231
Wilder, Thornton, 159
Wiley, Sen. Alexander, 134, 141
Williams, Sen. Harrison A., 171, 185, 187, 196–197
Williams, Sen. John, 242
Willkie, Wendell, 42
Wilson, Rep. Charles, 319
Wilson, Prime Minister Harold, 202
Wilson, Pres. Woodrow, 9, 99
Wise, David, 115
Wise, Stephen S., 9, 12, 13, 14, 15, 16, 18, 24, 30, 34
Wolff, Rep. Lester, 218–219

Wollack, Ken, 112, 286, 314
Wolman, Dr. Abel, 243
Woman's Army Corps (WAC), 71
Woods, George, 243
World Health Organization, 78, 268
World Jewish Congress, 21, 31
World Zionist Congress, 8
World Zionist Organization, 11, 14
Wright, Rep. James A., 17

Yaffi, Premier Abdullah, 231
Yakubovich, Hirsch, 44
Yamani, Sheikh Ahmed Zaki, 291
Yariv, Gen. Aharon, 165, 246, 325
Yates, Rep. Sidney, 145
Yost, Charles W., 211, 269
Young, Andrew, 330
Young, Sen. Stephen, 171
Yuval, Moshe, 37, 53

Zablocki, Rep. Clement, 125
Zalmanson, Wolf, 281
Zionist Organization of America, 10, 37, 97, 110, 122, 156